Strategy and Human Resource Management

2nd edition

Strategy and Human Resource Management

2nd edition

Peter Boxall and John Purcell

First edition 2003
Second edition 2008
Published by
PALGRAVE MACMILLAN
Houndmills, Basingstoke, Hampshire RG21 6XS and
175 Fifth Avenue, New York, N.Y. 10010
Companies and representatives throughout the world

PALGRAVE MACMILLAN is the global academic imprint of the Palgrave Macmillan division of St. Martin's Press, LLC and of Palgrave Macmillan Ltd. Macmillan® is a registered trademark in the United States, United Kingdom and other countries. Palgrave is a registered trademark in the European Union and other countries.

ISBN-13: 978–1–4039–9210–9
ISBN-10: 1–4039–9210–X

This book is printed on paper suitable for recycling and made from fully managed and sustained forest sources. Logging, pulping and manufacturing processes are expected to conform to the environmental regulations of the country of origin.

A catalogue record for this book is available from the British Library.

A catalog record for this book is available from the Library of Congress.

10   9   8   7   6   5   4   3   2   1
17 16 15 14 13 12 11 10 09 08

Printed and bound in China

Contents

Introduction

The last two decades of the twentieth century witnessed a major growth of interest in strategy and human resource management. Reacting to the dramatic growth of new technology, of competitive change, and of regulatory reform, business leaders (and their counterparts in the public sector) looked for ways to design and implement more successful strategies. Consultancy practices responded to this explosion of interest. So too did the academic field of strategic management. It moved on from its base in prescriptive texts on 'business policy'. Academically, strategic management is now characterised by a range of theoretical schools, by extensive research (published in such learned journals as *Strategic Management Journal*), and by large academic conferences. Business schools have invested enormous resources in the teaching of strategy, both in MBA programmes and in the 'capstone courses' of major undergraduate degrees.

The situation is much the same in HRM. The term first gained prominence in the United States where the most influential textbooks were initially published and where leading journals such as *Human Resource Management*, *Human Resource Management Review* and *Human Resource Planning* are based. Outside the United States, the significance of HRM has been recognised in the launch and growth of the *Human Resource Management Journal*, the *International Journal of Human Resource Management* and *Asia Pacific Journal of Human Resources*, among others. Within business schools, and across more traditional academic departments, there has been an explosion of courses and publications concerned with the management of work and people. It may have been fashionable to treat personnel management as a 'Cinderella' subject in the 1970s but few Universities today treat HRM with quite the same disdain.

The growth of interest in strategic management and HRM has not, however, been accompanied by sufficient concern for integrating these two important fields of theory and practice. This was our argument for writing the first edition of this book and remains our overriding goal in this second edition. Too much of the literature in strategic management continues to downplay or disregard the human issues which affect the viability and relative performance of firms. Similarly, too much of the literature in HRM carries on the preoccupation of the personnel management literature with individual techniques – such as particular types of selection tests or remuneration schemes – and fails to pay sufficient regard to the way that the value of particular techniques varies across contexts. Both bodies of literature have their characteristic weaknesses. On the strategy side, it is the failure to genuinely appreciate the ways in which the management of work and people is strategic to organisational success. On the HRM side, it is the failure to look up from the nooks and crannies of currently fashionable techniques to study the bigger picture, to perceive the ways in which patterns of HRM relate to broader management problems and need to vary with the organisation's particular environment.

Strategy and Human Resource Management is not organised around the classical sub-functions of HR practice – selection, appraisal, pay, training, and so on – with the word 'strategic' slipped in front. The sub-functional domains of micro-HRM do not dominate the design of chapters as if they were self-contained 'solutions'. Instead, the book is designed around the need for a critical overview of what is important in the way management tries to tackle HRM, of how HRM varies across important contexts, and in the face of different challenges.

Our approach in each chapter follows a style based on three elements: theory, research and illustration. We are committed to an 'analytical approach' to HRM. This means we first try to understand what managers do and why they do it before we offer any sort of prescription for what they should do or how they could do things better. This is an approach which is uncompromisingly about research but, wherever possible, we try to bring the story to life with the more interesting illustrations – cases and vignettes – with which we are familiar and have inserted more references to valuable internet sites.

The book retains the distinctive features of the first edition. It responds to Karen Legge's challenging questions (in her 1978 text) about the objectives of (what was then) personnel management by beginning with the question of goals in HRM. As before, we argue that HRM is an essential organisational process which serves multiple goals, and that these goals are subject to tensions and paradoxes. Not only are firms typically concerned with cost-effectiveness and with some degree of organisational flexibility but social legitimacy and managerial autonomy or power also play important roles in their HR activities. This framework of strategic goals is developed in the first chapter of the book and acts as a touchstone throughout. It has been critically reviewed and made more dynamic in this edition.

The book takes a distinctive approach to the definition of strategic management, arguing for the centrality of human resource strategy *within* any credible understanding of business strategy and not as some kind of dubious appendage to it. Our view is that an effective HR strategy is a necessary (though not a sufficient) condition of business viability. An outstanding HR strategy may help to lay a basis for sustained competitive advantage. In this edition, we strongly emphasise the value of understanding organisational HR strategies as clusters of HR systems. Each HR system is aimed at a different workforce group in the organisation but organisational processes and politics often ensure there are some overlapping features to a firm's HR systems.

We continue to analyse the debate within strategic HRM over the role of context ('best fit') and universalism ('best practice'). Our review of the evidence has been updated, including making better use of sources on national institutions and cultures. We retain and strengthen the conclusion that firms either adapt to their specific context or they fail, and we reject eclectic, de-contextualised lists of best practices. There is a basis, however, for a concept of best practice when it is based on underpinning principles that help managers to achieve better outcomes. The central part of the book aims to identify and expound major principles that underpin key choices in HR strategy. This means we are less interested in talking about specific HR practices than we are in pinpointing critical theoretical principles that run across HRM and its companion disciplines, Organisational Behaviour and Industrial Relations. All chapters have been updated, including ensuring we cover issues in services and the public sector more effectively. In addition, we have revised this part's structure, and now have a new chapter (Chapter 8) which draws the key ideas together through discussing different types of HR system and the key mediators linking HR systems to organisational performance. We think this will provide a better integration of this part, helping readers to see more easily overall patterns in HR strategy and key issues in the links from HR policies to outcomes.

A comment on the first edition was that we need to make better use of such collective or group-level concepts as social capital, organisational culture and workplace climate and we have sought to do so in this edition. This should be apparent in Chapter 1 and in Chapters 6 and 8, in particular. The material on internal labour markets which was formerly in its own chapter has been trimmed and redistributed (principally into Chapters 4 and 5).

As might be expected, we continue to work studiously with the contemporary emphasis on the resource-based view of the firm, with the notion that intangible assets can build enviable positions of competitive strength. In an era of knowledge-intensive competition, this remains a very important body of work which quite obviously links the strategy and HRM fields. Like others, we try in this area to make some of the abstruse ideas more accessible and to ensure we have an argument that goes beyond the self-evident truths. Areas much less often visited by writers on strategic HRM include the evolution of HR strategy across cycles of industry change and the shape of HR strategy within multidivisional and multinational firms. These have been concerns of ours – we see them as important in the dynamic picture and in the larger world of capitalist production – and they continue to play a key role in the final part of the book (in Chapters 9 and 10). The book's final chapter has been revised to include a summary of the main lessons of the book. Overall, we think that *Strategy and Human Resource Management* is a novel synthesis of the HRM–strategy nexus: you be the judge.

PETER BOXALL AND JOHN PURCELL

Acknowledgements

My journey into strategic HRM started in the late 1980s / early 1990s at Monash University where Peter Dowling was supervising my PhD and where the management school provided a stimulating and supportive environment. I am very grateful to Peter, to other colleagues there at the time, including Bernard Barry and Malcolm Rimmer, and to the Australian government's sponsorship of the National Key Centre in Industrial Relations. The funding of the Centre enabled me to conduct serious fieldwork on HR strategy in Australian firms facing growing international competition. I am also very grateful to two other institutions and sets of colleagues: to the Business School at the University of Auckland, my home base, and to the University of Bath, where I was a Visiting Professor in the Work and Employment Research Centre in 1998 and again in 2006. I am very grateful to the University of Auckland for the research and study leaves it has granted me and wish to take this opportunity to thank particularly Professors Alastair MacCormick and Barry Spicer for their support as Deans over the time I have been employed at Auckland. I am also indebted to colleagues, including Peter Haynes, Keith Macky and Giles Burch, whose insights have made a major difference to my work. In respect of the University of Bath, my sincere thanks go to Professor Andrew Pettigrew, to Cathy Aubin and Cathy Rowe, and to my friend and partner in this work, John Purcell, who has been an outstanding host during our sabbatical leaves. Working with John is always an enriching experience and I am very grateful for our collaboration, including the many conversations we have had, which have laid the basis of this book, and greatly improved its arguments. We both thank Palgrave Macmillan and our series editor, Mick Marchington, for their faith in, and patience with, this particular project. At Palgrave Macmillan, we especially thank Ursula Gavin, Lee Ann Tutton and Brian Morrison. As ever, my heartfelt thanks go to

Marijanne for her unfailing interest in my work and to our sons, Chris, Andy and David, who have a range of views on the costs and benefits of sabbatical leave.

PETER BOXALL

I first taught strategy and human resource management in 1995 to a group of Executive MBA students in the University of Bath. There was no textbook, at least none that I liked, and much of what we explored together was experimental – built, in part, on their own experiences as practising managers. Only rarely were any of them HR managers. Most were sceptical, at the start, about claims for the strategic importance of HRM but soon became enthusiastic as we tackled difficult questions linking HRM to performance and firm strategy. Supervising their projects, based on the experience of their companies, has taught me a great deal about how to link theory to practice and how to make theory practical. In a quite different way, final year undergraduates are terrific at theory and have a thirst for anything that tries to relate this to 'real' life. Linking theory with practice is central to my life as an academic in a business school. My colleagues in the Work and Employment Research Centre at the School of Management at Bath have worked with me in the last ten years on research projects concerned with 'leanness', telephone call centres, fostering and forcing change, contingent working and especially two projects funded by the Chartered Institute for Personnel and Development on what we call 'People and Performance'. More recently we have focused on the role of line managers in HRM and employee voice. The common thread in all these was seeking to link strategy with HRM. Insights from these projects were reflected in the first edition and are especially so in this second edition. I wish to record my debt, and my thanks, to Nick Kinnie, Sue Hutchinson and Juani Swart for their work on these projects but also for the stimulation, argument and debate we have had together in these ten years. It has been fun. I am very grateful to the Business School at the University of Auckland for helping to fund two visits there in 2001 and 2005. This allowed Peter and me to really get to grips with the core ideas in this new subject. Peter has been, as ever, a fund of knowledge and with a deep understanding of the critical issues. I cannot imagine a better collaborator and colleague. The lion's share of the task of revising the text for this edition fell to Peter while on sabbatical at Bath in 2006 at a time when I was deflected by management responsibilities in the University and by trying, still, to conduct field research. Our collaboration is deep rooted and seen in other projects, notably the *Oxford Handbook of*

HRM. I am very grateful to Annette Hayden, whose work on the permissions for many of the figures in this book was much appreciated. Kate Purcell has, as ever, been supportive but has also expressed cynicism 'as a sociologist' about the language and ideas of strategic human resource management. I value her for both more than, perhaps, she realises.

JOHN PURCELL

The authors and publishers wish to thank the following for permission to reproduce copyright material:

Academy of Management Review:
Hart, S. L. (1992) 'An integrative framework for strategy-making processes'. *Academy of Management Review* 17(2): 327–51. (Figure 2.3)

Professor M. Beer and Professor B Spector:
Beer, M., Spector, B., Lawrence, P., Quinn Mills, D. and Walton, R. (1984) *Managing Human Assets.* Copyright previously held by New York: Free Press. (Figure 3.4)

Blackwell Publishing Ltd:
Boxall, P. (2003) 'HR strategy and competitive advantage in the service sector'. *Human Resource Management Journal* 13(3): 5–20. (Figure 5.5)
Marchington, M. and Wilkinson, A. (2000) 'Direct participation'. In Bach, S. and Sisson, K. (eds) *Personnel Management: A Comprehensive Guide to Theory and Practice.* (Figure 6.2)
Pil, F. K. and MacDuffie, J. P. (1996) 'The adoption of high involvement work practices'. *Industrial Relations* 35(3): 423–55. (Figure 10.4)

California Management Review:
Williams, J. (1992) 'How sustainable is your competitive advantage?'. *California Management Review* 34(3): 29–51. (Figure 9.3)

Cornell University:
Herzenberg, S., Alic, J. and Wial, H. (1998) *New Rules for a New Economy: Employment and Opportunity in Postindustrial America.* Ithaca, NY: ILR Press. (Figure 5.4)

Elsevier:
Boxall, P. (1998) 'Achieving competitive advantage through human resource strategy: towards a theory of industry dynamics'. *Human Resource Management Review* 8(3): 265–8. (Figure 7.5)
Dyer, L. and Shafer, R. (1999) 'Creating organizational agility: implications for strategic human resource management'. In Wright, P., Dyer, L., Boudreau, J. and Milkovich, G. (eds) *Research in Personnel and Human*

Resource Management (Supplement 4: Strategic Human Resources Management in the Twenty First Century). Stamford, CT and London: JAI Press. (Figure 9.5)

Emerald Group Publishing Ltd:
Haynes, P. and Fryer, G. (2000) 'Human resources, service quality and performance: a case study'. *International Journal of Contemporary Hospitality Management* 12(4): 240–8. (Figure 5.6)

The Free Press:
Porter, M. (1985) *Competitive Advantage: Creating and Sustaining Superior Performance.* New York: Free Press. (Figure 3.5)

Harvard Business School Publishing:
Eisenhardt, K. M., Kahwajy, J. L. and Bourgeois, L. J. (1997) 'How management teams can have a good fight'. *Harvard Business Review* 75, July–August: 77–85. (Figure 2.5, p. 54)
Kaplan, R. and Norton, D. (1996) *The Balanced Scorecard: Translating Strategy into Action.* Boston, MA: Harvard Business School Press. (Figure 11.2, p. 297)
Kaplan, R. and Norton, D. (2001) *The Strategy-Focused Organization.* Boston, MA: Harvard Business School Press. (Figure 11.3, p. 298 and Figure 11.4, p. 302)
Leonard, D. (1998) *Wellsprings of Knowledge: Building and Sustaining the Sources of Innovation.* Boston, MA: Harvard Business School Press. (Figure 4.4, p. 95 and Figure 4.5, p. 98)
Walton, R. E., Cutcher-Gershenfeld, J. E. and McKersie, R. B. (1994) *Strategic Negotiations: A Theory of Change in Labor–Management Relations.* Boston, MA: Harvard Business School Press. (Figure 6.5, p. 165)

John Wiley & Sons Ltd:
Campbell, J. P., McCloy, R., Oppler, S. and Sager, C. (1993) 'A theory of performance'. In Schmitt, N. and Borman, W. (eds) *Personnel Selection in Organizations.* San Francisco: Jossey-Bass. (Figure 7.2)
Hedlund, G. (1994) 'A model of knowledge management and the n-form corporation'. *Strategic Management Journal* 15: 73–90. (Figure 4.6)
Whittington, R. and Mayer, M. (1997) 'Beyond or behind the M-form: The structures of European business'. In Thomas, H, O'Neal, D. and Ghertman, M. (eds) *Strategy, Structure and Style.* Chichester: Wiley. (Figure 10.3) This figure was adapted and used in Whittington, R. and Mayer, M. (2000) *The European Corporation: Strategy, Structure and Social Science.* Oxford: Oxford University Press. The figure used in this volume is taken from *The European Corporation.*

Oxford University Press:
Boxall, P. (2007) 'The goals of HRM'. In Boxall, P., Purcell, J. and Wright, P. (eds) *The Oxford Handbook of Human Resource Management.* Oxford: Oxford University Press. (Figure 1.3, p. 20)

Guest, D. (2007) 'Human resource management and the worker: towards a new psychological contract?'. In Boxall, P., Purcell, J. and Wright, P. (eds) *The Oxford Handbook of Human Resource Management*. Oxford: Oxford University Press. (Figure 7.9, p. 195)

Lepak, D. and Snell, S. (2007) 'Employment sub-systems and the "HR architecture"'. In Boxall, P., Purcell, J. and Wright, P. (eds) *The Oxford Handbook of Human Resource Management*. Oxford: Oxford University Press. (Figure 4.7, p. 102)

Rose, M. (1994) 'Job satisfaction, job skills, and personal skills'. In Penn, R., Rose, M. and Rubery, J. (eds) *Skill and Occupational Change*. Oxford: Oxford University Press. (Figure 7.11, p. 197)

Perseus Books Group:

Freeman, R. B. and Medoff, J. L. (1984) *What Do Unions Do?*. Originally published by Basic Books. (Figure 6.4)

Robertson Cooper Ltd:

Robertson Cooper Ltd (2003) *Teamable Technical Manual*. (Figure 2.4)

Sage Publications:

Barney, J. (1991) 'Firm resources and sustained competitive advantage'. *Journal of Management* 17(1): 99–120. (Figure 4.1)

Parker, S. and Wall, T. (1998) *Job and Work Design: Organizing Work to Promote Well-Being and Effectiveness*. Thousand Oaks, CA: Sage Publications. (Figure 5.1)

Rose, M. (2003) 'Good deal, bad deal? Job satisfaction in occupations'. *Work, Employment and Society* 17(3): 503–30. (Figure 7.10)

Rousseau, D. (1995) *Psychological Contracts in Organizations*. Thousand Oaks, CA: Sage Publications. (Figure 7.6 and Figure 7.7)

Vandenberg, R. J., Richardson, H. A. and Eastman, L. J. (1999) 'The impact of high involvement work processes on organizational effectiveness: a second-order latent variable approach'. *Group and Organization Management* 24(3): 300–39. (Figure 5.2)

Windolf, P. (1986) 'Recruitment, selection and internal labour markets in Britain and Germany'. *Organization Studies* 7(3): 235–54. (Figure 7.4)

Thomson Publishing Services:

Purcell, J. (1989) 'The impact of corporate strategy on human resource management'. In Storey, J. (ed.) *New Perspectives on Human Resource Management*. London: Routledge. (Figure 10.1)

Watson, T. (1986) *Management, Organisation and Employment Strategy: New Directions in Theory and Practice*. London: Routledge. (Figure 7.8)

Every effort has been made to contact all the copyright-holders, but if any have been inadvertently omitted the publishers will be pleased to make the necessary arrangement at the earliest opportunity.

1

The goals of human resource management

Our mission in this book is to explore the ways in which human resource management (HRM) is strategic to organisational success. We are interested in how HRM affects the viability and relative performance of firms and other formal organisations. In so doing, we take an 'analytical approach' to HRM (Boxall, Purcell and Wright 2007b). This means we are concerned, first and foremost, with research that tries to describe what managers do in practice and with theory which helps us understand why and how they do it. Only on this basis do we enter into discussion of what we think they ought to do or how we think they could do it better.

The logical place to begin is with the analysis of goals. What is management trying to achieve in employing people? What sort of motives underpin human resource management? This is the question we pose and seek to answer in this first chapter. The chapter begins by defining the key characteristics of HRM. We then identify and examine the principal goals or motives that can be discerned in management's HRM activities. This leads into a discussion of the strategic tensions and problems that management faces in pursuing these goals. We conclude with a summary and an outline of what lies ahead in the book.

Defining human resource management

HRM refers to all those activities associated with the management of work and people in firms and in other formal organisations. In this book, related terms such as 'employee relations', 'labour management' and 'people management' are used as synonyms for HRM. While there have been debates over the meaning of HRM since the term came into vogue in the 1980s, it has become the most widely recognised term in the English-speaking world referring to the activities of management in organising work and employing people. Appropriately translated, it is also popular in the Francophone and Spanish-speaking worlds.

We do not wish to use the term loosely, however. Definitions are important. They should not be rushed or glossed over because they indicate the intellectual terrain that is being addressed. They suggest the relevant 'problematics' of the field – that is, they suggest what needs to be discussed and explained. Before proceeding, our definition will be clarified and elaborated.

HRM: an inevitable process in organisations

Let's suppose you are a self-employed individual running your own small business. The business, however, is starting to take off. You have more orders from clients than you can cope with. You have some capital and your bank manager, who likes your financial performance so far and thinks you are a good risk, is prepared to lend you some more. The minute you decide you want to hire your first employee, you are engaged in the initial stages of human resource management. You are moving from a situation in which self-employment and self-management has been everything to one in which the employment and management of others will also be critical. Your ideas may not be well shaped at this stage but as you start to think more seriously about what kind of help you need and take some steps to make it happen (for example, by networking among talented friends or advertising the job on the internet), you are entering the world of HRM. Once someone has actually joined you as an employee, you have really begun the process of HRM in earnest. You have started to expand your business in the anticipation of improving its potential and, if you wish to survive, with the intention of making money through employing the talents of other people. You have embarked on a process that brings opportunity at the same time as it creates a whole new world of problems for you (for example, how are you going to involve this person in decision making?; what will you do if they are not much good at the job and coping with them turns out to be very time-consuming?; if they are good at it, how will you keep up with their income and career aspirations? . . .).

This simple illustration underlines the fact that it is virtually impossible to grow businesses (and, for that matter, any kind of formal organisation) without employing people. HRM is a process that accompanies the expansion of organisations: it is a correlate of entrepreneurial success and organisational growth. One of the key metrics commonly used to measure the size of organisations is the number of people employed. The world's largest company by revenue in 2006 – Wal-Mart Stores – employs 1.9 million people.[1] The second largest company by revenue but the most profitable firm in the world in 2006, Exxon Mobil, employs around 84,000 people.[2] These differences in employee numbers say something about the difference between retail organisations and oil production in terms of technological intensity (the oil industry requires huge capital investments while supermarkets remain relatively labour intensive) but both of these organisations need large numbers of people to do what they do. In the public sector, workforces can also be very large. The British national health system, for example, employs over 1.5 million people.[3]

The idea that we might need to justify the process of HRM in organisations is, thus, rather absurd. We may well wish to analyse the effectiveness of a firm's approach to HRM and make some changes but we inevitably come back to some kind of 'human resourcing' process (Watson 2005). You simply cannot grow and maintain organisations without at least some employment of other people. Longstanding firms may go through periods in which they need to lay off people – possibly very large numbers of people – to improve their cost structure but hardly any business will survive unless it is employing at least some people on a regular basis. If everyone is laid off and their final entitlements paid to them, the process of HRM will cease – but so will the firm.[4]

HRM: managing work and people

Our conception of HRM covers the policies and practices used to organise work and to employ people. In other words, HRM encompasses the management of work and the management of people to do the work. Work policies and practices are to do with the way the work itself is organised. This includes its fundamental structure, which can range from low-discretion jobs where supervisors exercise a high level of control through to highly autonomous jobs where individuals largely supervise themselves. It also

---

1 http://money.cnn.com/galleries/2007/fortune/0704/gallery.500top50.fortune/index.html
2 www.exxonmobil.co.uk/corporate/citizenship/ccr5/global_workforce.asp
3 www.skillsforhealth.org.uk/sector.php
4 Except in the case of 'shell companies' which are defunct but may be revived when someone acquires the rights to the name and decides to use them.

includes any associated opportunities to engage in problem-solving and change management regarding work processes (for example, through quality circles or team meetings). Employment policies and practices, on the other hand, are concerned with how firms try to hire and manage people. They include management activities in recruiting, selecting, deploying, motivating, appraising, training, developing and retaining individual employees. In addition, they include processes for informing, consulting and negotiating with individuals and groups and activities associated with disciplining employees, terminating their contracts and downsizing entire workforces. As this makes apparent, the management of work and people includes both individual and collective dimensions. People are managed through employing and relating to them as individuals and also through relating to them in larger groups.

HRM: involving line and specialist managers

Given this wide remit, it should be obvious that HRM can never be the exclusive property of HR specialists. As an essential organisational process, HRM is as an aspect of all management jobs. Line managers – those who directly supervise employees engaged in the operations of the firm – are intimately involved, usually hiring their own team and almost always held directly accountable for the performance of that team. In larger organisations, there may be permanent in-house HR specialists contributing specialist skills in such technical aspects of HRM as the design of selection processes, the formation of Equal Employment Opportunity (EEO) policies, the conduct of collective employment negotiations, and training needs analysis. There may also be specialist HR consultants contracted to provide such important services as executive search, and assistance with major reformulations of salary structure and performance incentives. In the UK and Ireland, there are currently around 81,000 HR specialists working in organisations and around 6,500 consultancy organisations providing HR advice or services.[5] This underlines the importance of this kind of work in advanced economies. All specialists, however, are engaged in 'selling' their services to other managers (senior, middle and first-line), in working together with other members of the management team to achieve the desired results. In this book, the acronym 'HRM' is used to refer to the totality of the firm's management of work and people and not simply to those aspects where HR specialists are involved.

---

5 www.apinfo.co.uk/pmy/

HRM: managerial efforts to build individual and organisational performance

HRM can usefully be understood as a set of activities aimed at building individual and organisational performance. On the individual level, HRM consists of managerial attempts to influence individual ability (A), motivation (M), and the opportunity to perform (O). If managers want to enhance individual performance, they need to influence these three variables positively (Blumberg and Pringle 1982, Campbell, McCloy, Oppler and Sager 1993). This is true in any model of HRM, whether we are talking of one in which employees have relatively basic skills (such as fast food services) or very advanced qualifications (such as brain surgery). Using mathematical notation:

$$P = f(A,M,O)$$

In other words, individuals perform when they have:

- the ability (A) to perform (they *can do* the job because they possess the necessary knowledge and skills);
- the motivation (M) to perform (they *will do* the job because they feel adequately interested and incentivised); and
- the opportunity (O) to perform (their work structure and its environment provides the necessary support and avenues for expression).

The AMO framework is depicted in Figure 1.1. We should note here that it is not only HRM that affects the AMO variables. Employees are motivated and enabled not only through incentives (such as pay and promotion) and work processes (such as supervisory help and co-worker support) but also through the wider organisational environment, including such things as the

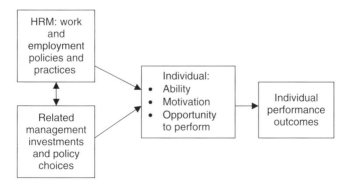

Figure 1.1 The AMO framework

quality of information systems and the level of funding available. It is easier to perform when a firm is financially successful and management decides to plough its wealth back into new technologies and better staffing budgets.

The mathematical shorthand we use here, $P = f(A,M,O)$, is not meant to be mystifying or off-putting. It is simply a useful way of indicating that no one knows the precise relationships among ability, motivation and opportunity. There is no exact formula here but we do know that all three factors are involved in creating employee performance. Good ability alone will not bring performance: the worker must want to apply it. Similarly, motivated workers with good abilities cannot achieve much if critical resources or organisational support are lacking. The AMO framework is something that we will refer to regularly, and develop in a more sophisticated way, in this book.

The managerial effort in human resource management, however, is not solely concerned with managing individuals as if they were independent of others. It does include this but, as we have indicated, it also includes efforts to organise and manage groups of employees and whole workforces. Figure 1.2 sketches the role of HRM on this collective level. Again, we do not know the precise relationships here but we do know that HRM plays an important role in building workforce organisation and capabilities and the general climate of employee attitudes. It typically includes attempts to build work systems that coordinate individuals in some kind of way, such as permanent teams, finite project groups and 'virtual teams' which coordinate through the internet. It may include attempts to build collaboration across departmental or hierarchical boundaries and networks operating across work sites, countries and time zones. These sorts of work organisation activities, along with various kinds of recruitment and development activities (including, at times, company takeovers), are attempts to build workforce capabilities. Managers try to build 'critical mass': the stock of knowledge and

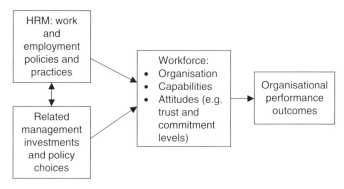

Figure 1.2 HRM and collective performance variables

skills they need to fulfil the firm's mission. Finally on the collective level, HRM includes management actions that affect the attitudinal climate of the workplace. Management's stance towards employee voice is a key influence here and a variety of collective variables – such as trust levels, commitment levels and the quality of cooperation – are in play.

HRM, then, needs to be understood as a management process that operates on more than one level. It includes attempts to manage individuals and attempts to build a functioning workplace society. Theorists increasingly argue that HRM is about building both 'human capital' (what individuals know and can do that is valuable to the firm) and 'social capital' (relationships and networks among individuals and groups that create value for the firm) (e.g. Goshal and Nahapiet 1998, Leana and van Buren 1999, Snell 1999). These levels are obviously connected. While there is often much that individuals can achieve through their own skills and drive, they are always acting within a larger social context. They are inevitably affected by the quality of workforce organisation and capabilities and the attitudinal climate in which they are embedded. The need to understand HRM as concerned with both human and social capital will be an important theme in this book.

HRM: incorporating a variety of management styles and ideologies

As our discussion so far should indicate, management often adopts a variety of approaches to managing employees. In the larger organisations, it is quite common for one approach to be taken to managing managers, another to permanent non-managerial employees, and yet another to temporary and 'contract' staff (e.g. Pinfield and Berner 1994, Harley 2001, Kalleberg et al. 2006). In unionised organisations, such as public sector hospitals, there can be different employment regimes for each professional group with each of these negotiated in separate contractual negotiations and then enforced or 'policed' with a high degree of seriousness. In this light, Osterman (1987) refers to a range of 'employment subsystems' in firms. Lepak and Snell (1999, 2002, 2007) talk of a 'human resource architecture' in which management chooses different HR systems for different groups based on their strategic value and the uniqueness of the skills that each group possesses.

Not only are there key differences in style within firms but differences in styles across firms are also widely observed. In terms of the way firms approach employee voice, we see a broad range of styles from paternalistic ones through to workplace 'partnerships' in which there is much greater recognition of employee rights and interests (e.g. Purcell and Ahlstrand 1994, Budd 2004).

Our definition of HRM, then, allows for a wide variety of management ideologies and styles. The notion of HRM is largely used in this sense in the United States where the term covers all management approaches to managing people in the workplace. Some approaches involve unions while others do not (see, for example, Noe *et al.* 2005). It must be admitted, however, that most styles of labour management in the US *private* sector do not involve dealing with unions.[6] This fact can mean that students of HRM there have much less exposure to theory on union–management relations than is typical in Europe and in the old Commonwealth countries of Canada, South Africa, Australia and New Zealand.

In Britain, the rise of practitioner and academic interest in HRM sparked a debate about the term's meaning, its ideological presuppositions, and its consequences for the teaching and practice of Industrial Relations. Storey (1995: 5) defined HRM as a 'distinctive approach to employment management', one which 'seeks to achieve competitive advantage through the strategic deployment of a highly committed and capable workforce, using an integrated array of cultural, structural and personnel techniques'. Similarly, Guest (1987) developed a model of HRM as a strongly integrated management approach in which high levels of commitment and flexibility are sought from a high quality staff. Some commentators went further and saw HRM as a workplace manifestation of Thatcherite 'enterprise culture', as an ideology that would make management prerogative the natural order of things (see, for example, Keenoy and Anthony 1992).

For research purposes, defining HRM as a particular style is obviously a legitimate way to proceed. It opens up useful questions such as: what practices constitute a high-commitment model of labour management?; in what contexts is such a model likely to occur?; and are the outcomes of such a model actually superior?

We are interested in all styles of labour management, and the ideologies associated with them, and pursue the sorts of questions about particular models just noted. However, for the purposes of exploring the links between strategic management and HRM, we find that a broad, inclusive definition of HRM is more appropriate. The terrain of HRM includes a variety of

---

6 In 2005, US private sector union density (based on membership) stood at 7.8 per cent of employed wage and salary earners: www.bls.gov/news.release/union2.t03.htm

styles. We are interested in which ones managers take in a particular context and why and we are interested in how different styles work. The strategy literature requires this kind of openness because it recognises variety in business strategy across varying contexts (see, for example, Miles and Snow 1984, Porter 1980, 1985). It implies that there is no 'one best way' to compete in markets and organise the internal operations of the firm. If we are to truly explore the HRM–strategy nexus, we need relatively open definitions on both sides of the equation.

HRM: embedded in industries and societies

HRM, then, is a process carried out in formal organisations – some small, some large, some very large, including multinational firms and the huge government departments of large countries. While recognition of this fact is essential, the academic study of HRM has been criticised by scholars in the companion discipline of Industrial or Employment Relations for focusing too much on the firm and ignoring the wider context of the markets, networks and societies in which the firm operates (see, for example, Rubery and Grimshaw 2003, Blyton and Turnbull 2004, Rubery, Earnshaw and Marchington 2005). We think this is a fair criticism. The different HR strategies of firms are better understood if they are examined in the wider context that helps to shape them, something we shall certainly be arguing throughout this book. Work and employment practices are not entirely developed within a firm or controlled by that firm's management.

We will shortly be arguing that HRM is profoundly affected by the characteristics of the industries in which the firm chooses to compete, as demonstrated long ago in Dunlop's (1958) classic analysis of industrial relations systems. Firms often adopt similar HR practices to other firms operating with the same know-how or technology or trying to serve the same type of client. Anyone with extensive experience of law firms, for example, will be able to explain important similarities in the way they hire their associates and set up arrangements to 'manage' their partners. Similarly, anyone with serious experience of production work in clothing manufacturers will see similarities in HR practices in this industry and will realise that there are major differences from law firms, not least in the work process and in the pay levels! We should point out that, in this sense, it is useful to consider the public sector as a set of 'industries', embracing core government departments, the armed services, public health providers, schools and many others. Organisations in these areas, just like firms in private sector industries, face similar challenges and demonstrate many similar responses in their approaches to HRM (e.g. Kalleberg *et al.* 2006, Bach and Kessler 2007).

We will also be arguing that along with industry differences, HRM is deeply affected by differences between societies. Although globalisation is a powerful set of forces, nation states still exercise a major impact on the HR strategies of firms. Nations provide resources of physical infrastructure, politico-economic systems, educated workforces and social order. These resources are of variable quality across nations but are always significant. In exchange for the use of these resources, national governments often impose regulations on how employees should be treated, with varying degrees of enforcement of these regulations. Firms, therefore, are always 'embedded in structures of social relations' (Granovetter 1985: 481).

The role of industry and societal factors in influencing the HR strategies of firms is an important theme in this book. The implicit model of HR practice as something entirely within the control of management in the individual firm is something we work hard to avoid.

What are the goals of HRM?

Human resource management, we have argued, covers a broad range of activities associated with managing work and people and shows a huge range of variations across such categories as occupations, hierarchical levels, firms, industries and societies. This confusing detail and profound diversity naturally begs a fundamental question: what are employers seeking through engaging in HRM and how do their goals for HRM relate to their broader organisational goals? What are the underpinning objectives of employers? In terms of the 'level of analysis' involved, our question concerns the goals that characterise whole employing units: that is, firms or, where these are diversified and devolved in labour management, business units or establishments within them.

The task is a difficult one. It has never been easy to define the goals of labour management in the firm. In a classic analysis, Karen Legge (1978: 3) noted that most textbooks on (what was then) personnel management sidestepped the issue by briefly referring to some statement such as, 'the optimum utilisation of human resources in order to achieve the goals and objectives of the organisation'. She pointed out that this kind of vague, ill-defined statement begged a number of important questions, including the question of *whose* interests were being served and what was meant by optimisation. Ignoring such troublesome questions, the textbooks moved quickly into the traditional exposition of personnel practices, depicted as ends in themselves (rather than as means or methods which might be relevant in some contexts and counter-productive in others).

One can, to some extent, sympathise. In asking about a firm's goals for HRM, we face the problem that that these goals are often implicit (Purcell and Ahlstrand 1994, Gratton *et al.* 1999b). Only the larger firms have formal or explicit goal statements for their HR strategies (Kersley *et al.* 2006). Even when they do, we need to be careful in taking them at face value. In HRM, aspirational rhetoric or ideology may mask a more opportunistic and pragmatic reality (Marchington and Grugulis 2000, Legge 2005). Broad policies are always open to the interpretations of managers, both general and specialist, and sometimes their active subversion. Furthermore, particular patterns of HRM are laid down or 'sedimented' at certain critical moments in an organisation's history (Poole 1986) and managers find themselves working within these traditions without necessarily being able to explain how all the pieces got there. Goals may not be seriously analysed unless some kind of crisis emerges in the firm's growth or performance that forces reconsideration and restructuring (e.g. Snape, Redman and Wilkinson 1993, Colling 1995). Our task, then, is better understood as trying to infer the general intentions or motives underpinning labour management, recognising that we are studying a complex, collective process, built up historically in firms and inevitably subject to a degree of interpretation, politicking and inconsistent practice. It helps if we analyse the goals of HRM in terms of two broad categories: economic and socio-political goals (Boxall 2007).

The economic goals of HRM

Cost-effectiveness

We argue in this book that the primary problem facing firms is to secure their economic viability in the industries in which they have chosen to compete. Viability means the firm is profitable enough to satisfy its shareholders and those who have lent it money. It is not essential for a firm to 'maximise' profits but it *is* essential to sustain the commitment of key investors or the firm will fail, be restructured or sold off.

To achieve viability, management needs to stabilise a production system that enables the firm to compete in its industry (Rubery 1994, Rubery and Grimshaw 2003). Industries vary in their 'underlying economic structure' (Porter 1980: 3) and the firm needs a reliable way of producing what its customers want at a price they are prepared to pay. If it is a public sector organisation, it will need to stabilise its operations (for example, run its school or its hospital) within the budget it has been allocated or the price set for its services. In order to support economic viability, managers are naturally concerned with the problem of how to make the kind of labour they need productive within a cost structure the firm can afford. In other words, management seeks to establish a cost-effective system of labour management (Geare 1977, Osterman 1987, Godard 2001).

The fundamental need for a firm's managers to relate their HR activities to the economic characteristics of the industry introduces a major source of variation into how HRM is conducted. Very expensive, high-skill models of labour management, incorporating rigorous selection, high pay, and extensive internal development, are unusual among firms in those services, such as fast food, gas stations and supermarkets, which are characterised by intense, cost-based competition (Boxall 2003). In such circumstances, firms typically adopt a low-skill model of HRM. They have some long-term managers and employees to provide a reliable 'backbone' to operations but otherwise simply offer enough money to attract less experienced workers such as students and new migrants. They do not expect most of these workers to stay very long. Their 'business model' turns on providing adequate rather than excellent service standards because customers are more price than quality sensitive: they will take part in service production (for example, weighing their own fruit and vegetables, packing their own groceries or pumping their own petrol) in order to buy more cheaply. On the other hand, as Godard and Delaney (2000: 488) explain, high-skill, high-commitment HR strategies are more often found where the production system is capital intensive or where high technology is involved. They cite the example of nuclear power plants:

> . . . in a nuclear power plant employing many workers, the costs of poor morale, (labour) turnover, and strikes can be high, so the benefits of HRM innovations will tend to be high. Firm size may also introduce important economies of scale, reducing the costs of HRM innovations per worker. Thus, in this plant, the benefits of new practices can be expected to exceed the costs. In a small, low-technology garment factory employing unskilled labour, the opposite may be true.

In capital-intensive conditions, the actual level of labour cost will be quite low (10 per cent or less of total cost) but workers will have a major effect on how well the technology is utilised or exploited (as Appleyard and Brown (2001) illustrate in the case of semiconductor manufacturing). It thus pays to remunerate and train them very well, making better use of their skills and ensuring their motivation is kept high. As they find ways of making the equipment meet or even exceed its specifications, the unit costs of labour fall and productivity rises. Thus, in this kind of context, the firm can easily sustain high wage levels. It is more important *not* to alienate this kind of labour, because of the productivity impacts of disruptions, than it is to worry about wage levels.

These examples help to illustrate the point that it is wrong to confuse wage levels with *unit* labour costs or to confuse cost minimisation with cost-effectiveness. In certain cases, where product markets are very competitive and where technology is limited and the work is labour intensive, labour costs are decisive in the assessment of cost-effectiveness (Boxall 2003). In these situations, cost-effectiveness does broadly equate with labour cost minimisation because labour cost levels have such a huge impact on the survival of firms. This is why so much clothing, footwear and toy manufacture has moved to low-wage countries such as China and Cambodia. On the other hand, more complex and capital-intensive research and design functions can often be kept in high-wage countries where a small team of well-paid designers uses advanced computing equipment and keeps in close contact with their marketing colleagues and with retail buyers external to the firm.

Clearly, then, the problem of securing cost-effective labour, of making labour productive at reasonable cost, invites some careful thinking about costs and benefits in the industry concerned. There are indeed situations where labour costs can make or break the firm. When this occurs in manufacturing, firms worry about where to site production facilities to take advantage of lower labour costs. When it occurs in services, firms typically use employment practices that keep their service costs competitive: wages paid are relative to 'the going rate' in the local labour market (but rarely superior to it), the training investment is only sufficient to ensure basic quality, and employee turnover levels can be high. Or, if the service can be offered over the internet, managers may think about outsourcing or offshoring it to lower-cost countries. Quality may be no better than average but this may be quite acceptable with customers if the price is right. On the other hand, there are situations where labour costs are not in competition but the interaction between labour and technology needs to be carefully managed to achieve high productivity. Here, high levels of HR investment pay high dividends and help to protect against disruption or downtime. Similarly, there are areas in the service sector, such as professional services, which are knowledge intensive. Here, managers see the value of investing in higher salaries, extensive career development, and time-consuming performance appraisal because these practices foster the kind of expert interactions with customers that make it possible for the firm to secure and retain high value-added business.

In summary, the fundamental economic motive that can be observed in HRM is concerned with making labour productive at an affordable cost in the industry concerned. In effect, managers ask: what HR systems are cost-effective or 'profit-rational' in our specific market context? In capitalist societies, the pursuit of cost-effectiveness runs across the management of labour in all business organisations and also makes its impact in public sector organisations through their budget constraints and contracting requirements.

Organisational flexibility

Cost-effectiveness is not, however, the only economic goal we can discern in HRM. It is something that is aimed for in a *given* context. In other words, given a particular market or budget and a certain type of technology (among other things), it is about management's drive to make labour productive at competitive cost. However, change is inevitable and many firms have, of necessity, adopted some HR practices designed to enhance capacity to change or build 'organisational flexibility' (Osterman 1987). The word 'organisational' is used here because employers typically seek forms of flexibility which extend beyond, but encompass, their labour management (Streeck 1987). Concern to achieve an appropriate degree of flexibility has grown since the 1980s.

Short-run responsiveness

In thinking about the HRM goals that firms pursue in the area of organisational flexibility, it is useful to distinguish between *short-run* responsiveness and *long-run* agility. Short-run responsiveness includes attempts to bring about greater numerical (or 'headcount') flexibility (measures which make it easier to hire and shed labour) and greater financial flexibility (attempts to bring greater flexibility into the price of labour) (Atkinson 1984). Thus, firms engaged in very cyclical activities often seek to relate their permanent staff numbers to their calculation of the troughs in business demand rather than the relatively unpredictable peaks, seeking to offer overtime and bring in temporary or 'seasonal' staff if, and when, the workload surges. In other cases, managers seek to pay workers a mix of wages and profit-related bonuses, with the latter fluctuating in line with company financial fortunes. In both these cases, the emphasis is on adjusting labour costs to fit with changes in business revenues. Short-run responsiveness also includes attempts to hire workers who are cross-trained or 'multi-skilled', combining roles that have historically been kept in separate job descriptions.

Such 'functional flexibility' (Atkinson 1984) helps the firm to maintain a lower headcount but cope better with marginal improvements in product design or production processes.

Long-run agility

Long-run agility, on the other hand, is a much more powerful, but rather ambiguous, concept (Dyer and Shafer 1999). It is concerned with the question of whether a firm can build the ability to survive in an environment that can change radically. Does the firm have the capacity to create, or at least cope with, long-run changes in products, costs and technologies? Can it adapt to change as fast or faster than its major rivals? What elements of its HR strategy might need to be flexible to achieve this? While some firms aspire to long-run agility, organisational ecologists such as Carroll and Hannan (1995), who study patterns of firm birth, growth and decline in industries, observe that it is very hard to achieve because core features of organisations are hard to change once laid down in the early stages of establishment and growth.

A key challenge to the agility of manufacturing firms in recent times has come from the major cost differences between companies with operations in the developed world and those with operations in newly industrialising nations. When manufacturers in lower-cost countries find ways of making the same products at the same quality and delivery benchmarks but do so at much lower prices, established firms operating in high-wage countries either adjust their HR strategies or go out of business. A case in point is one of Britain's most innovative manufacturing firms, Dyson. The firm, an international leader in vacuum cleaner technology, shifted its production facilities to Malaysia in the year 2000. Relocation to Malaysia not only delivered lower unit costs than was possible in the UK but also ensured proximity to key parts suppliers, thus improving the firm's location in its supply chain. Some 550 British workers were laid off in the process and HR strategy now revolves around managing a dual workforce: one in the UK where research and development (R&D) staff are employed and one in Malaysia where the products are assembled.[7] This shift in production facilities and labour forces has made Dyson a more agile firm, enabling it to invest more heavily in R&D and to expand production. The company sees its long-run ability to survive as relying on innovation in its core products or technologies. Making a difficult change to its production and HR strategy

---

7 For a summary of the company's history, see http://en.wikipedia.org/wiki/James_Dyson

has enabled it to focus more effectively on this goal. Agility, then, may mean that the firm needs the capacity to make quite radical changes in HRM.

What about competitive advantage?

Our discussion has focused on employer goals in relation to the viability problem of the firm. The pursuit of viability is clearly the fundamental driver that we observe in management behaviour: without securing economic viability, including its HRM dimensions, firms fail. However, a key question concerns the conditions under which firms can, and do, pursue sustained competitive advantage through HRM (e.g. Wright, McMahan and McWilliams 1994, Mueller 1996, Boxall and Steeneveld 1999). In thinking about this question, it is helpful to distinguish between labour-cost advantages and labour-differentiation advantages and to consider the extent to which either form of advantage can be sustained.

The sort of production switching we have just talked about is done for reasons of cost, including labour costs. This, however, is more likely to enhance viability than it is to bring about a *sustained* advantage: the firms that do it first enjoy some temporary advantages but, as others follow suit, profits typically return to normal. High-tech manufacturing firms, like Dyson, do not necessarily rest in this position. They may seek a more enduring form of advantage through some distinctive feature that is not so easily copied. This is where differentiation in labour quality becomes the issue, which is much more what people have in mind when they think of 'human resource advantage' (HRA). Boxall (1996, 1998) breaks HRA down into 'human capital advantage' (employing smarter people) and 'organisational process advantage' (developing better ways of working together). It is possible to hire brilliant individuals, and this can bring important breakthroughs for a time, but fail to take best advantage of this potential as a result of poor organisational processes in such areas as teamwork, communication and problem solving. Achieving both human capital and organisational process advantages is clearly more valuable.

When might firms embrace a goal of achieving some form of human resource advantage? Existing studies on service sector HR strategy, including Batt's (2000) study of US call centres and Hunter's (2000) study of US rest homes, indicate that firms rarely adopt this goal when they are locked into the cost-based competition that occurs in mass services. In mass services, customers are price sensitive and will typically take part in self-service if the price is right. The goal of HR advantage is more of a possibility in differentiated service markets where a group of more affluent customers is prepared to pay a premium for better quality (Boxall 2003). This often happens, for example, in professional services and in such services as luxury hotels and premium banking. We will explore this issue further in this book. What we wish to emphasise at this stage is that viability is the fundamental business goal that HRM must serve. There are, however, situations in which employers seek sustained competitive advantage through HRM and there are interesting questions around the conditions under which they might achieve it.

The socio-political objectives of HRM

Social legitimacy

While the pursuit of economic objectives is fundamental to HRM, it does not fully account for the strategic behaviour of employers. Firms are economic actors but they operate in societies, making use of human capacities that citizens and the state have nurtured (for example, through family support and through public education and training systems). In this light, governments typically exercise their right to regulate employment practices and constrain employer behaviour. We observe significant variation in HRM based on the way firms respond to different national regulations (e.g. Gooderham, Nordhaug and Ringdal 1999). There are fundamental differences, for example, between US employment systems and those that prevail in the 'Rhineland countries' of Germany, France and the Netherlands where 'social partnership' models accord a strong role to trade unions and works councils (Paauwe and Boselie 2003, 2007). This argument can be linked to the observation that capital markets and the governance systems of firms vary across 'varieties of capitalism' (Hall and Soskice 2001, Gospel and Pendleton 2003). Anglo-American firms, used to operating under more liberal market regimes, need to make adjustments when employing workforces in the more highly coordinated and regulated economies of continental Europe. Firms need to fit into their socio-political context and this inevitably means that packages of 'best practices' developed in one country, such as the USA, can rarely be exported 'holus-bolus' elsewhere.

The 'bottom line' is that most firms allocate some resources to ensuring their moral legitimacy or ethical standing in the society or the various societies in which they operate (Suchman 1995, Paauwe 2004). This is certainly true in societies where labour laws are not simply enacted but also effectively enforced through government agencies and/or trade union action. As Lees (1997) argues, social legitimacy should be understood as an employer goal alongside the more market-oriented ones. In general, employers are concerned with ensuring their social legitimacy *while simultaneously* pursuing cost-effective HRM (Boxall 2007). More broadly, of course, the quality of the firm's reputation as an employer is only one aspect of its social legitimacy, which also includes such things as its impacts on the natural environment. There is a range of contemporary movements designed to encourage greater social responsibility in business and broader corporate reporting, including the notion of the 'triple bottom line' (financial, environmental and social) (Elkington 1997).

In practice, we see significant variation in the extent to which employers take legitimacy goals into account in their labour management. At one extreme, there is a group of employers in any society who try to avoid their legal responsibilities. In the UK, for example, there is an ongoing problem with the employment of new migrants (some legal and some illegal) on wage rates below the legal minimum and in unsafe conditions. This was tragically illustrated in the drowning of 23 Chinese workers while harvesting shell-fish at Morecombe Bay in 2004.[8] There are sectors of the British economy where government enforcement activities (through HM Revenue and Customs) have revealed that a large number of employers do not pay the minimum wage. This has been estimated at one in three workplaces in pre-school childcare ('nurseries').[9] Most employers in Britain, however, comply with their responsibilities under employment law and under government regulations for occupational safety and health. Their legitimacy goal is legal compliance. Compliance is the baseline legitimacy goal for employers who wish to avoid prosecution and bad publicity, a risk in any society in which labour laws are efficiently enforced. It is apparent, however, that some firms, at least, operate beyond this baseline. For example, some firms are now actively competing for Equal Employment Opportunity (EEO) awards or for favourable rankings in lists of the 'best companies to work for', the 'great places to work' or the 'family-friendliest companies'.[10] These tend to be larger, better-known firms, but some are also innovative small firms, with a strong interest in building their standing as an 'employer of choice'. Some see the achievement of the Investors in People (IiP) standard as a dimension of legitimacy since it based on a commitment to training and development

---

8 See, for example: 'Another Morecombe Bay is waiting to happen', *Guardian*, 28 March 2006, p. 28.

9 www.gnn.gov.uk/environment/detail.asp?ReleaseID = 211711andNewsAreaID = 2and NavigatedFromDepartment = True

10 http://money.cnn.com/magazines/fortune/bestcompanies/; http://www.greatplaceto-work.co.uk/; www.workingwoman.com/100BEST_2005.html; http://business.times-online.co.uk/article/0,12190-2329654,00.html

linked to business needs[11] while for others being recognised for corporate social responsibility, including in employment, is a desirable goal.

Managerial autonomy or power to act

As with economic motives, where we see both attempts to stabilise cost-effectiveness in the short run and the need to build some capacity for change if firms are to survive into the long run, it is useful to think about management's socio-political motives in a dynamic way. All firms can be seen as political systems in which management holds authority but one in which management decisions are subject to legal and moral challenge (e.g. Donaldson and Preston 1995). What is management trying to achieve in the politics or governance of the workplace as time goes by? Whether consciously or not, the evidence suggests that management exhibits a fundamental desire to enhance its autonomy or power to act. In a classic study of management ideology, Reinhard Bendix (1956: xxiii) argued that 'ideologies of management are attempts by leaders of enterprises to justify the privilege of voluntary action and association for themselves, while imposing upon all subordinates the duty of obedience and of service to the best of their ability'. Similarly, Gospel (1973) refers to management as having a less openly acknowledged 'security objective' alongside the profit (cost-effectiveness) motive, a goal to maximise managerial control over an uncertain environment including threats to its power from work groups and trade unions. We can add to this the fact that management often feels constrained by sharemarket reporting pressures and scrutiny. De-listing from stockmarkets is growing among firms in which a dominant (often, family-based) interest has sufficient capital to buy out other shareholders.[12]

Most people would recognise that there is a natural tendency in positions of authority or in conditions of risk to try to ensure one can act effectively: it is unhelpful to firms if managers are hopelessly checked at every point when they need to take decisive action. Managers need some 'degrees of freedom' or the job is impossible. The issue we will shortly explore is the question of whether management's drive for power can undermine its other goals, including cost-effectiveness and social legitimacy.

Thus, while management is generally concerned about social legitimacy, at least to the extent of legal compliance in societies where there is a risk of legal enforcement, and sometimes well beyond this, we also observe management

---

11 www.iipuk.co.uk/IIP/Web/default.htm
12 See, for example, *The Economist*, 25 November–1 December 2006, p. 96.

playing a longer-run political game. The natural tendency of management is to act, over time, to enhance its room to manoeuvre. We see this in the way multinational firms tend to favour investment in countries with less demanding labour market regulations (Cooke 2001, 2007). We also see it at industry and societal levels, in the tendency of employer federations to lobby, over time, for greater freedom to manage and to resist new employment regulations seen to be diminishing managerial prerogative. And we see it in the actions of those firms which wish to minimise or eliminate the pressures exerted by external shareholders and watchdogs.

Strategic tensions and problems in HRM

We have identified, then, four fundamental or underpinning motives in HRM (Figure 1.3). We have split these into economic and socio-political goals because the firm is not simply an unconstrained economic entity: it is an economic entity located in a social and political context. In HRM, firms should pursue cost-effectiveness in the industries in which they compete while simultaneously aiming for legitimacy in the societies in which they are located. This is complicated enough but, over time, the firms that survive develop some degree of flexibility in HRM and their managers secure enough autonomy to be effective. Some firms may pursue sustained competitive advantage through HRM. Such a discussion naturally arouses suspicion that the pursuit of these goals is far from straightforward. This is indeed the case. The strategic management of work and people in the firm inevitably involves management wrestling with 'strategic tensions' and problems, including trade-offs between employer and employee interests. We turn now to a discussion of the key tensions and problems that management faces.

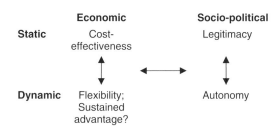

Source: Adapted from Boxall, P., 'The goals of HRM'. In Boxall, P., Purcell, J. and Wright, P. (eds) *The Oxford Handbook of Human Resource Management*. Oxford: Oxford University Press. © 2007 By permission of Oxford University Press.

Figure 1.3   The goals of HRM

One of the main problems facing management stems from the fact that firms need to compete not only in product markets but also in labour markets (Windolf 1986, Rubery 1994, Coff 1997). In all countries where forced labour has been eliminated, workers are free to resign and seek alternative employment. Firms must compete with others to secure appropriately skilled staff. Well-resourced and well-recognised organisations that have the ability to pay the going rate or better, and are able to offer good development opportunities, tend to dominate the labour market. As a result, many small firms remain fragile, tenuous organisations with ongoing recruitment problems (Storey 1985, Hendry, Arthur and Jones 1995, Hornsby and Kuratko 2003). The goals of building a stable production system, including a cost-effective supply of motivated employees, and building some capacity for development of the business, are seriously compromised if the firm cannot make competitive job offers and keep the labour it has. It then struggles to build the capabilities it needs to meet its business objectives or respond to its clients' demands. In the extreme, the tension associated with labour scarcity can become a full-blown 'capability crisis', threatening the firm's reputation and viability.

Labour scarcity is a problem that can afflict entire industries and not simply undercapitalised firms or new firms struggling for recognition. In the oil sector, shortages of managers, technical staff and offshore engineers are currently compromising the development of new production, leading to project delays, salary inflation and associated cost increases.[13] In the British trucking industry, there are major shortages of drivers because of difficult working conditions: drivers have responsibility for valuable vehicles and loads, work long hours in dangerous conditions and are often away from home (Marchington, Carroll and Boxall 2003). Many people who hold driving qualifications prefer to work in a local factory or service industry where their lifestyle can be more normal. In the health sector, labour scarcity is a worldwide phenomenon: competition for workers with internationally transferable skills continues to strain the resources of public and private health systems all over the world. The UK government's list of skill shortages, used to indicate immigration opportunities, currently includes over 50 categories of medical specialists.[14] As recruiters in rich countries comb the globe for scarce labour, there can be kick-on effects and ethical

---

13 *The Times*, 17 April 2006, p. 39; http://news.bbc.co.uk/1/hi/scotland/4302937.stm
14 www.skillclear.com/skilllist.asp#doctors

problems, unfortunately: health services in third-world countries can be denuded of expensively trained health professionals by first-world poaching.

The problem of labour motivation

As suggested by the AMO framework, a second major problem is associated with the motivation of employee behaviour if and when workers are actually hired. Motivation is a fragile variable. The employment contract is an exchange relationship but, unlike the sale and purchase of commodities, it involves an ongoing, unpredictable interaction between the parties. Future behaviour matters but neither party can accurately predict it when they sign up. Both are relying on some element of trust and are therefore taking risks. As the pioneering industrial relations writers, Sidney and Beatrice Webb (1902: 658) put it, the labour contract is 'indeterminate'. Will the worker offer a conscientious, consistent level of effort over time, helping the employer reach their productivity objectives? On the other side of the coin, will the employer impose work pressures that are intense or make the worker suffer working conditions that are unsafe? Will the level of work pressure be subtly (or, perhaps, crudely) increased over time without any renegotiation of rewards? Such a process of work intensification can undermine the initial trust extended to the employer by the worker and invite some form of retaliation which then damages the firm's performance (for example, reduction of work quality, absenteeism, disinclination to 'go the extra mile', and resignation). Overall, will the 'wage-effort bargain' become more or less satisfying for the parties? Will the parties achieve some kind of satisfactory balance in their relationship?

It is impossible to anticipate all this in advance and silly to think that any written contract of employment could cover all the possibilities (Williamson, Wachter and Harris 1975). As Cartier (1994: 182) puts it, 'the contract of employment is inherently incomplete'. As a result, the law gives employers the right to issue what are commonly known as 'lawful and reasonable orders', but the simple fact is that control of the behaviour of other human beings is always limited. When individuals are instructed to carry out work tasks, their discretion is never fully taken away from them (Bendix 1956). The employer, like the employee, must exercise some trust, relying to some extent on workers to use their judgement. For example, no matter how much 'scripting' there is of how to deal with customers in shops, restaurants or call centres, the individual employee can still decide not to be helpful or to be plainly rude in a way that alienates customers, something we have all experienced or may encounter on a regular basis. 'Discretionary behaviour' is something that employees can give and can withdraw (Appelbaum et al. 2000, Purcell et al. 2003). As Keenoy (1992: 95) argues, 'no matter how extensive the controls, in the final analysis, management is reliant on employee cooperation'.

There is a huge body of literature examining the relationships between employer and employee interests in the workplace and their implications for motivation, cooperation and workplace performance. In the Industrial Relations (IR) and Sociology of Work (SW) traditions, emphasis is placed on the fact that there are important conflicts of interest in the workplace (e.g. Clegg 1975, Kelly 1998, Blyton and Turnbull 2004). Conflicts over income (e.g. what share of revenue goes to profit and what to wages?; what relativities should there be across occupational groups?; to what extent is it fair to pay for performance differences within occupational groups?) and over the control of work (e.g. who makes decisions about work processes?; what staffing levels should be maintained?; how fair is the workload?) are seen to affect the basis for workplace cooperation. IR/SW scholars emphasise the role of voice institutions in improving the balance of interests (e.g. Budd 2004). The general argument is that management should work with worker representatives in processes of collective bargaining, information sharing and consultation, to enhance fairness and build a work climate characterised by trust and cooperation. A willingness on management's part to share control is seen as important to developing a stable 'social order' in which both the firm and its workers can work productively and reap rewards they value (e.g. Watson 2005, 2007).

Research in the Organisational Psychology (OP) and Organisational Behaviour (OB) traditions also emphasises fairness or equity concerns in the workplace, including employee concerns with distributive and procedural justice (e.g. Folger and Cropanzano 1998). The OP/OB traditions also include extensive work on the motivational properties of work itself, on the ways in which work can be made more interesting and challenging (e.g. Cordery and Parker 2007). In terms of conceptual frameworks, the notion that individuals have a 'psychological contract' with their employer has become increasingly important (e.g. Rousseau 1995, Guest 2007). A major gap between what management promises and what management delivers in the psychological contract inevitably affects an individual's capacity to trust and their level of motivation and commitment. The OP/OB tradition is important for its analytical focus on questions affecting the motivation of individual employees.

In this book, we bring together these perspectives on motivation. The key point both traditions emphasise is that a tension around employee motivation is endemic to the employment relationship. Motivation is an ongoing concern for individual managers and for management collectively. At their worst, motivational challenges can be expressed in forms of collective action (such as lowered work norms and strikes) or in high levels of individual action (such as dysfunctional levels of absenteeism and turnover). Such challenges can affect management's legitimacy, depress productivity and threaten the firm's viability.

Change tensions in labour management

The need to pursue stable production, while also pursuing some degree of flexibility, poses major dilemmas within management strategy (Osterman 1987, Brown and Reich 1997, Adler, Goldoftas and Levine 1999). How much weight should management place on strengthening its production routines and staffing arrangements to make the firm more efficient and how much weight should be placed on building flexibility for the future (Wright and Snell 1998)?

To illustrate the difficult choices involved, suppose a firm developing a new line of business decides it wants a high degree of flexibility. Unemployment levels are presently high and management thus employs all operating staff in the new business on short-term or temporary employment contracts. This means the firm can shed labour more easily if it has to. A problem emerges, however, as the labour market improves: many of the more highly skilled and productive workers move to more secure jobs elsewhere (why should they work on a short-term contract when they can obtain a permanent job, one that will help them gain home loans and make their families more secure?). In this labour market, the firm finds that it fails to recruit and retain as well as its competitors or to reach their level of production quality. Too much emphasis on flexible employment starts to threaten the firm's chances of survival. It will have to think again about how to employ people.

Imagine another firm, which employs all its labour on well-paid, permanent contracts to build a loyal workforce (traditionally called 'labour hoarding'). This works well for quite a time but the firm's sales are sensitive to consumer discretionary spending and decline sharply when a minor recession comes along. The firm has products with excellent long-term prospects but greater flexibility is needed in its staffing structure to ensure it can weather these sorts of short-term variations in demand. It is forced to make some lay-offs, a process that tarnishes its reputation with employees, and spurs management to think about whether all staff should actually be on permanent contracts.

As these illustrations makes apparent, both of these scenarios represent undesirable extremes. Both firms need to consider how to strike a better balance between short-run and long-run. Further, as the scenarios make clear, the problem of how to cope with change not only creates dilemmas within management strategy but brings trade-offs with the security interests of workers. In Hyman's (1987: 43) memorable phrase, capitalism is a system in which 'employers require workers to be *both* dependable *and* disposable'. The most resilient firms are those which can evolve a clever balance between stability and flexibility while maintaining employee trust and confidence. This is much easier said than done.

Legitimacy challenges in wider society

As emphasised above, some measure of social legitimacy typically matters to firms. The 'social order' within the firm which we have talked about in relation to the problem of motivation inevitably connects to the wider society. In countries such as the UK, France and the USA, the growth of trade unions in the early to mid parts of the twentieth century saw the legitimacy challenge spill over from the shopfloor onto the streets and vice versa. These countries and many others experienced waves of strikes and social disruption as unions sought recognition and the establishment of collective bargains. Unions also turned to national political activity, lobbying political parties and, in many countries, forming their own. As a result, progressive social legislation – which brings organising rights and minimum conditions to all workers – has largely eliminated this sort of challenge in advanced industrialised countries. There are exceptions, of course. Stubborn management resistance to employee influence is still apparent in a minority of firms, something which can require the intervention of government mediation services. There is also the fact that there are low-wage sectors in advanced countries which may be targeted by unions and community coalitions (see, for example, the 'living wage' campaigns in the USA described by Juravich and Hilgert (1999) and Nissen (2000)). More and more political concern, however, is now focused on working conditions in the Third World.

This does not mean Western companies are off the hook. An important development concerns the ethics of human resource management in global supply chains in which managers often seek out production sites which offer both lower costs and greater management autonomy (Cooke 2001, 2007). But problems can come. Multinational clothing and footwear companies are increasingly concerned that they do not acquire a reputation for sourcing their products from contractors employing Third World labour on exploitative terms.[15] Levi Strauss, for example, while no longer able to retain large production capacity in the United States because of major changes in the economics of production in its industry, is concerned to ensure that its foreign contractors comply with its code of employment ethics.[16]

A key question is whether companies can successfully audit their own performance in this area. To bring third-party scrutiny into the assessment of ethical employment practice, a New York-based organisation called Social Accountability International has developed an international standard called SA (Social Accountability) 8000.[17]. SA 8000 is based on key conventions drawn from the ILO (International Labour Organisation), the Universal Declaration of Human Rights and the UN Convention on the Rights of the Child. It thus incorporates standards on child and forced labour, union rights, employee discipline, and health and safety, among others. Companies seeking this standard must be audited and certified by an accredited audit agency. While modelled on the well-known ISO quality system, SA 8000 requires auditors to consult with workers and their unions, and includes a mechanism for workers to bring complaints about non-compliance. Companies which are signatory members of SA 8000 (meaning their own factories and their suppliers must comply) include the world's largest toy retailer, Toys R Us. Another way in which global companies can attest to the legitimacy of their HRM is through membership of the 'Ethical Trading Initiative', an alliance of companies, non-governmental organisations and trade unions, which requires independent verification that codes of employment practice are being implemented.[18]

These accountability standards underline the important role that trade unions and, in European countries, works councils have played in improving the legitimacy of employment practices. When management reaches employment agreements with worker organisations, and thus willingly constrains its own autonomy in certain ways, the legitimacy of the employment regime in the firm is usually enhanced. However, voice practices are now much more diverse with many initiatives having been developed by employers (Boxall, Freeman and Haynes 2007). How workers feel about these newer forms of voice is a question we explore in this book.

---

15 See, for example, 'Labour Behind the Label', www.cleanupfashion.co.uk/
16 www.levistrauss.com/Citizenship/
17 www.sa-intl.org/
18 www.ethicaltrade.org/

Complexity and politics in management

What we have said so far should indicate the kind of complexity that is involved in managing work and people. The fact that we can highlight the sorts of problems firms face in pursuing their HRM goals does not mean that it is easy to solve any of them. Complexity grows as organisations grow and as they become more diverse. Management faces 'cognitive limitations' in developing good strategy, a problem that has bedevilled management attempts to develop astute frameworks for problem analysis and goal setting in HRM. Despite the growing attention to HRM since the 1980s, boardroom and top management debates have often been hamstrung by lack of agreement on how reports on strategic HR matters should be structured. The problem was summed up by a group managing director in Purcell and Ahlstrand's (1994) study of HRM in multidivisional firms who commented that the board in his company 'had decided on thirty priorities in the last few years, with the people ones being the most woolly, the hardest to measure, and the easiest to forget'. In this light, much of this book is dedicated to examining confusing HR issues that affect management policy and exploring frameworks that can help structure the management of work and people in a way useful to managers.

But management's problems in HRM are not simply cognitive. Strategic management is not just mentally hard, it is politically fraught. Never mind the politics between management and labour, some of the worst politics are on one's own side. For example, if a senior HR executive in a large firm argues for a longer-term investment in building organisational agility through greater human resource development (e.g. greater use of off-the-job training and personal development for all workers), this idea is hardly likely to win universal support. It is an investment which needs to be justified. If the company is a multidivisional firm, business unit managers may not see the idea as helpful. If they are incentivised to produce short-run profit, why should they support activities which take people away from their jobs and which potentially make them less satisfied with their lot? This is just one example of internal politics but an important one in complex, multidivisional firms.

Variations in institutional supports and societal resources

Finally, supposing management understands the problems of HRM well enough and is well resourced and well disposed in political terms to handle them, we return to the fact that firms are embedded in industries and societies, as scholars of comparative employment institutions, such as Rubery and Grimshaw (2003), emphasise. Small firms are clearly very dependent on state support which includes, very critically, systems for vocational education and training in their sector (Winterton 2007). Firms in societies in which they and their competitors rely on 'poaching' rather than training to develop the staff they need are very vulnerable in a hot labour market: the undercapitalised ones may simply fail to attract the workers they need, finding that customers desert them and they lose their reputation.

It is wrong to assume that these issues simply afflict small firms. So-called 'global' firms are also affected by the dominant ways in which a society organises its human resource development. As is well known, large British manufacturers have been at a disadvantage for some time. German firms, for example, have enjoyed major advantages in manufacturing arising from superior technical training systems to those typically found in English-speaking countries (Steedman and Wagner 1989, Wever 1995). As Winterton (2007: 327) explains, 'the higher skill level of the German workforce is generally seen as a source of competitive advantage, permitting German firms to focus on higher value-added market niches'. On the other hand, he also explains that German firms do not have it all their own way: US and UK firms often find it easier to make the changes necessary to bring in 'lean production' and more flexible ways of working. The slow pace of the German institutional structure, with its layers of industrial negotiation and consultation, can act as a costly drag. Firms in the Anglophone world often take advantage of their more fluid decision-making structures. This helps to make the point that the industry and societal context both constrains and enables firms to perform.

In sum, then, firms are not masters of their own destiny in HRM even if they perceive the issues well and want to act effectively. We will be arguing that management does enjoy a realm of strategic choice to make distinctive decisions in HRM but the extent of that realm varies: the choices are never entirely in management's hands.

Summary and structure of the book

This book adopts a broad, inclusive definition of HRM because we aim to explore the various ways in which HRM is critical to the survival and relative performance of firms and other formal organisations. Human resource management includes the firm's work systems and its employment practices. It embraces both individual and collective aspects of people management. It is not restricted to any one style or ideology. It engages the energies of both line and specialist managers (where the latter exist) and typically entails a range of messages for a variety of workforce groups.

This chapter has discussed the goals or motives that we see underpinning the management of work and people. Human resource management is a process which serves more than one critical goal. Managers face the need to develop a cost-effective system of labour management to support the firm's economic viability in the industries in which it competes. At the same time, management typically aims to secure legitimacy in the societies in which the firm operates through, at the minimum, employing labour according to legal requirements. Over time, successful firms also embed elements of flexibility into their HRM to enable them to cope better with change and we observe management seeking to enhance its autonomy or power to act. Some firms pursue sustained competitive advantage through the way they manage labour.

Pursuing these goals inevitably involves grappling with strategic tensions and problems. The problem of labour scarcity hamstrings firms which are weak in the labour market. Labour motivation is a multi-layered challenge in all firms because control of human behaviour is inevitably limited. There is a fragile chain of links connecting what managers want to achieve with work and people and what they actually achieve. The need to grapple with change brings trade-offs between company survival and employee security. Wider social concern with the work and employment practices of firms can bring major challenges to legitimacy, including in global supply chains. The cognitive and political issues associated with these problems are a major problem in themselves. And, even where the firm is well resourced and astutely led, there are serious challenges posed by the industry and societal contexts in which firms are embedded.

We have a job to do, so what lies ahead? In Part 1, three chapters look at the key bridges that link strategy with HRM. Chapter 2 explores the meaning of strategy and the process of strategic management, including its (very human) cognitive and political dimensions. In Chapter 3, we set up definitions of strategic HRM and HR strategy and examine the debate between universalist ('best practice') and contingency ('best fit') models of strategic HRM. This chapter underlines the importance of a firm adapting its HRM to its context while also finding a useful role for general principles of labour management. Chapter 4 explores the implications for strategic HRM of the resource-based view of the firm. This is a key body of thought in contemporary strategic management which is richly laced with human issues. Along with an emphasis on the fact that firms are embedded in a web of social institutions and expectations, it is a perspective which informs much of the rest of the book.

In Part 2, the book contains four chapters which aim to lay the basis of a strategic theory of labour management after the previous part has undermined simplistic concepts of 'best practice'. It explores general principles that can be used to guide the strategic choices firms make in managing work and people. In Chapter 5, we examine work systems in the light of the changing economics of production. Then, in Chapter 6, we explore theory and research on the management of employee voice. This is followed by Chapter 7 which focuses on the management of individual performance and commitment. In Chapter 8, we draw the various pieces from this part of the book together through a typology outlining major HR systems and a model of the key links between HR systems and performance inside the 'black box' of the firm.

In Part 3 of the book, we apply strategy concepts and general principles of labour management to the analysis of HR strategy in complex and dynamic contexts. In Chapter 9, we set out a model of how HR strategy evolves across cycles of industry-based competition. Then, in Chapter 10, we discuss research on the nature of HRM in the most complex contexts currently known: multidivisional and multinational firms. The final chapter (Chapter 11) summarises the book's most important themes and asks the 'where to from here?' question, examining ways in which the understandings of strategy and HRM developed in this book might be practically applied to improve the strategic management processes in contemporary firms.

part 1

Connecting strategy and human resource management

2

Strategy and the process of strategic management

What do we mean by 'strategy' and 'strategic management' – and what role does HRM typically play in them? How might HRM play a more powerful, more effective role in strategic management? This part of the book is dedicated to these important questions. Because of diverse conceptions of strategy, the role of the first chapter in Part 1 is to establish a definition of this troublesome and over-worked word. In so doing, we consider the ways in which strategy is formed and re-formed in organisations – the *process* of strategic management. As the chapter will make clear, strategic management is a human process beset with all the pitfalls that characterise human attempts to make decisions in conditions of uncertainty, rivalry and limited resources. The major frameworks that have been used to understand the role of strategic HRM are covered in the two chapters that follow this one. In these chapters, we review the main theories that have been put forward on the strategy–HRM linkage.

Defining strategy

As many writers have pointed out, the notion of strategy is subject to a confusing variety of interpretations. Much of the early literature in the field of strategic HRM leapt into the fray with little recognition that the notion of strategy needs careful handling. In order to describe what we mean by the word, it helps if we start with the negative. What definitions or conceptions of strategy are *not* helpful?

First, as Henry Mintzberg (e.g. 1978, 1990, 1994) has long argued, it is unhelpful to equate strategy with 'strategic plan'. A strategic plan is a formal document setting out an organisation's goals and initiatives over a defined time period. Strategic plans are characterised by a variety of formats: the time horizons vary, as do the range of goals targeted, as do the activities that are planned for and the ways in which they are integrated with one another. Strategic plans are more likely to be found in large, complex companies which have major problems with coordinating efforts towards common goals (Grant 2005). It is hard to see how any multidivisional firm – facing the task of allocating its capital across business units – could cope without them. It is easy to see why such 'vast, diverse' firms as General Electric developed corporate planning in the 1960s (Whittington 1993: 71). Strategic plans are also more likely to be found in public sector organisations which generally have strict requirements to disclose their goals and principal activities to politicians and the public. There are also certain industries where formal planning is *de rigueur*. It is impossible, for example, to undertake major construction projects without formal planning for the financial, architectural, material, labour and environmental implications. Official permission is rarely forthcoming without it.

However, the formality of strategic planning is unusual in small businesses – which often account for as much as half the private sector economy. Does this mean these firms have no strategy? Certainly not. It is possible to find *strategy* in every business because it is embedded in the important choices the managers and staff of the firm make about what to do and how to do it. In other words, when careful observers (such as would-be owners) make the effort, it is possible to discern the firm's strategy in its behaviour, in the characteristic ways in which the organisation tries to cope with its environment (Freeman 1995). As will be explained further below, we intend to base our understanding of strategy on the 'strategic choice' perspective. This conception of strategy means we should also 'treat with a grain of salt' the strategic plans we do find in the kind of organisations that use them. Formal planning documents rarely describe all of the organisation's strategic behaviour or keep track of all of its 'strategic learning' over time (Mintzberg 1990). We are not wanting to imply, however, that planning is unhelpful. Far from it. As we will explain further in Part 3 of the book and in the final chapter, the research suggests that good planning is very valuable in HRM. We are not anti-planners. The point we are making here is that strategy is best discerned *in behaviour*.

Secondly, it is unhelpful to make a hard distinction between 'strategy' and 'tactics' or between 'strategy' and 'operations'. This is a problem that has crept into business (and the new public sector management) from the military origins of strategy. In classical Greek, '*strategos*' is associated with the role of the general (Bracker 1980). In popular usage, we still tend to associate strategy with the lofty, orchestrating overview of the military commander. There are lots of problems with this imagery – including its restricted model of leadership and communication – but one major problem is the way it tends to imply that tactics or operations are things that can be mopped up afterwards, things that we have to do but which are not really important. Nothing could be further from the truth – in business and, for that matter, in war.

Sound operational planning and reliable delivery of service is essential to the success of any business. Take a 'High Street' or 'Main Street' bank, for example. If it cannot reliably organise its information processing – its receiving, storing and analysis of transactions – its chances of staying in business are slim. If it cannot run branch offices according to official opening hours or fails to maintain its ATMs[1] or its internet sites, it will lose customer support. In other words, certain key operational practices are strategic to success in all organisations. Going back to the military sphere, much of the German success in the First World War is attributed to German 'tactical excellence': the adaptable behaviour of well-trained soldiers in the field who coped better than most with the chaos that the fighting inevitably created (Ferguson 1998: 308–10). Much of the ultimate German failure, however, can be attributed to serious difficulty in forming and re-forming appropriate 'war aims' (Ferguson 1998: 282–6).

Astute leaders realise the importance of operational disciplines. In the management jargon of the 1980s – the era of *In Search Of Excellence* (Peters and Waterman 1982) – they understand the importance of productive workplace 'culture'. This is a reason why, in some enduring organisations, only those who have worked their way up from fundamental roles in the firm's production or sales processes can ever hold the top management posts (Pascale 1985). On the way up the organisation they should have learnt that there are strategic dimensions of all the key disciplines that constitute the business. Making a business successful is about giving due attention to the critical aspects of all the essential parts of the system, ensuring they are genuinely supporting the firm's mission and one another.

---

1 Automatic teller machines

In adopting this perspective, some may think we are debasing the currency of strategy. If there are strategic aspects of all business disciplines, then there is no simple split between what the 'clever folk at headquarters' do and what the rest of us do. Where do we draw the line between the strategic and the non-strategic? It must be admitted that this is often a difficult thing to discern, not least because the environment changes in ways that surface new issues of strategic concern. Take the internet, for example. Ten to fifteen years ago it seemed that retailers, particularly the small ones, could ignore the kind of avant-garde information technology on which it is based and its implications for sales and distribution processes. Now hardly anyone in retail can afford to be complacent about it, large or small: web pages help potential customers to locate retailers of certain kinds of products, search for items in their stock and, in many cases, make purchases over the internet.

It seems we need some way of discerning where the strategic issues lie. One thing we must definitely avoid is the profligate application of strategy language simply to impress. This has become something of a disease in the HRM literature. Very often writers in HRM have slapped the word 'strategic' in front of the old sub-functional categories of selection, appraisal, pay, and training to produce, as if by magic, a book on 'strategic HRM'. David Guest makes exactly the same point about much of the transition from personnel management to HRM – the covers of some textbooks changed but very little in between them (Guest 1987: 506). As he points out, and as many managers know, the titles of personnel departments often changed with little attempt to review the nature of the work they do. This kind of self-serving use of language leaves students and practitioners with no basis for distinguishing between the critical or strategic issues involved in running firms successfully and those which are of lesser significance. In the definitions that follow, we will attempt to provide a more meaningful set of markers.

Strategic problems and the strategies of firms

We are now in a position to move from the negative to the positive. In our view, strategy is best defined by making a distinction between the 'strategic problems' firms face in their environment and the strategies they adopt to cope with them (Boxall 1998: 266). Naturally, this means we believe that there is a real business environment, a relatively objective reality 'out there' that firms must deal with. The environment – political, economic, social and technological[2] – is not a fiction or something that can be trivialised in highly subjective word-games. The stark fact is that sooner, rather than later, firms face 'intelligent opposition' from rivals (Quinn 1980). They can also face quite threatening regulation from the state and major fluctuations in markets. Even the most powerful firms, seemingly in control of their environment, will eventually face some kind of turbulence that threatens their position. Those who fail to understand their environment will fall foul of it.

The problem of viability

The most critical challenge that the firm faces is that of survival: the problem of becoming and remaining viable in its chosen market (Barnard 1938, Suarez and Utterback 2005). Unless the firm has the *savoir faire* to compete in its chosen market, it is not going to be taken seriously by potential customers and investors. Another way of putting this is to say that all firms require 'table stakes': a set of goals, resources and capable people that are appropriate to the industry concerned (Hamel and Prahalad 1994: 226, Boxall and Steeneveld 1999). Decisions about these 'table stakes' are strategic. They are make-or-break factors. Get the system of these choices right – or right enough – and the firm will be viable. Miss a key piece out and the firm will fail. In other words, when we use the word 'strategic' to describe something, we are saying it is critical to survival, it is seriously consequential. We take, in effect, the common sense view that the word 'strategic' should indicate something of genuine significance for the future of the firm (Johnson 1987, Purcell and Ahlstrand 1994: 51–2).

Continuing with our banking illustration, take the case of a company launching a new High Street or Main Street bank (Freeman 1995: 221). To be credible at all, it must have the same kinds of technology as other banks, a similar profile of products or services, the necessary levels of funding, systems of internal control, skilled staff who can make it happen 'with the gear' on the day, and a management team who can assemble these resources and focus the firm's energies on objectives that will satisfy its investors. Without an effective cluster of goals, resources and human capabilities, it is over before it starts (Figure 2.1). As Freeman (1995: 221) emphasises, much of the firm's strategy is formed in a 'package' when the original choice of industry is made. A bank has to act like a bank: it comes with the territory.

---

2 Readers will recognise the PEST framework here. See, for example, Johnson and Scholes (1997: 93–9).

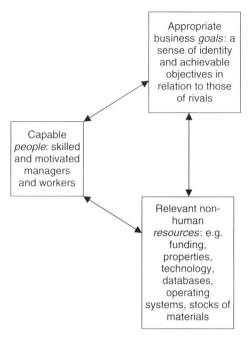

Figure 2.1 Three critical elements for the viability of the firm

The problem of viability is *the* fundamental strategic problem. While Figure 2.1 summarises the critical elements involved in it, it naturally over-simplifies the ambiguities, tensions and complexities involved. It is not necessarily straightforward to decide on the right mix of goals for the firm. Just take one example. Will the firm be more viable if it grows organically or by acquisition? There are costs and benefits in both strategies (Whittington 1993) and different firms in different sectors will read them in different ways at different times. Nor does a simple diagram like Figure 2.1 highlight the difficult relationships *among* resources that have to be managed. In business, different departments usually control some part of the firm's resources (Quinn 1980) but coordination among them is frequently difficult. As is often noted, 'marketing only promises what operations cannot deliver'.

What Figure 2.1 does highlight, however, is that there is no solution to the problem of viability *without* capable people. Appropriate human capabilities are strategic to the success of every firm. It is only people that pose the questions, 'What goals are appropriate for the business?' and 'What resources are relevant to our goals?', and take an interest in making the answers a reality. This is desperately obvious but it has to be said because there are dozens of books on strategic management which assume that good strategy appears out of nowhere: human beings do not seem to be involved.

Because the arrows go both ways, Figure 2.1 also highlights the fact that the three elements of goals, people, and other resources are *interactive* over time. While founding leaders are the first to develop goals (Boeker 1989), the sort of identity a firm acquires, and the sort of objectives it pursues, will attract some people to it and repel others from it. A firm like The Body Shop, with a reputation for environmentally friendly and 'cruelty-free' products, tends to draw in workers who identify with such goals.[3] Similarly, human capabilities and the firm's non-human resources interact with its goals over time. Take the example of a clothing manufacturing firm which hires workers who are not particularly flexible in their skills and invests very few funds in training. Such a firm may make lower-cost garments, with adequate quality standards, but never be able to make complex or high quality, branded clothing which commands a premium. The competitive goals of such a firm are limited by its historical investments in people and resources, a problem that will not be overcome quickly, if at all – a phenomenon noted in comparative studies of the British and German clothing industries (Steedman and Wagner 1989, Lane 1990). As is emphasised in the resource-based view of the firm (discussed in Chapter 4), the history of any firm is both a help and a hindrance: it enables management to contemplate some futures but makes other aspirations extremely difficult simply because the firm's 'routines' have been focused on other concerns (Nelson and Winter 1982).

The problem of viability, then, is the most critical problem facing the firm. It is a messy, interactive, dynamic set of concerns which we can simplify somewhat for theoretical purposes but never totally specify.

The problem of sustained advantage

While the problem of viability is the fundamental (though never static) strategic problem, there is a 'second-order' problem that lies beyond it. Firms which deal adequately with the viability problem have the chance to play in a higher-level 'tournament': the contest among leaders of sound businesses to see which firm can secure the best rate of return. They are sufficiently in control of the survival issues to contemplate superior performance. In effect,

---

3 The Body Shop's official company values can be found at: www.thebodyshop international.com/Values+and+Campaigns/Our+Values/Home.htm

this is not so much a problem as an opportunity, an opportunity to move beyond the pack and gain industry leadership (Boxall and Steeneveld 1999). It is, however, convenient to call it a problem because it is extremely difficult to achieve. As Chapter 4 will explain, it involves a complex mix of factors, human and non-human.

A firm which builds a relatively consistent pattern of superior returns for its shareholders has developed some form of 'competitive advantage' (Porter 1985) – or achieved what the economic theory of the firm has traditionally called 'rents': profits above what can normally be earned in conditions of 'perfect competition'. Chief executives are often incentivised for this higher-level game: they may, for example, be promised certain bonus sums if the firm's profitability significantly exceeds the industry average or if its share price beats the average of its rivals over a certain time-frame. Their goal, if you will, is not to support perfect competition (which might be a goal of politicians) but to engineer *im*perfect competition favouring their firm.

How long such superior performance can be sustained is, of course, variable. We should not think that superior performance can be maintained indefinitely. It doesn't take what economists call 'perfect competition' for imitative forces to set in. There simply have to be serious rivals – as there are in any oligopolistic market – who detect that someone has achieved an unusual level of profitability and seek to compete it away. It is better to think of 'barriers to imitation' as having different heights and different rates of decay or erosion (Reed and DeFillippi 1990). And, as Barney (1991) reminds us, there is always the possibility of 'Schumpeterian shocks'. This refers to the great Austrian economist, Joseph Schumpeter's view that capitalism involves 'gales of creative destruction' (Schumpeter 1950: 84). These are major innovations in products or processes which can destroy whole firms and the industries they inhabit. As he pointed out, this is a lot tougher than price-based competition.

The question of how to achieve competitive advantage is the dominant concern in the strategic management literature. Following theorists like Porter (1985, 1991), strategy textbooks in the last twenty years have typically assumed that competitive advantage is the dependent variable of interest in the whole subject. In our view, this emphasis is somewhat unbalanced. It focuses too much on how firms might make themselves different. Firms are inevitably different – in good, bad and ugly ways – but we think it is more balanced to use the notion of two strategic problems or dependent variables – viability and sustained advantage. In other words, firms must meet certain base-line conditions that make them similar to other firms (in the industries and societies in which they are based) while also having the opportunity to make gains from being positively different.

Our emphasis on the problem of viability is broadly consistent with the arguments of sociologists including 'organisational ecologists' (such as Carroll and Hannan 1995) and 'institutionalists' (such as DiMaggio and Powell 1983) who examine the processes that account for similarity among organisations. Recognition that firms face pressures to conform in order to gain social approval – or 'legitimacy' (one of the key goals, discussed in Chapter 1, that we discern in HRM) – and have economic reasons to adopt successful strategies in their industry has grown in the strategic management literature (see, for example, Oliver 1997, Peteraf and Shanley 1997, Deephouse 1999). In saying, then, that competitive advantage is a desirable end, we are not wanting to convey the impression that firms which pursue it will become completely different from their rivals. They will not. They will retain many similarities. If successful in securing competitive advantage, however, they will have some distinctive traits that give them superior profitability. Take the low-cost airline industry, for example. In this industry, companies like Ryanair and easyJet follow a very similar formula: they focus on the short-haul market (including the lucrative tourist market within Europe), tend to use one or two styles of airplane to reduce maintenance costs, carry higher loads of passengers, keep their aircraft airborne for longer, seriously reduce a range of staffing costs, and foster internet booking enormously.[4] All of this helps to keep prices low (despite the various price add-ons). While there are differences in their strategies (e.g. in the extent to which they use primary or secondary airports), these low-cost airlines have major similarities as opposed to 'full-service' and long-haul carriers.

The strategies of firms

In this context, the *strategies* of firms are their particular attempts to deal with the strategic problems they face. They are the characteristic ways in which the managers of firms understand their goals and develop resources – both human and non-human – to reach them. Some strategies are better than others in the context concerned: some address the problem of viability extremely well and others are simply disastrous – with every shade of effectiveness in between. The very best strategies are those which reach

---

4 See www.guardian.co.uk/airlines/story/0,1888934,00.html; and *Guardian*, 14 December 2006, G2, p. 21.

beyond the problem of viability to master the 'second-order' problem of sustained advantage. When key requirements for viability are not addressed by a firm's strategy, either its leaders learn quickly where they are failing or the firm will fold up. In this sense, all firms have strategies but some have strategies that are much smarter than those of other firms. This is exactly what we observe in practice. The fact that someone has a strategy does not mean they are successful. It simply means they have a characteristic way of behaving in their environment.

As noted earlier, we should not make the mistake of equating the strategies of firms with formal strategic plans. Following the 'strategic choice' perspective (Child 1972), it is better if we understand the strategies of firms as *sets of strategic choices*, some of which might stem from planning exercises and set-piece debates in senior management, and some of which emerge in a stream of action. The latter, called 'emergent strategy' by Mintzberg (1978) in a classic paper, is an inevitable feature of strategy. Once a firm commits to a particular strategy, such as a decision to enter internet banking, it is inevitable that the process of carrying out that commitment will involve learning which will shape the strategy over time. Resource commitments of this kind provide a structure or frame within which strategy evolves.

In defining a firm's strategy as a set of strategic choices we are saying that it includes critical choices about ends *and* means. A firm's strategy contains 'outward' and 'inward' elements. Firms face the problem of choosing suitable goals and the problem of choosing and organising appropriate resources to meet them. In effect, our 'strategic choice' definition draws on a 'configurational' or *gestalt* perspective (Miller 1981, Meyer, Tsui and Hinings 1993, Veliyath and Srinavasan 1995). To be successful, firms need an effective configuration of choices involving all the key dimensions of the business. At a minimum, these include choices about competitive strategy (which markets to enter and how to compete in them), financial strategy (how to fund the business over time), operational strategy (what supplies, technology and methods to use in producing the goods or services), and human resource strategy (how to recruit, organise and motivate the people needed now and over time).

This definition means we do not use the terms 'business strategy' and 'competitive strategy' interchangeably (Boxall 1996). Competitive strategy is a sub-set of business strategy, an aspect that interacts with, and evolves with, other aspects of the firm's strategy over time. This is not an attempt to downplay competitive strategy. There is no doubt that decisions about market positioning are extremely important, as we have already indicated.

In the course of the next chapter, we will examine theory and research on the relationship between competitive strategy and human resource strategy and other factors – such as the nature of the industry and its technologies – which can affect this relationship.

Our discussion so far implies that business strategy is composed of a cluster of strategies covering the various 'functional silos' of the business: marketing, operations, finance and human resources. Another way of putting this, using stakeholder theory, is to say that business strategy includes key choices involving all the stakeholder groups: it covers critical aspects of the firm's relations with investors, customers, employees, suppliers and regulators (Hill and Jones 1992, Donaldson and Preston 1995). Business strategy is the 'system' of the firm's important choices, a system that could be well integrated around common concerns or which might have various weak links and 'foul-ups'. As noted before, there is nothing in this definition to say that a firm's strategy is particularly clever.

A key issue associated with the strategic choice perspective is the question of what we are implying about the *extent of choice* available to firms. It is widely accepted in the strategy literature that firms in some sectors have greater 'degrees of freedom' than others enjoy (Porter 1985, Nelson 1991). Some environments are more benign – more 'munificent' – than others are (Pfeffer and Salancik 1978). Some firms are heavily constrained by competitive forces pushing them towards intense margin-based competition (something suppliers of supermarkets regularly complain about) while others enjoy a much more dominant position (companies like Microsoft come readily to mind). Consistent with John Child's (1997) re-formulation of the strategic choice perspective, we believe it is important to steer a path between 'hyper-determinism', on the one hand, and 'hyper-voluntarism', on the other. That is, firms are neither fully constrained by their environment nor fully able to create it. Adopting a strategic choice perspective means that we see firms as experiencing a varying blend of constraint and choice somewhere in between these two extremes. The 'choice' in 'strategic choice' is real but its extent is variable.

Before moving on, we should note that this definition of strategy is based at the business unit level. This level is, in fact, the most logical one at which to define strategy because different business units are organised around markets or segments of markets which require different goals and clusters of resources (Ghemawat and Costa 1993). Theory and analysis in strategy stems, almost entirely, from the business unit level (Porter 1985, Kaplan and Norton 1996). However, we should note that more complex frameworks are needed to encompass corporate strategy in multidivisional firms. Questions about 'parenting' – about which businesses to buy and sell, which to grow organically and so on – are vital in multidivisional firms. We examine the different ways multidivisional firms take these choices and the role of *corporate* human resource strategy in Chapter 10.

The process of strategic management

If we take this view of strategy, strategic management is best defined as a process. It is a process of strategy making: of forming and, if the firm survives, of re-forming its strategy over time. As we have already indicated, this may involve elements of formal planning, including the application of analytical techniques such as portfolio analysis (see, for example, Porter 1985, Whittington 1993, Grant 2005). It may involve set-piece debates among directors and executives, framed around policy papers and financial proposals. It may also involve *force majeure* if key power brokers – John Child's (1972, 1997) 'dominant coalition' – impose their will where they have the ability to do so. It will also, as Mintzberg emphasises (1978, 1990, 1994), *inevitably* involve a *learning* process as the managers of firms find out what works well in practice for them – or, we might add, what works better for their rivals. The transition in the strategy textbooks from titles such as 'Business Policy' and 'Strategic Planning' to 'Strategic Management' does indicate a realisation that strategy making is a mixed, impure, interactive kind of process.

This description of the strategic management process implies that it is hard to do it well. Following Eisenhardt and Zbaracki (1992) and Child (1997), we see strategic decision making as difficult in two key ways which need exploring in more depth: it is mentally or 'cognitively' tough and it is often politically fraught.

Strategic management and human cognition

Human cognition is a psychological term for thinking processes, for our ability to process information and make decisions. Research on cognition recognises the validity of Herbert Simon's observation, in his classic *Administrative Behavior*, that human beings are subject to 'bounded rationality' (Simon 1947). We cannot know everything about our environment, nor can we easily manipulate more than a handful of key ideas in a problem-solving situation: we are limited in the number of variables we can actively 'work on' as we wrestle with an environment which is much more complex than that. Our search for information is 'incomplete, often inadequate, based on uncertain information and partial ignorance, and usually terminated with the discovery of satisfactory, not optimal courses of action' (Simon 1985: 295).

While criticising the economics concept of optimisation or maximisation, we must be careful, however, to note that Simon was not saying that human behaviour is irrational:

> Skepticism about substituting a priori postulates about rationality for factual knowledge of human behavior should not be mistaken for a claim that people are generally 'irrational'. On the contrary, I think there is plenty of evidence that people are quite rational: that is to say, they usually have reasons for what they do. Even in madness, there is almost always method, as Freud was at great pains to point out. And putting madness aside for a moment, almost all human behavior consists of sequences of goal-oriented actions. (Simon 1985: 297)

As Simon indicates, we can generally find goals or the element of *intent* in human action. When studying strategy in firms, we can find intent in both formal planning and in Mintzberg's (1978) 'emergent strategy' of action, a point that Mintzberg, unfortunately, fails to make clear. The nature of the intent may shift, and it may not be very clever in the eyes of rivals or through our own hindsight, but it is there.

Following Simon (1947), management theory does not typically employ the assumptions of '*homo economicus*': that tradition within economics which keeps alive a view of economic agents acting with all the information they need and with no debilitating debates or frustrating compromises over the firm's desirable direction or internal organisation. As many academics have quipped, this view of business behaviour is largely unjustified but it makes the maths easier! Certainly, whoever thought of it first had no experience of University administration or any familiarity with the management of major organisations.

On a practical level, management can ill afford to assume it holds perfect knowledge or has outstanding problem-solving abilities. The work of strategic management, of finding a desirable path for the firm and managing its resources accordingly, is complex work that takes place in an environment of risk and uncertainty. As we have emphasised, it involves *systemic* factors – the problem of thinking not only within 'silos' but of identifying and coordinating a range of critical factors across the business. Figure 2.2, drawn from various sources (Belbin 1981, Isenberg 1984, Simon 1985, Barr, Stimpert and Huff 1992, Eisenhardt and Zbaracki 1992, Hambrick 1995), summarises some of the main findings of research on the cognitive problems of decision

1. We have reasons or goals for our actions but some of them are not very smart by other people's standards. Our powers of reasoning and our understanding of the world vary considerably.

2. We often have to act without knowing everything we'd like to: complexity and uncertainty are facts of life, especially in strategic management. Managers rely on 'mental models' which simplify and may distort the changing nature of their environment.

3. We often commit emotionally to a failing course of action and 'throw good money after bad'. People do not like to lose face.

4. We tend to search for confirming rather than disconfirming evidence to support our views (which is a common trap in employee selection, for example).

5. In problem solving, we often leap to a favourite or preferred solution without disciplining ourselves to diagnose the problem more deeply, mapping causes and consequences, generating real alternatives, and remaining truly open to the criticisms and refinements offered by others. Existing 'mental models' (about major cause-effect relationships in our world) tend to limit the range of our thinking about solutions to new problems.

6. No single executive in a large business is likely to have all the answers to complex, ambiguous problems: strategic management in large organisations needs teams of people with complementary strengths and styles.

7. Even if the need for management teamwork is recognised, knowledge of how things are done, and of how the firm might best respond to competitor threats or new technology, is dispersed throughout the firm, not held exclusively by far-sighted or 'heroic' executives or high-performing management teams.

8. The management process tends to repeat yesterday's success formula. It can take a long time to change the focus on 'what worked before' in a business. This opens up profitable opportunities for firms whose people can think differently. One firm's mindset or 'strong culture' is another firm's competitive opportunity.

Figure 2.2   Human cognitive issues affecting strategic management

making in firms. The overall effect of this research should be to induce some humility in the face of complex decisions. In respect of strategic decisions, it is much better to be 'often in doubt but seldom wrong' than 'seldom in doubt and often wrong'.

Barr, Stimpert and Huff (1992) provide an interesting illustration of the cognitive problems of strategic management. They examine the quality of strategic decision making in two US railway companies in the 1950s, a time when rail faced increasing competition from other transport modes (particularly the growing trucking industry). Between 1949 and 1973, the number of major railway companies roughly halved (down from 135 to 69). Barr *et al.* examined the efforts of two companies, the Chicago and North Western (C&NW) and the Chicago, Rock Island and Pacific (Rock Island), to handle this threatening environment. C&NW is still in business but Rock Island went bankrupt in the mid-1970s. Barr *et al.*'s analysis of 50 letters to shareholders written by the directors of these companies is revealing. As the environment began to turn against the rail companies in the 1950s, both companies blamed *external* factors for their poor performance – such as the weather, government programmes, and regulation. By about 1956, however, management at C&NW began to change its mental model, focusing efforts on *internal* factors (associated with costs and productivity) that management could control more effectively. This set in train (so to speak) a progressive learning process in which management strategies were improved by trail-and-error. This kind of shift in mental model did not occur at Rock Island until 1964, when an abrupt change of thinking occurred, by which time it was too late.

Barr *et al.* suggest that Rock Island's directors may have been caught in a 'success trap': having been prosperous for many years, they tended to dismiss the need for change even though the post-war environment was steadily moving against rail transport. This study is interesting because it demonstrates the way in which a dysfunctional mental model – one in which notions of cause-and-effect are well wide of the mark – can persist among the members of a senior management team. Not only was the environment clearly difficult but there were other firms – such as CN&W – that were handling it better.

Strategic management and organisational politics

Cases such as the demise of the Rock Island railway point to the role of cognitive strengths and weaknesses in strategic decision making. There is no doubt that cognition – cleverness – counts for a lot in company success. Most of the research on human cognition, however, overlooks the fact that strategic decision making is not simply about dealing with complex mental challenges in threatening environments. More than this is involved: politics matter, particularly in larger organisations. Strategic management is also about steering a course in a politically constituted organisation (Child 1972, 1997, Eisenhardt and Zbaracki 1992).

The point is well made in Child and Smith's (1987) study of Cadbury's attempts to transform itself in the 1960s and 70s. Facing the concentration and growth of retailer power and rising oligopolistic competition in a saturated home market, Cadbury needed strategic renewal. It needed to move away from some key elements of 'Cadburyism' – including a huge range of products and some key HR policies such as life-time commitment – towards a more efficient model of manufacturing with better technology and fewer but more flexible (and well-paid) workers. The leaders who made this change happen were people who handled the cognitive problems well (they cleverly perceived which parts of 'Cadburyism' needed to change and which ought to be enduring). However, as Child and Smith (1987: 588) explain, they also had the power to influence events, the political position and credibility needed within the firm to effect change: 'The Cadbury transformation relied on the exercise of power as well as on the persuasive force of vision and its attendant symbols'.

Because firms are networks of stakeholder groups, we must expect that any major initiative involves *political* management, particularly where investors must be persuaded to support the initiative or where employee groups are being asked to make changes that threaten their interests (as was the case in the Cadbury transformation). This is one of the straightforward implications of the stakeholder theory of the firm (Hill and Jones 1992, Donaldson and Preston 1995) and of 'resource-dependence' theory (Pfeffer and Salancik 1978). In a nutshell, firms are beholden to stockholders (who supply financial capital) but they are also dependent on any stakeholder group (such as suppliers and key customers) that contributes resources that are valuable to the firm. Labour is powerful in this sense, as we noted in Chapter 1. Workers – employees and contractors – do not need 'equal power' to have influence with management, they simply need the power to affect performance in some significant way. This is almost invariably the case. It follows that dealing with the power of labour is something that should concern executives in all firms, irrespective of whether the workforce is unionised. Theories of strategic change in work and employment systems are something we examine closely in Part 2 of this book.

Dealing with the power of non-management labour is one of the most visible of the power dynamics in firms. It often hits the media. Less eye catching but equally powerful is the loss of key employees who cannot be replaced, people with particularly scarce skills and good performance records who exercise their personal labour market power. The problem of retention of key workers began to stand out as a common problem in the 1990s and continues as a serious issue in the first decade of the twenty-first century.

Much of the political difficulty of strategic management occurs within the management structure itself. Organisations offer managers opportunities for personal aggrandisement. The large enterprises of our time – the *Fortune 500* companies and the like – provide management 'careerists' (Rousseau 1995) with a huge domain for self-serving behaviour. Intra-management political problems are of two main types. On the more 'macro' level, departments acquire power when they are central to the fundamental strategy on which a business is founded (Boeker 1989). Managers who head the historically strong departments often fight change even when the larger picture indicates that strategic change is now needed. For example, a firm in which production has historically led the way may well suffer from serious managerial in-fighting if the marketing department grows in significance and starts to challenge production's power base.

On the more 'micro' level, individual managers have personal reasons to advance their own interests irrespective of whether they are located in a powerful department. Perhaps the most significant problem presented by this feast of opportunity is the way consideration for one's personal future often encourages managers to keep quiet about problems, to filter the bad news. Alternatively, individuals may try to fix blame onto their supervisors, subordinates or peers as a way of displacing attention from their own performance.

When most managers in a team are afraid of introducing conflicting opinion, the organisation can suffer from 'groupthink' (Janis 1972), a syndrome where executives close down debate prematurely and take decisions with negative consequences. The decision by the US cabinet to invade Cuba at the Bay of Pigs in April 1961 is one of Janis's famous examples. In her classic study of flawed decision making in a selection of great historical events ('from Troy to Vietnam'), *The March of Folly*, Barbara Tuchman (1996: 302–3) finds many cases of the tendency:

> Adjustment is painful. For the ruler it is easier, once he (sic) has entered a policy box, to stay inside. For the lesser official it is better, for the sake of his (sic) position, not to make waves, not to press evidence that the chief will find painful to accept. Psychologists call the process of screening out discordant information 'cognitive dissonance', an academic disguise for 'Do not confuse me with the facts.' Cognitive dissonance is the tendency 'to suppress, gloss over, water down or 'waffle' issues that would produce conflict or 'psychological pain' within an organization.' It causes alternatives to be 'deselected since even thinking about them entails conflicts.' In the relations of subordinate to superior . . . , its object is the development of policies that upset no one.

The tendency to look after oneself is recognised by those branches of organisational economics (such as agency theory) which acknowledge that managerial interests can diverge from those of stockholders (see, for example, McMillan 1992, Rowlinson 1997). We cover these ideas (and their limitations) in Chapter 7. In the current chapter, it is simply important to note that the politics of executive ambition adds complexity to the broader stakeholder-based politics we find in organisations.

Improving strategic management processes

Given cognitive limitations and political complications, what can be done to improve the quality of strategic decision making in firms? And what role might human resource management play in this task?

The role of executive appointments

In the light of what we know about cognitive problems, including the fact that human performance becomes increasingly variable in jobs of high complexity (Hunter, Schmidt and Judiesch 1990), it seems obvious that HRM *should* play a major role in improving the quality of strategic management. The greater the uncertainty and discretion involved in work, the more important it is to hire (or promote) people of high ability, with a well-rounded intellectual *and* emotional profile, who have a capacity to think more creatively and flexibly. There is evidence that senior HR specialists act on this view. In a study of human resource directors in the largest New Zealand corporates, Hunt and Boxall (1998) found a strong emphasis in their work priorities on developing executive capability and performance. In line with findings in the UK (Marginson *et al.* 1988), the primary concern of most of the senior HR specialists in the study was the management of managers, including recruitment, remuneration, development, succession planning and termination. One stated that they 'worked constantly' with the CEO of the company: 'looking at managers, identifying strengths and weaknesses, seeing who will go further and who needs to go' (Hunt and Boxall 1998: 772–3).

As the research of Hambrick (1987, 1995) emphasises, improving top team performance must be substantially about getting well-qualified people into the management structure in the first place. But we should not think of this as solely about assessing and selecting for brilliance at the individual aspects of the job. Selection practices that enable firms to assess not only 'person-job fit' but also 'person-team fit' have something important to offer (Burch and Anderson 2004). Constituting and renewing the top team, including the chief executive, and building the overall capability of management in the firm, should perhaps be treated as the most strategic concern of all in human resource management (Boxall 1994).

The role of team building

While the core HR disciplines of recruiting and retaining highly talented people must be involved if strategic management is to be improved, they are

Descriptors	Command	Symbolic	Rational	Participative	Generative
Style	*Imperial*	*Cultural*	*Analytical*	*Procedural*	*Organic*
	Strategy driven by leader or small top team	Strategy driven by mission and a vision of the future	Strategy driven by formal structure and planning systems	Strategy driven by internal process and mutual adjustment	Strategy driven by organizational members' initiative
Role of top management	Commander: provide direction	Coach: motivate and inspire	Boss: evaluate and control	Facilitator: empower and enable	Sponsor: endorse and support
Role of organisational members	Soldier: obey orders	Player: respond to challenge	Subordinate: follow the system	Participant: learn and improve through self-evaluation against agreed criteria	Entrepreneur: experiment and take risks

Source: Adapted from Hart (1992)

Figure 2.3 Styles of strategy making

not, however, enough. Skills in developing leadership and group processes – which are not often discussed in HRM textbooks – must also be involved. This is emphasised in the work of Stuart Hart (1992) who defines five styles of strategy making (Figure 2.3). Hart's (1992) typology is useful because it specifies roles not only for executives but also for other members of the organisation under different modes of strategy making. We can see a major shift in the way senior managers and other members of the organisation are expected to behave from the command model at one end to the generative model at the other. Different modes might be appropriate to different contexts (a command style is needed in some crises) while firms might benefit from gaining the ability to combine different modes.

In a survey of the opinions of US chief executives, Hart and Banbury (1994: 266) find some evidence that 'firms which combine high levels of competence in multiple modes of strategy making appear to be the highest performers'. Consistent with resource-based view of the firm (which we explore in Chapter 4), they suggest that:

> . . . a firm dominated by the command mode of strategy-making relies on the idiosyncratic capabilities of a single (or a few) individual(s). Should this person(s) leave the organization or be attracted away by competitors, the firm's strategy making capability would be severely impaired. In contrast, a firm using symbolic, transactive,[5] and generative processes of strategy making demonstrates a more complex, deeply embedded capability requiring the concerted effort of hundreds

---

5 We have changed the 'transactive' label to 'participative' in Figure 2.3.

(or even thousands) of people. Such an organization possesses a difficult-to-copy asset that could yield competitive advantage. Thus, firms able to accumulate several process skills into a complex strategy-making capability should outperform less process-capable organisations. (Hart and Banbury 1994: 255)

The value of a mix of strategy-making abilities is an excellent point but Hart and Banbury's (1994) research does not tell us *how* firms can develop such a repertoire. A small group of researchers and consultants has, however, tried to identify ways in which management teamwork can be made more effective in organisations. One of the most celebrated frameworks is associated with the work of Belbin (1981). Belbin's model of team roles has been used to analyse the strengths and weaknesses of many senior management teams. According to this theory, it is a mistake to construct management teams simply based on the functional expertise of individuals (i.e. their abilities in marketing, finance, operations, information systems or other such work disciplines). Belbin argues that the most effective management teams enjoy a healthy mix of complementary *teamwork* styles (i.e. how people characteristically behave during team activities). Such teams have at least one clever and highly creative individual (a 'plant'), are chaired by someone who knows how to use the talents of others, and contain a spread of other useful styles (for example, a 'monitor-evaluator' to provide some dispassionate intellectual appraisal of the plant's ideas, and a 'completer-finisher' who will ensure sound organisation and follow-through) (Belbin 1981: 93–9). Belbin's ideas have been psychometrically evaluated and developed further by the British management consultancy, Robertson Cooper Ltd (2003).[6] A brief summary of their evolution of the Belbin team roles is shown in Figure 2.4. While they explain that individuals typically have strengths in one to three of these roles, they emphasise that it is not helpful to use role analysis to stereotype oneself or other people. It is much better if individuals participate as fully as possible in team activities and learn to develop new abilities.

The work of Kathleen Eisenhardt and her colleagues can also be used to help management teams perform more effectively – or learn to 'have good fights' (Eisenhardt, Kahwajy and Bourgeois 1997). Consistent with the view that strategic management involves both cognitive and political problems, she looks at ways to stimulate better conflicts, to avoid premature

---

6 www.robertsoncooper.com/products/Teamable.aspx

Team role	Offers the team:	Should aim to develop:
Specialist	Their technical skills and focus	A fuller involvement in the team beyond their technical skills
Leader Coordinator	An ability to encourage and coordinate others, to listen, to persuade and to build consensus	Their ability to move from decision making through to action
Driver	Urgency, a willingness to assume responsibility and a desire to make things happen	Their ability to consult others carefully and not simply rely on their personal drive to take others with them
Innovator	An ability to come up with creative ideas and original approaches in challenging circumstances	Their ability to listen to others and to connect with current priorities in the team
Explorer Networker	Strong interests in new ideas/opportunities and in people and an ability to network with them	Their ability to move from exploring and talking to making things happen
Analyst	Strong analytical abilities, a rigorous capacity to weigh up ideas and think through the implications	Their ability to empathise as well as challenge critically
Team coach	An ability to get on well with nearly all people they work with, listen to their feelings and offer personal support	Their ability to handle tough decisions where validating everyone's feelings is not going to work
Completer-Achiever	An ability to manage the details and ensure the job is done on time and to high standards	Their ability to see when their approach is too critical of the efforts of others or too 'perfectionist'

Source: Adapted from Robertson Cooper Ltd (2003)

Figure 2.4   A typology of team roles

closure when key decisions must be taken (Figure 2.5). These suggestions, if followed, would help to diminish the deadening effect of hierarchy on the level of debate about strategy in a firm. To achieve this, of course, we must note the obvious point that the power to stimulate greater participation in strategic management lies in the hands of the current chief executive. Even when a company has built a more a participative culture, every time a new chief executive is appointed there is potential for decision making to revert to an autocratic or closely held style. Business organisations are not constituted as democracies. Disproportionate power keeps reverting into the hands of senior management. This should remind us how central executive appointments are to the long-term success of the firm.

1. **Assemble a heterogeneous team, including diverse ages, genders, functional backgrounds, and industry experience**. If everyone in the executive meetings looks alike, then the chances are excellent they will probably think alike, too.

2. **Meet together as a team regularly and often**. Team members that do not know one another well do not know one another's positions on issues, impairing their ability to argue effectively. Frequent interaction builds the mutual confidence and familiarity team members require to express dissent.

3. **Encourage team members to assume roles beyond their obvious product, geographic, or functional responsibilities**. Devil's advocates, sky-gazing visionaries, and action-oriented executives can work together to ensure that all sides of an issue are considered.

4. **Apply multiple mind-sets to any issue**. Try role playing, putting yourselves in your competitor's shoes, or conducting war games. Such techniques create fresh perspectives and engage team members, spurring interest in problem solving.

5. **Actively manage conflict**. Do not let the team acquiesce too soon or too easily. Identify and treat apathy early, and do not confuse a lack of conflict with agreement. Often, what passes for consensus is really disengagement.

Figure 2.5 'Building a fighting team'

Conclusions

This chapter provides a basis for exploring the role of HRM in strategic management. It is important to pause and reflect on the nature of strategy and strategic management before leaping into theory and research on strategic HRM. Doing so will help to restrain us from superficial conclusions and misleading advice.

We have defined strategy by distinguishing between 'strategic problems' the firm faces in its environment and the characteristic ways it tries to cope with them (its 'strategy'). As common sense tells us, the word 'strategic' implies something that is seriously consequential for the future of the firm. The fundamental strategic problem is the problem of viability. To be viable, a firm needs an appropriate set of goals and a relevant set of human and non-human resources, a configuration or system of ends and means consistent with survival in the industries and societies in which it operates. This obviously means that without certain kinds of human capability, firms are simply not viable.

We take issue, then, with anyone who wants to downplay the significance of HRM in the firm. We find fault with those strategy texts which imply that key human resource concerns are not strategic. There is really no need for HR specialists to hang their heads in shame around the executive table, as if the critical dimensions of HRM were not important to the firm's success. As we shall argue further in the next two chapters, effective human resource strategy is a necessary, though not sufficient, condition of firm viability. We shall also examine the debate over the ways in which 'human assets' might lay the basis of sustained competitive advantage (which can be thought of as a 'second-order' or higher-level strategic problem). As we have argued in this chapter, however, firms which achieve some form of competitive advantage will not be completely different from those that do not – due to the need of all firms in the industry to have 'table stakes', features that make them similar to each other, and due to the need for firms that wish to be perceived as legitimate in society to comply with labour laws and social conventions.

Strategy, then, is a set of strategic choices, some of which may be formally planned. It is inevitable that much, if not most, of a firm's strategy emerges in a stream of action over time. Strategy has both 'outward' and 'inward' elements – it includes both the firm's goals and the important means it uses to pursue them. How well these elements are conceived and coordinated is very variable. Saying that firms have strategy does not mean they are successful in their environment. Some firms fail, some secure viability with adequate returns, and some find ways of out-performing others for periods of time.

Strategic management, therefore, is the process used in the firm to develop critical goals and resources. It is a mixed, impure, interactive process, fraught with difficulty, both intellectually and politically. Improving the process of strategic management has a lot to do with HRM. It involves making some key HR decisions (about the recruitment, development and promotion of key managers) but it also involves astute team-building activities, within the senior management team and throughout the organisation. There is some research suggesting that firms that develop multiple modes of strategy making are likely to be superior performers. Developing and sustaining highly participative styles of strategic management is not easy, however. Business organisations are not democracies. Power keeps reverting to those at the top, a phenomenon that reinforces the critical importance of people decisions at the apex of firms.

3

Strategic HRM: 'best fit' or 'best practice'?

Perhaps one message – more than any other – has been communicated in job advertisements for HR directors over the last few years: whatever you do, help the firm to make its HRM consistent with its strategic direction, *integrate* HR strategy with the wider business strategy. To many people this piece of advice seems obvious and straightforward. But is it? Could it be interpreted in quite different ways? Building on the concepts clarified in the previous chapter, our task in this one is to explain the main ways in which it has been argued that HRM should be integrated into strategic management and to consider the evidence for these claims.

The theory of strategic HRM does not, in fact, advocate a single way of linking HRM to strategy. Most theoretical debate around this nexus has been consumed with a contest between two approaches. One approach – the 'best fit' or contingency school – argues that firms must adapt their HR strategies to other elements of the firm's strategy and to its wider environment. This school invites a string of questions about which are the most critical contingencies in this complex context and how they are best connected. The other approach advocates 'best practice' or universalism. It argues that all firms will be better off if they identify and adopt best practices in the way they organise work and manage people. This is not straightforward either: it begs questions about how best practice models are defined and about who is best served by them. This chapter subjects these two approaches to a thorough review. We examine in each case what the research and theoretical critiques have to say and we reach an assessment of the relative merits of each approach. Readers will find that we take a very broad view of the research in reaching our conclusions and laying a basis for subsequent analysis in this book. To begin with, we need to flesh out our definition of strategic HRM and its companion term, human resource strategy.

Defining 'strategic HRM' and HR strategy

As Chapter 1 made clear, we do not associate HRM with any particular philosophy or style of management. Simply in terms of work organisation and opportunities for employee voice, we see all sorts of variations in employer behaviour. Work organisation varies from highly prescribed 'command and control' models through to high-involvement or high-discretion ones and employer strategies towards employee voice vary from very paternalistic and anti-union styles through to union–management 'partnerships'. The practice of HRM incorporates all of these patterns and many more. We are interested in identifying, analysing and tracking trends in all significant patterns of managerial behaviour over time.

What difference does it make, then, when we apply the adjective *strategic* to HRM? As explained in Chapter 2, our understanding of strategy is based on a 'strategic choice' perspective – something which can be applied to the whole of strategy and to its constituent parts, including human resource strategy. In this interpretation, the application of the adjective 'strategic' implies a concern with the ways in which HRM is critical to the firm's survival and to its relative success. There are always strategic choices associated with labour management in the firm – whether highly planned or largely emergent in management behaviour – and these choices are inevitably connected to the firm's performance. These choices are made over time by the whole management structure, including line managers and HR specialists (where they exist).

As explained in Chapter 2, it is helpful to think of strategic choices on two levels: they either play a role in underpinning the firm's viability (make-or-break choices) or they help to provide some kind of sustained competitive advantage, accounting for major, ongoing differences in the quality of business performance. In adopting this understanding, we follow Dyer (1984) in referring to a firm's *pattern* of strategic choices in labour management (including critical ends and means) as its 'organisational human resource strategy' – or its 'HR strategy', for short.

To illustrate what we mean by strategic choices in HRM, take the case of a management consulting firm that aims to join the elite cluster of firms which are global in their reach (Boxall and Purcell 2000). Firms such as PricewaterhouseCoopers, McKinsey and KPMG are among the leaders in this sector. What might it take to join them? There is no doubt that firms in this 'strategic group'[1] must have highly selective recruitment and strong development of staff to ensure they can consistently offer clients high quality service on complex business problems. In this elite group of professional firms, a synergistic blend of certain human resource practices – such as proactive recruitment channels, high entry standards, challenging, high-discretion work, high pay, the prospect of entering into partnership, and extensive professional education – is critical to business credibility. Firms of this type which are focused on competing through advanced and rare expertise need these sorts of HR practices to attract and retain the talented people they want (Dooreward and Meihuizen 2000). On the other hand, we can draw something of a line between these critical elements of HRM and other aspects which are not really important. It is unlikely, for example, that there is much hanging on the firm's choice of job evaluation systems. Job evaluation systems allocate jobs to pay grades based on the skill, effort and responsibility they involve. If any one of a range of such systems supports its remuneration goals in recruiting and retaining highly qualified consultants, or does not perversely undermine them, then the choice among different systems is not critical. Similarly, the contracting out of payroll or benefits administration in such a firm is not a strategic dimension of its HRM. It is not difficult to meet the requirements of employment contracts in these areas and elite firms are not differentiated from lesser firms on this basis. What is vital, however, is that the firm's leaders put together the *system* of truly critical HR practices and investments that will help the firm to join the elite group of professional firms in this sector. However, it would be unwise to think that the firm's labour market reputation will be made quickly or that viability in the sector will be achieved solely through HR strategy (as our discussion of the resource-based view of the firm in the next chapter will make clear).

As a field of study, then, strategic HRM is concerned with the strategic choices associated with the organisation of work and the use of labour in firms and with explaining why some firms manage them more effectively than others. It is helpful to spell out this definition in a very practical manner. Suppose an HR Director is asked by a chief executive to conduct a review of the quality of HR strategy in a firm. What should such a review entail? We suggest the questions shown in Figure 3.1:

---

1 A strategic group is a cluster of firms in the same industry that compete for clients in the same kind of way and develop strong 'mutual understandings' (Suarez and Utterback 1995, Peteraf and Shanley 1997).

1. *Strengths and weaknesses in human resources*
   How well does the firm's human and social capital help it to perform? In terms of cost-effectiveness, social legitimacy and organisational flexibility, what strengths and weaknesses are apparent in the firm's management of its main employee groups?
2. *Competitive risks and potential in HRM*
   What threats does the firm face in its HRM (e.g. from under-performing work systems, from employee dissatisfaction or from labour market competition)? What opportunities does the firm have to improve its HR performance relative to its industry rivals? Does the firm have the potential to generate some form of sustained competitive advantage through HRM? If so, how?
3. *Assessment of strategic HR management processes*
   How effective are the firm's HR planning and reporting processes? What data are available on HR performance and how are they used for evidence-based strategic decisions, especially when linked to data on other critical variables like customer satisfaction, product quality etc? How can such strategic management processes be improved?

Figure 3.1 Three sets of questions for a review of HR strategy in a firm

As the three sets of questions in Figure 3.1 make clear, this kind of analysis is far from straightforward. In many firms, a major effort in data gathering would be needed to answer the questions. A study of these questions nearly always reveals the need for better ways of measuring HR performance in the firm, as advocates of the 'balanced scorecard' have noted (Kaplan and Norton 1996: 144–5). There is still a marked tendency in firms to treat HR practices as ends in themselves and a lot of work is needed to map their links to one another, to other management activities and to important performance variables (an issue we explore in Chapters 8 and 11). The second question involves not only data analysis but some kind of theory about how to make HRM more effective in the firm, about how to improve the strategic management of human resources in it. This is the nub of the debate between advocates of 'best fit' and 'best practice', which is the focus of this chapter.

Before exploring this interesting debate, we should note some complications in our conception of human resource strategy. First, as noted in our definition of HRM in Chapter 1, we should not assume that HR strategies are uniform within firms. It is wrong to conjure up the image of HR strategy as a single set of critical practices for managing work and people in the firm. The vast bulk of the evidence suggests otherwise: firms rarely adopt a single style of management for all their employee groups (see, for example, Osterman 1987, Pinfield and Berner 1994, Harley 2001). It is better to think of HR strategy as a cluster of HR systems, as depicted in Figure 3.2. Questions of social legitimacy and internal political pressures mean there

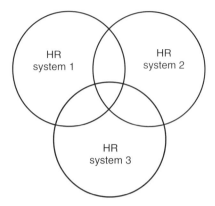

Figure 3.2   An organisation's HR strategy as a cluster of HR systems

will usually be some overlaps in HR practices across HR systems within an organisation: for example, there may be common ways of handling leave entitlements and common ways of dealing with personal grievances. There are some companies in which opportunities for shareholding are opened to all employees, and so on. However, there are also substantial differences across HR systems. Each HR system is aimed at organising the work and managing the employment of a major workforce group. It is quite common for there to be one HR system for management, another for core operating staff, and one or more models for support workers of various kinds. This is something we explore more fully in Chapters 4 and 8.

Secondly, we have been talking as if the firm is a single business unit. As explained in our definition of strategy in Chapter 2, this is the easiest way to develop theory in strategic management. Reality, however, is much more complicated. Difficulties arise with multidivisional firms, operating across a variety of market or industry contexts. To what extent should lower levels of management be free to adapt HR strategies suited to their unique contexts? If they do this (and it is common), is there a role for corporate HR strategy in such firms and, if so, what should it be? Can corporate HR strategy provide some form of 'parenting advantage' which adds value to what business units can achieve without corporate influence? This question is explored in Chapter 10.

A third complication arises with international firms (as many multidivisional firms are). Where firms compete across national boundaries, in what ways should they adapt their HR strategies to local conditions? How should HRM be organised when the firm operates in more than one society? This is one of the key concerns of the field of international HRM

> **Human resource (HR) strategy:**
> - consists of critical goals and means for organising work and managing people
> - inevitably affects the firm's chances of survival and its relative performance
> - is made by the whole management structure and not simply by HR specialists (where they exist)
> - is likely to be partly planned and partly 'emergent' in management behaviour
> - is typically 'variegated' – while there are some overlaps, firms typically have different HR systems for different employee groups (e.g. different models for management, for core operating workers, and for support staff)
> - like strategy generally, is easiest to define at the business-unit level
> - is more complex in multidivisional firms in which different business units face different market or industry contexts and in which there are political interactions between the corporate and the divisional and business-unit levels
> - is more complex in firms that operate across national boundaries because of the impact of different societal contexts

Figure 3.3   Key characteristics of human resource strategy

(e.g. Brewster and Harris 1999, Evans, Pucik and Barsoux 2002, Dowling and Welch 2004). We address this problem in the course of this chapter and extend our analysis in Chapter 10. Overall, our understanding of HR strategy is summarised in Figure 3.3.

On the basis of these definitions and clarifications, we are now in a position to examine the debate between 'best fit' and 'best practice' in strategic HRM.

Strategic HRM: the 'best fit' school

As indicated in our chapter introduction, the 'best fit' or contingency school of strategic HRM argues that the variety we see in HRM across hierarchical levels, occupations, firms, industries and societies implies that managers inevitably tailor their HRM to their specific context. Furthermore, they are wise to do so: firms under-perform and may fail if they do not adapt to their environment. The 'best fit' literature contains both broad analytical models and more specific theories. In this section of the chapter, we will outline these and consider the research evidence and conceptual critiques.

'Best fit': broad analytical frameworks

As was widely noted in the late 1980s and early 1990s (e.g. Poole 1990, Boxall 1992), the Harvard framework (Beer *et al.* 1984) provided one of the first major statements in the HRM canon on the issue of how managers should

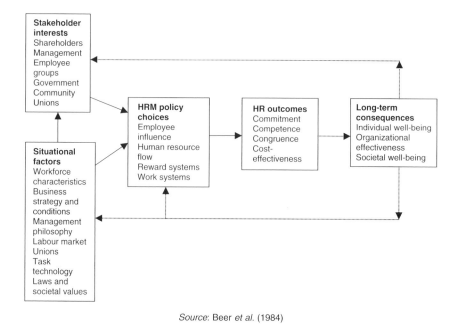

Source: Beer *et al.* (1984)

Figure 3.4   The Harvard 'map of the HRM territory'

make strategic choices in HRM (Figure 3.4). In this analytical framework, managers in firms are encouraged to set their own priorities in HRM based on a consideration of stakeholder interests and situational factors. HR outcomes, in turn, are seen as having longer-term impacts on organisational effectiveness and on societal and individual well-being.

In terms of our understanding of HR strategy, the most important chapter in the Harvard text was the last one in which the authors sought to integrate the huge range of HR choices that might be adopted by considering the differences between 'bureaucratic', 'market' and 'clan' models of HRM, a set of categories that draws on the work of Ouchi (1980). The bureaucratic model is seen as concerned with 'control and efficiency', using traditional authority and such staples of personnel management as job descriptions and job evaluation to provide order and equity (Beer *et al.* 1984: 179). This HRM approach is regarded as relevant to markets with stable technology and employment levels. The market HRM approach, on the other hand, aims to treat employees more like sub-contractors, fostering short-term exchanges and performance-related pay systems. This is seen as relevant to fast-changing environments such as high-fashion merchandising, advertising and professional sports (*ibid.*: 180). Finally, clan HRM systems are seen as building more diffuse kinship links, fostering shared values, teamwork and strong commitment in organisations seeking 'long-term adaptability' (*ibid.*: 181). This is seen as relevant to firms pursuing quality and innovation. Combining aspects of two or even three models is seen as useful when facing complex environments (*ibid.*: 184).

While the links between HRM goals and the firm's business strategy and environment are only very briefly sketched in the book, the main message is that HR strategies can, and should, vary based on contextual factors and that firms should aim to develop a relatively consistent style. Beer *et al.* (1984: 178, 184) argue that 'HRM policies need to fit with business strategy' and with 'situational constraints' while also envisaging a role for management values (*ibid.*: 190–1). The goal of fit with broader business strategy and context, followed by internal consistency in HR choices, was argued to be the essential purpose of HRM.

The Harvard framework was followed by a range of similar models (e.g. Dyer and Holder 1988, Baron and Kreps 1999). In Dyer and Holder's (1988) framework, management is advised to aim for 'consistency between HR goals . . . and the underlying business strategy and relevant environmental conditions' (with the latter, like the Harvard framework, including influences such as labour law, unions, labour markets, technology and management values). In Baron and Kreps's (1999) framework, managers are advised to consider the impact of 'five forces' on HR policy choices: the external environment (social, political, legal and economic), the workforce, the organisation's culture, its strategy and the technology of production and organisation of work. This advice is not offered in a simple, deterministic fashion: managers still have choices (such as where to locate plants in manufacturing) but once some choices are made, certain environmental consequences do follow: so, if you locate in the USA, rather than Honduras, US laws, culture and workforce characteristics inevitably come into play. The goal of achieving internal consistency in whatever model of HRM is adopted – otherwise known as 'internal' or 'horizontal' fit – is then strongly emphasised by Baron and Kreps (1999).

Like the Harvard authors, if not more emphatically, Dyer and Holder (1988) and Baron and Kreps (1999) argue for a contingent understanding of HR strategy or the necessity of moulding HRM to the firm's particular context. Dyer and Holder (1988: 31) conclude that 'the inescapable conclusion is that what is best, depends'. Baron and Kreps (1999: 33) assert that 'in HRM, there is no one size that fits every situation' and argue that no model should be adopted unless the benefits outweigh the costs. None of these frameworks is inherently anti-union or takes the view that HRM is restricted to one style. The message in terms of HR strategy is one of fit or adaptation to the firm's broader business goals and its environmental context.

'Best fit': research and critique

The broad frameworks just described have been important as analytical models that help managers to identify options and make choices in their own environments. In terms of theoretical development, however, progress depends on picking particular variables in these frameworks and subjecting them to formal research (typically through surveys and/or case studies). Theorists tend to be motivated by a desire to reduce complexity and seek to build more tightly defined, 'parsimonious' models.

In one of the earliest sources, Baird and Meshoulam (1988) claimed that HR activities, like structure and systems, should fit the organisation's stage of development – something they call 'external fit' and which others sometimes call 'vertical fit'. Developed from in-depth case studies, their argument is that while start-up firms exhibit more informal, more flexible styles of HRM, more sophisticated, professionalised styles become necessary to handle greater complexity as firms become larger and more mature.

Does research support this proposition? There is clearly strong support for the idea that the size of an organisation makes a major difference to the kind of HR policies and practices management adopts. In a major review of research on contextual influences in HRM, Jackson and Schuler (1995) show that larger organisations are more likely to have 'due process' procedures, use more sophisticated staffing and training practices and have more developed 'internal labour markets' (i.e. a structure of more specialised jobs and more extensive career hierarchies which provide greater scope to promote and develop people from within), among other features. None of this will come as a surprise to anyone who has worked in both small and large firms or in the same organisation which started small and became much bigger. Larger firms inevitably need more formalised practices to manage larger numbers of people and to cope with more diverse occupational groups. Individuals being recruited to larger organisations are likely to be screened through multiple channels and will often ask to see a job description and ask questions about how their pay fits into the job hierarchy. Those joining a small firm are much more likely to agree the details directly with one person – the owner – and are much less likely to see formal documentation.

There is also research support for the idea that the HR problems managers respond to vary across organisational life-cycle stages. For example, in a study of 2,903 small to medium-sized US family firms, Rutherford, Buller and McMullen (2003) find that managers in firms experiencing high rates of growth consider employee development their biggest problem but perceive much less difficulty with employee retention. This is not surprising: fast growth can make a company exciting to join but stretches managers in terms of trying to develop the employee capabilities they need. In comparison, firms not experiencing growth have the greatest difficulty recruiting. These could be failing firms which are stymied in terms of their ability to grow precisely because no one wants to join them. We think life-cycle theory is an important line of analysis in HR strategy and explore it more fully in Chapter 9.

Theoretically, however, most models of 'best fit' in HRM did not follow Baird and Meshoulam's (1988) emphasis on adapting HRM to organisational size and stage of development but argued that the key goal was to achieve fit with the firm's competitive strategy. The notion of external or vertical fit in strategic HRM is more often used in this sense. In this line of thinking, the basic recipe for strategic HRM involves bringing HR strategy into line with the firm's desired position in its product market. There are some complexities here and we need to be careful with the language we use. First, when theorists advocate fitting HR strategy to competitive strategy, they are usually talking about matching HR practices to the competitive strategy of a *particular business unit* which operates in a particular industry. This should not be confused with the role of HRM in the corporate strategy of a parent company, something we discuss in Chapter 10. Second, theorists are generally talking about how management should manage *core operating workers*: those most intimately involved in making the product or providing the service. Theoretical models in this area are not generally about how managers themselves should be managed, which is a different question altogether (Boxall 1992, Boxall and Gilbert 2007).

The most heavily cited work on external fit in strategic HRM is associated with a theoretical model developed by Schuler and Jackson (1987). This model, and a subsequent stream of papers (e.g. Schuler 1989, 1996), has proven very influential for the way it spells out the connections between competitive strategies, desired employee behaviours and particular HR practices. Schuler and Jackson (1987) argue that HR practices should be designed to reinforce the behavioural implications of the various 'generic' competitive strategies defined by Porter (1985). A giant in the strategy field, Porter (1985) advises firms to specialise carefully in competitive strategy (Figure 3.5). In his view, firms should choose between cost leadership (achieving lowest unit costs in the industry), differentiation (based, for

Competitive advantage

Lower cost | Differentiation

		Lower cost	Differentiation
Competitive scope	Broad target	Cost leadership	Differentiation
	Narrow target	Focus: Cost leadership	Focus: Differentiation

Source: Porter (1985)

Figure 3.5 Porter's typology of competitive strategies

example, on superior quality or service) or focus (a 'niche play' in cost or differentiation). They should avoid getting 'stuck in the middle' or caught in a strategic posture which is mixed – neither fish nor fowl, one might say.

Schuler and Jackson (1987) used Porter's framework to argue that performance will improve when the HR practices in a business mutually reinforce competitive strategy (Figure 3.6). To arrive at a desirable set of HR practices, Schuler and Jackson (1987) argue that different competitive strategies imply different kinds or blends of employee behaviour. These inferences are drawn from a major review of existing literature. If, for example, management chooses a competitive strategy of differentiation through continuous product innovation, this would call for high levels of creative, risk-oriented and cooperative behaviour. The company's HR practices would therefore need to emphasise '. . . selecting highly skilled individuals, giving employees more discretion, using minimal controls, making greater investment in human resources, providing more resources for experimentation, allowing and even rewarding occasional failure, and appraising performance for its long-run implications' (Schuler and Jackson 1987: 210).

On the other hand, if management wants to pursue cost leadership (i.e. to attain lowest unit costs in the sector), the Schuler and Jackson model implies something a lot less attractive to the average employee. It suggests designing jobs which are fairly repetitive, reducing employee numbers and wage levels, training workers as little as is practical, and rewarding short-term results.

Although competitive posture can be complex and typologies such as Porter's can oversimplify it (Murray 1988, Miller 1992, Cronshaw, Davis

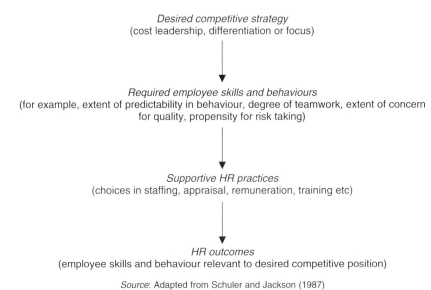

Desired competitive strategy
(cost leadership, differentiation or focus)

Required employee skills and behaviours
(for example, extent of predictability in behaviour, degree of teamwork, extent of concern
for quality, propensity for risk taking)

Supportive HR practices
(choices in staffing, appraisal, remuneration, training etc)

HR outcomes
(employee skills and behaviour relevant to desired competitive position)

Source: Adapted from Schuler and Jackson (1987)

Figure 3.6   Linking HR practices to competitive strategy

and Kay 1994), the fundamental premiss is that business performance will be better when there is alignment between competitive strategy and the management of core operating workers inside the business. Clearly, there are two issues here. First of all, do managers relate their HR policies and practices to their competitive strategies? Secondly, are they wise to do so? In line with our emphasis on 'analytical HRM' (Boxall, Purcell and Wright 2007b), our task first of all is to answer the descriptive question: what do managers in firms actually do? We will come back to the question of whether they are wise to behave in a certain way when we examine research and critique on the notion of 'best practice' later in the chapter.

In answering the first question, we need to distinguish between firms operating in service sectors and those operating in manufacturing. This is because research suggests that the links between competitive strategy and HRM are stronger in services than they are in manufacturing. A leading study in services is Batt's (2000) analysis of four market segments in call-centre work in the US telecommunications industry. These segments vary in terms of the complexity and value of the employee–customer interaction. At the low end, there are low-margin interactions of short duration, typically with predetermined scripts and with strong technological monitoring of call-centre workers. At the high end, there are high-margin, low-volume interactions relying far more on employee skill and discretion where technology is much more of an enabler than a monitor. One statistic alone is telling: at the low-margin end, operators deal with an average of 465 customers per day, in the two mid-range segments they deal with 100 and 64, and at the top end they deal with an average of 32 (Batt 2000: 550). Batt (2000) finds significant differences in the contours of HR strategy across these market segments with skill requirements, the degree of discretion allowed to employees and pay levels all higher among firms competing at the high-margin end of the call-centre market.

Studies of specific service industries like this one on call centres generally support the notion that HR strategy is closely related to competitive differentiation in services. Other compelling examples can be found in US studies of rest homes (Eaton 2000, Hunter 2000) where HR investments (in training, pay, career structures and staffing levels) are greater in firms that target higher-value niches and in studies of hotels where those at the luxury end invest more heavily in their staff in order to deliver superior customer service (Lashley 1998, Haynes and Fryer 2000, Knox and Walsh 2005). A close relationship between competitive strategy and HRM can also be discerned in professional services. In their study of Dutch and German management consultancies, Dooreward and Meihuizen (2000) discern two broad strategic types: firms oriented to efficiency and firms oriented to expertise. The former offer 'standard solution(s) to familiar problems in an efficient way' while the latter promote 'an individual professional's ability to offer new, client-specific solutions to new, unusual problems' (Dooreward and Meihuizen 2000: 43). These are tendencies, not hard and fast categories, but they are associated with differentiation in HR strategies. Expertise-driven firms try to hire highly intelligent 'free spirits' and retain them through challenging, high-discretion work, while those oriented to efficiency have a much more bureaucratic model of HRM.

When it comes to firms operating in services, then, research suggests there are quite strong links between competitive positioning and patterns of HRM. What about manufacturing? As indicated in our discussion of cost-effectiveness in Chapter 1, we cannot really answer this question without considering the role of technology. Unlike service workers, employees in manufacturing do not generally deal directly with customers: instead, they work with machinery to make products (Combs *et al.* 2006). As a result, how managers try to organise HRM for a manufacturing firm's core workers tends to be related to technological choices, which form a key part of operating strategy (Purcell 1999). Snell and Dean's (1992) study of 512 US metal manufacturing plants shows that heavier investments in individual employees, including more extensive screening and training practices, are associated with plants using advanced technologies such as computer-integrated manufacturing systems. When a manufacturing firm has expensive investments in advanced technology, which requires highly skilled and careful handling, managers are likely to spend money building employee competencies and fostering employee commitment, *even if* their competitive goal is to achieve the lowest unit costs in the industry (Steedman and Wagner 1989, Godard 1991). In effect, where there are high 'interaction risks' between specialised capital assets (in which the firm has major 'sunk costs') and the behaviour of workers, managers are likely to adopt employment models that foster greater expertise and buy greater loyalty and care. The value of such investments, however, is likely to be questioned by managers when the industry they are operating in is characterised by a stable, low-technology environment (Kintana, Alonso and Olaverri 2006). Labour-intensive, low-tech manufacturing is much more likely to be associated with pressures to outsource production to low-wage countries, as we shall explain in Chapter 5.

The notion of fitting HR strategy to competitive strategy, therefore, stands up better in services than it does in manufacturing but in both cases we see contingencies in play. Whether it is about organisational size, life-cycle stage, competitive strategy or technology (or all of these), we are seeing a process of adaptation to context. The importance of fit is further emphasised when we consider the characteristics of employees and the state of labour markets (e.g. Boxall 1996, Lees 1997). Firms with complex workforces often have multiple HR systems: they may adopt one model for managing their management and professional cadres, another for core operating staff and yet another for support workers (e.g. Pinfield and Berner 1994, Kalleberg *et al.* 2006). Some of these differences reflect different union contracts and some reflect differences in the degree to which the type of labour is critical to production (e.g. Osterman 1987, Godard 1991). When economic growth is strong and labour markets are tight, we see firms adjusting their models of HRM to cope: managers tend to respond with more generous employment offers and more motivating conditions (e.g. Jackson and Schuler 1995).

Furthermore, as explained in Chapter 1, labour regulation, social norms and national educational/training institutions have a major impact on the process of adaptation to context that takes place in a firm's HRM, as emphasised in reviews and studies conducted by Tayeb (1995), Gooderham, Nordhaug and Ringdal (1999), Paauwe and Boselie (2003, 2007), Rubery and Grimshaw (2003), Pudelko (2006), Winterton (2007) and many others. In respect of social norms, there is now a major body of literature on international and cross-cultural HRM which underlines the way in which different cultures affect HR practices. All societies contain one or more major cultures: deep-seated value structures and belief systems that reflect the ways groups of people have learnt to live and work together. In a major review of this literature, Aycan (2005) describes a wide range of research showing that practices in such areas as selection, performance appraisal and pay are affected by such dimensions of culture as the extent to which individualism is fostered over collectivism and the extent to which it is considered legitimate to challenge authority. In Anglo-Saxon and in Dutch cultural contexts, it is common to consider people as individuals who can be selected, evaluated, rewarded and dispensed with on their individual merits but such assumptions risk failure in more collectivist cultures where an over-emphasis on individuals can threaten group harmony and challenge important status differences. In a celebrated study, *Riding the Waves of Culture*, Trompenaars and Hampden-Turner (1997: 4–5) comment that:

> Pay-for-performance ... can work out well in the USA, the Netherlands and the UK. In more communitarian cultures like France, Germany and large parts of Asia it may not be so successful, at least not the Anglo-Saxon version of pay-for-performance. Employees may not accept that individual members of the group should excel in a way that reveals the shortcomings of other members. Their definition of an 'outstanding individual' is one who benefits those closest to him or her ....

Managers operating within only one society, especially a monolingual one, can be blind to much of this but those working in firms operating across national boundaries soon become aware of it. What do they do? How do they cope? The evidence suggests that managers in multinational firms adapt to national institutions and cultural norms while still seeking to take advantage of their proprietary technologies and production systems to make desired rates of economic return.

This process is well illustrated in a study by Doeringer, Lorenz and Terkla (2003) of the HR practices of Japanese multinationals with transplants in the USA, the UK and France. These plants are required to meet Japanese productivity benchmarks and usually have Japanese managers appointed to them to lead and monitor local management. Examination of the ways they have sought to organise work and employment over the last 20 to 30 years provides a kind of 'natural experiment' on the interaction between HRM and societal institutions and cultural norms. Doeringer *et al.* (2003: 271) conclude that there is 'almost no evidence' of Japanese management practices 'being transferred intact to Japanese transplants'. What they do show, however, is that *work* processes associated with Japanese quality-oriented production systems (such as problem solving in quality circles, teamworking, and worker responsibility for quality) are much more likely to have been diffused than *employment* practices associated with pay, skill, promotion systems and the like. This makes a lot of sense: the transplants need work processes that are consistent with the economics of production in the industry but can be much more flexible in relation to employment practices. The latter are much more driven by national laws, by union contracts and by established social attitudes.

In the UK, for example, Japanese firms have learnt to work with a higher level of unionisation than they find in the USA and have been found to adapt to British attitudes to bonus systems (which often favour simpler and 'less subjective' systems to those found in Japan) and to the status differences between technicians and production workers. In France, among other things, Japanese firms have learnt to accept that supervisors will typically be appointed directly to a position of responsibility based on their personal achievements in France's national system of educational qualifications and without any prior experience. The French elite model of education, with all its hierarchical rungs, is not easily sidestepped. This contrasts sharply with the Japanese practice of promoting from within based on extensive shopfloor experience.

Overall, Doeringer *et al.*'s (2003) study is useful in two ways. On the one hand, it helps us to see that national boundaries are far from impermeable barriers in HRM: multinational firms find ways of making money through transferring the core elements of production systems across them and, indeed, search out national regimes that will offer them better profit opportunities. On the other hand, national labour laws, cultural attitudes, educational systems and trade unions all act as filters in HRM, ensuring that a large measure of adaptation to the customary employment practices in the particular production locality takes place.

Readers will have noticed that we are back into complexity. The idea that we can develop parsimonious models of the factors that influence HR strategy is attractive but flawed: we do need to incorporate a wide range of factors. Bearing in mind our discussion so far, but trying to keep complexity to a minimum, Figure 3.7 offers our view of the range of factors that research suggests affect HR strategy in a firm (more accurately, a business unit in a firm). For convenience, it organises the relevant factors into two broad categories. Economic factors, both inside and outside the firm, do influence many of the choices managers make in HR strategy. Here we include the firm's competitive strategy but we also include the economics of production in the industry concerned, including the kind of technologies involved. We then include the firm's size, structure and life-cycle stage, general economic

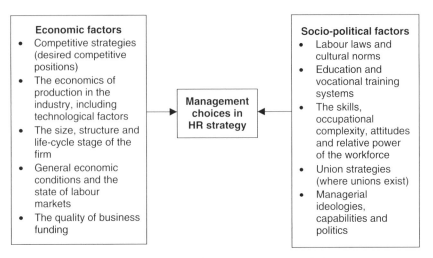

Economic factors
- Competitive strategies (desired competitive positions)
- The economics of production in the industry, including technological factors
- The size, structure and life-cycle stage of the firm
- General economic conditions and the state of labour markets
- The quality of business funding

Management choices in HR strategy

Socio-political factors
- Labour laws and cultural norms
- Education and vocational training systems
- The skills, occupational complexity, attitudes and relative power of the workforce
- Union strategies (where unions exist)
- Managerial ideologies, capabilities and politics

Figure 3.7 Major contextual factors affecting management choices in HR strategy

conditions, the state of the labour market, and the quality of the firm's funding. The figure also recognises that HR strategy will be shaped by a range of socio-political factors. Labour laws and cultural norms exert a major influence, as do national educational and training systems. Very importantly, employee skills, occupational complexities, attitudes and power must be considered, as we have just noted in the case of Japanese transplants in the West. Employees are rarely passive: they will not necessarily buy into management policies if they offend cultural norms or if they feel betrayed by past events. In any initiative in HRM, likely reactions from current and potential employees ought to be considered, and an assessment made of union strategies where unions exist. Management itself has issues to do with ideology, capability and politics which inevitably affect HR decision making. As noted in Chapters 1 and 2, management does not necessarily make a good set of choices in HRM: limitations in ideologies and cognitive abilities and debilitating politics within the management structure will lower performance and may lead to outright failure.

Before leaving the picture offered in Figure 3.7, a key point should be emphasised about it. Anyone deciding to use it as an analytical framework would be advised to bear in mind, as we argued in Chapter 1 and above, that firms have multiple goals in HRM. It is unwise to treat the notion of 'fit' as simply about alignment between HRM and economic performance. Managers do need to achieve healthy levels of cost-effectiveness. They must survive in markets where they compete for revenues and face cost pressures while public sector agencies must work within government-imposed budget constraints. But, at the same time, organisations need an adequate fit with the socio-political environment to achieve acceptable levels of social legitimacy. Both economic and social goals should be 'bottom lines' for formal organisations. They are priorities that ought to be worked on simultaneously. Furthermore, firms that want to survive into the longer run need some HR practices that will enhance organisational flexibility, as Wright and Snell (1998) emphasise. HR strategy should give effect to the firm's current competitive goals, by recruiting, developing and retaining people with the sort of skills needed in the firm's industry. However, it is also highly desirable that HR strategy encourages staff to think 'outside the square', that it helps to build the sort of skills needed for business capabilities in the future. Managers, at the very least, should not be managed in such a way that they are locked into only one kind of strategy (Boxall 1992). In effect, the firm needs multiple fits with its environment.

Strategic HRM: the 'best practice' school

Those who advocate the 'best practice' approach start from a different premiss to contingency theorists. In best-practice thinking, a universal prescription is preferred. The staunchest advocates of best practice argue that all firms will see performance improvements if they identify and implement best practices. This brings quite a different understanding of the problem of integrating HR strategy with the rest of business strategy. Integration with strategic management, in this conception, is about top management identifying the 'leading edge' of best practice, publicising commitments to best practices, measuring progress towards them and rewarding lower-level managers for implementing them consistently.

Before proceeding, we should note an initial difficulty with this school of thought: a lot of writing on 'best practice' moves fairly quickly into prescription without making its basic assumptions explicit. In a classic critique of the 'best practice' genre in what was then personnel management, Legge (1978) asked the question: for *whom* is 'best practice' best? *Whose* goals or interests are being served? If 'best practice' serves both shareholder and worker interests, it is hard to object to it.[2] Similarly, if we agree that

---

2 Although consumers and environmentalists might still object to some practices (for example, when a firm is making high profits and paying high wages but prices are extortionate or the firm is a bad polluter).

some practice is bad for both parties and should be avoided. But what if a practice is good for corporate returns but bad for workers? This is often the case with downsizing: sharemarkets seem to rate companies more highly for doing it, a cold comfort for the workers laid off and for those left behind whose workload may just have become much more stressful. When this kind of trade-off emerges, do workers get a real voice in deciding the issue (Marchington and Grugulis 2000)? Best-practice models are typically silent on these sorts of tensions. Those emanating from the United States do not typically mention or argue for the sort of strong employee voice institutions seen in Europe, such as unions and works councils, which can help to protect employee interests when trade-offs occur. This point is explored in Chapter 6.

Furthermore, what if a practice is good for executives but not good for either shareholders or waged workers? This is the problem, arguably, with many exit packages used for senior executives dismissed or 'let go' because of disappointing performance: *they* benefit but the company and its other employees typically lose out. In fact, the whole area of executive remuneration – staying or going – has become controversial, particularly in the USA. As Kochan (2007: 604) explains, American 'CEO pay relative to the average worker (has) exploded from a ratio of 40:1 in the 1960s and 70s to over 400:1 today'. This trend may be best for senior US executives but many others, both within the USA and looking at US practices from the outside, regard the trend as an aspect of American HR practice which is socially divisive and undesirable.

How are we going to proceed with a discussion of 'best practice' in the light of the problem of interest conflicts? Given that explicit assumptions are largely lacking, we need to consider implicit ones. In our view, the most common implicit assumption in the 'best practice' literature is that 'best practices' as those that enhance shareholder value. We think, however, that a useful test of any best-practice claim is the extent to which it also serves employee interests. One would not expect to see a perfect alignment of interests but it is likely that the most sustainable models of HRM over the long run are those that enjoy high levels of legitimacy within the firm and in wider society. On the basis of this caveat, we step gingerly forward.

'Best practice': micro foundations and macro models

Despite their tendency to gloss over basic assumptions, studies of individual best practices within the major categories of micro HRM – such as selection, training and appraisal – do have a very long tradition in

Western psychology and management theory. During both World Wars, for example, a lot of British and American energy went into improving practices for officer selection and also into the training and motivation of (non-combatant) production workers (Eilbert 1959, Crichton 1968). The academic discipline of Industrial Psychology gained great momentum as industrial psychologists studied the prediction and development of human performance. In the area of employee selection, for example, they usefully compared different practices for selecting individual employees (such as ability tests, personality inventories, 'biodata' obtained through application forms or from an individual's curriculum vitae ('cv'), references, and various types of interviews), assessing their validity in terms of subsequent performance (usually as rated by supervisors).

Based on this tradition of work, some micro aspects of best practice *are* widely acknowledged by researchers and practitioners (Delery and Doty 1996: 806, Youndt *et al.* 1996: 838). In the selection area, hardly anyone would advocate unstructured interviewing over interviews carefully designed around job-relevant factors. Similarly, no one would advocate input-based performance appraisal for senior executives (such as measures of timekeeping) over processes that examine results achieved (such as profit generated and growth in market share) or the kind of behaviour demonstrated in working with colleagues and clients. The selection and performance appraisal fields are two areas where we can point to an extensive body of research that assists management to carry out these processes more effectively. While there are still major debates and a raft of new problems, as recent reviews attest (Latham, Sulsky and MacDonald 2007, Schmitt and Kim 2007), there is quite a lot of agreement on what constitutes 'bad' or 'stupid' practice when we talk about practices in selection and performance appraisal.

At least, this is a fair generalisation *within* our specific cultural mind-set or 'blinkers'. We are talking here about selection and appraisal within a Western cultural frame of reference, dominated by US and British research. In this cultural tradition, we are generally comfortable with the idea that management should try to predict, appraise and reward *individual* performance (Trompenaars and Hampden-Turner 1997). In fact, a lot of high-performing employees will be angry and disloyal if their individual merit is not recognised (e.g. Trevor, Gerhart and Boudreau 1997). The sort of research discussed earlier helps us to remember, however, that such a high emphasis on individualism may be considered counter-cultural or subversive in societies which place a heavier emphasis on group identification and interpersonal humility. As a result of this, many industrial psychologists nowadays will acknowledge that cultural factors are important and will identify themselves as working on a specific HR practice *within* a particular cultural domain. Within this tradition, they will usually focus on problems relating to a restricted micro domain of HRM, such as selection processes for executives or performance management techniques for sales representatives.

The interesting and difficult question we face in a book about strategic HRM is whether 'best practice' thinking can work on a more macro level, on the level of *HR systems* (Becker and Gerhart 1996), a notion that is critical to our understanding of HR strategy. As noted in the definitions at the beginning of this chapter, firms often have more than one HR system. HR systems are aggregations of HR practices that managers have built over time to organise the work and manage the employment of a major workforce group. In most theoretical models, the key group of workers is the firm's core operational workers: the largest category of workers who make the products or deliver the services. Research often tries to identify what proportion of this core group is covered by a particular set of practices (e.g. Osterman 1994, 2000). A key theme that these models share with the literature on 'best fit' discussed above is the idea that HR systems should be synergistic (e.g. Dyer and Reeves 1995, Delery and Shaw 2001): that practices should be 'bundled' or clustered to reinforce desired effects.

There are, in fact, writers who have set out to offer models at this higher, more systemic level. In the United States, one model that has attracted a high profile is associated with Jeffrey Pfeffer's (1998) seven practices 'for building profits by putting people first', shown in Figure 3.8.

What comes through Pfeffer's list is a desire to carefully hire and develop talented people, organising them into highly cooperative teams, and employing them in a way that builds their commitment over the long run (through high pay, employment security and as much egalitarianism

| 1. Employment security |
| 2. Selective hiring |
| 3. Self-managed teams or teamworking |
| 4. High pay contingent on company performance |
| 5. Extensive training |
| 6. Reduction of status differences |
| 7. Sharing information |

Source: Pfeffer (1998)

Figure 3.8   Pfeffer's 7 practices

and openness as possible). Recruiting and retaining talented, team-oriented, highly motivated people is seen to lay a basis for superior business performance or competitive advantage. This is one well-known model which has been widely propagated through books and conferences.

It does not, however, stand up well on a reality test – that is, when we look at the actual HR strategies of US firms. There are cases of individual firms aiming to behave in the way Pfeffer advocates but when we observe the general trends in pay in the US, noted above, the trend is actually towards executive elitism and away from the egalitarianism that Pfeffer (1998) advocates. Similarly, the US data on the diffusion of HR practices suggest that employee insecurity grew in the 1990s and teamworking, present in around 40 per cent of firms with at least 50 employees, did not expand (Osterman 2000, Batt 2004). This is not, however, the point with best-practice models. Pfeffer (1998) is making a normative argument, an argument about what *ought* to be, not what is. He is challenging the wisdom of the contingency position we outlined in the first half of this chapter.

There is now a major body of literature in which various academics have attempted to define macro models of best HR practice. This literature is very diverse and at least three terms have been employed. One stream of literature stems from the work of the Harvard academic, Walton (1985), and is commonly called 'high-commitment management' (HCM) (Wood 1996). As this implies, the emphasis in this model is on winning employee commitment to the organisation's goals through positive incentives and identification with company culture rather than trying to control their behaviour through routine, short-cycle jobs and direct supervision. Another school of thought traces back to Lawler (1986) and is concerned with 'high-involvement work systems' (HIWSs). Here, the emphasis is on redesigning work to involve employees more fully in decision making and on the skill and motivational practices that are needed to support this process (e.g. Vandenberg, Richardson and Eastman 1999). A third term, 'high-performance work systems' (HPWSs) has sparked widespread interest over the last 10 to 15 years and is now the terminology many people use when they talk of 'best practice' models of HRM. Cappelli and Neumark (2001) trace the term's popularity to an influential public report, *America's Choice: High Skills or Low Wages!* (Commission on the Skills of the American Workforce 1990). This report, concerned about the fate of US jobs and highly critical of traditional work organisation, argues the case for substantial investment in 'high-performance work organisation' and higher skills. HPWSs are commonly understood to involve reforms to work practices to increase employee involvement in decision making and companion investments in employee skills and changes to performance incentives to ensure they can undertake these greater responsibilities and want to do so (Appelbaum *et al.* 2000). They constitute an attempt to roll back the kind of 'Taylorist' or highly specialised, de-skilled jobs which were a key part of the US system of mass production (something we will discuss further in Chapter 5).

'Best practice': research and critique

What, then, does research and theoretical critique have to say about the best-practice approach to HR systems? The first and most obvious difficulty with the approach was pointed out early on by Becker and Gerhart (1996): there is too much diversity in lists of best practices. Pfeffer's (1998) list of seven practices is actually reduced from an earlier list of 16 practices (Pfeffer 1994) and there have been major variations between theorists not only in the number of practices needed for an HR system but in which ones to include. A big part of the problem, as Becker and Gerhart (1996) and Purcell (1999) point out, is that many theorists simply list practices and do not specify the pathway or intervening variables through which they are supposed to improve business performance.

Leaving aside definitional issues, the major objection to the idea of a universally valid set of best HR practices is the socio-cultural one. As emphasised in our review of the best-fit literature, there is overwhelming research evidence that firms adapt their HR practices to their unique contexts. And this is the key point: they are *wise* to do so because social legitimacy is an important aspect of a firm's multidimensional HR performance. Some practices – such as an employee grievance procedure and forms of consultation – are legal requirements in countries like the UK. Governments have decided they should form part of employer practice for ethical and political reasons. Simply on the fact of societal regulation of labour markets, we must discount the idea that there can be universally valid lists of best practice.

Similarly, as Trompenaars and Hampden-Turner (1997) and many others remind us, there really is a problem with trying to specify a set of cross-culturally best HR practices because there are significant differences in cultural values. Even if we are talking about the same practice, such as selection interviewing, the application of it can vary very significantly across cultures. In New Zealand, for example, where government policy supports biculturalism (English and Maori are both official languages), it is not uncommon for Maori job applicants to request a *whanau* (family, kinship-supported) interview. In such an interview, family members and close friends speak to the merits of the job applicant because it is considered culturally offensive to indulge in self-praise or 'blow your own trumpet'. This is still a selection interview but it is not what American or British writers think of when they use the term.

As Becker and Gerhart (1996) imply, we would be wise to dispense with the idea that there can be lists of HR practices that are universally relevant. A more appropriate line of thinking is to accept that there will always be socio-cultural variations in how HRM is organised and look to systems or configurations of HR practices that have a kind of 'functional equivalence' or 'equifinality' (Delery and Doty 1996). In other words, it is possible to envisage systems that are designed to serve certain underpinning principles (such as supporting high levels of employee involvement in decision making) but which recognise variety in the actual practices that are used in different industries and different societies to express these principles.

In effect, Appelbaum and Batt (1994), whose work on models of high-performance work systems has been highly influential, adopt this kind of approach. When looking beyond the USA for HPWS models, they identify four that are worth discussion: Swedish 'socio-technical systems', Japanese 'lean production', Italian 'flexible specialisation' and German 'diversified quality production'. Each of these models (all of which have internal variations) are embedded in national laws, customs and management styles that vary from those of the USA. Just comparing three of these countries shows major differences (Figure 3.9). As Appelbaum and Batt argue, it is very difficult to transplant foreign models of high-performance work systems to the USA

	USA	Japan	Germany
Unionisation	Very low level (below 10 % of private sector workers)	Well-established enterprise unions in the large corporations	Strong, industry-based unions with key involvement in vocational training (among other areas)
Power sharing: institutions	Collective bargaining only in workplaces where there is majority worker support	Collective bargaining at set annual time ('shunto' – the Spring Offensive) plus well-established consultative processes	Industry-based collective bargaining plus very established tradition of codetermination (works councils and worker directors)
Management attitudes to joint governance	Apart from some cases of union–management 'partnerships', strong management resistance to any form of power sharing with unions	Japanese executives work with strong cultural norms that emphasise consultation and have often been officials in the enterprise union	German managers have adjusted to codetermination and, while grappling with flexibility problems, see advantages in consensual decision making

Sources: Taira (1993), Appelbaum and Batt (1994), Wever (1995), Towers (1997), Freeman (2007)

Figure 3.9 Some key differences in employment relations in three national contexts

because of these socio-political contexts. While they support the idea of greater voice mechanisms for US workers, they realise that this will have to be worked out in an American way. Most commentators on the USA recognise that the chances of major reform there towards European-style works councils or worker directors are extremely small (e.g. Towers 1997, Freeman 2007).

The line of argument found in the work of Appelbaum and Batt (1994) has now been reinforced with the publication of *Manufacturing Advantage* (Appelbaum *et al.* 2000). This book looks at US-style HPWSs in three industries: steel making, clothing manufacturing and medical electronics manufacturing. The studies in this book were all conducted at the plant level, identifying the particular HR practices used in each industry and measuring performance as objectively as possible in terms of the productivity indices relevant to the production processes concerned. They involve surveys of worker responses to HR reforms and do not rely on managerial reports of either company results or worker attitudes. In the main, the studies are supportive of the idea that both companies and employees have benefited where HPWSs have been implemented in these industries. There are other influential studies in the steel industry (Ichniowski, Shaw and Prennushi 1997, Ichniowski and Shaw 1999) and in automobile manufacturing (MacDuffie 1995). The latter studies have actually looked at HR systems in similar plants across countries (most notably comparing the US and Japan). This has enabled these studies to pick up principles of work design that have become common across the two countries while also observing culturally embedded HR practices that have not.

As Ichniowski and Shaw (1999) show in their study of US and Japanese steel plants, the US plants that have achieved similar operational performance to Japanese ones have done so through adopting the principles of employee-driven problem solving seen in Japanese plants while customising employment practices (such as selection tests and pay systems) in a way that is more compatible with US law and cultural norms. Their work indicates the way in which the debate about best practice needs to evolve: away from the idea that we can have 'exact replicas' of 'best practices' in all industries towards studies of HR systems or models that are established on a core set of common principles but inevitably show intelligent adaptation of specific practices across contexts.

Do studies such as those by Ichniowski and Shaw (1999) in steel plants and MacDuffie (1995) in automobile manufacturing give us a basis for asserting that there are best HR practices which will deliver higher value across all industries? No, they do not. These studies have the virtue of identifying the technologies, work processes and employment practices actually used in these industries and measuring the operational outcomes relevant to them. Understanding these distinctive features means we are less likely to assume they will work in other production environments. Appleyard and Brown (2001) underline this point in a study of the semiconductor manufacturing industry, contrasting the role of key occupational groups in this industry with that described by MacDuffie (1995) in automobiles and Ichniowski *et al.* (1997) in steel. In semiconductor production, problem-solving processes are dominated by highly skilled professional engineers and not by operators or technicians. The latter two occupational groups have an important role to play but the production process is more technologically intensive than in either steel or automobile manufacturing. While operators and technicians bring their knowledge into problem-solving activities, it is the involvement and skills of highly qualified professional engineers, including software and equipment engineers, which are decisive in finding solutions to production quality issues and breakdowns.

What the sets of studies we have just cited offer is a thorough examination of production and HR systems *in the field* and a rigorous assessment of whether new HR systems will pay off in terms of the economics of production *in that industry*. We can be pretty confident from studies of steel-finishing production systems that HR approaches which significantly enhance operator engagement in problem solving do improve machine up-time, quality and on-time delivery in this industry (Ichniowski *et al.* 1997, Ichniowski and Shaw 1999, Appelbaum *et al.* 2000). Within this particular environment, we can envisage improvements in shareholder value from these HR systems.

We can be more confident of such findings when research exercises use longitudinal methodologies that rule out or heavily discount other causes of performance variation. We have this with the steel industry studies just mentioned but it is far from easy to conduct this kind of study (Wright *et al.* 2005, Gerhart 2007). The only research we have that addresses the cost-effectiveness of HPWSs across a broad swathe of industries over time, and at a high level of rigour, is not flattering. This is the work of Cappelli and Neumark (2001), who use a national probability sample of US manufacturing establishments, assessing work practices and outcomes in firms in 1977 and then again some 20 years later. They conclude that HPWSs raise labour costs and that this implies that employees benefit through average remuneration rises, a picture reinforced by Osterman's (2006) study of the wage impacts of high-performance work organisation in US manufacturers. However, the statistical case for productivity benefits is weaker and the effects on profitability are unclear. In this context, firms would be wise to be sceptical about the economics of such systems, as Godard (2004) argues. They may well offer benefits but they will not be costless and the relationship between benefit and cost needs careful assessment in their *particular* context.

Conclusions: reconciling 'best fit' and 'best practice'

In the light of all this, where do things stand in the debate between 'best fit' and 'best practice'? If we want to identify a winner, it is obviously a clear win to the best-fit camp on the evidence of what firms actually do. Research on what firms do – descriptive research – makes life very difficult for the more extreme advocates of 'best practice'. It demonstrates that methods of labour management are inevitably influenced by context, including a range of economic and socio-political factors. And it also shows that there are very good reasons for adaptation to context including the needs to fit in with social values and to adapt to industry characteristics. Does this fact invalidate all best-practice thinking? Should the best-practice people pack up their tents and go home?

We think there are three ways in which it is possible to take some value out of the best-practice approach rather than discarding it completely. First, as we explained above, there are aspects of 'best practice' in the micro domains of HRM which are important. When companies commit to an executive selection process, for example, they are well advised to avoid invalid predictors and to learn from research on how to make the process effective for both the firm and the chosen candidate. Similarly, if they commit to performance appraisal, they are well advised to work hard on dealing with the 'rating errors' that research has shown will inevitably rear their ugly heads (Latham, Sulsky and MacDonald 2007). However, all of this takes place within a cultural and legal context. The relevant best-practice prescriptions in these domains have been developed in an Anglo-American frame of reference and should have regard to Anglo-American laws on discrimination and equal opportunity (e.g. Kossek and Pichler 2007).

Second, when we come to study specific industries, it is clearly possible to identify HR systems that embody a set of principles while fostering astute local adaptations in different production sites around the world. The research by Doeringer, Lorenz and Terkla (2003) and by Ichniowski and Shaw (1999), among others, shows the way in which management might emulate a core set of principles while cannily adapting to the specific context. Tayeb (1995: 600), for example, underlines the astute capacity of Japanese managers in Britain to implement their core philosophies on 'quality and built-in control . . . and harmonious employee-management relationships' while adjusting sensitively to 'British employees' cultural attitudes and values'. In a high-tech firm she studied, Japanese managers did not require 'the famous morning rituals performed in many Japanese companies . . . nor did they experiment with just-in-time or plant-based unions' (*ibid.*: 600). There is a role for identifying better HR systems within particular industry contexts as these evolve, bearing in mind that such systems will more likely be based on 'equifinality' (applying the same kind of principles and aiming to achieve similar performance outcomes) than on exact lists of practices.

The second point leads us to a third, more general one. Following Becker and Gerhart (1996), we think there is scope to identify some general principles in HRM and, in fact, much of this book is dedicated to this task. Building on the arguments in this chapter, it is helpful to make an analytical distinction between the surface level of HR policy and practices in a firm and an underpinning level of HR principles (Figure 3.10). This is not a perfect distinction but it helps to reconcile the tension between 'best fit' and 'best practice' in strategic HRM. We are most unlikely to find that any theorist's selection of best practices (the surface layer) will have universal relevance because context always matters. It is, however, possible to argue that at the level of the underpinning layer there are some desirable principles which, if applied, will bring about more effective management of people. In effect, it is possible to argue that, *ceteris paribus* (other things being equal), all firms are better off when they pursue certain principles in HRM (Youndt *et al.* 1996: 837, Edwards and Wright 2001).

What sort of principles do we have in mind? We have, in effect, already been arguing for three underpinning principles. First, both in this chapter and in Chapter 1, we have claimed that a good performance in HRM involves dealing with multiple goals. There are multiple 'bottom lines' in HRM, including economic and social legitimacy goals which involve managing trade-offs and dynamic tensions. This is a fundamental perspective or principle that informs all of our analysis. Second, the pursuit of economic and socio-political goals means that firms inevitably adapt their HRM to their specific context *and* they are wise to do so. This is the 'law of context', if you like. Third, we have argued that all models of HRM work through their impacts on employees: they all work through the 'AMO' variables, on the individual level, and through employee attitudes, on the collective level, as we described in Chapter 1. At the heart of this is a principle concerned with alignment: with the need to align management and employee interests,

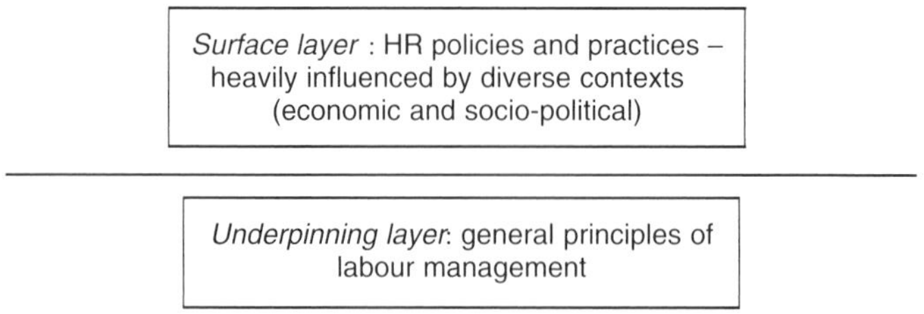

```
┌─────────────────────────────────────────┐
│  Surface layer : HR policies and practices – │
│  heavily influenced by diverse contexts  │
│  (economic and socio-political)          │
└─────────────────────────────────────────┘

┌─────────────────────────────────────────┐
│  Underpinning layer: general principles of │
│  labour management                       │
└─────────────────────────────────────────┘
```

Figure 3.10   The 'best fit' versus 'best practice' debate: two levels of analysis

at least at the level of a contract that meets the baseline requirements of both parties. As a general rule, all firms benefit from policies and practices that help them to align their interests with those of employees. In any context where workers have good labour market choice or develop powerful organisation or enjoy strongly enforced labour market standards, this principle becomes more apparent – but it is always there. Research on how employees respond to different kinds of managerial policy and behaviour, and the links from these responses to the firm's performance, is going to be very important in this book and is likely to lead us to other important principles.

In Part 2 of the book, we engage in a process of 'searching for general principles' in the management of work and people and in the final part we look at how these play out in dynamic and complex contexts. In effect, the book is grounded on the assumption that *both* general principles *and* specific contexts play an important role in the theory and practice of strategic HRM. No one can seriously argue against the importance of 'best fit' or contextual thinking in HRM. However, there is still a valuable role for a concept of 'best practice' if it means a concern for underpinning principles of labour management which help all firms to manage work and people more effectively.

4

Strategic HRM and the resource-based view of the firm

In this part of the book, we are concerned with fundamental concepts of strategic management and with their links to the management of work and people in firms. Chapter 2 established our preferred definitions of the major terms involved in studying strategy. It made the point that strategic management is a human process, dependent on human strengths, but also affected by our cognitive weaknesses and political agendas. This means that, at the very least, key choices about *whom* to place in leadership roles and *how* to build strategy-making processes are critical to the success of firms. Chapter 3 built on this basis to define what we mean by strategic HRM and HR strategy. It discussed the debate in the strategic HRM literature between contingency theory ('best fit') and universalism ('best practice'). The chapter underlined the compelling evidence in favour of a contingency approach but also argued that it is possible to identify some underpinning *principles* of labour management which managers will benefit from following if they aim to make the firm more successful.

The broad debate around the merits of contingency theory and universalism dominated the field of strategic HRM as it emerged into the limelight in the 1980s and remains very important in any kind of theory building. Since the early 1990s, however, another body of thought has grown in significance. The strategic HRM literature has increasingly been influenced by a branch of strategic management known as the resource-based view of the firm (RBV). Relating the RBV to the best-fit/best-practice debate we have just been discussing, one might say that strategy theorists who work with the RBV aim to discover how a firm can build an *exclusive* form of fit. How might a firm develop and manipulate its resources – human and non-human – to become the *best adapted*, the most consistently profitable of all firms in its industry? This chapter aims to explain what is meant by the RBV, defining key concepts and exploring major models. In so doing, it examines the implications of the RBV for the strategic management of labour, helping to lay the basis for the rest of this book.

The resource-based view: origins and assumptions

The resource-based view is usually sourced to a remarkable book by a University of London Professor of Economics, Edith Penrose (1959). At the time, texts on the economics of the firm were dominated by discussion of 'equilibrium' conditions under different forms of competition. The main focus of these texts was on the relative merits of different types of market, including 'perfect competition', oligopoly and monopoly. While valuable in debates about market regulation, the traditional analysis ignored very important issues inside the 'black box' of the firm's operations, leaving the study of entrepreneurship and business management in a very rudimentary state within the discipline of Economics.

Arguing that her interest was different from that of the standard texts on the firm, Penrose set out to build a theory of the growth of firms. She made the basic, but critical, observation that the firm is 'an administrative organisation and a collection of productive resources', distinguishing between 'physical' and 'human resources' (Penrose 1959: 31, 24).[1] Her understanding of the quality of the firm's human resources placed heavy emphasis on the knowledge and experience of the 'management team' and their subjective interpretation (or 'images') of the firm's environment (showing an early grasp of the kind of cognitive problems of strategic management discussed in Chapter 2). Her analysis proceeded from what has become a fundamental premiss in the theory of business strategy: firms are 'heterogeneous' (Penrose 1959: 74–8). As Nelson (1991: 61) puts it, competition ('perfect' or otherwise) never entirely eliminates 'differences among firms in the same line of business' and these differences account for major performance variations.

Penrose's ideas lay dormant for some time. Her work was not brought within the mainstream of strategic management theory until it was

---

1 In passing, we might note that Penrose was one of the first theorists to adopt the 'human resources' terminology.

rediscovered by Wernerfelt (1984) and then by a string of other strategy writers from the late 1980s (e.g. Dierickx and Cool 1989, Barney 1991, Conner 1991, Grant 1991, Mahoney and Pandian 1992, Amit and Shoemaker 1993, Peteraf 1993). The result has been an explosion of interest in the resource-based perspective, focusing on the ways in which firms might build unique clusters or 'bundles' of human and technical resources that generate enviable levels of performance. Major reviews of the strategic management literature now routinely recognise the RBV as a major body of thought concerned with explaining sources of competitive advantage (e.g. Hoskisson *et al.* 1999).

In effect, the growth of the RBV has provided a counterweight to the marketing-oriented models of strategic management which were dominant in the strategy textbooks of the 1980s. The best known of these models was associated with the works of Michael Porter (1980, 1985), discussed in the context of best-fit theory in Chapter 3. These models place greatest emphasis on critical choices associated with competitive strategy – primarily, choices about which industry to enter and which competitive position to seek in it. In so doing, these models make some fairly heroic assumptions (Boxall 1992, 1996). For example, they assume that the firm already has a clever leadership team which can make these sorts of choices effectively. They assume that the human resource issues that arise when particular paths are chosen, such as hiring and motivating a capable workforce, are straightforward. They assume that culture change, when it might be needed to shift direction, is also unproblematic. In contrast, it is *exactly* these sorts of people issues that the resource-based view regards as strategic. In the RBV, the quality of the management process and of the firm's workplace culture are seen as major factors that explain enduring differences in business performance (e.g. Barney 1991).

It can, however, be argued that the RBV is itself imbalanced, placing undue emphasis on the internal side of the old SWOT acronym (strengths, weaknesses, opportunities, threats). In a response to criticism from resource-based theorists, Michael Porter argues that 'resources are not valuable in and of themselves, but because they allow firms to perform activities that create advantages in particular markets' (Porter 1991: 108). Similarly, Miller and Shamsie (1996: 520) argue that the RBV needs 'to consider the contexts within which various kinds of resources will have the best influence on performance.' In a study of the Hollywood film studios from 1936 to 1965, they demonstrate how knowledge-based resources (such as the exceptionally creative skills of key writers and cinematographers, and big-budget coordinating abilities) were more valuable to the studios in the

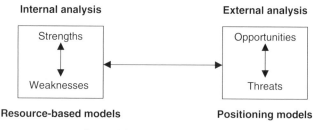

Source: Adapted from Barney (1991)

Figure 4.1 Internal and external dimensions of the strategic problem

relatively uncertain and turbulent environment of the 1950s when the advent of television seriously affected movie-going habits. On the other hand, in the more stable conditions of the late 1930s and the 1940s (Wasn't everyone watching films in the war?), property-based resources (such as networks of theatres and long-term, exclusive contracts with particular actors) were more valuable for studio performance. In other words, the human talents that helped the studios to 'think and act outside the square' were indeed valuable when the context became less predictable.

Wernerfelt (1984: 173) did recognise the interplay of resources and markets when he said there is a 'duality between products and resources'. In other words, the strategic problem has both internal (strengths, weaknesses) and external (opportunities, threats) dimensions (Figure 4.1). These dimensions – what Baden-Fuller (1995) calls the 'inside-out' and the 'outside-in' perspectives on the strategic problem – are interactive over time. The point is well made. One should not get carried away with either external or internal perspectives: both are necessary for a sufficient view of a firm's strategy. It seems safe, however, to suggest that what the resource-based perspective has achieved is a *re-balancing* of the literature on strategy, reminding people of the strategic significance of internal resources and their development over time.

Resources and barriers to imitation

What, then, are the basic definitions and concepts associated with the RBV? In the resource-based perspective, resources are not simply understood as assets in the formal accounting sense (which can be disclosed on a balance sheet) but include any feature of the firm with value-creating properties (Hunt 1995: 322). This means that aspects of the business that are not formally owned by it, such as the talents and interactions of the people who work in it, are not ignored but come within the realm of analytical interest. Wernerfelt (1984: 172) defined resources in the following way:

> By a resource is meant anything which could be thought of as a strength or weakness of a given firm. More formally, a firm's resources at a given time could be defined as those (tangible and intangible) assets which are tied semipermanently to the firm. Examples of resources are: brand names, in-house knowledge of technology, employment of skilled personnel, trade contacts, machinery, efficient procedures, capital etc.

In an interesting study of chief executive opinion about the value of different kinds of resource, Hall (1993) found that CEOs rated the quality of employee know-how and their firm's reputation with customers as their most strategic assets. It is easy to see why the RBV is so attractive to human resource specialists – here at last is a body of thought within strategic management in which people issues figure prominently.

Clusters of resources, understood in this broader way, can be sources of competitive advantage. Barney (1991), one of the most influential and accessible theorists in the RBV school, distinguishes between a competitive advantage which a firm presently enjoys, but which others will be able to copy, and 'sustained competitive advantage', a characteristic which rivals find themselves unable to compete away, despite their best efforts. In his conception, resources are valuable when they enable the firm to take advantage of market opportunities or deal particularly well with market threats in a way that competitors are not currently able to. The task is to manage these valuable resources in such a way that rivals are frustrated in their efforts to imitate or out-flank them.

Using some fairly awkward terminology, RBV theorists are interested in the conditions that make desirable resources 'inimitable' and 'non-substitutable' (Barney 1991). What can be done to ensure others do not simply imitate or copy a firm's strengths or find ways of substituting for them that achieve the same ends? The key characteristics of desirable resources, then, are that they are valuable and inimitable (with inimitability covering both direct and indirect forms of copying) (Hoopes, Madsen and Walker 2003).

As Coff (1997, 1999) and others point out (for example, Grant 1991, Kamoche 1996), it is important to add 'appropriability' to this list of traits. Not only must the firm be able to generate and defend sources of high

Desirable resources are:

- valuable: capable of delivering superior competitive results
- inimitable: very hard to imitate or copy, either directly or indirectly
- appropriable: capable of benefiting the firm's shareholders

Figure 4.2 Qualities of desirable resources

performance,[2] but the RBV assumes that the firm is able to capture the benefits for its shareholders. This is easier said than done because the firm is a network of *stake*holders. Some stakeholders, such as senior executives, have access to the kind of information and power which can enlarge their share of the firm's bounty. Where they are concentrated in a small geographical area, such as the City of London, the result can be quite extreme competition for very high bonus payments in millions of pounds. Qualities of desirable resources are shown in Figure 4.2.

Having defined these sorts of desirable traits, Barney (1991) notes that such resources are not immune to 'Schumpeterian shocks'. The great Austrian economist, Joseph Schumpeter, referred to the propensity for capitalism to generate 'gales of creative destruction' – radical breakthroughs which disturb technologies or basic concepts of business in the particular business sector (Schumpeter 1950). In the transportation sector, for example, inventions such as railroads, automobiles, and airplanes have had enormous impacts on the ways of providing transport that preceded them. We are currently living through a time when computerisation, telecommunications and the internet are making a major impact across various sectors of business. The vast majority of firms cannot insulate themselves from such radical trends but there is scope for firms to differentiate themselves in ways which are relatively sustainable in a *given* competitive context.

The issue is one of how management might build valuable, firm-specific characteristics and 'barriers to imitation' (Rumelt 1987, Reed and deFillippi 1990), which make it hard for others to copy or ape what the successful firm is doing. What, then, are the key barriers to imitation noted by resource-based theorists?

2 In the RBV literature, high financial performance is often described as 'rent', an old-fashioned term in Economics for profits above the normal level in competitive markets.

Unique timing and learning

Models proposed in the RBV typically place emphasis on the way that historical learning acts as a barrier to newcomers and slower rivals. Theorists cite the value to firms of 'unique historical conditions' (Barney 1991: 107), 'first mover advantages' (Wernerfelt 1984: 173) and 'path dependency' (Leonard 1998: 35). They argue that valuable, specialised resources (sometimes called 'asset specificity') are developed over time through opportunities that do not repeat themselves (or not in quite the same way). Competitive success does not come simply from making choices in the present (as positioning models of strategic management seem to imply) but stems from building up distinctive capabilities over significant periods of time.

In simple terms, RBV theorists argue that a sense of time and place matters: if you are not there at the time things are happening, you cannot expect to be successful. Others will take up the unique learning opportunity. As Woody Allen once quipped, 'fifty percent of success is turning up'. Shakespeare expressed the same sentiment in a famous line from *Julius Caesar*: 'there is a tide in the affairs of men, which taken at the flood, leads on to fortune'. Or as Wernerfelt (1984: 174) puts it, in the rather prosaic language of business theory, 'if the leader executes the experience curve strategy correctly, then later resource producers have to get their experience in an uphill battle with earlier producers who have lower costs'.

The special value of timing and learning is widely understood in the business community. The difficulty of securing a firm's presence in an area where it has no experience is often a reason for take-overs. Directors of firms often feel they cannot make a mark in a new sector (or a new region) without buying an established player who has built up the necessary client base, employee skills and operating systems. The international accounting firms very often expanded this way in the 1970s and 1980s, taking over much smaller, but well-regarded, firms around the world. The small firms thus absorbed provided important political connections, a pool of appropriately qualified staff and a well-established client base. Naturally, the owners of these firms also benefited enormously from the learning of the international firm, gaining access, for example, to special audit techniques, management consulting methodologies, and training systems developed at considerable expense elsewhere.

Social complexity

The phenomenon of historical learning or 'path dependency' is intimately linked to a second barrier to imitation – 'social complexity' (Barney 1991,

Wright, McMahan and McWilliams 1994). As firms grow, they inevitably become characterised by complex patterns of teamwork and coordination, both inside and outside the firm. As we emphasised in Chapter 1, successful firms become strong clusters of 'human and social capital' (Lovas and Goshal 2000: 883). Productive work communities, such as outstanding schools and universities, take time to build and are inherently complex systems. The network of these internal and external connections is a kind of natural barrier to imitation by rivals, a prime reason why firms in some industries try to recruit an entire team of employees. Loss of all or most of an outstanding team of staff can decimate an organisation's reputation. Something like this happened in 1957 when eight scientists and engineers working on the development of the silicon chip resigned from the Shockley Semiconductor Laboratory, a research and development company led by the Nobel laureate physicist, Bill Shockley: 'Their mass departure cut the productive heart out of the laboratory, leaving behind a carcass of men working . . . on the four-layer diode project plus a bunch of aimless technicians and secretaries . . . ' (Riordan and Hoddeson 1997: 252). The group left to form Fairchild Semiconductor. The rest, as they say, is history.

Mueller's (1996) discussion of 'resource mobility barriers' is one that places strong emphasis on socially complex attributes of firms. Mueller argues that sustained advantage stems from hard-to-imitate routines deeply embedded in a firm's 'social architecture' (Mueller 1996: 774). By contrast, he sees little enduring value accruing to the firm from top management's codified policy positions (which are easily imitated because of their public visibility). Indeed, he implies that little value is created by those senior managers who are highly mobile:

> Corporate prosperity not seldom rests in the social architecture that has emerged incrementally over time, and might often predate the tenure of current senior management. . . . The social architecture is created and re-created not only or even primarily at senior management levels in the organization, but at other levels too, including at workgroup level on the shopfloor. (Mueller 1996: 771, 777)

According to Mueller, outstanding *organisational* value is more likely to come from persistent, patient management processes that, over time, encourage skill formation and powerful forms of cooperation deep within the firm. These processes generate valuable new combinations or 'bundles' of human and non-human resources for the firm.

Causal ambiguity

A third type of resource barrier noted in the RBV literature – causal ambiguity – is more controversial. As with social complexity, ambiguity about the cause/effect relationships involved in the firm's performance is an inevitable outcome of firm growth (Reed and deFillippi 1990, Barney 1991). It can take some time to figure why an established firm has become successful and to discern how successful it really is. There is no doubt that firms wanting to acquire other firms should be very careful in the 'due diligence' process that precedes (or ought to precede) the purchase of another business. There are inevitably elements of ambiguity about a firm's performance, as there are about the performance of individuals and teams.

Having said this, it is likely that causal ambiguity is over-rated as a barrier to imitation (McWilliams and Smart 1995). Human rationality is always bounded, as was noted in Chapter 2, but if one pushes the notion of causal ambiguity too far, management is virtually meaningless, as is theory (Priem and Butler 2001). The 'paradox of causal ambiguity' has been explored by a study in two US industries: textiles and hospitals (King and Zeithaml 2001). This study examined the way senior and middle managers perceive the competencies of their organisations and their links to competitive advantage. Interestingly, the study was one in which chief executives were very keen to participate (which is quite unusual given 'survey fatigue' among managers in the USA). It involved finding out how other members of their senior team and a cross-section of middle managers understood the firm's resources and their impacts. CEOs were interviewed and the other managers selected in the 17 firms were surveyed (with very high response rates). The study contains evidence that high-performing firms benefit from building consensus across management levels about the resources that enable them to out-perform rivals. Understanding of the key competencies and the most important links among them *ought* to be high. This does not mean, however, that all the micro aspects of particular competencies will be transparent because there is always some degree of ambiguity embedded in organisational culture and employee know-how. As we explore further below, 'tacit knowledge' is always present in organisations.

The findings of this study are consistent with the arguments of advocates of the 'balanced scorecard' (Kaplan and Norton 1996, 2001, 2004, 2006) who claim that, given enough effort, it must be possible within business units to evolve a broad theory of how the business works or might work better (see Chapter 11). Not only this, but the benefits of having agreement about where we are going and how we can get there must be more valuable than confusion and working at cross-purposes! It seems, then, that while causal ambiguity will always be present to some degree, it is likely to be a less important barrier to imitation than the processes of historical learning and social interaction that characterise established firms.

Applying the resource-based view

The discussion so far might convince us that the RBV contains some important insights but leave us wondering what we can do about it. How can all this talk of valuable resources and barriers to imitation be made useful?

One of the more popular frameworks is associated with the work of Hamel and Prahalad (1993, 1994). They argue that competitive advantage, over the long run, stems from building 'core competencies' in a firm which are superior to those of rivals. Their notion of core competence is very close to the concept of 'distinctive competence' discussed in the older strategy texts as something the firm does particularly well. Their definitions of the term (shown in Figure 4.3) place strong emphasis on analysing a firm's collective skills: skills found in the complex teamwork embedded in the firm.

The writings of Hamel and Prahalad are important for leaders of multidivisional firms (discussed in Chapter 10). CEOs and directors of these firms are encouraged to identify the underlying clusters of know-how in their companies which transcend the artificial divisions of 'strategic business units' – or which might do so, if they were appropriately managed. Sony's 'unrelenting pursuit of leadership in miniaturisation' – manifesting itself in various products over time – is one of Hamel and Prahalad's standard examples (Hamel and Prahalad 1994: 119). Another example,

---

A 'core competence':

- is a bundle of skills and technologies that enables a company to provide particular benefits to customers
- is not product specific
- represents . . . the sum of learning across individual skill sets and individual organisational units
- must . . . be competitively unique
- is not an 'asset' in the accounting sense of the word
- represents a 'broad opportunity arena' or 'gateway to the future'

Source: Excerpted from Hamel and Prahalad (1994: 217–28)

Figure 4.3   Hamel and Prahalad's notion of 'core competence'

offered by Goold, Campbell and Alexander (1994) is that of Canon which has deliberately sought to integrate development engineers in different strands of the business to exploit fibre-optic technology. Hamel and Prahalad (1994) argue that companies which make the effort to understand their core competencies (and envision the core competencies they ought to build) are much less likely to get left with outdated products or miss important new applications of a knowledge base. In effect, their work is an argument for developing a 'knowledge-based', rather than a product-based, understanding of the firm. This might be a simple distinction to make but it suggests quite a profound change in the way corporate directors review company strengths and analyse their strategic opportunities.

A similar analysis is advanced by Leonard (1998) who uses the word 'capability' instead of 'competence' (but is concerned with the same idea). Her framework helps executives to identify the distinctive or 'core capabilities' underpinning their products or services. Core capabilities are 'knowledge sets' composed of four dimensions: the 'content' dimensions which include the relevant employee skills and knowledge and technical systems, and the 'process' dimensions which include managerial systems, and values and norms (Figure 4.4). Her framework is perhaps the most helpful in terms of spelling out the HR implications. This is because managerial systems include the critical HR policies needed to recruit, develop and motivate employees with the relevant skills and aptitudes (Leonard 1998: 19). Employee development and incentive systems are a key part of her notion of core capability. She also emphasises the interlocking, systemic nature of the

---

1. *Employee knowledge and skill*: This dimension is the most obvious one.

2. *Physical technical systems*: But technological competence accumulates not only in the heads of people; it also accumulates in the physical systems that they build over time – databases, machinery, and software programs.

3. *Managerial systems*: The accumulation of employee knowledge is guided and monitored by the company's systems of education, rewards, and incentives. These managerial systems – particularly incentive structures – create the channels through which knowledge is accessed and flows; they also set up barriers to undesired knowledge-creation activities.

4. *Values and norms*: These determine what kinds of knowledge are sought and nurtured, what kinds of knowledge-building activities are tolerated and encouraged. These are systems of caste and status, rituals of behavior, and passionate beliefs associated with various kinds of technological knowledge that are as rigid and complex as those associated with religion. Therefore, values serve as knowledge-screening and -control mechanisms.

Figure 4.4 The four dimensions of a 'core capability'

four dimensions and the resulting tendency of core capabilities to become 'core rigidities' over time, unless firms learn to practise continuous renewal. According to Leonard (1998: 30), every strength is also simultaneously a weakness. The recognition that firms can also have weaknesses or 'distinctive inadequacies' is an aspect of the RBV that ought to be given greater attention (West and DeCastro 2001). Some weaknesses can result from having 'too much of a good thing', as Leonard implies, while others can simply be 'bad things' (such as not developing sufficient skills in environmental analysis and change management).

In outlining her model of how firms might develop outstanding capabilities, Leonard (1998: 5–16) discusses the interesting case of Chaparral Steel, a very successful US 'minimill'. While only the tenth largest steel producer in the USA at the time of this study, Chaparral enjoyed a reputation as a world leader in productivity:

> . . . in 1990, its 1.5 person-hours per rolled ton of steel compared to a US average of 5.3, a Japanese average of 5.6, and a German average of 5.7. Chaparral was the first American steel company (and only the second company outside of Japan at the time) to be awarded the right to use the Japanese Industrial Standard certification on its general structural steel products. (Leonard 1998: 6)

With strong values and incentives supporting the creation of new knowledge, Chaparral employees have pushed the company's equipment well beyond its original specifications:

> The rolling mill equipment its vendor believed (was) limited to 8-inch slabs is turning out 14-inch slabs, and the vendor has tried to buy back the redesign. The two electric arc furnaces, designed originally to melt annual rates of 250,000 and 500,000 tons of scrap metal, now produce over 600,000 and 1 million tons, respectively. (Leonard 1998: 11)

Leonard explains how Chaparral has achieved these results through building an 'interdependent system' of employee skills and technical systems supported by HR policies, practices and cultural values:

> Chaparral's skills, physical systems, learning activities, values and managerial philosophies and practices are obviously highly interdependent. Competitively advantageous equipment can be designed and constantly improved *only* if the workforce is highly skilled. Continuous education is attractive *only* if employees are carefully selected for their willingness to learn. Sending workers throughout the world to garner ideas is cost-effective *only* if they are empowered to apply what they have learned to production problems. (Leonard 1998: 15–16, italics in the original)

Leonard's model, then, places emphasis on the fact that cleverly developed systems of this kind – where the parts do reinforce each other in powerful ways – are very hard to imitate. This is certainly the view within Chaparral. Leonard (1998: 7) notes that the CEO is happy to give visitors a full plant tour, showing them almost 'everything and . . . giving away nothing because they cannot take it home with them'. This kind of story lends some support to the argument made earlier that even if we have a good understanding of why a firm is successful (low 'causal ambiguity'), the unique path that company has travelled and the social complexity this brings remain significant barriers to imitation.

'Table stakes' and distinctive capabilities

While sources of valuable differentiation are very important in the RBV, it is worth injecting a note of caution here. A problem with some writing in the RBV is the tendency of authors to focus only on sources of idiosyncrasy, thus exaggerating differences between firms in the same industry. As we argued in Chapter 2, all viable firms in an industry need some similar resources in order to establish their identity in the minds of customers and to help secure legitimacy in broader society (Carroll and Hannan 1995, Peteraf and Shanley 1997, Deephouse 1999). For example, banks must act like banks (having the requisite information technology and the typical range of services, for instance). They must satisfy investors and regulators that they can behave as responsible repositories and lenders of funds. Without these baseline features, banks lack recognition in their industry and legitimacy in wider society.

Some writers in the RBV are so focused on the firm that they do not recognise these wider connections. However, it is a strength of the frameworks outlined here that the authors do see the importance of 'table stakes' (Hamel and Prahalad 1994) or 'enabling capabilities' (Leonard 1998). These are features of the business which enable participation in the industry but which do not make the firm distinctive or account for superior performance.

Leonard (1998) makes useful distinctions among three kinds of capabilities: core (which are superior and cannot be easily imitated), supplemental (which add value to core capabilities but can be easily copied) and enabling (which are necessary conditions of being in the industry). These distinctions are shown in Figure 4.5. Both Leonard (1998) and Hamel and Prahalad (1994) note the dynamic nature of capabilities: over time: one company's distinctive or core capability (such as outstanding quality) tends to be emulated by other firms. It then becomes part of the 'table

Low   **High**

Figure 4.5   Strategic importance of capabilities to the firm

stakes' in the industry and firms that seek superior performance must search for other ways to differentiate themselves. Hamel and Prahalad (1994: 232) note this dynamic in a case most of us can attest to – that of automobile manufacturing:

> . . . in the 1970s and 1980s quality, as measured by defects per vehicle, was undoubtedly a core competence for Japanese car companies. Superior reliability was an important value element for customers and a genuine differentiator for Japanese car producers. It took more than a decade for Western car companies to close the quality gap with their Japanese competitors, but by the mid-1990s quality, in terms of initial defects per vehicle, has become a prerequisite for every car maker. There is a dynamic at work here that is common to other industries. Over long periods of time, what was once a core competence may become a base-line capability.

From an HR perspective, 'table stakes' or 'enabling capabilities' include the minimum HR policies and practices required by each firm to play the competitive game (including similar types of work organisation and employment conditions) (Boxall and Steeneveld 1999, Boxall and Purcell 2000). The types of minimum 'HR system' needed inevitably vary by industry or, more accurately, strategic groups or customer segments within industries (Boxall 2003). There are, for example, strong similarities in the way car plants employ labour and strong similarities among retail chain stores. The differences between these two industries in skills required, working conditions, team processes and so on are very significant. The key point is that viable firms in a particular industry are *partially* rather than totally idiosyncratic. Valuable resources, then, include some elements in common with other firms in the industry and some differences.

Dynamism in the RBV: the role of knowledge and learning

Standing back from the commentary so far, it should be clear that the management of knowledge plays a key role in resource-based models of the firm. For Hamel and Prahalad (1994), building a focus on knowledge management is much more important than the historical focus of Western firms on product management. For Leonard (1998), understanding the 'wellsprings of knowledge' is the key issue in the long-run renewal of the firm. On a practical level, a lot of interest in the area is directed towards models of knowledge management, of how to identify, protect and enlarge a firm's 'intellectual capital' (e.g. Edvinsson and Malone 1997, Stewart 1998).

The RBV, then, encourages researchers to focus on knowledge and its creation and exploitation within firms (Grant 1991, Hoskisson *et al.* 1999). How to build the organisation's capacity for learning or its *dynamic* capability becomes the fundamental issue (Teece, Pisano and Shuen 1997, Helfat and Peteraf 2003). Some go so far as to talk of a 'knowledge-based view' (KBV) of the firm (e.g. Grant 1996) but we think this is generally unwise: knowledge is extremely important to organisational success but access to money, properties and natural resources also continue to be vital. In an energy-strapped world, for example, companies which can access cheap and plentiful energy sources are definitely at an advantage.

Where the KBV comes into its own is in those companies where the knowledge and brain-power of employees is the only substantial source of competitive advantage (Kinnie *et al.* 2006). These are 'professional service companies' in such sectors as consultancy practice, media, law and IT. They own very few assets in terms of natural resources and property yet often have a very high market value, like Microsoft. In these firms, professionally qualified employees often have distinctive needs concerned with multiple identities. Do they, or indeed should they, identify with their employer, their major client, their team or their profession (Swart 2007)? The assumption of the KBV is that the firm is able to leverage this professional knowledge and intellectual capital in a unique way that others cannot copy, to gain competitive advantage and appropriate value. However, rival firms will seek to poach talented staff, often forcing up pay and rewards, thus challenging the level of appropriation. And managing talent is not just about pay. It includes ensuring that professionals work on stretching projects with other talented colleagues in project teams at the forefront of their profession. This in turn will have a strong influence on the business strategy of these knowledge-intensive firms since the need to keep talented staff drives the search for innovative and creative work.

It is clearly important that we build an analysis in which we are able to explain why some firms are better at learning and renewal than others. Why do some firms have greater dynamic capability? A large part of the answer must be associated with the people involved and with how they are managed.

The RBV and human resource strategy

It should be obvious, then, that resource-based models of strategic management are replete with references to the human dimensions of resources. A major part of any firm's strengths – and weaknesses – does stem from the calibre of the people employed and the quality of their working relationships.

At the most elementary level, the resource-based view of the firm provides a conceptual basis, if we were ever in any doubt about the matter, for asserting that key human resources can be sources of competitive advantage. Taxonomies of valuable resources always incorporate an important category for 'human capital' (Barney 1991) or 'employee know-how' (Hall 1993) and resource-based theorists stress the value of the complex interrelationships between the firm's human resources and its other resources: physical, financial, legal, informational and so on (e.g. Penrose 1959, Grant 1991, Mueller 1996). This much is self-evident: as we emphasised in Chapter 2, a firm is a system of interconnected parts and the firm's human resources form a necessary (though not a sufficient) part of this system.

But this does not get us very far. The key questions raised by the RBV are twofold: *what* is it that can be exceptionally valuable about human resources and *how* might a firm develop and defend these sources of value? Identifying what is most valuable and protecting it with 'barriers to imitation' is at the heart of resource-based thinking.

We can certainly rule out the value of formal policy positions in HRM (what top management says the firm should do in managing work and people). These can simply be run off on a photocopier or downloaded from the internet. As Muller (1996) argues, it is hard to see any distinctive and inimitable value in policy positions *per se*. Furthermore, when there are major disconnections between senior management's formal HR policy and the actual HR practices of line managers, this can be a source of competitive *dis*advantage (Purcell 1999). There is always a danger in gaps between management rhetorics and workplace reality (Legge 1995, 2005, Grant 1999).

Since people vary in their capabilities and cannot work for all firms at once, Wright *et al.* (1994) argue that we are more likely to find value residing in the human resources themselves, in the human capital pool. Human capital is the quality of the individual human talent recruited to the firm and retained in it. All firms need certain kinds of individual talent relevant to implementing the organisation's mission and, if they wish to survive over the long run, capable of helping the organisation to adapt to change or, better still, lead it (Boxall and Steeneveld 1999). As we noted in

Chapter 2, all firms need a relevant set of human resources to be viable, in order simply to survive or attain 'competitive parity'. Firms which recruit and retain exceptional individuals have the possibility of generating 'human capital advantage' (Boxall 1996, 1998).

Why can individuals be so valuable? The answer lies in Polanyi's (1962) classic distinction between 'tacit' and 'explicit' (or 'articulated') knowledge. Tacit knowledge is 'nonverbalized or even nonverbalizable, intuitive' while explicit or articulated knowledge is 'specified either verbally or in writing, computer programs, patents, drawings or the like' (Hedlund 1994: 75). Figure 4.6 illustrates this distinction with examples across four levels of analysis, starting with the individual and moving up to the 'inter-organisational' domain. The distinction helps to explain why firms are vulnerable to labour turnover (Coff 1997, 1999). They can never entirely capture what individuals know. Some of what and whom we know – including many of our best skills – cannot be reduced to writing or to formulas. When we leave the firm, we take our job know-how and networking knowledge with us. No two individuals are exactly alike and the differences are particularly noticeable in high-skill jobs: as job complexity increases, so does the range of human performance (Hunter, Schmidt and Judiesch 1990). When whole teams of highly talented individuals leave, as was noted earlier in a case from the semiconductor industry, the effect can be devastating.

Moreover, individual human capital is embedded in a social context. The quality of social capital – of human relationships in the firm and with its environment – plays a major role in whether or not firms make outstanding returns from their human capital (e.g. Goshal and Nahapiet 1998, Swart and Kinnie 2003, Collins and Smith 2006). In other words, firms need 'organisational process advantages' if they are to realise the potential of human capital (Boxall 1996, 1998). Organisational process advantage

Type	Individual	Group	Organisation	Inter-organisational domain
Explicit knowledge	Knowing calculus	A quality circle's documented analysis of its performance	Organisation chart	A supplier's patents and documented practices
Tacit knowledge	Cross-cultural negotiation skills	Team coordination in complex work	Corporate culture	Customer attitudes to products and expectations

Source: Adapted from Hedlund (1994: 75)

Figure 4.6   Types of knowledge

is a function of historically evolved, socially complex, causally ambiguous *processes* such as team-based learning, and high levels of trust and cooperation between management and labour and among co-workers, processes which are very difficult to imitate. Both human capital and social capital can generate exceptional value but are likely to do so much more powerfully when they reinforce each other. Kay (1993) refers to this as the 'passing game', nicely indicating that teams may have highly talented players (high human capital) but it is the capacity to play together that is important. Thus, we can say that under the RBV, a firm's distinctive human resource advantage (HRA) is a combination of appropriately talented people (human capital advantage) and the way they work together (organisational process advantage). In mathematical notation,

$$HRA = f(HCA,OPA).$$

But does the resource-based view imply that all employee groups in a firm are strategically valuable? In a nutshell, no: it suggests that there some critical, 'core' workers in all firms, while other individuals are less critical or more peripheral (Purcell 1999). Lepak and Snell (1999, 2007) have picked up on this aspect of the RBV (and related economic theories) in developing what they call an 'HR architectural perspective' (Figure 4.7). This framework

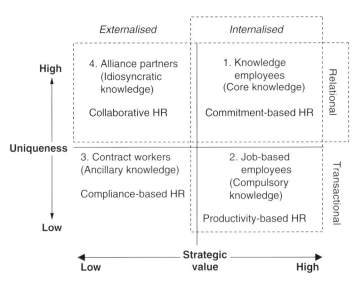

Source: Adapted from Lepak, D. and Snell, S., 'Employment sub-systems and the "HR architecture"'. In Boxall, P., Purcell, J. and Wright, P. (eds) *The Oxford Handbook of Human Resource Management*. Oxford: Oxford University Press. © 2007 By permission of Oxford University Press.

Figure 4.7   Lepak and Snell's 'HR architectural perspective'

utilises two dimensions: the extent to which the particular form of human capital represents a valuable resource for the firm and the extent to which it is unique or firm specific. This leads to four types of HR system that fit different sets of human resources.

Lepak and Snell argue that firms need a commitment-oriented HR system for employees whose skills are critical to a firm's core or distinctive capabilities (Quadrant 1). Firms should invest heavily in the motivation, empowerment and development of those who hold critical knowledge. Thus, when workers are perceived as especially valuable to the firm's strategy, the question of how to defend them turns on adopting HR systems which build their loyalty and, thus, exclusiveness to the firm. Protecting special human resources depends on building high employee commitment and low rates of employee turnover within this core group. The relationship is much more of a long-term, 'relational' kind than a short-term 'transactional' kind (Rousseau 1995). However, firms can adopt a more productivity-based approach to those, such as accounting staff, whose work is valuable in the labour market but not unique (Quadrant 2). This means hiring people who can be productive quickly and rewarding them on a more short-term, results-oriented basis. Those whose skills are low in value and generic are prime candidates for contracting out (Quadrant 3) while individuals whose skills may be 'unique in some way but not directly instrumental for creating customer value' (Lepak and Snell 1999: 40), such as a firm's attorneys, are likely to be engaged in some form of longer-term alliance (Quadrant 4).

This model, then, offers a way of helping firms to distinguish which types of HR system are appropriate for different kinds of human capital. An important, ongoing issue is the question of whom managers consider 'core' in a particular firm. We often observe strategic choice here: managers make different interpretations, as illustrated in the bottled gas market in the UK in the mid 1990s (Purcell 1996). British Oxygen was a long-established player in the market with a dominant share. Air Products was a relatively new entrant but with lots of experience in the USA. In 1992, British Oxygen needed to improve delivery, cut costs and get customers to trade up where possible. They had a large existing distribution fleet. Painful negotiations with the drivers' union led to new hours of working, wider job responsibilities including customer relations, more training and cab-based information technology. Drivers became seen as key staff in direct contact with customers. At the same time, Air Products decided to outsource distribution to a specialist haulage contractor. There was no expectation here that drivers would know anything about gas beyond safety considerations. In the case of British Oxygen, drivers were considered a core part of the firm because they always had been, not because they possessed distinctive organisational knowledge or skills. Indeed this knowledge of the customer and the skill about gas systems had to be learned once the decision was made to give them customer relations responsibilities. A similar case in New Zealand involved the privatisation of gas companies. Meters in domestic properties need to be read, but are meter readers just 'data harvesters' (carrying out single-task jobs suitable for outsourcing) or are they front-line customer service representatives (Peel and Boxall 2005)?

In practice, firms come up with different answers. Some choose the core for historical or institutional reasons and then design the jobs and the employment relationship to fit these core attributes, as in the case of British Oxygen. This seems very explicable: 'Many activities in firms . . . are so taken for granted or so strongly endorsed by the firm's prevailing culture and power structure that decision-makers no longer even question the appropriateness or the rationality of these activities' (Oliver 1997: 700). To put it another way, the moral (legitimacy) as well as the financial exit costs can be too high. Arguably, Lepak and Snell over-emphasise the potential to differentiate between types of workers within the same organisation, especially where people share the same site and where family ties are frequently found. However, Baron and Kreps (1999: 460) suggest subtly different criteria in choosing whether to externalise certain jobs or manage them internally. First, they suggest that 'the degree to which the task is strategically important for the firm, that is, whether it is a 'core competence' is critical. Here, they are on similar ground to Lepak and Snell with their emphasis on 'strategic value'. Baron and Kreps's second criterion is not the uniqueness of the skill but 'the degree to which the activity displays high technical or social interdependence with tasks done by regular employees' (Baron and Kreps 1999: 460). In this regard, Purcell, Purcell and Tailby (2004) studied a call centre where the failure to appreciate the social interdependences of staff – where agency 'temps' worked alongside permanent staff – led to escalating labour turnover among both temps and experienced staff.

Recall that Leonard (1998) made the distinction between core, enabling and supplemental capabilities. While these are analytically distinct, and similar to the knowledge categories in Lepak and Snell's quadrants, it is important to appreciate that they are, simultaneously, cumulative. Exploiting core capability requires that the firm holds enabling and supplemental capabilities. Boxall (1998: 268) makes a distinction between inner- and outer-core workforces. The 'inner core . . . provides the "adaptive capacity" of the firm while the outer core provides it with "credible operational capacity" '. One cannot operate effectively without both capabilities. In Chapters 6 and 8, we draw attention to the firm as a social entity, a community with a distinctive culture. Too much differentiation between core and periphery along the lines of Lepak and Snell's quadrants can damage the creation of a sense of community and challenge perceptions of fairness. For example, in 2005, an American company in the UK established an employee forum for the first time. One of the first items raised was the fact that management and professional staff were given free health insurance but other staff members were not. This was deemed unfair and at odds with the company's aspiration to be 'an employer of choice' and its emphasis on 'togetherness' (i.e. social interdependency). Free health insurance was subsequently extended to all employees.

Despite the point we make here, a key trend over the late 1990s and into the twenty-first century has been the rise of outsourcing or offshoring in manufacturing and in services (such as call centres), an important issue we will discuss in Chapters 5 and 8. Location on a separate site, and performance of technically different tasks from those in home base, means that both technical and social interdependencies can be minimised. Outsourced sites, especially those offshored to third-world countries, can quickly be 'out of sight and out of mind'. As Lepak and Snell (2007) recognise, many firms now locate operating workers in countries with lower labour costs. In Chapter 1, we considered the case of the British manufacturer, Dyson, which has done exactly this, offshoring its assembly operations to Malaysia. The intention in these situations might be to treat these workers as core resources employed within the firm but management is doing so within a much lower cost structure or is using either a sub-contractor or an alliance partner (Quadrant 3 or 4) who does this. The critical core in the firm is thus defined even more parsimoniously, as the firm's key executives and the R&D, marketing and logistics specialists it still employs in its home-country head office.

Leaving aside these labour cost issues, which we will explore in Chapter 5, a key implication of the argument so far must be that carefully enacted HR systems can be sources of superior and hard-to-imitate value. Arguably, the scarce and hard-to-imitate value stems from the historically developed, socially complex elements, including the way in which these have formed important systemic connections over time. Thus, while knowledge of individual HR policies is not rare, the knowledge of how to build and customise appropriate HR systems and create a positively reinforcing blend of HR systems *within* a particular context is likely to be very rare. The value is greater when these astute HR decisions are complemented by a mix of other intangible and tangible assets: senior management commitment, consistent line manager support for critical HR practices over significant time periods, (at least) adequate financial resourcing, sympathetic management accounting systems, and so on (Boxall 1998, 2003). A commitment-oriented HR strategy, which Lepak and Snell (1999, 2007) argue firms need for their core workforce, depends on a sympathetic social context within the firm (Collins and Smith 2006). We take this argument further in Chapters 8 and 9 in our discussion of the 'mediators' between HR systems and company performance and in our discussion of the role of HR strategy across cycles of change in industries.

In summary, then, human resource strategy, supported by other sympathetic elements, can enable a firm to build sources of sustained competitive advantage. In any industry, there are likely to be particular firms which have built 'human resource advantage' in this sense. The evidence discussed by Leonard (1998) certainly implies that Chaparral Steel has built human resource advantage in the US steel sector.[3] On the other hand, the majority of surviving firms in an industry are likely to have HR strategies which support their survival but which do not confer advantage. Arguably, most (surviving) firms are 'mainstream' or 'median' employers whose HRM is sufficient to underpin their viability but not otherwise impressive. And, as we have noted, this may well mean shifting production 'offshore' to keep labour costs competitive. Firms that fail altogether have often fallen short in the critical human and social capital they need to be viable, as studies of young, vulnerable firms attest (e.g. Storey 1985, Bates 1990).

Before moving on, let us recall again that there is a problem with thinking about resources only at the level of the firm. Clusters of valuable resources occur at both industry and societal levels. Industry clusters can benefit all firms through providing a skilled labour pool and networking connections across the supply chain, one of the reasons why Dyson found it attractive to locate in Malaysia, as noted in Chapter 1. In addition, countries provide variable resources of infrastructure, politico-economic systems, social order and so on. Some firms have a 'head start' in international competition because they are located in societies which have much better educational and technical infrastructure than others (Porter 1990, Boxall 1995). American, British, German and French firms, for example, are all assisted by the existence of long-established traditions of excellence in higher education which enhance the knowledge-creating capacities of business organisations.

---

3 As of 2006, Chaparral Steel had become the second largest producer of structural steel products in the USA and now has two mini-mills. See: www.chaparralsteel.com/

The point here is that the potential to develop competitive advantage through human resources does not lie solely in the hands of managers within individual firms.

Conclusions

There is no doubting the fact that the resource-based perspective is an important set of spectacles for viewing the strategic problems facing the firm. It focuses on the analysis of internal strengths and weaknesses, paying particular attention to the ways in which firms can develop valuable resources and erect barriers to imitation of them. It is not, however, without conceptual weaknesses. Key strategy theorists, such as Porter (1991), remind us that firms always exist in environments: resources are not ends in themselves but are useful when they create value in markets. More broadly, resources are valuable when they win some form of stakeholder support for the firm. The stakeholders that matter include not only shareholders but also employees, the state and the public at large who have expectations that the firm will use society's resources in legitimate ways. We must also avoid getting carried away with the resource-based notion of idiosyncrasy or heterogeneity. To be sure, superior firms have distinctive features but all firms in an industry need some similar resources in order to identify their line of business and meet standard customer expectations. From the perspective of HRM, we should note that the RBV, like most of the strategy literature, can become too absorbed with the firm as the unit of analysis. Human resources vary in quality across industries and nations and this variability does affect the strengths that firms are capable of building.

As the name itself implies, resource-based frameworks present an account of strategic management which is richly laced with *human* resource issues. These HR issues include strong concerns with the management of human knowledge or with the development of learning capabilities. Managing knowledge inevitably means managing both the company's proprietary technologies and systems (which do not walk out the door at the end of the day) and the people (who do). It implies management of the ongoing interaction between these two aspects of a firm's knowledge system. Clearly, then, when we take a resource-based perspective on the strategic problem, questions of human resource strategy are going to loom large. How to build human capital by attracting, motivating and developing individuals is going to be central. So is the question of how to build the kind of organisational processes which enable individuals to function effectively. Much hinges on how firms build socially complex clusters of human and social capital. The reader will not be surprised that we regard this line of analysis as extremely important. Our exploration of the resource-based view continues in various parts of the rest of the book. We aim, however, to build on the RBV while staying alert to its weaknesses.

part *2*

Managing work and people: searching for general principles

5

Work systems and the changing economics of production

As we concluded in Chapter 3, firms fit in with their contexts or they fail. It is not therefore possible to identify a set of best HR practices that will be universally beneficial to firms. Furthermore, as we saw in Chapter 4, the resource-based view of the firm argues that firms have something to gain from being the fittest of the fit, from evolving their HR systems in such a way that they build and exploit valuable differences in human and social capital. On the other hand, both these chapters explain that firms face similar challenges in trying to manage work and people in the industries and societies in which they operate. As long as we recognise the strict limits of prescription at the level of specific practices, there is merit in searching for general or underpinning principles in labour management. This is the concern of this part of the book.

The logical place to begin is with the analysis of work systems. In Chapter 3, we indicated that the HR strategy of a firm typically embraces a number of different HR systems. For example, there are often somewhat different HR systems for managers, core operating workers, and support staff. In complex professional environments, such as hospitals, there can be a different system for each professional group. An organisation's HR strategy is a cluster of such systems. How well HR systems work in their own terms and how well they relate to each other in any firm is a moot point.

As indicated in our definition of HRM in Chapter 1, there are two key elements to each HR system: the kind of *work* organisation involved and the *employment* practices that are used to hire and manage the people doing the work. The function of this chapter is to analyse work systems while the next two chapters will look at principles underpinning the collective and individual aspects of employing people. Chapter 6 will focus on employee voice, which has traditionally had strong collective elements, while Chapter 7 will examine the management of individual employees. In Chapter 8, we will draw the pieces together, summarising the most common types of HR system, and outlining the key intervening variables that link HR systems to employee and organisational outcomes.

Work systems involve choices about what work needs to be done, about who will do it, and about where and how they will do it. This means work systems vary enormously across industries and occupations: consider the different ways in which work is organised in car plants, schools, call centres, merchant shipping and supermarkets. Work system choices are fundamental to both operations management and human resource management in an organisation (e.g. Cordery and Parker 2007). They are inevitably connected to an organisation's chances of economic survival and its relative performance.

We therefore emphasise in this chapter the way in which work systems are linked to the *economics* of production. Capitalism is a system in which firms need to evolve work systems that will pay. This has always been true but has become graphically apparent over the last thirty years. Since the breakdown in the 1970s of the boom conditions that followed World War II, there have been waves of economic reform and restructuring. There has been a process of economic 'globalisation' in which new industrial powerhouses have emerged and challenged the economic elites in Europe and the USA. Japan was the major challenge in the 1970s and 1980s and now market reforms and rapid industrialisation in China and India, among other countries, are changing the old economic order. This is not simply about manufacturing. The growth of cheap computing power and the advent of the internet have made it much more possible to offer services across national boundaries. At the Brookings Institution Trade Forum in 2005 on the 'offshoring' of white collar work, Jensen and Kletzer (2005) reported that over the period from 2001 to 2003, 70 per cent of the US workers displaced by global competition worked in services, not manufacturing.

Massive companies or whole sectors in previously secure national markets have been forced to change the way they operate to meet threats to their financial viability or they have simply failed. Management responses that have involved changing the sales pitch or 'rebranding' the same old offering without substantive change to technology, operations management and HRM have been swept aside by firms in newly developing countries which can offer the same quality (or better) but at much lower prices. Companies have been forced to accept the strategic significance of how their work is organised. They have been forced to look internally at all aspects of the way the organisation functions in order to reduce costs while delivering better value. A recent case in point concerns Aviva, Britain's largest insurer, which owns Norwich Union and RAC, among others. On 14 September 2006, the company announced a cut of 4,000 jobs, made possible by more sales being handled over the internet and a merging of back-office functions. When union leaders protested, Norwich Union's chief executive commented that the company was working in a 'self-service world' and was 'always looking for ways of working smarter with fewer people'.[1] As this example illustrates, the cost-effectiveness of how work is organised does matter to firms and changes in technology and customer habits do alter the economics of work systems over time.

Our intention in this chapter is to look at the economics of work organisation in the major sectors of the modern economy: manufacturing, private sector services and the public sector. Because it has been the most important source of ideas about work organisation historically, we begin with manufacturing, describing its traditional work patterns in Britain and the USA and then examining social and economic challenges to these patterns. This leads into a fuller discussion of the emergence of 'high-involvement' or 'high-performance' work systems, which we noted in Chapter 3. Having laid out much of the key terminology through this discussion, we then turn to the impact on both manufacturing and services (private and public) of key contextual changes: globalisation, market reforms and the growth of production offshoring. This sets the scene for us to discuss contemporary work systems in private sector services and the public sector. We do not stop at manufacturing but it is the natural place to start.

Work systems in manufacturing

The origins and evolution of the factory system

At the time when Adam Smith was writing his famous text in 1776, *The Wealth of Nations*, with its analysis of the massive efficiency gains to be achieved by the detailed division of labour, factory owners in the emerging British industry of cotton manufacture were taking advantage of new mechanised processes, like power looms, to create radically new forms of work organisation. Initially employing large numbers of children, usually

---

1   As quoted by Phillip Inman, 'Union attacks "brutal" Aviva for 4,000 jobs cut', *Guardian*, 15 September 2006.

taken from the parish work-houses, owners like Samuel Gregg in Styal, just outside Manchester, and Robert Owen in New Lanark near Glasgow, brought to an end the centuries-old system of 'putting-out' whereby merchants would contract home workers using the hand-powered, hand-built looms they owned, to produce bundles of fabric or clothing. In an age of horse-drawn transport, putting-out was slow and inefficient, and at harvest time family members would work in the fields. Families worked to the rhythm of the seasons but exercised greater control over their time as long as they did so. The great advantage of the factory system, then as now, was that it allowed capitalist, or managerial, control to be exerted over the whole work process, gathering workers into a single location around a common power source. New forms of power (water and steam) applied to newly invented machinery like power looms and the spinning jenny made it important and profitable to concentrate workers together at the point of production rather than have them dispersed (Deane 1969: 87, Jones 1994). The technological revolution in power sources and machinery led to a migration of workers from villages into the factory towns and growing cities.

Under the factory system, operators became machine minders working at the pace set by the machines owned by the capitalists and the factory's time clock, not by themselves. They were paid a wage, often linked to output and, working very long hours, undertook a single task or a small number of linked tasks requiring some dexterity but little intellectual skill. Each task took no more than a few seconds or minutes and then had to be repeated again, and again. As Adam Smith understood, workers who specialised at a simple set of tasks learnt to do them quickly. Benevolent owners, like the two just mentioned, would provide housing, schooling and (compulsory) Sunday worship but little in terms of training or career development. Discipline was strict and power was vested in overseers or foremen. The language at the time, and common throughout the nineteenth century, and even into the twentieth, of 'the master and his hands', is especially instructive. The implication, as Watson (1986) observes, was that workers were machines using motor not mental skills.

Factories were designed by engineers to function as large engines of cogs and wheels rationally linked together. This metaphor of organisations as rationally coordinated, interlocking parts is still prevalent today and still brings with it a denial of human emotional and social life (see Morgan (1997) for a wonderful analysis of the ways of thinking about or imagining organisation). As work was 'de-skilled' through breaking it down into the simplest tasks, and as workers no longer owned their own means of production, being reliant, as 'wage slaves', on the owner and his management agents, much about the process seemed dehumanising. In a wider sense, this was no more than a reflection of social structures and beliefs in society at the time on the brutish nature of the emerging working class. However, questions were increasingly being asked by British novelists like Dickens and Mrs Gaskill, and social reformers like Seebohm Rowntree, about the social consequences of the 'dark satanic mills', as William Blake called them.

The mental models of the early factory owners about the way work should be organised became the standard or 'default' model for the design of work organisation in industrialised societies. In what Cordery and Parker (2007) call the 'mechanistic' model of work design, managers did the thinking and directing while workers were required to obey instructions and mind the machines. As this implies, factories depended on two HR systems operating under different principles: one for workers involving low discretion, low scope and low skill and one for managers involving much higher levels of discretion, responsibility and skill. A pattern of low trust of workers and high trust of managers was born (Fox 1974). Subsequent developments, whether that pioneered by Henry Ford, or turned into a new science of management by F. W. Taylor, continued to rest on these premises.

The key figures we have just mentioned – F. W. Taylor and Henry Ford I – were both Americans. While Britain may have industrialised first, the United States rapidly caught up in the nineteenth century and it was American consultants and business leaders who kick-started the theory of industrial management. What Taylor advocated and Ford put into practice was the application of more rigorous work measurement processes and the ruthless division of responsibility between management and labour (e.g. Braverman 1974, Meyer 1981, Warner 1998). Formal processes, such as 'time and motion study', were used to investigate the informal methods workers had developed on the job, quantifying how long it took them to carry out their tasks and how they moved within the work space, interacting with materials, tools and machines. Work practices were then redesigned by a management-appointed 'work study' expert to make human activities more efficient and to create a basis for identifying normal output and for linking pay incentives ('bonus systems') to higher levels of output. Under Taylor's concept of 'Scientific Management', the efficiency gains inherent in task specialisation were heightened and incentivised.

While it is wrong to suggest that the Taylorist practice of 'de-skilling' work permeated all manufacturing industries or all manufacturing jobs (e.g. Burawoy 1979, Littler 1982), the process of reducing core operating jobs to a set of simple tasks was widespread in the development of the factory system in the nineteenth and early twentieth centuries. Henry Ford's particular contribution came in linking these highly specialised jobs to the *moving* assembly line (e.g. Lacey 1986). This minimised the need for operating workers to move around the floor to pick up tools or parts: instead, they remained at their work station and the work came directly to them, creating the basis for 'speed-up' and massive productivity improvements. The Ford Motor Company smashed production records and used these gains to deliver major reductions in the price of cars and thus expand the market, fostering a process in which car ownership eventually spread beyond the upper and middle classes to factory workers themselves. Although these principles had their precursors, the innovations of Taylor and Ford, more than anything, epitomised the American system of 'mass production'.

Political and trade union challenges to the factory system

Work systems matter enormously to workers. The organisation of work deeply affects the level of skill needed, the extent to which individuals can use their abilities, and their levels of job satisfaction and job loyalty (e.g. Boxall, Macky and Rasmussen 2003, Cordery and Parker 2007). Workers did not necessarily take these new production methods lying down, nor did they meekly accept working conditions where wages were low or work pressures too great. Early factory legislation, bitterly opposed by the owners, outlawed the employment of the youngest children and limited some of the worst excesses of dangerous working conditions. This forced the factory system to adapt and it did so despite the warnings of dire consequences of economic collapse from capitalist leaders. New efficiencies were found, often by replacing people with advances in technology.

However, 'employee voice' became, and remains, a key concern in the governance of the workplace, as we shall explain more fully in Chapter 6. Suffice it to say here that from the late nineteenth century onwards, governments, disturbed by threats to social order, began to enact progressive labour legislation supportive of worker rights. This responded to, and was accompanied by, the growth of trade unions. From such beginnings in the nineteenth century, unions grew more strongly in the first part of the twentieth century: at the end of the First World War, throughout the Great Depression of the 1930s, and during the Second World War (e.g. Clegg 1994, Hannan 1995, Kaufman 2004).

Inside the factory, managers responded with steps to shore up the order and stability of the 'labour process' embedded in the factory system. Wherever workplaces were big (and large factories in steelmaking, ship-building, textiles and automotive assembly could employ several thousand workers at one site), unions tended to be strong, and senior management moved to appoint labour relations specialists to their staff. These specialists worked on mechanisms to channel industrial conflict. This meant working with unions through a process of collective bargaining to jointly regulate the terms and conditions of work and employment. It led to the adoption of such bureaucratic control systems as job evaluation, intended as a way of bringing greater order into payment methods by developing a strict hierarchy of jobs and pay grades. Through such methods, the role of industrial relations managers was to keep the peace with the unions and help to ensure continuity of production. However, while the accommodations to organised labour that came through this process significantly improved levels of wages and benefits, they rarely challenged the structure of the work itself. What unions with strong shopfloor power did achieve was improvements in pay, employment security, staffing levels and work norms. They helped to build what academic economists call the 'internal labour market' (ILM) (Doeringer and Piore 1971, Jacoby 1984).

This is a strange term because the whole idea of an ILM is to minimise market influences. ILMs are administrative codes, not markets. They are a system of bureaucratic rules for defining jobs, allocating workers to them, enhancing employment security and determining pay. In the most developed systems, recruitment at the bottom levels of the job ladder led into a structure which offered promotion from within and a set of benefits in pay escalation, training, pensions and security which were very hard to obtain working in smaller firms. Unions played a major role in fostering such systems. However, they rarely challenged the division of labour (between managers and workers and between different types of worker) on which the Fordist production regime rested. In many cases, they magnified it through inter-union 'demarcation' disputes in which boundaries between different types of labour (and, thus, union memberships) were contested and policed.

Management was not entirely insensitive to worker reactions to mechanistic work systems and management theory was not entirely moribund. New ideas did emerge on how to boost productivity through enhancing worker autonomy and job scope and thus reducing boredom with repetitive tasks. In the middle decades of the twentieth century, the 'Human Relations School', showed interest in how work and supervisory practices affected employee motivation and in the role of informal groups in the workplace (see Watson (1986) for an excellent analysis). Similarly, in the 1950s, theory developed on 'socio-technical work systems', which aimed to enhance both social and economic outcomes in the workplace (e.g. Trist and Bamforth 1951). In the 1960s and 1970s, psychologists

```
┌─────────────────────────────────────────────────────────────────────┐
│                      'Motivational' strategies                        │
│                                                                       │
│  1. Arrange work in a way that allows the individual employee to      │
│     influence his or her own working situation, work methods, and     │
│     pace. Devise methods to eliminate or minimise pacing.             │
│  2. Where possible, combine interdependent tasks into a job.          │
│  3. Aim to group tasks into a meaningful job that allows for an        │
│     overview and understanding of the work process as a whole.        │
│     Employees should be able to perceive the end product or service   │
│     as contributing to some part of the organisation's objectives.    │
│  4. Provide a sufficient variety of tasks within the job, and include │
│     tasks that offer some degree of employee responsibility and make  │
│     use of the skills and knowledge valued by the individual.         │
│  5. Arrange work in a way that makes it possible for the individual   │
│     employee to satisfy time claims from roles and obligations        │
│     outside work (e.g. family commitments).                           │
│  6. Provide opportunities for an employee to achieve outcomes that    │
│     he or she perceives as desirable (e.g. personal advancement in    │
│     the form of increased salary, scope for development of expertise, │
│     improved status within a work group, and a more challenging job). │
│  7. Ensure that employees get feedback on their performance, ideally  │
│     from the task as well as from the supervisor. Provide internal    │
│     and external customer feedback directly to employees.             │
│  8. Provide employees with the information they need to make          │
│     decisions.                                                        │
└─────────────────────────────────────────────────────────────────────┘
```

Source: Parker and Wall (1998: 20)

Figure 5.1   Recommended strategies to create a more 'motivational model' of work design

laid increasing emphasis on ways of enhancing employee discretion and increasing responsibility through 'job enrichment' (Herzberg 1968, Hackman and Oldham 1980). Job enrichment was seen to improve satisfaction with the work itself and thus employee commitment, an issue whenever labour markets were tight. Parker and Wall (1998) summarise the shape of what Cordery and Parker (2007) call a 'motivational model' of work design based on these innovations (Figure 5.1). Most of these ideas, however, made little substantive impact in factories. There were celebrated experiments with work redesign, such as Volvo's attempts to introduce 'semi-autonomous' teamwork at its Uddevalla plant (Berggren 1992), but these were often marginal and short-lived (e.g. MacDuffie 1995).

Competitive challenges to Fordism and Scientific Management

It was not until the 1970s that management thinking about the organisation of factory work really started to change. While the sort of ideas we have just noted had been talked about in management research and education for some time, the impetus for sustained changes to work systems had much more of its origin in serious *competitive* challenges – challenges transmitted through product markets – that started to shake management confidence. The oil shocks of the mid-1970s undermined management complacency by triggering major rises in energy prices and ushering in a period of declining productivity. Alongside this macroeconomic change, Japanese manufacturing firms began to show they had mastered a new form of production which delivered better quality products at lower prices. Japanese factories had adopted ways of manufacturing that reduced wasteful stock levels and involved workers (and not simply managers) in enhancing production quality. Ironically, they had taken American quality gurus, such as Deming (1982), much more seriously than had managers in the West and had used post-war reconstruction to build a manufacturing model which directly challenged Western manufacturers through the way it created higher levels of skill and identification with company goals. Japanese methods of 'lean manufacturing' (Womack, Jones and Roos 1990, Delbridge 2007) and 'total quality management' (e.g. Wilkinson and Willmott 1995) began to take their toll, surprising Western manufacturers by the way in which quality improvements could reduce waste and costs. The British motorcycle industry, flatfooted by Japanese production of a range of more reliable, cheaper and more stylish bikes, was one of the early casualties.[2] In the United States, smaller, more fuel-efficient Japanese cars began to gain market share and challenge the hegemony of such household-name institutions as Ford and General Motors, a process which continues to unfold as energy prices rise again.[3]

What was painfully realised in the light of Japanese manufacturing success, seen most graphically in the Toyota Production System (Ohno 1988), was that HR systems for operating workers could no longer be ignored by senior managers. Unchanged, the old forms of work organisation could become a source of competitive *dis*advantage. On the other hand, transformed to focus more on quality and on more flexible types of working, new forms of work organisation had the potential to contribute to competitive advantage in a way unimaginable in the 1960s. The implications were well put by the

---

2 For an excellent analysis of the rise and decline of the British motorcycle industry, see Ian Chadwick's website: www.ianchadwick.com/motorcycles/britbikes/index.html

3 The *Guardian* reports that 'Ford has lost market share in the US for 10 successive years': 'Job cuts and sales slump could put Ford $9bn in red', *Guardian*, 16 September 2006.

founder of one the major Japanese manufacturing companies to a group of visiting Western business leaders in 1985:

> Your firms are built on the Taylor model: even worse, so are your heads. With your bosses doing the thinking, while the workers wield the screwdrivers, you are convinced deep down that this is the right way to run a business. For you, the essence of management is getting the ideas out of the heads of the bosses and into the hands of labour. We are beyond the Taylor model: business, we know, is now so complex and difficult, the survival of the firms so hazardous in an environment increasingly unpredictable, competitive and fraught with danger that their continued existence depends on the day-to-day mobilisation of every ounce of intelligence. For us, the core of management is the art of pulling together the intellectual resources of all employees in the service of the firm. Only by drawing on the combined brain power of all its employees can a firm face up to the turbulence and constraints of today's environment. (Konosuke Matsushita)

The development of 'high-involvement work systems'

The threat to Western manufacturing associated with Japanese production systems generated enormous interest in the 1970s and 1980s and forced significant changes in work organisation in key industries (e.g. Piore and Sabel 1994, Wallace 1998, Delbridge 2007). In the iconic industry of automobile manufacturing, which deeply concerns public policy makers because its tentacles reach out into a whole host of manufacturers of parts and advanced materials, Western firms made major efforts to reform Fordism, adopting Japanese techniques of 'just-in-time' manufacturing and moving away from low-discretion work systems towards what Lawler (1986) calls 'high-involvement' work systems (HIWSs).

Some use this term synonymously with 'high-performance work systems' (HPWSs), which we discussed in Chapter 3 in our examination of best-practice models of HR systems. While the HPWS terminology has become very prevalent, we think that talking of high involvement is more useful because it is a more descriptive term. There must be multiple routes to high performance, only some of which involve reforms designed to empower workers (Orlitzky and Frenkel 2005). While leading HPWS authorities such as Appelbaum et al. (2000) do use the HPWS terminology to signify a change to a more empowering type of work design, we prefer to make the point more plainly by speaking of high-involvement work systems. This clearly signals a shift away from the low-involvement characteristics of traditional Taylorist-Fordist work models.

As emphasised in Chapter 3, it is not possible to argue that HIWSs are generally relevant across all industries or manufacturing occupations.

In high-tech semiconductor manufacturing, for example, an industry which has emerged since World War II (and especially since the use of silicon chips in personal computers in the 1980s), the role of highly skilled professional engineers, who enjoy high levels of involvement, is very important (Appleyard and Brown 2001). These workers hardly need job enrichment: they already experience it. However, HIWSs do constitute an important part of a reformed production model which has been adopted in those Western manufacturing industries where managers want to move to higher quality production systems and where historical practices of de-skilling and demarcation stand in the way of this.

Management moves to reform production systems in these industries often start with investments in advanced manufacturing technologies, such as robots, computer-aided design (CAD), computer numerical control (CNC) machine tools, and electronic data interchange (EDI) systems. Research shows that advanced manufacturing technologies reach more of their potential when the work of production operators is redesigned and their skills improved to enable them to enhance the operating performance of these technologies (Wall *et al.* 1990, Boyer *et al.* 1997, Challis, Samson and Lawson 2005). It is the combination of company investments in new manufacturing and information technologies *and* in the related work practices and employee skills that brings the greatest productivity benefits (Brynjolfsson and Hitt 2000, Black and Lynch 2001).

As Wall *et al.* (1990, 1992) explain, work redesign and training that enables production operators to solve technical problems as they occur reduces reliance on the need to call in specialist technicians for problem solving and thereby enhances productivity. The productivity benefits come from two sources (Wall *et al.* 1992: 354). The first is simply due to time savings: the more that machine operators are empowered to address routine machinery problems, the quicker the response to these problems and the lower the amount of machine downtime. With highly automated technology, higher levels of error-free machine operation during a worker's shift translate directly into higher output and revenue. The second source is 'anticipatory' or based on more effective use of the capacity of operators for learning: operators who enjoy greater empowerment learn more about the reasons why faults occur in the first place and find ways to reduce their incidence.

In terms of their role in production reforms, it is thus apparent that high-involvement work systems encompass a range of practices that attempt to reverse the Taylorist process of centralising decision making and problem solving in the hands of management and technical specialists. Some elements of decision making and problem solving always remain with management and advanced specialists but high-involvement work practices grant greater autonomy to production workers and enhance their responsibilities, thereby necessitating a greater investment in employee development. As opposed to the traditional Fordist factory, the goal becomes one of making better use of operator skills, capacity for initiative, and potential for learning (e.g. Delbridge, Kenney and Lowe 1998, Florida, Jenkins and Smith 1998).

The components of a high-involvement approach to work design are usefully spelt out by Vandenberg, Richardson and Eastman (1999) in the framework shown in Figure 5.2. This is based on Lawler's (1986) 'PIRK' model in which high-involvement work processes encompass workplace power (P), information (I), rewards (R) and knowledge (K). These four variables are seen as mutually reinforcing. In other words, high-involvement work processes empower workers to make more decisions, enhance the information and knowledge they need to do so, and reward them for doing so.

In effect, this parallels the set of lenses in the AMO framework we introduced in Chapter 1: for the high-involvement model to work, it must positively affect employee abilities, motivations, and opportunities to contribute. Improvements in knowledge enhance ability while empowerment and information enhance the opportunity to contribute. Rewards are a direct attempt to enhance motivation, which may also be improved through empowerment (enjoying more autonomous work), information (feeling better informed) and knowledge (enjoying a growth in skills).

Figure 5.2 identifies two paths through which the PIRK variables affect outcomes: a 'cognitive path' in which they take 'greater advantage of the skills and abilities' employees possess and a 'motivational path' in which

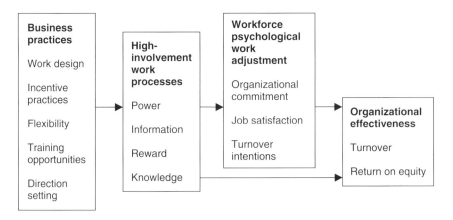

Source: Vandenberg *et al.* (1999: 307)

Figure 5.2   Conceptual model of high-involvement work processes

involvement processes increase 'workers' satisfaction and other affective reactions' (Vandenberg *et al.* (1999: 304). This parallels Batt's (2002) identification of a 'direct' path (enhancing employee skill levels and firm-specific knowledge) and an 'indirect' path (enhancing employee motivation and satisfaction and lowering quit rates). The direct path is important for enabling workers (individually and collectively) to solve work problems more effectively and the indirect path is important to ensuring they want to do so and continue to take responsibility for doing so.

We must, however, avoid thinking there is a best-practice 'silver bullet' here. As underlined in Chapter 3, the specific work practices that will bring about greater employee involvement can be expected to vary across industries (Appleyard and Brown 2001, Kalleberg *et al.* 2006). In some (but not all) situations, HIWSs will involve reforms to create greater teamworking, either on-line (during production) or off-line (away from the production process), as has become increasingly common in automobile manufacturing (Pil and MacDuffie 1996: 438). There are shades of 'teamness' but moving to a situation where a group of workers agree their own roles and help each other with problem solving when quality problems occur constitutes a major change in philosophy after years of highly individualised jobs and supervisor control. Such a process encourages something of a reintegration of mental (traditionally, management-dominated) and manual (traditionally, worker-dominated) work. A very good example of this type of integration is in the Toyota NUMMI plant in California where performance in efficiency and flexibility has been well above average (Adler, Goldoftas and Levine 1999).

Reintegration of work in HIWSs often encompasses more than the vertical dimension. A second form of integration comes from the efficiency improvements associated with combining specialist work roles within operational teams. This means, for example, that responsibility for maintenance and quality inspection, previously carried out by specialists in different departments, is brought within the ambit of the team as far as the members have technical competence to do so. In some cases, individuals with special skills will work as team members. A third form of integration can occur across organisational boundaries when manufacturing workers are linked to suppliers and customers. In some car assembly plants, for example, assembly workers are members of teams that meet with suppliers to discuss problems and improvements. Electronic data interchange and the internet, accessed by computer-literate workers, can facilitate these links. A fourth kind of reintegration occurs when there are attempts to better integrate workers into the cultural or organisational fabric of the firm, rather than treat them as outsiders or lesser citizens. At a trivial, yet symbolic level, this is seen in the adoption of the language of inclusion: in some companies, senior managers start to talk of employees as 'associates' or 'members'. They attempt to blur the old rigid distinction between managers and workers. More significantly, some managerial tasks are devolved to team leaders who usually work alongside and with their team members, compared to traditional foremen, for example, who often sat in glass-fronted offices on the shop floor. In this way, front-line management is less remote and the task of front-line managers and team leaders changes to give more emphasis to training, coaching and encouraging better performance.

As explained in Chapter 3, the evidence suggests there are industries in which a transition to HIWSs helps to significantly improve operating performance. Assessments of the pay-off are much more believable when they are grounded in in-depth, industry-based studies. On this basis, some of the best evidence we have is based on high-involvement changes in US steelmaking (Arthur 1994, Inchniowski *et al.* 1997, Ichniowski and Shaw 1999, Appelbaum *et al.* 2000), in US medical electronics manufacturing (Appelbaum *et al.* 2000) and in the worldwide automobile assembly industry (MacDuffie 1995). In thinking about the strategic value of HIWSs, it is helpful here to return to the notion of 'table stakes', a concept we introduced in Chapters 2 and 4. It is likely that in the automobile industry, for example, customer demand for higher quality standards means that nearly all car manufacturers now require higher employee involvement as part of industry 'table stakes'. In other words, such work systems have become part of the price of being in the game: survival depends on having them, along with other key investments in new technologies. This is not, however, true in all industries and whether HIWSs offer gains more generally is still a moot point. As mentioned in Chapter 3, the best assessment we have, a very careful longitudinal study of US manufacturing by Cappelli and Neumark (2001), concludes that the effects of HIWSs on profitability are unclear. A study of some 3,000 small US firms (less than 100 employees) by Sean Way (2002) also calls for caution. It indicates that the costs may outweigh the benefits in small organisations.

Where there is potential to make HIWSs pay off, however, we should not imagine that top results can be easily achieved. As we shall emphasise in Chapter 8, an important part of what brings these new systems alive is the behaviour of managers, especially the immediate managers or team leaders. Many of the HR policies designed to suit high-involvement work systems can only be applied by line managers. Studies of lean methods of working (e.g. Hutchinson *et al.* 1996, 1998), however, frequently cite growing levels of stress among team leaders, who feel caught in the middle as both team worker (one of 'us') and as manager (one of 'them'). The ability of front-line managers to enact change is an outcome of the way these managers are themselves selected, motivated, monitored and rewarded. An environment which also includes cost cutting and downsizing can put intense pressure on line managers.

Furthermore, as Figure 5.2 makes plain, HIWSs hinge on the responses of employees. Survey evidence indicates that HIWSs which bring improvements in employee autonomy, greater development and use of their skills, and greater financial rewards appeal strongly to workers, significantly lifting job satisfaction (Berg 1999, Vandenberg, Richardson and Eastman 1999, Macky and Boxall 2006). However, the gains to workers are most likely to occur when increases in their responsibilities do not come with unwanted pressures (Mackie, Holahan and Gottlieb 2001, Macky and Boxall 2006). Case studies often point to a 'dark side' of lean manufacturing, including increases in stress (Delbridge 2005).

There can, for example, be a problem with inappropriate applications of teamwork. Research by Sprigg, Jackson and Parker (2000) illustrates how greater use of teamworking is much more likely to appeal to workers when they are working in a highly interdependent production process, where they must interact at a high level to improve how things are done. In situations where workers are largely independent of each other, however, imposing teamworking can undermine individual autonomy and job satisfaction. In Appelbaum *et al.*'s (2000: 113–14, 180) study of high-involvement work reforms in three manufacturing industries, the job satisfaction and commitment of workers in US apparel firms was actually lower among those in self-directed teams. Thus, we repeat again the caution that it is important to avoid over-generalising about *particular* work practices, such as teamworking. Some workers undoubtedly feel that some forms of teamwork undermine, rather than enhance, their personal autonomy (Berg 1999, Harley 2001).

All of this underlines the fact that success with work reforms is far from assured. The quality of implementation is extremely variable. This means, however, returning to the resource-based view of the firm discussed in Chapter 4, that HIWSs can be competitively valuable. Where management does successfully build an HIWS with operating workers, Lepak and Snell (1999, 2007) argue this will merit protection through a high-commitment HR system (see Figure 4.7). The need to protect HIWSs through higher levels of employee loyalty is underlined in Guthrie's (2001) study of 164 New Zealand firms. This survey shows that when firms pursue high-involvement work practices, lower employee turnover is associated with higher productivity.

Conversely, when firms pursue more control-oriented (Taylorist) forms of work organisation, higher employee turnover is associated with higher productivity. In other words, firms which make the costly investment in high-involvement work processes, and the related skills, will have better economic performance in conditions of low labour turnover. Worker loyalty might be taken for granted when the introduction of HIWSs occurs alongside major lay-offs, as happened in the steel industry in the 1990s (Bacon and Blyton 2001), but when labour markets are tight, employers who have invested in HIWSs will need to take measures to improve employee commitment if they are to achieve low labour turnover.

We must note here, however, that Guthrie's (2001) study gives us no basis for arguing that HIWSs are generally good for productivity. His study shows *two* paths to higher productivity, one of which works through HIWSs and the other through low involvement and high employee turnover. This is a key point because it is now apparent that many firms, faced with insurmountable pressures from low-cost producers, have given up on the idea of HIWSs in high-wage countries, if they ever entertained it (e.g. Konzelmann, Forrant and Wilkinson 2004). They have decided instead to *offshore* their production.

Globalisation, market reform and production offshoring

'Globalisation' of production was strong in the nineteenth century under the 'Pax Victoriana', when Britain ruled the waves (e.g. Krugman 1997), and under the continuing impetus of industrial innovations, including the growth from the 1820s of steam shipping (e.g. Solar 2006). International trade, however, suffered major setbacks in the first half of the twentieth century as a result of the two world wars and the Great Depression. Globalisation is not a new phenomenon but is something that has reasserted itself since the Second World War through a process of significant reduction in tariffs and other trade barriers between countries and regions. This has been a fraught, imperfect process but other factors, such as the liberalisation of financial markets, the collapse of Communism as an alternative economic system, the growth of improved modes of transport (better air travel and containerised shipping) and higher-speed and more comprehensive communications through the internet, have all played their part in opening up the world to higher levels of trade in goods, services and ideas. Globalisation has also been associated with the growth in the number of mergers and strategic alliances

Country	US$ per hour, 2004
Germany	32.53
Netherlands	30.76
United States	24.71
United Kingdom	23.17
Australia	23.09
Japan	21.90
Canada	21.42
New Zealand	12.89
Korea	11.52
Taiwan	5.97
Hong Kong (special administrative region of China)	5.51
Mexico	2.50

Note: Hourly compensation costs include total hourly pay before tax (including pay for time worked, holiday pay and any wage premia and bonuses regularly paid) plus employer social insurance expenditures and other labour taxes.
Source: U.S. Department of Labor, Bureau of Labor Statistics, November 2005, www.bls.gov/news.release/ichcc.t02.htm

Figure 5.3 Hourly compensation costs in US dollars for production workers in manufacturing, 2004: selected countries

stretching across national borders, for example in pharmaceuticals, motor cars and management consultancy companies (see Chapter 10).

Globalisation has made a major impact in those manufacturing industries where technology has been less successful in automating production and, thus, the ratio of labour costs to total cost remains fairly high. This is the case, for example, in clothing, footwear, and toy manufacture. In these sorts of industries, as Figure 5.3 indicates, operations in high-wage countries are extremely vulnerable to differences in labour costs. The US and the UK have relatively similar levels of labour costs, somewhat more competitive than some of the higher-cost European countries such as the Netherlands and Germany. However, hourly compensation costs in Korea are currently around half of those in the US and UK, while those in Taiwan and in the Hong Kong Special Administrative Region of China are around 20 to 25 per cent of US/UK levels and those in Mexico are around 10 per cent.

These are national labour cost figures and do not necessarily give an accurate picture of comparative labour costs in an industry. This information is readily available on the internet, making comparisons much easier than in the past, and thus informing company strategies on offshoring, or reacting to competitive threats. For example, steel industry data for labour costs in the production of crude steel show that the unit cost in the USA in 2005 was US$23.8. It was US$26.0 in the UK but as low as US$0.9 in India and US$1.1 in China. This very low level of labour cost is not just a Far Eastern phenomenon. Costs in the Ukraine were US$0.8 while in the Czech Republic they were US$6.1. Meanwhile, Mexico, a member of NAFTA (the North America Free Trade Association) and thus in a tariff-free zone, can produce steel for US$2.5, roughly a tenth of the cost in its northern neighbour, the USA.[4]

These numbers speak for themselves. Such marked differences in labour costs place intense pressure on the cost structures of labour-intensive operations in the advanced industrial nations. These pressures are by no means restricted to manufacturing. Governments and regional economic areas such as the European Union have dismantled regulations that protected service industries in the past, whether the abolition of retail price maintenance, or the deregulation of particular sectors such as banking and airlines. In airline deregulation, which took place in the USA in the 1980s and in Europe was begun in the 1990s, the effect was that the protected routes 'owned' by a national airline or a favoured few were opened up to competition. Now labour cost increases could no longer be passed on automatically to the captive customer. New, low-cost airlines, which we noted in Chapter 2, entered the market like People's Express in the 1980s in the USA and easyJet and Ryanair in Britain ten years later. As labour costs are the largest component of variable costs in the airline industry, huge pressure was placed on finding means of achieving cost reduction (Batt 2005).

The pattern of low-cost, new-entrant firms rapidly taking market share from long-established companies repeated itself in many service industries like telecommunications, information systems, and banking, insurance and finance. In each case, established players found that the rules of the competitive game had changed. Now they, too, had to find ways of rapidly introducing new technologies or systems in order to reduce costs drastically while improving quality and the speed of customer service. This had to be done by finding better ways of managing operations and people. It is no wonder that the managerial preoccupations of the 1990s included 'benchmarking', 'business process re-engineering' and 'change management'.

Similar forces have been at work in the public sector. Pressures to reduce government expenditure as a proportion of gross domestic product, for example, in order to meet the criteria for joining the Euro, and to reduce government debt, were associated with the large-scale privatisation of government-owned industries (e.g. Bach and Kessler 2007). Pioneered by Mrs Thatcher's government in the UK in the 1980s, this approach to minimise the role of the state quickly spread around the globe and was enthusiastically

---

4 www.steelonthenet.com/labour_cost.html

supported by the International Monetary Fund and the World Bank. New forms of government action came in the form of state-sponsored regulators and auditors whose jobs were to ensure that privatised firms were not exploiting 'captive' customers. Regulators had the power to order significant reductions in prices, as they did, for example, in British water companies in 2000. This had dramatic consequences for jobs in the industry. Governments, whether national or supra-national like the European Union, ordered the opening up of sheltered service markets to competition, as for example in telecommunications. Utilising the latest technologies and building on the changing nature of customer preferences with the growth of mobile phone and internet access, new companies were able to enter the market. They had significantly lower cost structures compared to the existing, long-established firms which were burdened with sunk costs. Pressure to reduce these costs while improving quality and adopting new technologies was, and remains, intense.

The force of change was experienced, too, in those parts of the public sector that could not be privatised. This is the sphere of public hospitals, state schools and other central and local government services which have few independent sources of revenue beyond taxes. Here the import of the 'new public management' (Hood 1991, Ferlie *et al.* 1996) sought to replicate private sector competitive strategies. This could involve compulsory competitive tendering of service provision, such as school meals, refuse disposal or hospital facilities management, or the creation of proxy markets to force competition. This was achieved in health care through the artificial splitting of 'purchasers' from the 'providers' of services.

The initial response of many organisations affected by these cost pressures was often to lay off workers. Downsizing, one of the dark sides of HRM, is now a prevalent business strategy (e.g. Baron and Kreps 1999, Batt 2005). Unless technology is improved at the same time or client demand falls, downsizing leaves a smaller workforce which works longer hours or works the same hours under a greater sense of pressure. The first half of the 1990s, in fact, witnessed a general rise in work intensity in many European countries (Green and McIntosh 2001). In an extensive study using a variety of data sources, Green (2001) noted that in 1986 some 37 per cent of employees in the UK said they were subject to work pressure from clients or customers but by 1997 this had risen to 54 per cent. In the same period, the proportion who reported that they were subject to work pressure from fellow workers or colleagues rose remarkably from 29 to 57 per cent. 'It seems that peer pressure has come into its own as a source of labour intensification' (Green 2001: 70). This is strongly confirmed by the Bath *People and Performance* study (Hutchinson *et al.* 1996, 1998). Many of those interviewed said that 'they could not let their mates down'. This type of 'concertive' control by team members over themselves is, suggests Barker (1993), more powerful than other, more traditional methods of control to gain worker compliance with management's requirements.

However, while there are major variations in working hours and work pressure across countries, with Britain and Ireland and other neo-liberal economies exhibiting relatively high levels, working hours generally declined in European countries in the late 1990s (Gallie 2005). To be sure, this masks variations across the labour market. There are high stress levels in public-sector professional services and, in the private sector, high-income, highly skilled workers often find themselves in companies with long working hours cultures where they eventually experience problems of work-life imbalance. But the fact that we have now entered a period in which working hours seem to have stabilised suggests that work intensification has peaked for the time being.

There is an important clue here as to how companies have increasingly reacted to low-cost competition. In the private sector, work intensification is a limited strategy which will rarely bridge the gulf in costs we have talked about. In globalised manufacturing and service industries, firms either downsize their workforces, but in tandem with advanced technologies and work reforms which drive a productivity revolution (Brynjolffson and Hitt 2000), or they transfer their operations to attractive low-cost countries. Offshoring production to countries in which labour costs are markedly lower, and labour regulations are less demanding, has become one of the preferred HR strategies of multinational companies (Cooke 2001, 2007). Multinational companies with factories and offices in diverse countries have often been able to play one location off against another, rewarding the efficient with new investment and new-model work (as in the motor industry), and bargaining with governments for development grants as an inducement to keep existing plants open (Mueller and Purcell 1992). In many cases, established firms have ceased manufacturing altogether in high-wage countries. We saw this in the case of Dyson, referred to in Chapter 1, which shifted its assembly operations to Malaysia. Another iconic British case is that of the shoe company, Clarks, which closed its last factory in Weston-Super-Mare in 2001, moving production to Taiwan.

We thus see a range of strategies playing out as firms in advanced economies respond to a globalising economic order. Some have adopted new technologies, including, quite critically, an escalation of investment in new information technologies, and made companion investments in high-involvement work systems. This is easiest in capital-intensive or high-tech industries where workforce numbers and labour cost levels are already relatively low. For example, BMW, in its Oxford UK plant, making the highly successful Mini, announced the move of engine production from Brazil to its engine plant nearby in Ham Hall in 2006 despite labour costs in Brazil being two thirds of British costs.[5] BMW Oxford, the old Cowley works of Morris Motors and British Leyland, was notorious for poor industrial relations in the 1960s and 70s. It is now a classic case of successful HIWSs. This probably contributed to the decision. More important was the fact that labour costs only contributed 15–20 per cent to total costs and, by getting major suppliers within one hour of Oxford, significantly reduced transportation costs and increased flexibility, for example in engine choice.

Others, in industries more limited in their technological options, may have initially tried to downsize and intensify work. However, this is a much more limited strategy which can rarely bridge the cost gap that exists in such labour-intensive industries as clothing manufacturing and call centres between the high-wage economies of North America and Western Europe and the newly industrialising economies of Southern Asia, Central and South America and Africa. Here the unfolding story is that we see large-scale offshoring to sites where labour costs are so much lower that traditional Taylorist-Fordist work systems can be used without any difficulty.

Work systems in services and the public sector

Our discussion of the origin and evolution of work systems in manufacturing has given us much of the terminology and theory we need to discuss work systems in services, both private and public. Moreover, our discussion of the effects of globalisation and market reforms has underlined issues that are critical to analysing trends in service industries. Services are typically much more labour intensive than manufacturing, with ratios of labour to total costs that typically exceed 50 per cent (Batt 2005) and are often around 60 to 70 per cent, including in the public sector (Bach and Kessler 2007).

---

5 *Guardian*, 14 September 2006.

Work systems	Tightly constrained	Unrationalised labour intensive	Semi-autonomous	High-skill autonomous
Examples	Telephone operators, fast-food workers, cheque proofers	Some nurses' aides, hotel maids, domestics, long-distance truck drivers, child care workers, clerical home workers	Clerical and administrative jobs with relatively broad responsibilities, low-level managers, some sales workers, UPS truck drivers	Physicians, high-level managers, laboratory technicians, electricians, engineers
Markets served	High volume, low cost; standardised quality	Low cost, low volume; often low or uneven quality	Volume and quality vary	Low volume (each job may differ); quality often in the eye of the beholder
Task supervision	Tight	Loose	Moderate	Little
Formal education of workers	Low to moderate	Low to moderate (skill often unrecognised)	Moderate	High
On-the-job training	Limited	Some informal, unrecognised learning from other workers	Limited to moderate	Substantial

Source: Abridged from Herzenberg *et al.* (1998: 42–3)

Figure 5.4   Herzenberg *et al.*'s (1998) typology of work systems

To broaden our discussion into services, it helps to refer to a typology of work systems developed by Herzenberg, Alic and Wial (1998: 41) (see also Frenkel *et al.* 1999 and Batt 2000). This typology is shown in Figure 5.4. It has the value of summarising four readily discernible categories of work. Typologies can never recognise all the complexity or nuances that exist in work organisation but the framework in Figure 5.4 usefully stretches from Taylorist work design, first developed in manufacturing, to high-discretion systems, such as high-skill professional services where Taylorism has rarely intruded. In between are two other categories. One category recognises the large amount of work which is labour intensive, less skilled and largely 'unrationalised' by management systems. A lot of personal services are very informal and have remained this way. Examples include a host of jobs in small shops, in family-owned restaurants, in nurse aiding, and in services offered directly to households including child care and gardening. These jobs may draw heavily on the interpersonal skills and physical stamina of the individuals involved but they have not required the high levels of educational and experiential preparation that are associated with professional services in such spheres as education, accountancy, engineering, medicine and the law. The other intermediate category recognises semi-autonomous work which requires mid-range skills and is neither high in discretion nor highly constrained. This latter category covers a lot of sales, clerical and associate-professional work. It is very prevalent in large, private sector bureaucracies, such as the major banks and insurance companies, and in the administrative cadres of central and local government.

We will turn our attention first of all to private sector services. Boxall (2003) draws on the work of Herzenberg *et al.* (1998) and on the economic and strategic management theory we discuss in this book to define three broad types of competition and work organisation in private sector services (Figure 5.5). Where the interaction between technology and people is typically critical to the choice of work systems in manufacturing, the interaction with customers, and the level of knowledge needed for this encounter, is critical in services.

Service market type	Competitive dynamics	Knowledge content of service	Typical work design
Type One: Mass service markets (e.g. gas stations, fast food, supermarkets)	Cost-based competition except to the extent limited by unions and state regulation; substitution of labour for technology and self-service	Low: key managers or franchisees have critical knowledge but general labour uses limited, mostly generic know-how	Low discretion; may be highly 'Taylorised' in international franchises or major chains; otherwise unrationalised, low-skill work
Type Two: A mix of mass markets and higher value-added segments (e.g. elder care, hotels, call centres)	A mix of cost and quality-based competition; greater profit opportunities for firms that identify higher value-added segments	Low to moderate knowledge levels; mix of skill levels needed in the workforce	Traditionally low to moderate discretion but potential for HIWSs
Type Three: Highly differentiated markets (e.g. high-level professional services)	Expertise and quality-based competition but with some anchors on relative pricing; some services may be routinised and migrate back to Type Two competition	High knowledge intensity except where some professional services become routinised	Generally high discretion; the natural home of HIWSs

Source: Adapted from Boxall (2003)

Figure 5.5 Types of work design in private sector services

Mass service markets

In mass service markets, such as gas stations, fast-food outlets, and supermarkets, customers tend to have choice in where to buy and quality differences are either non-existent or not that important. Customers are therefore very price sensitive. Because this is the low-skill end of services, customers will often *co-produce* the service, one of the defining features of basic, everyday services (e.g. Batt 2005, 2007, Combs *et al.* 2006). This may include pumping their own gas, queuing at a counter and then carrying their food to a table at a fast-food outlet, and weighing their own fruit and vegetables in the supermarket. The more firms engage customers in co-production and the more they can automate services or offshore 'back-office' functions to lower-cost countries, the lower unit costs will be. Once one firm in an industry pioneers a major cost-saving innovation, virtually everyone has to follow to stay in business. The key managers or franchisees who run operations must have critical knowledge to establish, maintain and renew their business model as competition unfolds but general labour in these services uses limited, mostly generic know-how.

Work design here typically involves one of two types in the Herzenberg *et al.* (1998) framework. Some mass-service firms adopt Taylorism. We see this, for example, in the high-volume, inbound call centre industry where management may rationalise work practices by measuring such variables as call length against prescribed time, the calls waiting to be answered, the abandoned call rate, and the time taken to 'wrap up' (e.g. Cordery and Parker 2007). In addition, there will frequently be recording of calls and remote monitoring where managers listen in to ensure that scripts and greetings are used properly. In these situations, an equivalent of the manufacturing 'speed-up' occurs, and stress levels and employee turnover can rise (e.g. Deery, Iverson and Walsh 2002). We see similar work formalisation strategies in the large-scale retailing sector, including the national or regional chain stores. These organisations often use surveillance via closed-circuit TV and video cameras and may use 'mystery shoppers', who secretly score sales assistants on their willingness to smile and be helpful (e.g. Guy 2003). Training in the chain stores and supermarkets often includes 'scripting' in an attempt to ensure that customers are greeted in a standard way and handled in preferred ways when problems arise. These attempts to prescribe and enlist 'emotional labour' can be highly stressful (Hochschild 1986, Cordery and Parker 2007).

Alongside the mass service providers are many smaller organisations which try to make a living by keeping out of the way of the 'big boys' and offering more localised and personal services. This includes many small shops, service agencies, regional taxi services and a host of local bars and restaurants.

The owners of these businesses have hardly ever used the bureaucratic, rationalised practices that the big players need for their large workforces, relying instead on the personal contacts and control of the owner or a 'hands-on' manager (e.g. Marchington, Carroll and Boxall 2003). This can actually be a much more enjoyable working environment because people are not alienated by huge layers between them and the owners. The owner is a real individual who may well engage in a certain degree of 'give-and-take' over working conditions to build the loyalty of the people he or she trusts.

As our discussion indicates, cost pressures in basic services mean that work systems that involve higher levels of employee discretion and skill are rare in this sector. This does not rule out creative responses by individual firms but high levels of competitive pressure do constrain management behaviour. They mean that large firms offering low-priced services to a mass market are continually looking for ways to take out labour costs through self-service, offshoring and labour-saving technology. Small firms competing at the fringes of these markets may be able to 'keep their heads down', at least until a large trader threatens their patch, but they are often working with low margins and with their personal wealth at stake. When labour markets are hot, high levels of employee turnover can undermine even basic service levels and firms are forced to raise wages and improve conditions to hold the higher-performing, better experienced workers. However, the general pressure of cost cutting tends to reassert itself over time in mass services and this means that state regulation of pay levels and working conditions, and trade union activity, are very important to creating a floor of rights and more dignified conditions for workers.

Mass service markets with some quality differentiation

There is an important shift in the economics of production when firms find segments of mass markets where customers will pay a premium for a better quality of service (Boxall 2003, Batt 2005, 2007). We see this in such service markets as elder care, hotels, and call centres, where there is major variation in customer preferences and higher value-added customers can be targeted for better service (e.g. Batt 2000, Eaton 2000, Hunter 2000). A study by Haynes and Fryer (2000) of a five-star hotel located in a large New Zealand city illustrates the point (Figure 5.6). Like all luxury hotels, physical amenities and the refurbishment of properties drive one aspect of the hotel's strategy but tend to fall into the category of 'table stakes'. With enough money, hotel owners can create the kind of opulent surroundings that position them in the luxury hotel segment. However, the bricks and mortar

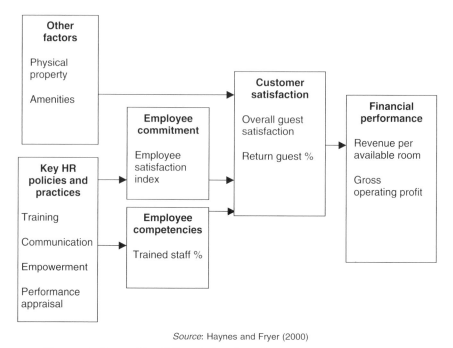

Source: Haynes and Fryer (2000)

Figure 5.6 Competitive differentiation through HR strategy in a luxury hotel

(or, in this case, the marble and polished wood) do not confer any form of advantage in the segment. Superior returns also turn on the way staff deal with customers in the context of these surroundings. This includes the way in which guest preferences are discovered and catered for in successive visits. It means that there is a role for investments in the more intangible variables: in broader, more empowering job design, in development reviews and more comprehensive training, and in staff committees and surveys through which management learns about employee motivators.

When firms aim for higher value-added segments in services, then, investments in creating HIWSs are more likely to be economically justified (Boxall 2003). At this point, however, it is vital to underline a key distinction between the economics of higher quality production in manufacturing and in services. As we saw earlier, Japanese manufacturers in such spheres as automobiles and motorbikes showed that it was possible to create improvements in quality and reductions in price at the same time. This process has now unfolded in many capital-intensive manufacturing industries (e.g. consumer electronics) where customers have got used to buying better models as they are released at lower prices. There are many service industries, however, where improvements in quality will *only* come at a higher price.

This is the case when the larger part of the service is geographically fixed. For example, if you want to stay in a luxury hotel in Paris, the hotel will be in Paris and, despite the internet and outsourcing, the bulk of the service provision will take place with staff working in Paris and being paid Parisian wages. While companies in differentiated services continue to apply new technologies and offshoring wherever they can to reduce costs, higher quality service in the geographically fixed components of services translates into higher costs and prices.

Highly differentiated service markets

We now come to another major point of contrast with work design in manufacturing. In high-level, professional services and other knowledge-intensive services, work organisation has traditionally involved high levels of employee discretion. Workers in high-skill services typically have advanced educational qualifications. How they work depends much more on how these professions educate and train their own people (e.g. Combs *et al.* 2006). We are not therefore talking about a situation where work practices have traditionally been imposed by managers but one in which managers are typically senior professionals themselves. They have to deal with major performance differences among professionals but their effectiveness typically depends on working in a way that is sympathetic to professional discretion. Managerial attempts to increase control over professional behaviour often meet with professional resistance.

Recent research by Kalleberg *et al.* (2006) in the US underlines key differences between work practices in professional services and those in manufacturing and less skilled services. While professional organisations, such as schools and health care services, are big users of team meetings, where professionals collectively discuss goals and problems, they are significantly less likely to use job rotation: you simply cannot rotate professionals across jobs unless they have the relevant professional qualifications. Employee growth in professional services tends to come as individuals deepen and extend the experience they have in their particular specialisation.

In the private sector, we therefore see a conjunction of high discretion, high quality and high pay in advanced, complex services. This implies, as just noted in our discussion of quality differentiation, that customers or clients have to pay higher prices if they want the service in question. Access to the top lawyers and financial advisers, for example, depends on being able to pay their 'professional fees'. To be sure, some advanced services become 'routinised'. This happens where consulting firms roll out standardised solutions to more common business problems and use more junior professionals to deliver them (e.g. Dooreward and Meihuizen 2000). There is also a growth now of 'knowledge-processing offshoring' where aspects of such services as insurance underwriting and legal and financial research are conducted in low-wage countries, most notably in India.[6] However, the more complex or esoteric the knowledge, requiring a high level of adaptation to each client's needs, the higher the control exercised by the professional and the higher the price that will be charged.

Public sector services

We have already said a lot about the public sector, which has been affected by the same sort of cost pressures as the private sector. Downsizing and budget constraints have been applied while client demands, as in public education and health, have risen. These pressures have often been as intense as anything in the private sector or worse (Green 2001, Smith 2001, Kersley *et al.* 2006). Many public services are geographically fixed and work intensification pressures, unless effectively resisted by trade unions or undermined by high levels of employee turnover, can operate for long periods of time.

Two broad patterns of work organisation are important in the public sector. One occurs in the public service ministries and local government departments, which are typically much larger and much older than private sector establishments (Kalleberg *et al.* 2006). They have therefore relied heavily on tall hierarchies and such bureaucratic devices as job descriptions, job evaluation and performance appraisal systems. The public service has historically rivalled the largest manufacturers and the high-street banks in growing huge 'internal labour markets'. To ensure governments can account to taxpayers for how public funds are spent, pressures for standardisation of conditions have been strong, as have procedures which help to show equity of treatment across different grades of workers and across different individuals (Bach and Kessler 2007). As in large-scale manufacturing, but arriving somewhat later, the public sector has been, and remains, a strong site of unionisation. As there, unions have had the effect of increasing the number of work rules adopted in the internal labour market. Given these large organisations and pressures for joint regulation, government clerical and administrative work has been closest to the 'semi-autonomous' pattern shown in Figure 5.4. It often involves a degree of discretionary judgement

---

6 Randeep Ramesh, 'Analyse this: Wall Street looks to India', *Guardian*, 6 November 2006, p. 26.

(e.g. should a sole parent receive a benefit or not?; should this taxpayer be granted this exemption?; should this child be granted entry to this school?) but this is typically exercised within a prescribed policy framework and a set of operating rules.

The other major pattern in the public sector is the existence of a high degree of highly skilled professional work, which we have just discussed in talking about highly differentiated service markets. In the United States, 6 out of 10 public sector establishments operate in professional services (Kalleberg *et al.* 2006: 282). Being in the public sector, where there are large organisations with tall hierarchies, this means a higher level of bureaucracy than one finds in private sector professional firms but it also means a high level of independent action by professionals, both acting as individuals and working through trade unions.

Bach and Kessler (2007) outline the way in which these traditional models of public sector work have been challenged by the 'new public management', referred to above. Governments from the Thatcher era on have sought to constrain the growth of, and get greater control over, the huge amount of public money that is invested in public sector workforces. This has included attempts to split 'purchasers' from 'providers' in the public sector in order to create organisational contracts which promise a certain level of services for a given amount of public money and which enable regular audits of performance. On the individual level, it includes greater mechanisms for accountability such as individual performance targets and performance-related pay. There is little doubt that the target/audit culture has brought work intensification of a kind that has antagonised public sector professionals, lowering levels of trust in the public sector (e.g. Guest and Conway 2002) and exacerbating problems of recruitment and retention (Audit Commission 2002). In the British health service, it has actually led to an explosion in the number of people who are categorised as managers (Kirkpatrick, Ackroyd and Walker 2005).

Governments may now be starting to appreciate the limits to the 'new public management' but this does not predicate a return to the public sector of old. Increasingly, governments have sought to separate the provision of a service free at the point of delivery from the ownership of the service provider. Increasingly, we see privately run prisons, hospitals and schools alongside, and to a growing degree competing with, the traditional public sector, much to the fury of the unions. This has strong parallels with multidivisional companies, as we discuss in Chapter 10, where performance comparisons are linked to investment decisions. Any idea that the public sector is immune from job cuts and efficiency comparisons has been almost completely removed with the arrival of private sector competitors subject to less stringent rules and procedures governing work organisation. With much about all this that is highly contentious, the public sector continues to provide an important case study of what can go wrong in the HR strategies of large organisations, as we will argue more fully in Chapter 8.

Conclusions

Work systems – choices about what work needs to be done, about who will do it, and about where and how they will do it – are fundamental to both operations management and human resource management in organisations. The appropriateness of a firm's work systems is inevitably connected to its chances of economic survival and to its relative performance. And they matter enormously to workers, being a principal source of job satisfaction or dissatisfaction and a major factor in employee turnover.

Many of our ideas in work design have originated in manufacturing. The growth of manufacturing in Britain and the USA in the nineteenth century depended heavily on highly specialised work systems in which operating work was characterised by low discretion, low scope and low skill. This kind of work design emerged in the early factories and was reinforced by Taylorist principles of 'Scientific Management' and Henry Ford's moving assembly line. Political and trade union challenges forced the model to adapt, leading to better incorporation of worker interests, including higher pay levels and better conditions, and encouraging the growth of 'internal labour markets' in which employee security and promotion prospects were enhanced.

It was not until Japanese competition exposed the weaknesses of Western manufacturing that principles of work design began to be seriously reformed. High-involvement work systems (HIWSs) now constitute an important alternative to traditional Taylorism-Fordism. These systems, which enhance employee discretion and skills, have been adopted in various parts of Western manufacturing where firms had become vulnerable to higher quality and lower-priced competition. In certain industries, including steel manufacturing and automobile assembly, a transition to HIWSs and greater investments in computerised technologies has enhanced the chances of survival or significantly lifted performance. There is also evidence to indicate that HIWSs can bring improvements in employee autonomy, greater development and use of their skills, and greater financial rewards, significantly lifting job satisfaction. However, in the case of both firms and workers, the relative costs and benefits of HIWSs depend heavily on the context in which they are attempted and how they are implemented.

In terms of the context facing firms, industry deregulation, tariff reductions, new information technologies and the growth of the internet have opened up greater competition from new producers and from newly industrialising countries with much lower labour costs. These forces have had major impacts in those industries where the ratio of labour costs to total costs remains fairly high. This is not simply an issue in labour-intensive parts of manufacturing but applies to many services given their high labour content. Strategies of downsizing and work intensification have played their part in industry restructuring but tend to be limited. In some globalised industries, the dramatic improvement in labour costs needed can only be achieved by offshoring operations or those parts of service production which do not need to be geographically fixed.

Mass services are subject to major pressures for cost reductions, which are increasingly pursued through strategies of customer self-service, offshoring of 'back-room' functions and new technologies, such as internet shopping. Large firms often adopt Taylorist work design in mass services while smaller firms, operating at the fringes, rely on more informal methods of control. There is less scope in basic services for the kinds of work reform seen in high-tech or capital-intensive manufacturing. In higher quality segments of service markets, however, there are possibilities for firms to offer higher quality at a higher price, thus making investments in work redesign and higher skill more worthwhile. In professional services, Taylorism has rarely intruded and high discretion, high quality and high pay are typical, though even here there are some service activities which are not geographically sensitive and thus have offshoring potential. The public sector embraces a mix of bureaucratic work systems in which workers exercise moderate levels of discretion and a host of professional jobs. In recent years, budget constraints, workforce downsizing and a rise in bureaucratic controls have met with a very mixed response from the public sector workforce, a theme to which we will return.

6

Managing employee voice

In our discussion of the rise of the factory system in Chapter 5, we explained how employee voice became a controversial area for management. We are concerned with underpinning principles of HRM in this part of the book and the fundamental question here is how much influence employees should have over decisions that affect them at work. This is not simply a matter of the economic performance of the firm but concerns social legitimacy and the extent to which employers should be compelled by the state to give voice to employees and, where they exist, their trade unions.

Even the definitions of employee voice are controversial. 'Employee voice' is a relatively new term designed to cover all forms of opportunities where employees can have their say and exert some influence. But, as George Strauss comments, 'voice is meaningless if the message is ignored' (2006: 803). He much prefers the term 'participation'. Participation is 'a process that allows employees to exercise some influence over their work and the conditions under which they work' (Heller *et al.* 1998: 15). Strauss adds, 'that for me, it is *actual* influence, not a *feeling* of influence that is important' (Strauss 2006: 778). Others take a much softer approach. In the same journal where Strauss's stringent definition is found, the editors define ' "participation" to encompass the range of mechanisms used to involve the workforce in decisions at all levels of the organization' (Gollan, Poutsma and Veersma 2006: 499). Managers are often happier with 'involvement' on the job than they are with employees exerting influence at higher levels. Marchington (2007) expresses the dilemma neatly: 'Voice is probably the area of HRM where tensions between organisational and worker goals, and between shareholder and stakeholder views, are most apparent because it connects with the question of managerial prerogatives and social legitimacy'. The 'problem' of worker voice is compounded, for multinational companies at the least, by the markedly different approach taken in the USA from other Anglo-American countries and from practice and law in continental Europe. Meanwhile, in rapidly industrialising countries, worker rights and the way multinational firms are responding to them are a matter of international concern (e.g. Cooke 2007), as we explained in Chapter 1.

Over many decades, indeed since industrialisation, voice mechanisms have taken many forms and been labelled with a wide variety of terms. The way these have changed indicates the shifting priorities and values associated with different types of voice systems. 'Worker participation', favoured in the 1960s and 1970s, gave way to 'employee involvement' (EI) in the 1980s while, for a short period in the 1970s, the term 'industrial democracy' was used to imply the need for wider employee rights through the appointment of worker directors. There has always been an interest too, albeit a minority one, in forms of worker self-management and worker cooperatives where changes in ownership are seen as providing the best means of exerting influence (Bradley and Gelb 1983, Oakeshott 2000). The best-known firm in the UK owned by its employees, or 'partners' as they called, is the John Lewis Partnership. It is a highly successful chain of department stores and associated supermarkets, the latter trading as Waitrose. This model of a very different type of company is receiving increased interest. It has been suggested by senior management in the Royal Mail, for example, that it could move from public ownership into a partnership based on the John Lewis model. There is now a growing interest in 'social enterprises' providing an alternative organisational form to the traditional joint stock company and the public corporation.[1] These ownership types of EI might be seen as an innovative form of corporate social responsibility. One thing is certain: controversies over what type of voice workers should have, and how shareholders and senior managers should respond, will never be resolved since at their heart they are about ethics, social legitimacy and power.

Many of the ideas for employee participation come not from the 'best practice' school of human resource management, which we examined in Chapter 3, but from political philosophy and from trade union action in the political economy. Thus, while many chapters in this book are concerned with the links between HRM and the economic performance of the firm, here our concern is more with the social and political forces which impinge on management's approach to employee interests. We need to ask how, and how extensively, employees should have a voice in organisational decision

---

1 See www.socialenterprise.org.uk

making. In the chapter, we look at the political and institutional forces which set the context for voice practices, and note some fundamental and far-reaching changes. We examine the implications of these trends for trade unions, the traditional champions of worker interests, and consider one of the most fundamental issues in strategic HRM: what sort of style can, and should, managers adopt in relation to employee voice? Virtually every analysis of voice points to the critically important part that management plays in supporting or opposing different forms of worker voice.

The growth and changing contours of employee voice

The link between politics and worker voice is important since in this area of human resource management, trade unions and the state have often played a major role and what has been learned in political science and philosophy has echoes within the modern enterprise. It is not possible, even if it were desirable, to look at questions of employee voice only through the economic lens of cost-effectiveness. Rather, the issue of social legitimacy (as we discussed in Chapters 1 and 3) is fundamental and few nation states leave this to the owners of capital to resolve themselves, unfettered by legislation or social stigma ('the unacceptable face of capitalism', as one British Conservative Prime Minister once said of a major employer which suddenly closed a shipyard without any discussion or warning). If the British monarchy's royal prerogative, the God-given right to rule, came spectacularly to an end on the executioner's block on 30 January 1649, so the issue in the world of work is not whether, but *how much*, restriction should be placed on managerial prerogative, on the right to manage. If modern democracies are based upon political citizenship, how far should there also be a concept of industrial citizenship? If the exercise of arbitrary power by those in authority in government is constrained by laws giving rights to citizens, and enforced by the judiciary, how far should equivalent rights be applied in the world of paid employment and how far can they be enforced?

There are not, and never can be, any conclusive answers to these questions, just as there can be no finite, universally accepted code of ethics. It may be convenient to justify the utility of various forms of employee voice against the template of economic performance, and we will do so later in this chapter, but it is never sufficient since, ultimately, questions of human rights and social legitimacy have also to be faced. In seeking to evaluate the outcomes of particular forms of voice, it would be more sensible to use the reverse test of degrees of damage caused. Do employee voice arrangements significantly endanger the enterprise by reducing performance and creating conditions of competitive *dis*advantage? Using this test, it is hard to think of any employee voice mechanism, as currently practised, which is economically seriously damaging. Even this test, however, is flawed since it confuses ends and means. Ultimately the justification for employee voice is as an end value in its own right. As such, it is always contentious and subject to reinterpretation as different generations of power-holders in enterprises and the wider political system deal with the ethics of employment relations.

These problems in the first half of the twentieth century, when the foundations of industrial relations were laid, were mainly about strikes and cycles of intense industrial unrest which threatened social order, as noted in Chapter 5. The solution then was to foster the recognition of trade unions and to emphasise the process of collective bargaining, described by one leading American professor in the 1950s as 'the great social invention that has institutionalised industrial conflict' (Dubin 1954: 44). The state, in many Anglo-American countries especially, but also in the Nordic countries, persuaded employers to engage in formal discussions with trade unions, often at industry or sectoral level through employers' associations, and strongly endorsed this in the way it ran public sector organisations.

The linkage between social democratic or labour parties in the political arena and trade unions in the industrial sphere meant also, especially in the post Second World War period, that workers' interests were reflected in political agendas with unions recognised as 'social partners' at the national level in many European countries, and legislation was passed to enhance worker rights to information and consultation (e.g. Frege and Kelly 2004, Heery and Adler 2004). Within the Anglo-American tradition, the emphasis was on worker rights 'won' at the bargaining table by strong, well-organised trade unions (e.g. Hyman 1975, Clegg 1994). The principle was one of 'voluntarism', where the state would abstain from regulation, leaving it to unions and management to determine their own solutions. In so doing, the assumption was that the unions were the legitimate representatives of labour. The unions themselves fiercely defended their role as the one, and only, formal channel of communications and negotiation between management and employees. Employee participation, in the main, meant dealing with and through trade unions.

The alternative route, more often found in continental European, or more specifically Northern European countries, was the provision of rights enshrined in law and applied universally across the economy. In the UK, but also in Canada and the USA, voluntary agreements on information, consultation and joint regulation were found in many different forms in a patchwork of agreements in individual companies and sectors. In the Netherlands and Germany, however, rights were established in law (e.g. Paauwe and Boselie 2003, 2007). Collective bargaining agreements became legal minima applied to all firms in a sector whether they had union members or not, and all firms beyond the very smallest were required to have a works council, a form of employee forum to provide information and discuss a range of issues to do with the organisation and future direction of the firm. In some of the larger companies in Germany, especially, a further requirement was for worker directors to work with other board members to 'co-determine' key aspects of company strategy.

These two very different approaches to the role of the state, reflected in very different paths to worker representation and voice systems, were profoundly affected by the foundation and subsequent enlargement of the European Union (EU) in the last three decades of the twentieth century, taken in the context of a decline in union membership and union power in many countries. The EU has led to marked changes in the landscape of worker participation and to a degree of convergence in systems of employee representation. With it has come a new language of 'partnership' and a search for more effective ways of incorporating employee opinion into company decision making (e.g. Haynes and Allen 2000, Belanger, Giles and Murray 2002). The right of employees to a say in company decisions is a fundamental tenet of EU policy in employment relations. A series of regulations has provided a requirement for representatives of employees to be consulted at times of major organisational change: for example, in large-scale redundancies and in mergers between organisations.[2] Originally, the assumption in the UK was that where trade unions were recognised by the employer, their representatives, the shop stewards and full-time officers, would be consulted. Where there was no union recognition, the regulations would not apply. At a time when a growing number of employees work in companies that do not recognise trade unions, their apparent lack of rights to consultation has become a cause for concern. The European Court of Justice, in a series of rulings, has established that all workers have the right to be consulted and trade union exclusivity can no longer be sustained.

Two further regulations reinforce the contemporary view that consultation is a worker right and not something provided only through trade unions.

---

2 Transfer of Undertakings, Protection of Employees Regulations or TUPE, for short.

Large, 1,000-worker-plus multinational companies with establishments of over 150 employees in two or more member states are now required to establish European Works Councils (EWCs) to receive information on future plans and performance and discuss appropriate action, if 10 per cent of workers express a wish for this. So far, of the 2,204 companies this applies to, just over a third have established an EWC (European Works Councils Bulletin No. 64, 2006: 4–6). In the UK, 41 per cent have done so. In 2002, a further, potentially much more significant Directive was adopted: the Information and Consultation of Employees Regulation (ICE). This came into force in the UK for enterprises with 150 workers in 2005 and by 2008 will be extended to those with 50 or more workers. It establishes the right of employees, if 10 per cent or more ask for it, to be provided with information on company matters and to be consulted (normally through elected representatives in what are often called employee forums but sometimes works councils or joint consultative committees (JCCs)).

We need to draw out three important implications here. First, while some question how effective EWCs are (Marginson *et al.* 2004, Waddington 2006), and there has initially been a cool response to the ICE regulations (Hall 2006), these regulations do establish rights for employees to elect representatives to meet management at the highest levels of their companies and discuss 'big' issues. Second, the combination of these new institutions providing substance to employee voice systems, and the very different environment in which unions now operate in the global economy, has had marked effects on the role and operation of trade unions. This is discussed in detail later in this chapter but here it is necessary to note that the move from union-only-based rights to universal employee rights to forms of voice is a fundamental change and the consequences have yet to be worked through. Third, this type of employee voice through elected representatives on works councils or employee forums is long established and deeply embedded in most of continental Europe. Gumbrell-McCormick and Hyman (2006) call it 'embedded collectivism'. However, it is simply unknown, and 'off the radar' in the USA, the world's largest economy. Partly for reasons of labour law which prohibits 'company unions' (and elected employee bodies like works councils are seen as such) and partly because of employer antipathy to collective voice, there is little experience of representative voice in America. A large proportion of workers notice this 'representation gap' (Freeman 2007). This draws attention to the 'varieties of capitalism' debate (Hall and Soskice 2001) where US capitalism is dominated by shareholder concerns whereas in parts of continental Europe a more stakeholder approach is evident, as exemplified by the role of the state in the development of worker representational rights (Paauwe 2004). These different traditions and mental maps are powerful forces of path dependency, a concept central to the resource-based view of the firm (see Chapter 4). All this calls attention to the role of the state in determining or influencing forms of employee voice.

This American blind spot to worker representation as a form of worker voice does not mean that American managers are uninterested in voice systems. Their concern has typically been with the link between employee voice and economic performance. Along with state and trade union interventions, managerial concern with business performance has been a second major influence in the growth of employee involvement (e.g. Boxall, Purcell and Wright 2007b). The interest is especially in direct forms of voice at the level of the task in 'on-line' and 'off-line' arrangements for worker influence. On-line voice is seen in such things as semi-autonomous team working where workers have greater influence over deciding how the work is done. Off-line voice usually involves taking part in problem-solving groups like quality circles and continuous improvement or 'kaizen' teams. These types of voice practices are central to high-involvement work systems, as discussed in Chapter 5. The aim is not generally to provide workers with a voice *per se* but to secure worker cooperation in improving the productivity and flexibility of the firm.

Thus, we have two sets of forces helping to build employee voice institutions: one involves the state and the actions, through it and alongside it, of trade unions, primarily concerned with enhancing the interests of workers and with wider issues of social legitimacy. The other is management itself, primarily in those firms which are concerned to enhance their economic performance through better kinds of employee involvement and higher levels of employee commitment. These two forces are driving a wide variety of employee voice practices and, before we can proceed meaningfully, we need to sort out some definitions and pinpoint the key trends.

Choices and change in employee voice systems

In any analysis of voice systems allowing for, or encouraging, employees to have a say, and thus influence in decision making, five linked questions need to be addressed:

1 How much say/involvement/participation is envisaged in the scheme?
2 Over what sort of decisions?
3 Taken at what level in the enterprise, or beyond in the wider political economy?

4 Who is involved and, if a representative, how elected or selected?
5 What are the enforcement mechanisms, both to keep the system going and to ensure that action follows?

The first question is the most important since it will strongly influence the form the answers to subsequent questions take. In the German co-determination and consultation legal framework, there is a clear delineation of degrees of influence or types of involvement (information to be provided, topics subject to consultation etc). Elsewhere, especially in Anglo-American societies, there is much more ambiguity but it is still possible to suggest a scale based on the extent of influence allowed or expected. This is shown in Figure 6.1. Marchington and Wilkinson (2000: 343) display this diagrammatically as an 'escalator' of participation (Figure 6.2).

The types of decision and their location in the managerial hierarchy can attract different degrees of involvement. For example, decisions on health and safety will often (and, in many countries, must by law) involve employee representatives in the evaluation of risks and their avoidance in current operations and in the purchase of new technology. In some extreme cases, safety representatives have the right to delay or veto a decision if there is a danger to life and limb. In the same firm, it would be most unusual for employees to have the same degree of voice, or any voice, over product marketing or distribution decisions. In a thriving system of consultation, however, it may be that management will explain and account for these decisions. Examples of such joint discussions in recent years have included consideration of declining quality in a car manufacturer and exploring means to correct it (Purcell *et al.* 2003), the pricing and shelf display of a biscuit maker's products concerning the relationship with a dominant

None:	Unilateral management
A little:	Information provided
Downward:	Right to be told
Some:	Opportunity to make some suggestions
Two-way:	Consulted / Opinion sought during decision making
:	Consulted / Opinion sought at all stages of decision making and implementation
A lot:	The right to delay a decision
Power to affect outcomes:	The right (or power) to veto a decision
Substantial:	Equality or co-determination in decision making
Complete:	Employee self-management and ownership

Figure 6.1 Scale of participation or involvement allowed to employees and their representatives

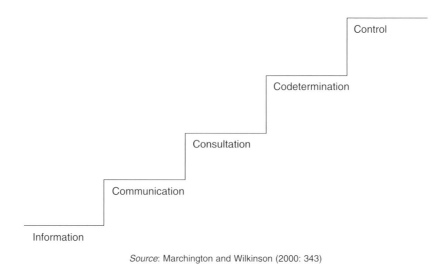

Source: Marchington and Wilkinson (2000: 343)

Figure 6.2   Marchington and Wilkinson's escalator of participation

supermarket (Purcell and Ahlstrand 1994), and a major plant location and investment decision in a multinational company (*ibid.*). In these cases of consultation, the 'right of last say' still rested with management but the desire to justify decisions and the subsequent discussions did influence management's approach. The extent to which employees believe their views are listened to, and have influence, affects the way employees evaluate voice systems and judge management effectiveness. If positive, this can increase job satisfaction and organisational commitment (Guest and Conway 1997, Appelbaum *et al.* 2000).

If the scale of involvement varies by type of decision and by its location (in the corporate board in the case of a major plant location; at the plant, department or level of the team in the example of declining quality), then this in turn strongly influences the nature of the voice system. Some types of involvement in all but the smallest companies will require a system of representation with a few employees elected or selected to represent their co-workers. Here involvement is indirect and questions are posed on how the tenor and outcome of joint meetings is communicated amongst 'constituents', and how, and to what extent, representatives take soundings before meetings, especially when dealing with confidential information. The quality of the underlying relationship in terms of levels of trust is crucial if the exchange is to be anything more than 'white knuckle' adversarial posturing (Walton and McKersie 1965, Purcell 1974, Marchington 1989).

In contrast, other types of voice systems provide individual employees a direct say. This can happen through their membership of teams, through problem-solving groups like quality circles, through the way their jobs are designed, through attitude surveys or through their involvement as individual shareholders. Figure 6.3 combines direct and indirect forms of employee voice systems with the location of decisions. We use the terms 'power-centred', 'ownership-centred' and 'task-centred' to categorise voice practices. For example, power-centred types of schemes can be indirect forms allowing for high-level dialogue at meetings in joint partnership committees or company-level works councils between senior managers or directors and employee representatives. Power-centred schemes can also involve employees directly. Employee attitude surveys are growing in popularity and now occur in around two fifths of British workplaces (Kersley *et al.* 2006: 68). We call these 'power-centred' because the results can question, and bring changes in, the actions of senior management. They are increasingly seen as important, as we note in Chapter 11, when combined with customer

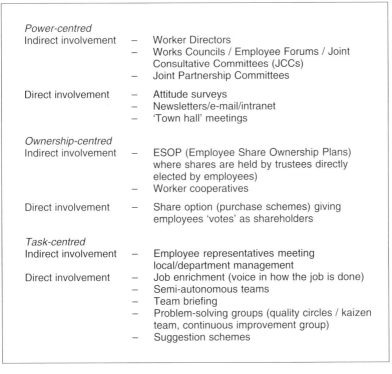

Figure 6.3 Types of employee voice mechanisms

satisfaction surveys since there is often a strong correlation between employee commitment, customer satisfaction and company performance (Fulmer, Gerhart, and Scott 2003, Gelade and Ivery 2003). Another form of power-centred, direct involvement includes meetings between management and all employees on site, called 'town hall meetings' in the USA. These are now very common, happening in 79 per cent of UK workplaces with at least 10 employees (Kersley *et al.* 2006: 134). A generation ago, such workforce meetings only happened in a third of workplaces (Millward and Stevens 1986: 152).

The evidence is clear that direct types of employee voice have grown since the 1980s across the industrialised world, both in Anglo-American countries (Boxall, Freeman and Haynes 2007) and in continental Europe (Poutsma, Ligthart and Veersma 2006). In the UK, forms of communication between management and employees are widely used with 91 per cent of workplaces having face-to-face meetings, 83 per cent using one form or another of downward communication, like an intranet (34 per cent) or communication chains (sometimes called cascade briefing) (64 per cent), and written two-way communication methods like e-mail or suggestion schemes evident in two thirds of workplaces (Kersley *et al.* 2006: 135). Team working is also widespread in Britain (72 per cent of workplaces) although in only half of these establishments are all employees in teams. The evidence suggests that adoption of such employee involvement practices is much more likely where there is a strategic need for worker cooperation and a reliance on skilled human capital (Benson and Lawler 2005: 166), especially since high-involvement work systems raise costs (Cappelli and Neumark 2001). Poutsma *et al.* (2006: 520) report that in Europe 'collaborative practices' appear to be 'more often practiced in innovative workplaces facing intense competition, with highly qualified personnel, where management considers direct participation a competitive advantage'.

Other factors positively influencing the adoption of voice systems include being a foreign-owned firm, making more extensive use of information technology and the size of the company and the workplace. Large enterprises are much more likely to have formal voice systems in place (e.g. Kersley *et al.* 2006). We know that in small firms the perception of employees of the 'influence gap' is lower (Boxall *et al.* 2007). Formal systems of worker voice are rare, yet worker satisfaction with communication is often relatively high (Forth, Bewley and Bryson 2006). The reason, of course, is that there is likely to be much more personal face-to-face contact between senior management and workers; something which fades rapidly when the workplace gets above 50 employees. This rather forcibly makes the point that big firms tend to be more impersonal, bureaucratic and rule-driven. The social and power distance between the managed and top decision makers is much greater. Formal systems of worker voice can be imagined as antidotes to these tendencies, but it must be doubted how successful they can be unless management themselves give support and bring them to life.

What of indirect schemes such as works councils, employee forums or joint consultative committees? Here the picture is very different and varies significantly between countries. In most of continental Europe, the legal requirement for works councils ensures that such forms of indirect voice are widespread, but not universal. In the USA, they are virtually unheard of but there is evidence of significant growth in the other Anglophone countries in recent years (Boxall *et al.* 2007). The UK, in which joint consultative committees are important, provides comprehensive data from the most recent WERS[3] survey (Kersley *et al.* 2006: 126–32). While they are unusual in small firms (and small firms make up a growing proportion of British firms (*ibid.*: 19)), two thirds of workplaces with 100–199 workers have JCCs, either at the workplace itself or through access to one at a higher corporate level. This figure rises to 72 per cent in respect of workplaces with between 200 and 500 workers and 82 per cent in workplaces with 500 or more employees. Indeed, there is some evidence that in these larger companies the use of JCCs might be spreading. The employers' body, the Confederation of British Industry (CBI), recorded a 10 per cent growth in 'permanent information and consultation bodies' in their annual employment survey in 2006 (*IRS Employment Review* 856, October 2006: 7). One of the most significant features of JCCs is their composition since, as we discuss later in the chapter, management's response to dealing with these consultation forums varies significantly if they are based on union representation or are non-union committees. Overall, in 2004, 11 per cent of JCCs were composed exclusively of union representatives, 67 per cent of them were non-union and a further 22 per cent were mixed with both union and non-union representatives sitting alongside each other in discussions with management (Kersley *et al.* 2006: 131).

Right throughout the Anglo-American world, then, direct forms of employee influence have become more important – particularly in companies

---

3 This is the UK's *Workplace Employment Relations Survey*. Five surveys have been conducted over the last 26 years. They are comprehensive, representative assessments of employee and managerial opinion and financial performance in British workplaces. Arguably, they provide the UK with much better data on the state of its workplace relations than any other country in the world. We use data from these surveys frequently in this chapter and in this book.

trying to meet tougher competition through higher levels of employee skill and commitment. Apart from the USA, indirect forms of employee voice, such as joint consultative committees, are also important. These are typically used to enhance levels of information, consultation and trust in large workplaces and can operate either alongside or instead of trade unions.

What are the impacts of employee voice systems?

There is plenty of evidence that voice arrangements can be no more than 'bolt-ons' which become an additional burden on line managers who fail to provide the necessary support to make them effective (Marchington 1989, 1995). This is particularly clear in the chequered history of quality circles (Collard and Dale 1989, Hill 1991). Here, developing and encouraging employee voice in problem solving can be a fashionable fad, or worse, a sop, with little expected or experienced from its introduction. Not surprisingly, voice systems which are disconnected from organisational decision making, and are irritants to line managers, have a short life.

However, when linked to wider changes in work organisation, as we discussed in Chapter 5, these systems very much form part of the capital O in AMO: the opportunity to participate. We know that employee perceptions of the extent to which they are provided with information by their manager, the degree to which she or he provides a chance to comment and respond to suggestions, is associated with higher levels of job satisfaction and organisational commitment, and these variables are linked to performance (e.g. Appelbaum *et al.* 2000). Millward , Bryson and Forth (2000: 130) show how positive responses in employee attitude surveys on these variables are strongly associated with the existence of direct voice arrangements. Gallie and White (1993: 44), in their large-scale survey of employees in the UK, concluded that:

> Participation is of fundamental importance for employees' attitude to the organisation for which they work. It is strongly related to the way they respond to changes in work organisation and with their perception of the quality of the overall relationship between management and employees.

What Cox, Zagelmeyer and Marchington (2006) call 'embedded' voice systems, where the majority of employees take part in direct schemes and JCC meetings are held regularly, often lead managers in these firms to assert that they produce positive outcomes (Marchington *et al.* 2001). It is more difficult, however, to find hard evidence on the financial performance of voice systems. The crucial variable is *how*, and *to what extent*, line managers support and activate employee involvement as a process. Research which asks if a practice exists, or even what proportion of the workforce is covered by a practice, is not particularly helpful. Structure does not equate with process (Purcell 1999). In the area of voice arrangements, the supporting organisational climate, especially the level of trust, is crucial in providing the seed-bed for effective participation to germinate (Ichniowski, Shaw and Prennushi 1997). There are often hard-to-measure changes over time in the effectiveness of voice processes. While employee financial participation is often associated with positive performance outcomes (see Pendleton (2000, 2006) and Hyman (2000) for reviews of the evidence), Bhargava (1994) suggests that, in respect of profit sharing (which can be a form of voice mechanism if linked to firm ownership), there may be an effect, but it is one-off at the point of implementation and not subsequently. Thus, positive effects can be transitory and restricted to employees who are able to compare the new arrangements with what took place before. New starters can see these developments in a different light and memories have a habit of fading.

Despite the difficulties in evaluating performance effects, we do have some clues if justification is required. Coyle-Shapiro (1999: 45), in a careful time-series study, found that 'the extent of employee involvement is positively related to the assessment of the benefits of TQM'. In particular, and echoing earlier comments on the crucial role of line managers, she found that 'supervisors have a positive role in getting employees involved in TQM' (*ibid.*). Kessler and Purcell (1996) in a study of joint working parties found that, according to both the managers and the employee representatives involved, the level of trust between them increased markedly. This was especially the case where employee representatives, and the employees themselves, were actively involved in all stages of the change process overseen by a joint working party. Where this happened well, over half of the managers considered that their organisation had benefited 'a lot' from this form of involvement.

Research by Sako (1998), on the impact of employee voice in the European car components industry, is particularly interesting. It shows how it is the combination of direct and indirect forms ('dual' voice systems) which has the strongest effect in this industry. She was able to use both 'hard' measures of faulty products and softer attitudinal dimensions in the analysis. Thus, rather than direct and indirect forms of voice systems being alternatives, it was the combination of the two which linked to better operating performance. The outcome effect of combined types of voice arrangements was also clear in a large-scale European survey of participation in the mid-1990s. The greater the forms of participation used, the more likely it was that managers reported benefits from increased output through to declining absenteeism (Sisson 2000). This makes a lot of sense, since different forms of involvement play different roles in different organisational settings and at different levels. It is the climate and style of participation in the organisation as a whole which seems to be crucial, as we shall explain further in the chapter.

In recent years, the search for evidence on the impact of voice systems has changed from a concern with direct 'bottom-line' business outcomes to a focus on the mediating effects on employee attitudes and behaviour which then relate to outcomes such as levels of labour turnover and more 'distal' (or distant) measures of organisational performance. For example, Vandenberg, Richardson and Eastman (1999) found in the insurance industry in North America that employees' perceptions of the quality of involvement processes was related to their job satisfaction and commitment and to the organisation's level of employee turnover and return on equity (see Chapter 5).

The use of surveys of employees, itself a form of upward voice expression, can thus provide good evidence of the impact of different types of voice mechanisms. They can be used to address three important questions. First, to what extent is there a relationship between employee voice and employee job satisfaction and commitment? Second, do surveys show that worker needs or problems are resolved by the use of voice systems? Third, do managements and managers become more responsive to workers when voice systems are in place? We look at each of these in turn, drawing distinctions, where relevant, between direct, indirect and dual voice systems.

Purcell and Georgiades (2007), using the WERS 1998 database of employee and management responses, show that, even when other potential influences on employee attitudes have been controlled for, like the presence of other HR practices, well-embedded voice systems are strongly associated with higher levels of organisational commitment, job satisfaction and the amount of discretion workers say they have in their job. The effect is strongest in relation to direct involvement while indirect systems have a modest link to attitudinal outcomes. However, where direct and indirect voice practices are well embedded, the outcome is 10 per cent stronger than for direct-only systems, thus confirming previous research (for example, Delbridge and Whitfield (2001) who focused on employees' perceptions of their job influence).

These findings are repeated when the question of worker needs or problems is assessed. This approach was adopted in a recent set of studies in the Anglo-American world comparing what workers want and what they experience in voice practices (Freeman, Boxall and Haynes 2007). For example, Bryson and Freeman (2007) show that a combination of JCCs and 'open door' policies reduces the number of needs reported by British employees. Voice systems can allow needs to be expressed and dealt with and can help to minimise the causes of problems. The use of open-door policies, meetings with the workforce, and quality circles or similar problem-solving groups in direct involvement, and JCCs in indirect involvement, seems particularly effective. Interestingly, these authors find that the mere existence of an HR department has no effect in reducing worker needs or problems. It is those HR departments which foster effective systems of employee voice which add better value.

Surveys of employee perceptions of management responsiveness are similarly revealing. In these, the focus is on the extent to which managers seek the views of employees, respond to suggestions, share information, and treat employees fairly. Both Purcell and Georgiades (2007) and Bryson, Charlwood and Forth (2006) find that the experience of direct involvement is closely associated with positive worker evaluations of management responsiveness while the effect of indirect schemes is more muted. Bryson et al. (2006: 448–9) relate responsiveness to productivity. Their data, based on the WERS 2004 survey, show very clearly that managers who report that their firm's labour productivity is much higher than that of their competitors are much more likely to have employees who say that their managers are responsive to worker voice.

We might say that responsiveness is a form of accountability to workers: treating them fairly, giving information and responding to suggestions. Purcell and Georgiades (2007) use WERS 1998 data to show that managers in firms with well-embedded forms of direct involvement are significantly more likely, compared with the year before, to have devolved responsibility for employee relations to supervisors, to have given more importance to employee relations in objective setting, to have provided more information, and to have increased employee influence in decision making. Where well-embedded dual systems of worker voice are present, the effect is even stronger.

A different type of responsiveness is seen in the link between employee voice and the acceptance of change or resistance to it. One of the justifications for the development of voice regimes is that they can contribute to the successful management of change. Employees with voice know more about what needs to happen, and why, and are able to contribute ideas to the change programme. The facilitation of change is sometimes strategically more important than a fixation with bottom-line outcomes (Purcell 1999). In Chapter 1, we referred to the achievement of organisational flexibility as one of the key goals of employers alongside cost-effectiveness, social legitimacy and management autonomy. Employee involvement is clearly critical to the achievement of social legitimacy but there is evidence, too, of its role in the pursuit of flexibility or responsiveness to change. We see this at various levels in the organisational hierarchy. Giangreco and Peccei (2005: 1825) looked at middle managers and their responsiveness to change, reminding us that managers are employees too. They concluded that 'the more deeply involved . . . middle managers were in the various aspects of the development and implementation of the change programme [in the Italian firm they studied], the more positive they were about the change and the lower the level of resistance to change that they exhibited'.

Overall, then, employee voice has a number of critical impacts and we affirm here one of the key themes of this book: HRM needs to serve multiple goals. First and foremost, employee voice institutions are important for reasons of social legitimacy. They help to ensure that companies serve a wider public of 'stakeholders' and not only the economic interests of shareholders. But well-implemented, well-embedded voice practices also have economic value, both in the short run through reducing problems in the workplace and, in the long run, through helping to facilitate the management of change. The economic benefits are more important to firms seeking to compete through higher levels of employee skill and commitment. It is management in these firms which is most likely to see the costs of implementing comprehensive, dual (direct and indirect) systems of employee voice as worth the investment.

Trade unions and change in employee voice

The growth in direct forms of involvement and the legislative preference in Europe for non-union forms of indirect employee voice clearly pose a challenge to trade unions, the traditional vehicle for employee voice. They can also pose dilemmas for management in well-established companies where trade unions have long been recognised as the legitimate representatives of employees, or at least representing union members. This dilemma is especially acute where less than half of employees covered by collective bargaining, the 'bargaining unit', are union members. In these circumstances, should the company set up a consultative committee with representatives directly chosen by the workforce, and how will the union react to this? Alternatively, should management stick with the union, encourage employees to join if they want a voice, and seek to build a 'partnership' to achieve mutual gains? These are very real questions.

Does it make a difference if the management are dealing with union or non-union representatives in JCCs? Recent British evidence could be interpreted as very threatening to trade unions. Bryson (2004: 234) observed that 'in general, non-union voice is more effective than union voice in eliciting managerial responsiveness in British workplaces, and direct voice is more effective than representative voice (whether union or non-union)'. He notes that the combination of non-union representative voice with direct voice is 'more effective (in delivering benefits to employees) than any other voice regime' (*ibid.*). It reduces the number of problems or issues and the desire for unionisation dissipates.

The better success rate of non-union JCCs in dealing with worker needs is explained in a number of interlocking ways. There is clear evidence that union members report more needs and problems than non-union employees and 'on-site union representation engenders greater critical awareness on the part of workers and perhaps increases voice-inducing complaining' (Bryson 2004: 235). Union representatives have much lower levels of trust in management than non-union representatives do and this tends to be reciprocated by management. Trust and distrust is nearly always mutual. A recent test showed that in only 31 per cent of workplaces was there mutual trust between management and union representatives whereas it was double that (64 per cent) where non-union elected representatives held office (Kersley *et al.* 2006: 172). Not surprisingly, in these circumstances, non-union representatives report a higher level of collaborative working with management than their union counterparts. They work more closely with management over change, and report that management is more inclined to value representatives' opinions and share information (*ibid.*: 170). Managers tend to discuss a much wider range of issues, such as production issues and future plans, with non-union representatives than they do with union reps (*ibid.*: 165). One of the reasons for this may be that employee forums made up of directly elected representatives usually cover the whole workplace, representing everyone. Union representatives will be concerned to look after the interests of their members and negotiate on their behalf in collective bargaining. This tends to be more of an issue in the Anglophone world than in continental Europe where there is a much clearer separation between the union role in collective bargaining and employee representation in the workplace through the works council. Labour law in Germany, for example, requires cooperative working between the works councillors and management.

The British evidence is that managers are much more likely to be working in relatively low-trust, adversarial environments when dealing with union representatives than they are when interacting with non-union representatives. We are not suggesting that it is unions which primarily cause low levels of trust. Indeed, most evidence points to management as the dominant force in creating collaborative or adversarial employee relations. The choice of employee relations styles is largely, but not entirely, in management hands (Purcell 1987). There is a paradox here for trade unions. Union shop stewards have relatively low levels of trust in management and spend more time in dealing with disputes than non-union representatives, yet seem to be less effective at resolving issues as reported by employees. While there is some evidence of more collaborative working between British management and union representatives in 2004 compared with 1998 (Kersley *et al.* 2006: 170), it is still at a low level compared with the way managements deal with non-union representatives. This, of course, may be deliberate since non-union systems can be used as union substitution devices (Purcell and Georgiades 2007).

It would, however, be folly for management to ignore trade unions in countries like the UK where just under half of employees work in places where a union is recognised (Kersley *et al.* 2006: 120). In the public sector, this is true for 92 per cent of employees while, in the private sector, one third are covered by collective bargaining (*ibid.*). Union membership may be stabilising after 25 years of continuous decline (*ibid.*: 143). The number of employers recognising trade unions has been growing in the UK, partly in response to the introduction of legal rights supporting recognition in certain circumstances (Gall 2004).

The attitude of management toward unions is a crucial dimension in explaining how successful unions are in recruiting and keeping members. Kersley *et al.* (2006: 113) show that 60 per cent of the more than 2,000 managers they interviewed for WERS 2004 were neutral about union membership while just under a quarter were either in favour or actively encouraged membership. Only 3 per cent actively discouraged union membership. Where managers were in favour, or proactively supportive, around 60 per cent of employees belonged to the union. Where membership was discouraged, membership was around the 5 per cent mark (*ibid.*: 114).

Shifts in union strategy?

Unions themselves have been changing in the way they see their role in the global economy. In a review of the role of trade unions at the time of the 1997 general election, when the Labour government came to power, the British Trades Union Congress (TUC), representing all major unions, said 'trade unions must not be seen as part of Britain's problems but as part of the solution to the country's problems' (TUC 1997: 1). The title of this authoritative publication was *Partners For Progress*. Since then, 'partnership' has become widely accepted in the lexicon of industrial relations, and has been implemented in some workplaces, although it is impossible to say how many. As a rhetoric, it is very powerful, implying a major shift toward a less adversarial, more cooperative relationship with employers (Haynes and Allen 2000). In its idealised form, as Tailby and Winchester (2000: 365) put it, 'a qualitatively different form of indirect participation or employee representation . . . offers each of the parties significant gains: employers are able to secure a greater degree of job flexibility and stronger commitment of employees and union representatives to organisational goals; trade unions are offered a more cooperative form of involvement in enterprise-level employment regulation; and employees are promised greater employment security and the opportunity to participate in new forms of consultation'.

This type of partnership, if possible and sustainable, stands in marked contrast to the historic role of unions (which is why some sceptical managers – and employees – doubt 'partnership' since 'the leopard cannot change its spots'). Unions which fail to perceive that a changing context calls for a shift in strategy can sometimes be by-passed. Storey (1993: 544) recalls the comment of a senior manager in the Rover Motor Company at the time of its major rescue restructuring in 1991–92: 'Unions were invited to the party but they didn't want to come. So the party went ahead without them'. Subsequently, the unions did accept the invitation and the company concluded that it was foolish to try to exclude them. Many trade unions representing workers in private sector firms have discovered that fighting to preserve the existing rules and structures is rendered especially hard in a more globalised economy. If union power is only a function of the propensity to go on strike, then fear of offshoring and plant shut-down emasculates this.

But union influence is more than the imposition of veto power to stop change occurring. Despite the stereotypical imagery of conflict and adversarialism, there have always been examples of 'integrative bargaining' and collaborative relationships between unions and employers (Walton and McKersie 1965). This was evident in the era of productivity bargaining in the 1960s and 1970s in the UK (McKersie and Hunter 1973). What is different now, and it is this which helps explain the change to the language of 'partnership' and 'being part of the solution', is that the traditional union roles of job protection through restrictive work rules and gaining above-average pay rises through collective bargaining have been eroded. What is left is what Freedman and Medoff (1984) call 'voice-response interaction': that is, dialogue and discussion with management about the operation of the firm in general and the management of people in particular. Union roles are depicted in Figure 6.4.

The ability of unions to gain 'monopoly' power in wage bargaining (the top line in Figure 6.4) has been reduced as the coverage of collective bargaining has shrunk and more contracts of employment have been individualised (Brown *et al.* 1998). The dilemma, too, as the model makes clear, is that there is often a trade-off between pay and jobs. Higher labour costs, unless these can be passed on to the customer, make it more attractive to move work overseas and/or invest in labour-saving technologies and work methods which increase productivity. The middle line in Figure 6.4, showing restrictive work practices and 'featherbedding', was common in the 1960s and 70s in established manufacturing firms and in whole sectors like the newspaper industry (Martin 1981) and the waterfront where 'custom and practice', or what were rather oddly called 'Spanish customs', controlled actual hours of work, who did what job, and restricted the adoption of new technology (Turnbull, Woolfson and Kelly 1992). Many of these practices have been

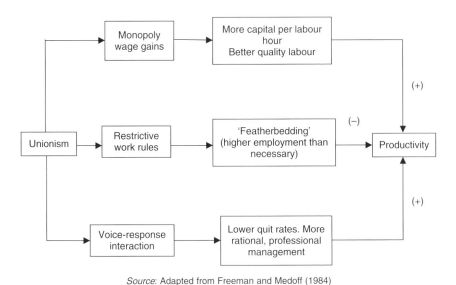

Source: Adapted from Freeman and Medoff (1984)

Figure 6.4 What unions do

swept away in the last 30 years, either because of the virtual collapse of the industry, as in ship-building, or by new entrants to the market able to utilise the opportunities of greenfield sites, as we explained in Chapter 5. In other cases, change has been imposed on the workforce, as in the fire service in the UK in 2003. There are relatively few places left where such controls remain.

The type of transformational change required to sweep away restrictive practices has sometimes been achieved by union de-recognition, for example by the Murdoch newspapers. More often, it has been the outcome of painful and protracted negotiations with trade unions leading to agreements establishing 'full flexibility' with management. These agreements have achieved or regained the right to design jobs and allocate labour: in other words, they have allowed a rediscovery of the management prerogative. This process is particularly evident in sectors where global competitive pressures have intensified, but it is not universal. In the public sector, for example in teaching and health services, union roles have changed more slowly and adversarial industrial relations remains the norm. Here, where public funding is constrained and governments take the key decisions, rather than local managers, adversarialism can remain the only avenue for unions to exert influence (Boxall and Haynes 1997).

The bottom line of Figure 6.4 is more diffuse and ambiguous and is centred on the union role in having a positive voice, responding to management proposals in consultative forums, and working with management on change agendas. This is where 'partnership' fits in since, if the relationships remain marked by distrust and adversarial posturing by either, and therefore nearly always by both sides, management is unlikely to discuss proposed changes and will not be prepared to listen. Unions in these circumstances will be unwilling to discuss proposed changes without knowing the price beforehand in terms of pay and job security. In effect, with the collapse of unions' traditional roles in many, but not all sectors, they are left with a difficult choice of either being marginalised and continuing to lose members, or of seeking new forms of relationship based on cooperation and joint problem solving. This presupposes that management is willing to accept a joint philosophy and work to make it meaningful (Haynes and Allen 2000). It is management's response which is critical here. It is extremely difficult for unions to insist on a high level of cooperation or a climate of 'partnership' (Boxall and Haynes 1997).

Underlying this new focus on unions as productive transmitters of employee voice is an economic need for a greater emphasis on organisational survival and flexibility. The old industrial relations was more about defending management control within a fundamentally profitable regime: gaining agreements to keep the production system going and minimising disruptive conflict. Management needed to make marginal adjustments in terms and conditions of employment and in responding to worker disquiet while preserving managerial prerogatives as far as possible at what was sometimes called the 'frontier of control' (Goodrich 1975). All of the partnership deals analysed by Marks *et al.* (1998), Haynes and Allen (2000), Tailby and Winchester (2000) and Martínez Lucio and Stuart (2004) have been about the management of major change. However, the outcomes have been mixed. Partnership is not the panacea portrayed by politicians hoping to engender a 'new' social contract but, like much else, is dependent on the mix of circumstances and beliefs, especially the mutual need for viability or survival.

The fundamental question in unionised work settings is how far the union representatives should be 'invited to the party' (included) or, as critics on the left would say, 'incorporated' in the change process. Or should unions be by-passed with change imposed by management? This requires unions to decide how far they can go in working with management's change agenda. Both parties in change and restructuring have to choose between what Walton, Cutcher-Gershenfeld and McKersie (1994) call 'fostering' and 'forcing' strategies or a subtle mixture of both (Figure 6.5). Sometimes the strategy for the employer may be 'escaping' through plant relocation and the threat of this can also be part of a forcing strategy.

Fostering and forcing as strategies are not simply about the nature of union–management relations but cover management's relationships with individual employees, with different degrees of emphasis placed on obtaining behavioural 'compliance' and generating employee 'commitment'. Walton *et al.* (1994) call the patterns that emerge from these choices 'social contracts' and suggest that, when management wants a social contract based on high individual commitment and strong labour–management cooperation, it will be likely to emphasise fostering in industrial relations, although there may be elements of forcing in order to kick-start the change process.

Walton *et al.* (1994) suggest that an employer will be likely to adopt a forcing strategy, as in the British fire service in 2003, when major, dramatic changes are required and when they believe there is no point in extended dialogue with the unions (Figure 6.5). Management also has to believe it can win, or has the resources to survive a long, drawn-out battle to destroy labour resistance. Fostering strategies typically focus on the need for a move to new ways of working that require, or are predicated on employees embracing high-involvement work practices, as described in Chapter 5. Here the presumed union role is one of helping the management of change. The union stands to gain in terms of greater institutional security,

	Conditions that promote	
	Forcing	Fostering
Objectives of initiating party (management)		
Priority for and ambitiousness of substantive change?	High*	Low
Priority for improvement in social contract?	Low*	High
Expected responses (labour)		
Labour expected to be persuaded by business rationale?	Unpersuaded*	Persuaded
Labour believed to be receptive to social contract changes sought by management?	Unreceptive*	Receptive
Power equation		
Management confident it can force substantive change?	Confident*+	_ ‡

* The more strongly these conditions are fulfilled, the more likely there will be *unrestrained* forcing.
+ When labour and management are both confident of their power, *unrestrained* forcing becomes even more likely.
‡ No hypothesis for this power condition and fostering.

Source: Walton, Cutcher-Gershenfeld and Mckersie (1994: 57)

Figure 6.5　Conditions that affect choices to force and foster: Walton *et al.*'s propositions

better consultation and a greater role in supporting skill formation. It may gain some guarantees of employment security although this is now much less likely. Thus, in forcing, the union is seen to be the blocker of change while, in fostering, its role is legitimised by management as an ally in the process of change.

Unions, then, are faced with a new context which calls for new strategic thinking. To some extent, they still have their traditional business in sectors where wages are low, conditions poor and management is resistant to independent employee voice and in the budget-constrained, conflict-prone parts of the public sector (Boxall *et al.* 2007). However, they also need to develop a new business model, to reinvent themselves in industries in which management and employees have embraced new voice practices and moved on to a more development-oriented agenda, as we shall explain further in Chapter 7. For its part, management needs to avoid stereotyping of trade unions. Each union needs to be judged on its own merits. Has it shifted in terms of its strategic orientation and to what extent is it in tune with the aspirations of the contemporary workforce?

Management style in employee relations

This discussion of choices in relations with unions and in the management of change leads to the most fundamental managerial question in the realm of employee voice. What sort of management style does the company want with its employees? Management style can be defined as 'a distinctive set of guiding principles, written or otherwise, which set parameters to, and signposts for, management action regarding the way employees are treated and how particular events are handled' (Purcell and Ahlstrand 1994: 177).

A highly consistent management style is an attribute of 'strong' HR systems (Bowen and Ostroff 2004). This includes the role of line managers in engaging in supportive behaviour and being responsive to employees in the 'leader-member exchange' (Uhl-Bien, Graen and Scandura 2000). It cannot be assumed that what top management seeks in terms of management style in employee voice will necessarily be enacted by middle and line managers. The fundamental role of such managers in 'bringing policies to life' is increasingly recognised (Purcell and Hutchinson 2007), as explained in Chapter 5. Batt (2004: 206–7) provides a vivid illustration of this point where a successful initiative introducing self-managing teams, measured in terms of economic benefits, was abandoned because 'the voluntary cooperation of supervisors and middle managers was not forthcoming'. These front-line managers felt threatened. In the ensuing company politics, the cost of pushing through worker voice in the form or autonomous teams, even though it had great benefits, was too high when opposed by them. Such an illustration reinforces the point that employee voice is as much about politics and power within management, as it is about economic rationality.

It is top management who should make the critical design choices on what sort of relationships they want with employees directly, with trade unions, and with employee representatives in works councils and JCCs. That is, choices in voice arrangements, while to a greater or lesser extent constrained by legislation and wider beliefs on legitimacy, need to be taken by senior management. Do they wish to avoid, live with, or embrace forms of partnership with representatives and with employees directly? The way these systems of involvement, participation and negotiation are designed and operated is at the heart of management style. Relationships with unions (and to a lesser extent with works councils and JCCs) range along a continuum from avoidance to high levels of cooperation (Boxall and Haynes 1997). Some, often American firms, seek to avoid all forms of collective worker representation. Others have to come to terms with unions that have gained recognition, or reluctantly accept the JCC imposed by law, but choose to do so with a minimal level of interaction: a 'hands-off' approach. A third group is more positive, seeking collaborative working with employee representatives, providing information, valuing their opinion and working closely in the management of change.

These choices are strongly mediated by the type of line-manager behaviour expressed in the way individual workers are managed. In crude terms, the choice is between a 'command and control' style and a commitment-oriented one. It is here that the extent of direct employee involvement comes into play. We have noted that this is more likely to be extensive where workers are highly skilled and where their cooperation is critical to the achievement of strategic objectives. Here, high-involvement, high-commitment management is more likely to be found. In contrast, where labour is easily recruited, where investment in terms of training and skill formation is low, and where work is repetitive with short job-cycle times, a command and control style of managing individual workers may predominate.

Figure 6.6 shows the main choices. Choices in such countries as the Netherlands or Sweden, with long traditions and acceptance of collective worker representation, may well be different from those taken by the same type of firm in the USA or the UK. While the figure stylistically describes six distinctive management styles, in practice each of the axes is a continuum and, as we argued in Chapter 3, all styles are the outcome of the complex interplay of tensions and choices between conflicting demands.

Organisations operating with an avoidance strategy, seeking to prevent trade unionism and trivialise legislative voice systems, do so either by forceful opposition (Box 1) or by competition in the sense of preferring to provide very competitive conditions of employment and extensive use of direct voice

Commitment/ Involvement		Individual-based high-commitment management Extensive direct voice systems *Box 2*	Emphasis on high-commitment management and direct voice Hands-off relationship with representatives Low trust of external unions *Box 4*	High-commitment management Partnership with unions or non-union representatives Extensive direct and indirect voice systems High trust *Box 6*
Relationship with employees				
	Command/ Control	Low trust No voice *Box 1*	Low trust Restricted voice Conflict *Box 3*	Emasculated representatives No real voice 'Sweetheart unionism' *Box 5*

Avoidance   Adversarial   Cooperative

Relationship with trade unions and elected works councils / JCCs

Figure 6.6 Voice systems and management style

arrangements (Box 2). The former, described by Guest (1995) as 'black hole' firms, have neither high-commitment policies in their relationship with their employees, nor any industrial relations policies of working with trade unions. Most typically, these firms will utilise low-skill employees and minimise investment in people, as seen in low pay, little training and little job discretion. Box 2 firms, like management consultancy organisations or software houses, place emphasis on human capital and knowledge management, seeking to get the best out of their core employees and emphasising policies which encourage high performance and retention of the best. They eschew any form of collective representation but emphasise direct voice through e-mail, intranet, employee surveys and regular management meetings.

Boxes 3 and 4 include companies caught in adversarial, hands-off relationships with trade unions. Traditional patterns of conflict, and Scientific Management control systems, are found in Box 3. These still exist in some manufacturing companies (especially in developing countries), in parts of the public sector and in parts of the service economy like routine, short-transaction call centres. While formal methods of consultation may exist at corporate and workplace levels, they are generally seen to be ineffective, being marked by distrust and posturing.

Box 4 organisations are usually in transition. While formal relationships with trade unions or works councils are marked with distrust and a failure by each party to communicate effectively with each other, direct forms of voice are used, often to by-pass and undermine the unions while work organisation places emphasis on HIWSs. It is here that non-union JCCs can be created as a union substitution device in the hope that union membership will fade away. Box 5 is where work organisation is traditionally 'command and control' but relationships with unions or works councils are cooperative. This is sometimes called 'sweetheart unionism' and exists where the union is concerned more with its own survival, or its representatives with their own career and benefits, than with fighting for their members' interests. Collective voice systems are shallow. While examples are rare, they are most likely to be found where company unions or staff associations exist, in part to keep out external unions. Some JCCs designed more as union substitution mechanisms than effective involvement channels fit here since listening to employee voice is not seen as a necessary feature of management behaviour.

Box 6 firms exhibit strong voice arrangements, combining both direct and indirect arrangements. It is likely that a wide variety of schemes operate in tandem and are embedded in a bundle of HR practices which encourage high involvement and employee well-being. The leading HIWS adopters, described in Chapter 5, have these types of voice arrangements, especially those that recognise trade unions and where union–management 'partnership' is accepted as appropriate.

Management styles, like the organisational culture of which they are a part, evolve over time but once established become difficult to change radically since it is hard to eradicate embedded assumptions and values held by employees and key groups such as middle managers (Martin 1992, Legge 1995). They set the parameters of 'how we do things here'. Studies in supermarkets by Rosenthal, Hill and Peccei (1997) and Ogbonna and Harris (1998) show the difficulties that planned cultural change programmes can run into. The assumption that senior management has the power to easily change workplace culture is severely challenged in such studies.

Conclusions

A critical choice at the heart of HR strategy in any firm concerns the extent to which employees are considered central to the achievement of firm performance or are deemed peripheral. In any review of HR strategy, this is an issue which senior management should consider very seriously. Particular employee voice arrangements will be deeply influenced by senior management's values in this respect and by what line managers actually do in practice. The more central are employees, the more likely voice – involvement and participation in management decisions – will need to be developed, and the more likely management will be to see the need to do so within the societal context in which the firm operates. This may include direct means, or indirect means through employee representatives, or both in combination. Employee voice practices are highly relevant for those firms which see employee initiative and innovation as central to their business strategy. On the other hand, where employees are more like a factor of production to be controlled, with labour costs minimised, employer incentives to engage in voice activities with them are often minimal.

However, we have emphasised in this chapter that it is important not to create the impression that voice arrangements are solely about the economic performance of firms. The beliefs and values of employees, and of the society of which they are part, provide a crucial extra dimension. Few voice systems and positive union–management relations will exist, or exist for long, unless they are valued in their own right as legitimate and morally necessary activities *irrespective* of economic outcomes. They are there for reasons of social legitimacy.

Such beliefs and value systems amongst the powerful in society can vary from one generation to another and from one society to another. The move to market individualism or neo-liberalism in the last two decades of the previous century, especially in Anglo-American societies, has challenged notions of legitimacy, especially in regard to the role of trade unions (Boxall and Haynes 1997). Now, in the UK, as a part of Europe, there is a renewed emphasis on the rights of employees, especially a right to have a voice in the affairs of the company for which they work (Purcell and Georgiades 2007).

Legislation, to be effective, needs to have a catalytic effect on beliefs and values, especially on those of the managers who are required to share power and to be accountable to their subordinates, as in most voice systems. The growth in partnership arrangements may be one clue to a change in perspective in some British and Irish companies but, in general, it is much too early to say whether underlying changes in values and beliefs are occurring or what form they might take.

The development of voice systems giving employees access to, and involvement in, management decisions is dependent, then, on strategic choices at both national and organisational levels. Historically, many employers have opposed legislation yet adapted to it as a political expedient. Taken in isolation, and grudgingly accommodated, voice systems have little impact, or can become a focus for negative adversarial relationships between management and labour. On the other hand, seen as an important ingredient in high-involvement models of human resource management, employee voice can positively influence the way people are managed and impact on their sense of commitment to the organisation.

Questions of employee voice are ethical choices with profound implications for every other aspect of HR policy. There are many ways in which they can be approached, as we have reviewed in this chapter. For those seeking to compete through a high level of employee skill and commitment, evidence points to the way in which well-embedded, dual channels of employee voice (using direct and indirect practices), appropriately integrated, can bring positive outcomes for both the organisation and its members. Trust is critical here and it is this, or rather the lack of it, which limits the effectiveness of dual systems of worker voice. To build trust, senior executives need to be clear on the fundamental style of employee relations, or the preferred ways of providing people with a voice, that should be adopted in their firm and they need to build high levels of consistency within the whole management team, as we shall argue in Chapter 8.

7

Managing individual performance and commitment

Chapters 5 and 6 explored principles associated with the organisation of work and with the management of employee voice. These two chapters deal with a lot that is inherently collective in the workplace or which sets the context into which individuals are hired. We turn now to issues associated with managing *individual* performance and commitment within this framework. Without compromising the importance of the specific contexts in which the organisation is located, what guiding principles might inform the management of individuals in the firm? Performance and commitment are words which summarise two key variables that are of importance where individual employees are concerned. Employers are looking for some kind of performance and are seeking some degree of commitment. How much they seek of each, and how much they get, are quite variable.

Traditional personnel management (now sometimes called 'micro' HRM (Boxall, Purcell and Wright 2007b)) and the discipline of industrial psychology have always been concerned with managing individuals within the given structure of the firm's work systems and its employee relations style. The focus (or 'level of analysis') has usually been on how to use individual HR practices (such as particular selection, appraisal or training techniques) to build employee performance and/or commitment. Textbooks in this tradition typically cover a range of practices across the 'individual human resource cycle', a framework based on the idea that most employment relationships are intended to be long-term (Figure 7.1). This is very often true for those employees management deems to hold core, strategic value, as discussed in Chapter 4. The cycle of employing and managing such individuals includes a trail of techniques stretching from job analysis through selection, pay, appraisal, training and so on. In most cases, the performance

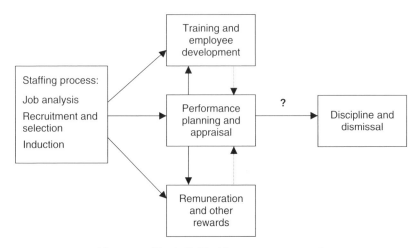

Figure 7.1 The individual human resource cycle

of the individuals recruited is acceptable or better and the cycle is concerned with the links from performance appraisal to training, to remuneration, and to other forms of reward (such as promotion systems). However, in some cases, performance management will identify the sort of poor performance or misconduct that leads to discipline and, in some cases, dismissal.

Those readers wanting an in-depth commentary on particular practices within the individual human resource cycle should consult one of the books available in their home country. As we emphasised in Chapter 3, different countries have different laws and institutions in the labour market and their people often approach the same employment practices from different cultural values and assumptions. Our interest in this chapter is with the critical, underlying principles or connecting theory as one passes through these HR sub-functions. This is important for general managers and any other managers, including HR specialists, wanting to participate in the strategic debate in the firm. We need underpinning theory on the management of individual performance and commitment to enable senior managers to take a more strategic approach to the management of people in the firm. What theory will help firms to attract and manage human capital more intelligently?

The performance equation

If we are concerned to manage individual human performance more effectively, we should actually start with a model of human performance. In

Chapter 1, we referred to the 'AMO' framework. This argues that individual performance is some function of the individual's abilities, motivation, and their opportunity to perform in the specific context (which covers factors like the quality of resources available and the channels for influencing management decisions discussed in Chapter 6):

$$P = f(A,M,O)$$

On the colloquial level, this model has been around for a long time. Academically, a more formal version of AMO theory can be found in the work of the industrial psychologists, Campbell *et al.* (1993) (Figure 7.2). In this model, ability is broken down into 'declarative' knowledge (what we know about things) and 'procedural knowledge and skill' (how we actually go about things). The elements of motivation are also usefully identified. They include the choice to perform, the level of effort applied and the degree of persistence. However, the role of 'opportunity' is not clearly acknowledged. Like Blumberg and Pringle (1982), we think it is important to have an O factor in the equation because this helps to make the point that individual performance is embedded in a context. To be sure, individual attributes have a huge impact but even the most able and motivated people cannot perform well if they lack 'the tools to finish the job'[1] or work in an unsupportive social environment.

What, then, are the implications of the performance equation? For one thing, it clearly reminds us that firms should aim to hire, develop and retain 'motivated capability': people who have the *can do* (ability or capability) and the *will do* (motivational) factors relevant to the job. From this basic premise, some authors have developed broad-brush typologies of human performance

---

$P = f$ {Declarative Knowledge} × {Procedural Knowledge and Skill} × {Motivation}

Facts	Cognitive skill	Choice to perform
Principles	Psychomotor skill	Level of effort
Goals	Physical skill	Persistence of effort
Self-knowledge	Self-management skill	
	Interpersonal skill	

Source: Campbell *et al.* (1993)

Figure 7.2   Determinants of job performance

---

1 One of war-time Prime Minister, Winston Churchill's most famous pleas was: 'Give us the tools and we'll finish the job'. British motivation was not in question but resources were certainly scarce.

to assist employee development and succession management activities. One such model, adapted from Odiorne's (1985) 'human resources portfolio', is shown in Figure 7.3. The implicit argument here is that performance management and employee development needs to be adjusted to handle different individual types effectively. All firms need some blend of 'stars' and 'solid citizens' while aiming to minimise the numbers who fall into the problematic categories – 'marginal performers' and 'chronic under-achievers'. Star employees have the sort of qualities that are important for innovation and path-finding. In knowledge-intensive industries, such individuals can make a disproportionate impact, as is increasingly recognised in what some call the global 'war for talent' (e.g. Wooldridge 2006). It thus pays to think very carefully about their rewards, development and retention.

Stars	*Ability*: advanced, highly respected technical experts, very capable general managers or highly creative business winners; over time, perceived as having star abilities by most people in the workplace and possibly the industry.
	Motivation: always operate with the necessary motivation; often capable of several periods of outstanding achievement in a single year; but may be vulnerable to 'burnout' and 'workaholism'.
Solid citizens	*Ability*: possess valued technical or managerial know-how related to established business operations; help to ensure the organisation can reliably deliver what it has promised its customers.
	Motivation: always operate with the necessary motivation; generally capable of sustaining performance through some periods of high pressure in a single year.
Marginal performers	*Ability*: could be generally adequate but not able to handle high-pressure situations or weak in a couple of critical performance domains; or slightly below most performance standards but capable of improvement through greater personal efforts to improve know-how.
	Motivation: may be inconsistent in motivation ('blowing hot and cold'); or generally motivated but occasionally depressed.
Chronic under-achievers	*Ability*: may have misrepresented their abilities at recruitment; or may be carrying major intellectual or emotional weaknesses which have never been appropriately dealt with; or may be an example of the 'Peter Principle' (promoted to the level of their incompetence).
	Motivation: may be seriously depressed; or annoyingly inconsistent in motivation; or perversely motivated; or may be highly motivated but unable to bridge major gaps in their experience and abilities.

Source: Adapted from Odiorne (1985)

Figure 7.3 A typology of performance types

Solid citizens are also vital: they make things happen reliably once direction has been decided. This should never be underestimated because customers want to deal with companies that deliver on promises. The idea of an 'all star' company is therefore impractical. Firms need to manage *both* change *and* stability: they need to find a way forward while also reaping the profits to be made in a given context (Boxall 1998). A high-performing team is much more likely to exhibit a blend of team roles, as Belbin (1981) demonstrated (see Chapter 2).

The sort of model shown in Figure 7.3 is sometimes used by firms to map the talent they have in particular teams, and plan their employee development and retention strategies accordingly. Figure 7.3 is not, however, a precise framework. It is simply a loose approximation to reality. Reality is always more complex. While recognising the important role of ability and motivation, we ought to base our conceptions of how to manage individuals on a more secure footing. Our concern in the rest of the chapter is to outline theory and research that can assist.

Managing employee ability

Levels and types of ability vary enormously across the human population. Research consistently demonstrates the huge impact of intelligence or 'general cognitive ability' on performance (Hunter and Hunter 1984, Judge *et al.* 1999, Hunter *et al.* 2000). Besides intelligence, education and life (including work) experience make key impacts on a person's abilities. Except in cases of very discouraging or traumatised backgrounds, more intelligent people secure a better education and gravitate towards more demanding work (Baumeister and Bacharach 2000). The process of tackling more challenging work develops their abilities further, increasing their value to potential employers and thus further enhancing their advantages over others. It is not surprising that more intelligent people earn more and get promoted more often (Judge *et al.* 1999, Baumeister and Bacharach 2000). They may not be happier with the intrinsic dimensions of their work or less stressed, something we shall explore further below, but they do get employed in more complex and better paid work.

The crucial role of recruitment and selection

When one looks at the size of the recruitment industry around the world, it seems that practitioners act as if recruitment and selection is the most important human resource function. The research on the critical role of ability in explaining performance suggests they are *not* wrong to do so. Failure to recruit workers with appropriate competencies will doom the firm to failure or, at the very least, to stunted growth. Firms need to attract and nurture people with the kind of abilities that will make the firm productive in its chosen industry.

While firms should aim to recruit effectively at all levels of ability, the need to recruit astutely is particularly important where higher levels of discretion or specialised blends of skills are required in the work. As job complexity increases, so does the range of human performance (Hunter, Schmidt and Judiesch 1990). Thus, as we move up from low-complexity work (such as routine clerical work) to jobs where greater ambiguity is involved in decision making, differences in skills and judgement become more pronounced and are more consequential for the organisation. It is quite possible for one professional, such as a lawyer or an IT consultant, to be several times better than another at the same task. The phenomenon of large performance variation is also commonly recognised in sales work, such as insurance sales (Hunter *et al.* 1990). Some people simply lack the blend of cognitive abilities and personality traits needed (such as a friendly manner plus the ability to close the sales deal) and should not be recruited at all. Among those who do have the threshold abilities, the performance range will still be enormous. In Anglo-American countries, at least, firms commonly find they need 'sales compensation packages' which allow high achievers to earn a higher pay packet better linked to their personal productivity.

Recognising the crucial role of ability in performance, the literature on recruitment and selection is vast. Our concern is not to summarise it but to point to underlying principles. In terms of highlighting the key messages in this literature, it is important to make a distinction between selection practices and recruitment strategies. Selection is about choosing among job candidates. It is about how to make fair and relevant assessments of the strengths and weaknesses of applicants. It is concerned with the value of particular selection techniques. Recruitment strategy is best understood as the way in which a firm tries to source or attract the people among whom it will ultimately make selections. Recruitment strategies include attempts to make the organisation an attractive place to work and attempts to reach better pools of candidates. Recruitment or attraction strategies are now critical in globalised industries where there is a shortage of top talent (Wooldridge 2006).

As has been noted before in this book (Chapter 3), the literature on selection is an area where concepts of 'best practice' do have a logical place, as long as we bear in mind that such concepts are embedded in a cultural context. In the Anglo-American context, the fundamental issue is how to make selection more 'valid': how to define performance appropriately and how to use techniques that improve the ability of firms to predict which individuals will be good performers (e.g. Rynes, Barber and Varma 2000, Schmitt and Kim 2007). Hardly anyone would recommend unstructured interviews over interviews where questions have been based on a careful job analysis or over the use of work sample or cognitive ability tests. Across a variety of jobs, the selection literature offers valuable insights into how the process can be made more effective for employers and fairer for job candidates.

The focus of the recruitment literature is somewhat different. The literature here has many more gaps (for recent reviews, see Taylor and Collins 2000, Orlitzky 2007) and the notion of 'recruitment strategy' needs further development. One of the few papers in the area which is useful for considering the strategic questions was written by Windolf (1986). Windolf identifies the task of profiling the ideal kind of candidate and the choice of recruitment channels (among search, advertisements, networking etc) as key dimensions of recruitment strategy. We would add a third dimension to these: the quantity and quality of inducements offered to job candidates. Some firms are powerful recruiters because they are sufficiently well-resourced to be able to pay wage premia, which increases their ability to pick and choose in the labour market (Guthrie 2007). The capacity to offer better pay and greater internal development makes it easier for firms to build high-involvement work systems and out-compete under-capitalised firms (see Chapters 5 and 9). Some firms competing for scarce talent are developing an 'employment value proposition': a formal statement of the particular benefits they can offer potential recruits (Wooldridge 2006: 16). This may include superior pay, training and career opportunities but can also extend to such things as the company's reputation for social responsibility (Orlitzky 2007).

Recognising the need to identify what the firm offers by way of inducements, we find the typology of recruitment strategies developed by Windolf (1986: 238–46) a useful framework. An adapted version is shown in Figure 7.4. Firms vary in their labour market power (the vertical axis). They also vary in the extent to which management is creative and proactive in forming and reviewing recruitment strategies (the horizontal axis). This framework usefully makes the point that some firms ('status quo' recruiters) have resource advantages but do not use them thoughtfully. Their recruitment practices tend to be conservative, often recruiting from the same

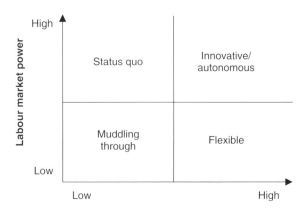

Source: Windolf (1986: 239)

Figure 7.4 A typology of recruitment strategies

social strata and age groups without challenging the way this can discriminate against certain kinds of job seekers. One the other hand, 'innovative' firms attempt to recruit talented people who can help them develop a stream of new products and processes. They therefore use all possible channels to generate a 'heterogenous group of applicants'. Another proactive type, the 'autonomous' firm, plans very carefully for all types of recruitment and aims to 'cream off' the best candidates whatever the condition of the labour market. Most firms classified as 'muddling through' or 'flexible' are small or medium-sized and cannot offer above average conditions. They do gain some power in slack labour markets but face serious difficulties when labour markets are tight. The two types of firm are differentiated on the basis of the HR expertise they bring to their problems. Flexible firms are more thoughtful: they make more astute use of what little power they have.

The key implication of Windolf's (1986) framework is that firms have something to gain from more creative use of their resources. This is particularly so for small firms competing against much better-resourced rivals. As a general rule, more proactive employers do better in tight labour markets. At the present time, this may include opening up channels for workers over the age of 50. A lot of companies, including many which are well-resourced, still imagine recruitment to be about attracting young workers, fresh from colleges, or after only a few years in the labour market. Such conservatism is out-of-step with the rise in the average age of the workforce and with the fact that age discrimination is increasingly illegal in developed economies. Similarly, the more creative companies have become better at sourcing talent internationally. This includes outsourcing activities to countries such as India – for example, in software engineering – and opening branches internationally to build the firm's human capital pool in growth markets (Wooldridge 2006).

It is also outdated to think that firms can always recruit exactly the experience they want in individuals. Sometimes they can but this should not always be the primary focus of the recruiter. Providing candidates have the base-line qualifications needed in the role, a more creative approach is to focus on hiring the underlying characteristics and potential of individuals. If trying to build a strong core of workers around whom a high-involvement work system will be based, or if trying to create 'organisational agility', it is important to recruit for long-run adaptability (see Chapter 9). Specific know-how of company routines can be developed over time if the individual has the ability to learn, the motivation to keep learning, and the willingness to work cooperatively with others.

The complementary role of training and development

This discussion of the crucial role of recruitment and selection ('buy') helps to put training and development ('make') in its context. As our discussion indicates, 'make' cannot be a total alternative to 'buy'. This is obviously true on quantitative grounds: at some point, there has to be an inflow of talent even in companies with extensive 'internal labour markets'. More importantly, it is true on qualitative grounds. Given the fact of major ability differences in the population, which companies can rarely compensate for, training should be seen as a complement to, rather than a substitute for, careful recruitment.

Having said this, all companies have something to gain from encouraging informal and incidental learning on the job (Marsick and Watkins 1990, Hendry, Arthur and Jones 1995). Besides encouraging individuals to try new things and thus learn by trial-and-error, it is typical to expose new workers to the skills of experienced performers. This approach is sometimes colloquially referred to as the 'SBN' system – 'sit by Nellie' (with the sub-text: 'and do what she does').[2] This may be complemented by some formal on- and/or off-the-job training in technical skills where the expense can be justified by

---

2 For an historical reference to the role of 'Nellie' in employee training, see Crichton (1968: 33–4).

the fact that such skills are needed for acceptable job performance. Much training in the use of new computer software is of this nature.

Informal learning and short-run training are probably the most common approach among small firms in English-speaking countries. The expense is kept down and the costs of losing good workers through 'poaching' – an ever-present risk in tight labour markets – is minimised. The overall approach is often described as a 'deficit model' (simply based on bridging obvious performance gaps). It is wrong to criticise small firms for this kind of pragmatic attitude to training investment. They are acting in an economically rational manner and the problem of under-investing in employee development lies in wider national and industry institutions over which they have no control (e.g. Lane 1990, Winterton 2007).

The opportunity to use education and training more powerfully really arises where firms have invested more comprehensively in recruitment, and thus built a labour pool with greater long-run potential (and consequently greater aspirations). Such firms would be wise to maximise their greater investment in human resources. In this context, training and development offers the kind of complementary potential recognised in models of high-involvement work systems (see Chapter 5). Such firms are well placed to consider more ambitious training strategies which involve moving beyond immediate demands in jobs to longer-run employee development. The key principle here is that, in the context of a superior investment in work and employment practices, employee development should not be restricted to a deficit model. Rather, it should aim to build employee potential and the firm's agility over the long run (Dyer and Shafer 1999, see Chapter 9).

Unlike short-run training, long-run development plans involve a more balanced mix of formal training and education (typically off-the-job) and informal coaching and team building (typically on-the-job). Formal learning is important to enhance the individual's grasp of relevant theory (the template through which they understand their experience) and their ability to tackle abstract problem solving. This kind of development becomes more powerful when individuals also, or subsequently, face a more challenging work environment in which their informal learning is extended (Marsick and Watkins 1990). There are stages in careers when a mix of abstract, theory-based learning and more difficult assignments help to extend individual abilities and open up more satisfying work, as we shall argue below.

Performance appraisal systems: valuable, if astutely managed

The argument so far implies that the most important thing a firm can do to improve individual performance is to learn to recruit and retain more effectively. We have stressed the crucial role of thoughtful recruitment strategies and valid selection practices and the complementary role of training and development, especially where significant investment has been made in the staffing process. Improving retention is something we shall explore further below. What about performance planning and appraisal systems? Performance appraisal (PA) systems are formal methods of planning and evaluating employee performance which involve employee interviewing (typically annually). Quite commonly, they include some form of employee development planning, although some firms separate these activities.

Clearly, our argument implies that it is wrong to conflate performance appraisal systems with 'performance management'. Individual performance is managed through a variety of techniques – from recruitment to termination (Figure 7.1). Current reviews stress that PA systems can play a productive role in this mix of techniques, but only if they are managed astutely (Latham and Latham 2000, Marshall and Wood 2000, Bradley and Ashkanasy 2001, Latham, Sulsky and MacDonald 2007). People have long been able to see a valid and important role for formal performance appraisal, particularly in large organisations with major numbers of salaried staff (Huber and Fuller 1998).

Research in Britain shows that PA systems are growing as a key way of managing individual performance, particularly in managerial and professional work (Gallie *et al.* 1998, Kersley *et al.* 2006). As noted above, the spread of performances in work with higher levels of discretion is vast and it seems only logical to manage each 'human asset' in an individualised manner. PA systems can form a basis for individual work planning, for discussing 'critical success factors' in the job, and can provide the key (if not the only) input to decisions on training, promotions, merit-based salary increases, and international transfers. It is hard to see how multinational firms, involved in time-consuming expatriate management, can operate without a formal PA system for assessing performance and potential (Dowling and Welch 2004).

The problem we must wrestle with is that good intentions in the PA area have often been associated with disappointing outcomes (Latham *et al.* 2007). As well as huge variability in how (or even whether) managers conduct formal interviews, research has long confirmed the existence of 'rater bias', stemming from use of invalid performance criteria and lack of representative data on performance (amongst other things). As a result, some industrial psychologists now routinely distinguish between 'objective' and 'rated' performance in organisations (Hunter *et al.* 2000). The implication is that good performers are insufficiently recognised. They also tend to be frustrated with senior management because PA systems raise expectations of links to rewards and development which are often not forthcoming. Too many managers see appraisal interviews as a chore to be got out of the way (as another management system with which they are forced to comply). Their staff typically see them as an opportunity to have their good work rewarded and further developed. Staff are often concerned with the links to the other parts of the HR cycle (Figure 7.1). Not surprisingly, then, a key concern in the appraisal literature over many years has been similar to that in the selection field: how to make the whole process more valid or how to improve its 'cognitive properties' (Huber and Fuller 1998).

Cognitive problems must have something to do with the frustration with PA systems and better management training is bound to be part of the answer, providing it actually involves effective practice at better techniques (Latham and Latham 2000). However, in recent years, some key writers in the literature have started to realise that the problem is not simply cognitive. The idea that better training is the answer assumes that managers are not perversely motivated. The work of writers such as Murphy and Cleveland (1991), who point out that managers have goals of their own which may not include giving accurate appraisals and who act in a political context, is attracting greater attention (Huber and Fuller 1998, Latham and Latham 2000). This kind of approach resonates with the work of Kets De Vries and Miller (1984) who discuss a range of dysfunctional managerial behavioural and personality syndromes including 'powerholic' and 'workaholic' problems, and infantile jealousies of more productive people.

Admitting the possibility of motivational, personality and political problems implies that senior managers must improve accountability mechanisms around PA systems – for example, requiring lower-level managers to summarise and justify all proposed evaluations in advance of interviewing any employees (Marshall and Wood 2000). Senior managers can also improve systems by spending better time clarifying their purposes and how key linkages to rewards and development will actually be achieved consistently in practice (*ibid.*). All of this is a tall order. It seems, then, that PA systems can be used effectively when they are well-led and well-resourced. In this light, small firms might be well advised to stick with good informal performance management and some 'golden rules' (such as aiming to hire as well as they can, intervening early in any case of poor performance, and doing what they can to retain the best performers). In large organisations, however, such as large public companies and government ministries, the scale of the problems associated with planning work and rewarding performance is simply too great to rely on informal methods, as we see in the fact that the use of PA systems continues to grow in large organisations (Kersley *et al.* 2006). The challenge in these contexts remains one of making formal PA systems reach more of their potential.

Managing employee motivation

Vital and substantial though it is (Hunter *et al.* 2000), ability is not the only factor explaining performance. In order for performance to occur, workers must also choose to apply their capabilities with some level of effort and consistency. Motivated capability is the quality that firms most need from individuals. This means that firms must offer workers sufficient incentives to attend work and do an adequate job. Like the employer, the employee is motivated to enter an employment relationship when:

- the benefits of doing so (such as wages, intrinsic enjoyment, social standing) outweigh the costs (such as increased stress, fatigue and travelling costs)
- and in the light of alternatives to that employment (such as alternative job offers or staying at home).

In other words, there must be sufficient levels of mutuality in the relationship if employment is to be stable (e.g. Barnard 1938, Watson 1986, Shore *et al.* 2004). The extent to which employment relationships meet both parties' needs is, of course, variable. It is possible to imagine a range of implications depending on the extent to which business and employee interests are mutual or aligned (Boxall 1998) (Figure 7.5).

The key question, then, becomes one of finding ways in which firms can create the motivational environment they desire. Motivation is a variable. What explains high and low levels? There are so many theoretical perspectives that could be cited here that we must be very selective (for a recent review, see Latham and Pinder 2005). We consider two perspectives that we think help to highlight critical issues for management – agency theory (drawn from organisational economics) and the theory of psychological contracting. We round the chapter out with a discussion of job satisfaction and long-run development, and of the problem of retaining highly motivated workers over significant periods of time.

Agency theory and incentive alignment

While economists recognise the role that different levels of ability or 'human capital' play in the lifetime earnings of workers (see, for example, McConnell

Quality of alignment between business and employee interests	Short-term business context	Long-term business context
Weak	Likely to have chronic HR problems (e.g. high labour turnover, low productivity) which create, or contribute to, business failure	Likely to become victim of major market changes because of loss of key value generators and low motivation among remaining staff
Adequate	Likely to recruit and retain a competent workforce but motivational levels are unlikely to support any forms of 'human resource advantage'	Likely to survive as a credible member of the industry but not to develop any leadership position through human resources
Strong	Helps create the motivational basis to move beyond basic viability issues and develop superior short-run productivity	Helps to create the motivational basis to secure the employees likely to play a decisive role in the long-run direction of industry change

Source: Boxall (1998)

Figure 7.5   Likely implications of different levels of employment mutuality

and Brue 1995), by far their main focus in performance management is on the question of motivation. In organisational and personnel economics, the problem of individual performance is largely seen as one of aligning the incentives of employers and employees (e.g. Lazear 1999, Tomer 2001, Grimshaw and Rubery 2007). Much of this thinking derives from a classic paper by Jensen and Meckling (1976: 308) which helped establish the field of 'agency theory':

> We define an agency relationship as a contract under which one or more persons (the principal(s)) engage another person (the agent) to perform some service on their behalf which involves delegating some decision-making authority to the agent. If both parties to the relationship are utility maximizers, there is good reason to believe that the agent will not always act in the best interests of the principal. The principal may limit divergences from his/her interests by establishing appropriate incentives for the agent and by incurring monitoring costs designed to limit the aberrant activities of the agent.

Employer–employee relationships are seen as a class of principal–agent relationships, all of which are defined by the fact that the interests of the two parties may diverge. As we argued in Chapter 1, this is a realistic assumption: employers ('principals') and employees ('agents') should be seen as having mixed motives. Some of their interests overlap while others move in different directions.

The standard prescription in agency theory is that employers should find ways of ensuring win/win outcomes with their employee agents. The typical employee in mind is a manager and the context is one in which the principal cannot know all that the manager knows about running the firm. The manager could behave opportunistically, serving their own interests to the detriment of the firm. One of the key techniques advanced to deal with this possibility is the individual bonus or incentive scheme (Grimshaw and Rubery 2007). The idea is to ensure that the agent benefits only when the principal benefits (e.g. through a sustained rise in share price relative to rival firms in the same industry).

In effect, agency theory argues that extrinsic rewards matter to employees and that making such rewards contingent on some form of measured performance will help the firm perform better. The first part of this proposition is certainly something that employers should keep in mind. The main reason for working is the need to earn money to live – sometimes called the 'provisioning motive' (Rose 2000, 2003). This should never be underestimated. A primary motive for changing jobs is to get higher levels of income (e.g. Griffeth, Hom and Gaertner 2000, Boxall *et al.* 2003, Guthrie 2007).

However, the other part of the agency proposition, that *contingent* rewards – performance-related pay (PRP) systems – are good for firms is something that needs careful qualification. It is important to look at the conditions under which PRP schemes will work well. One of the more useful contributions in this regard is contained in a study of worker bonuses conducted by Edward Lazear (1999). Lazear gained access to the records of the Safelite company, a firm which installs automobile window glass, and which changed in 1994 from time-based to piece-based pay (with a minimum hourly wage guarantee). Full data were available on worker output before and after the change in the pay system. The data revealed that overall productivity increased by 44 per cent after the change to performance-related pay. Lazear was able to show that the firm benefited in two ways: high-potential workers increased their output (an 'incentive effect', as predicted by the theory). But he was also able to show a 'sorting effect': the rate of labour turnover of higher performers dropped and more workers of high ability were attracted to the firm. At the same time, those of lower ability tended to leave in search of more secure payment regimes elsewhere. This is functional, not dysfunctional labour turnover. By the end of 1995, Safelite's workforce was on average much more productive than it had been when associated with time-based wages alone. The study is valuable because Lazear (1999) notes some of the critical contingencies which make it a case where individual bonuses will work well: the work is actually very individualised, it is quite observable, and cooperation in teams (which is better assisted by pay compression and group bonuses) is not important in this company's business.

Most pay researchers would validate the importance of these contingent factors and also argue that other factors will come into play over time (e.g. Kessler 1998, Guthrie 2007). Performance pay systems always have the potential to become demoralised. This can happen where there is an initial incentive effect but changes in the business context that employees cannot control – such as a downturn in the economy or the entry of a powerful, new rival firm – mean that the bonuses disappear or fall to a level that is no longer significant enough to motivate. There are also the issues that arise when performance pay is based on qualitative assessments of performance. This means that subjectivity ('rated' performance) plays a key role (Kessler and Purcell 1992). The PRP scheme is dependent on the quality of the performance appraisal system that feeds into it. As we have seen, this can be enormously variable. It is little wonder that even in firms that are very committed to some form of PRP, management finds it necessary to tread very carefully in the way it designs links from appraisal to pay adjustments (Kessler and Purcell 1992).

Generally speaking, agency theory could do better at spelling out the contingent factors that foster or limit the use of 'at risk' models of performance-related pay. Research outside the agency frame can help to refine the contingent factors that affect pay system design. Wood's (1996) study of pay systems in a sample of British manufacturing firms pursuing 'high-commitment management' is instructive. Most US models would advise such firms to adopt a serious element of contingent remuneration but Wood finds that UK manufacturers pursuing higher employee commitment are circumspect about bonuses. If using any form of PRP, they are more likely to add merit pay permanently into the salary (so it is not 'at risk' from year to year). When one reflects on Wood's findings there is a strong, intuitive logic to them. Employers may well avoid individual bonus systems if they discourage the kind of involvement the firm seeks (Wood 1996: 65, 72). One of the risks in bonus systems is that they will create 'perverse incentives': behaviour which produces rewards but which channels the worker's actions too narrowly and which does not help to build a more flexible and comprehensive awareness of the firm's unfolding needs (Kessler and Purcell 1992).

The greatest concern currently with PRP schemes relates to their use by company directors and senior executives who have been benefiting from the explosion of performance pay schemes and the related inflation in executive pay (Bartol and Durham 2000). Along with them, strategically placed staff, in such industries as financial services and investment banking, have been enjoying a bonus boom. In 2006, it was estimated that some 4,200 individuals in the City of London, now possibly the world's leading financial centre, would earn an annual bonus of over 1 million pounds.[3] With this enormous largesse has come an expansion of expectations: some 93 per cent of financial sector staff in London expect a bigger bonus than the previous year. Given the amount of money allocated to these schemes and the escalation of expectations, it is less obvious that shareholders are benefiting. This is the problem of appropriation, of particular concern in the resource-based view of the firm (Chapter 4). As such, elite PRP schemes have created more, rather than less, shareholder concern with agency problems in companies (e.g. Bruce and Buck 1997, Conyon 1997) and have also fuelled concerns about the social legitimacy of extreme pay inequalities within companies (e.g. Kochan 2007).

What can companies do to minimise the potential for managerial PRP schemes to get out of hand? In one US study, Martell and Carroll (1995) obtained detailed responses on HR practices for managing top management members, as well as assessments of business performance, in a sample of 115 strategic business units based in 89 *Fortune 500* companies. The study found that the practices associated with better management performance were:

- very selective recruitment (but whether executives were hired from within or outside the group did not have an impact)
- high external relativity in pay (implying that firms should try to pay executives well in terms of the labour market)
- rigorous use of performance planning and appraisal (while there were no relationships between the bonus systems used in these firms and business performance).

Martell and Carroll's study reinforces the argument in this chapter about the crucial role of recruiting for good ability in the first instance. It also produces interesting evidence that having ongoing dialogue around desirable

---

3 Teather, D., 'The bonus bonanza', *Guardian*, 4 November 2006, 27–8.

objectives for executives (a well-led, well-implemented performance appraisal system) is more important in fostering good performance than having bonus systems. Of course, this does not invalidate the need to pay people well in terms of the external labour market, something which correlates with hiring the best candidates (Guthrie 2007). What the study suggests is that the desired results of bonus systems (getting managers to focus on the right things) can be achieved more effectively (and, almost certainly, more cheaply) by strong attention to performance planning and feedback.

All of this underlines the point that the question of the best ways in which to align interests through pay needs careful handling (Kessler 1998, Guthrie 2007). As a general rule, pay systems should be designed to recruit and retain the people the firm needs, as Martell and Carroll's (1995) study demonstrates. After that, they can be used to incentivise certain kinds of valued behaviour but they work best when certain key conditions are met. With individual bonuses, this typically means ensuring that team effects are not important and that workers are able to reach high performance through their own discretionary efforts, and without company resources, management politics or other factors limiting them. In field-based sales work, these conditions can quite often be achieved and sustained for serious amounts of time. If, however, such conditions cannot be carefully orchestrated or are not desirable (because high levels of team cooperation are wanted), firms should tread warily or consider more group-based options (such as team or company-wide incentives). The sort of difficulties that can arise mean that careful firms ensure that full consultation with the workers and managers concerned is undertaken in any new form of pay system design (Bowey and Thorpe 1986, Purcell 1999). The area of pay incentives is one of those areas in micro-HRM that is extremely sensitive to the 'how' of implementation: many a bright idea has come to grief because of failure to study the particular context and consult the stakeholders, including both the target employee group and their direct managers.

Psychological contracting and employee commitment

As our discussion implies, social and psychological processes, including what people in the team or company consider fair, play a major role in the employment relationship alongside individualistic economic ones. While agency theory constitutes an attempt to understand individual performance management from an economic perspective, the emerging theory of psychological contracting represents an attempt to do so from a more psychological and socially aware stance.

Early sources on the notion of psychological contract placed their emphasis on shared expectations between the employer and the employee (Wolfe Morrison and Robinson 1997, Coyle-Shapiro and Kessler 2000, Shore *et al.* 2004). Schein (1978: 48) defined the psychological contract as 'a set of unwritten *reciprocal expectations* between an individual employee and the organisation'. He developed a simple model which argued that successful employment relationships involve *matching* organisational needs with individual needs (Schein 1977, 1978). Individual needs are seen to be changing across early career, mid-career and late career phases. There was really very little theory in the model except the basic point that long-term employment requires an ongoing alignment of interests between employers and employees.

In recent years, Denise Rousseau (1995) has become the most prominent writer on psychological contracting in employment relationships. She defines the psychological contract as an individual's beliefs about the terms of their relationship with the organisation that employs them. Spot or 'transactional' contracts have very little psychological content but the standard, open-ended employment relationship has lots of 'relational' content (MacNeil 1985, McLean Parks and Kidder 1994). The distinction between the two is particularly relevant to the consideration of differences between core and more peripheral types of employees, as discussed in Chapter 4. A range of contrasts is usually made between transactional and relational contracting (Figure 7.6). These types are best understood as located at the ends of a continuum, rather than as absolute categories.

An example of how a psychological contract is formed is shown in Figure 7.7. For Rousseau, the employment contract is 'fundamentally psychological – agreement exists in the eye of the beholder' (1995: 6). The rectangular boxes indicate the individual's thinking and work orientations while the words in the ovals indicate processes from the organisational side. The formation of the individual's psychological contract is shaped by recruitment claims and company policies but also by social cues in the work environment. The diagram helps to illustrate how difficulties can arise. The individual in this case forms the view that they are being promised early promotion in exchange for hard work. People often conflate 'hard work' with performance, concepts which may overlap but which do not perfectly coincide because of ability and resourcing differences. Their personal assumption that they can be promoted in a single year is just that: a personal assumption. It may have been encouraged by the recruitment rhetoric but it is not grounded in anything the employer has specifically promised. In actual fact, something like 2 per cent of individuals are promoted in this organisation in a single year (Rousseau 1995: 34),

Transactional contracts	Relational contracts
Specific economic conditions (e.g. wage rate) as primary incentive	Emotional attachment as well as economic exchange
Limited personal involvement in the job (e.g. working relatively few hours, low emotional attachment)	Whole person relations (e.g. growth, development)
Close-ended timeframe (e.g. seasonal employment, 2 to 3 years on the job at most)	Open-ended time frames (i.e. indefinitely)
Commitments linked to well-specified conditions	Both written and unwritten terms (e.g. some terms emerge over time)
Little flexibility (change requires renegotiation of contract)	Dynamic and subject to change during the life of the contract
Use of existing skills	Pervasive conditions (e.g. affects personal and family life)
Unambiguous terms readily understood by outsiders	Subjective and implicitly understood (i.e. conditions difficult for third party to understand)

Source: Rousseau (1995: 91–2)

Figure 7.6 The continuum from transactional to relational contracting

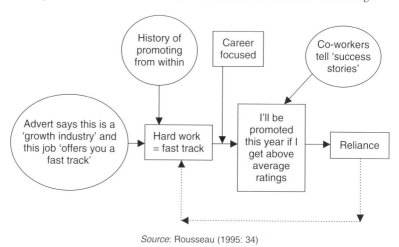

Source: Rousseau (1995: 34)

Figure 7.7 An illustration of the formation of a psychological contract

so the individual is more than likely heading for disappointment and disillusionment.

Given the prevalence of scenarios like that depicted in Figure 7.7, it is not surprising that research on psychological contracting finds that psychological contracts are frequently 'violated' (Wolfe Morrison and Robinson 1997). A widely cited study by Robinson and Rousseau (1994) argues that violation of the psychological contract is the norm rather than the exception. The study tracked 128 MBA graduates two years after their graduation. Some 55 per cent said their psychological contract had been violated over this short time frame. Robinson and Rousseau (1994) inject a sense of proportion into this: there are obviously degrees of violation. Some aspects of an employee's psychological contract are more significant than others. It is therefore helpful, as Morrison and Robinson (1997) suggest, to make a distinction between 'violation' and a less damaging kind of 'breach'. It is also helpful to recognise that some violations are owned up to and explained by management. In certain situations, employees do accept as credible the explanations they are given for violations (Rousseau 1995: 127).

The risk, however, with more serious violations of psychological contracts is that they undermine employee commitment and valuable employees leave prematurely (before the employer has had a good payback) or stay and adjust what Organ (1988) calls their 'organisational citizenship behaviours' (OCBs). OCBs include a range of cooperative and caring behaviours that can be very valuable to collegial relations, teamwork and client service in a firm. If an employee who has tried to work hard feels violated in some important aspect of their psychological contract, the argument runs that they are less likely to work sacrificially in future. Much as predicted by Adams' (1965) famous 'equity theory', they adjust their work inputs (effort) to take account of the lowered outputs (rewards) they are actually experiencing at work.

There are, however, serious problems with the approach that Rousseau (1995) takes to the notion of psychological contract. As Guest (1998) argues, Rousseau's model makes the psychological contract entirely subjective, something only in the head of the employee. This means that it cannot be seen in any meaningful way as 'contractual'. If one cares about the plain meaning of words, Rousseau's definition cannot be supported. To have a psychological contract must mean that employer and employee *share* some common understandings that go beyond what was written in their employment agreement, as earlier writers on psychological contracting argued (Coyle-Shapiro and Kessler 2000, Shore *et al.* 2004).

Guest (1998) also points to the huge difficulty that multiple agency presents in large organisations. Given the fact that so many managerial actors can be involved in the recruitment and then the ongoing performance management of an individual, it is hard to see how management can ever maintain a consistent set of psychological messages. Breach and violation are virtually inevitable and perhaps employees come to realise and accept this. While these are serious difficulties, Guest (1998) still sees some value in the notion of psychological contract as a way of analysing the variety of individual employment relationships that exist in today's labour market. As suggested in Chapter 4, it can be used in the analysis of core-periphery employment models in firms. In core-periphery models, management is often trying to send a different set of messages to different groups which vary in their centrality to the firm's mission (e.g. Lepak and Snell 1999, 2007). The notion of psychological contracting is also important for the way in which it helps us to understand the dynamics of employment relationships.

Expectations and trust dynamics in psychological contracting

A key paper which underlines the dynamic nature of psychological contracting has been written by David Grant (1999). Grant points out that concepts of psychological contracting really stem from expectancy theories of motivation. The key dimensions of expectancy (or expectations) theory are shown in Figure 7.8. The text boxes with borders are the elements of the pure theory of expectancy while the other parts of the diagram have been inserted to build a more comprehensive model of individual performance. We have done this by drawing on the work of Tony Watson (1986), whose concept of the implicit contract is synonymous with the psychological contract, and by drawing on the performance equation which is fundamental to this chapter.

Expectancy theories of motivation do not tell us about the content of human motivations (about pay, status and intrinsic job satisfaction, for example) but make the fundamental point that our *ongoing* motivation at work is affected by the expectations we form *and* our experience of whether these are met over time. On a practical level, expectancy theory tells us three quite important things. First, impossible goals will frustrate rather than motivate. There is no point in putting forth effort if we are being set up for failure. We might try once or twice but, over time, we need to believe that our efforts can achieve the results desired. Second, unrewarded goals may well be ignored. In other words, people are indeed motivated by obtaining rewards that are important to them. These may be money-based or more intangible like praise, a sense of worth, or as sense of achievement. This, of course, is something to be very careful about when designing PRP schemes, as noted earlier. Companies should avoid rewarding certain kinds of behaviour that are ultimately dysfunctional for the firm. Third, expectancy theory implies that firms cannot motivate good performers at all unless they have rewards that these people value. It is impossible to employ some people, for example, unless the work interests them and the pay meets at least their threshold expectations. Over time, to keep people motivated, the firm needs

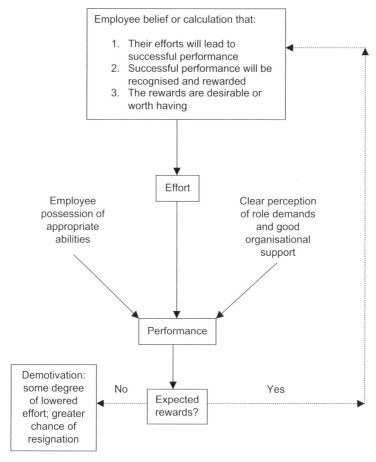

Source: Adapted from Watson (1986: 119)

Figure 7.8   The expectancy theory of motivation and performance (with added factors to recognise the full 'performance equation')

a virtuous cycle in which the rewards that people value do come to them when they perform.

Like agency theory, then, expectancy theory says that employees must be offered the incentives that appeal to them (which typically, of course, extend beyond monetary rewards). However, expectancy theory implies that faith in the management process is something that needs to be built and maintained over time. Those writing on psychological contracting increasingly draw on the notion of 'social exchange' (e.g. Gouldner 1960, Blau 1964) to argue that employees reciprocate the kind of treatment they receive from management as the employment relationship unfolds (e.g. Whitener *et al.* 1998, Whitener 2001, Shore *et al.* 2004).

The critical principle at stake here is that employee trust and commitment to the firm tend to be based on their perceptions of fairness and trustworthiness in management decision making (Guest 2007). If firms are only interested in a short-term exchange (e.g. so much money for a small task or a very finite project), this is not so much of an issue. Where, however, management wants a particular employee to stay over the long term because their skills and experience are of ongoing value, there is an important issue with trust dynamics. Eisenberger *et al.* (1986, 2002) use the notion of 'perceived organisational support' in this connection. The argument is that employees who perceive good organisational support in their employment relationship respond with increased trust in management and greater commitment to the organisation. As Chapter 4 on the resource-based view of the firm argues, the trust and commitment of core employees can be very valuable 'intangible assets' for organisations. Higher levels of trust foster greater collaboration and can facilitate change management while greater commitment can bring benefits in retaining valuable experience in the business (e.g. Whitener 2001, Macky and Boxall 2007). In service firms, for example, this greater experience can help to win and hold important customers who are unimpressed by firms where employees lack the expertise to solve their problems or do not recall their preferences and interests.

Figure 7.9, modified from the work of Guest (2007), underlines the key insights involved here. Where employee commitment is valuable to the firm, employee trust in management matters and this trust is sensitive to the state of the psychological contract: to whether the employee perceives management to have made and have kept important promises in their

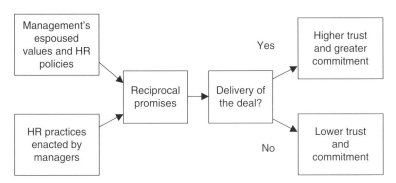

Source: Modified from Guest, D., 'Human resource management and the worker: towards a new psychological contract?'. In Boxall, P., Purcell, J. and Wright, P. (eds) *The Oxford Handbook of Human Resource Mangement*. Oxford: Oxford University Press. © (2007) By permission of Oxford University Press.

Figure 7.9   Promises, trust and commitment in the psychological contract

employment relationship. As we shall argue further in Chapter 8, employee perceptions of management values, policies and practices are critical in the chain of variables that link HRM to company performance.

Intrinsic and extrinsic motivators

The theory of psychological contracting and social exchange helps to highlight the important question of how to sustain employee motivation and commitment. It highlights the importance of a process of building trust over time (Whitener *et al.* 1998). It has very little to say, however, about the typical content of employee motivation: what sort of rewards matter to employees? Perhaps the most useful work in this context is associated with studies of job satisfaction. Studies of job satisfaction and of labour turnover tell us some important things about 'what workers want' (Rose 2000, Boxall *et al.* 2003).

It is standard to distinguish between intrinsic and extrinsic sources of employee motivation. Intrinsic sources are to do with the nature of the work itself (the extent to which the individual finds it enjoyable and interesting and how well they get on with supervisors and colleagues) while extrinsic factors are to do with benefits the job brings with it (the level of pay; the prospect of promotion; the degree of security; the level of status and so on). Figure 7.10 lists the results from a survey of some 7,000 British workers conducted in 1999–2000, showing the top factors they rated as their priorities in searching for a job (Rose 2003). The nature of the work itself is clearly very important. This is chosen first by 27 per cent of people and adding the two columns in Figure 7.10 shows that some 45 per cent of people give it as either their first or their second priority. Pay and job security are also highly valued, rated either first or second priority by 48 per cent and 43 per cent respectively. This underlines once again that extrinsic motivators should not be underestimated, including what some people would now regard as old-fashioned: the desire for employment security.

The nature of work varies enormously, so what makes a person happy with the work they do? As a general rule, people like jobs they personally

Job facet priorities	Chosen first %	Chosen second %
The actual work	27	18
Job security	25	18
Pay	22	26
Using initiative	10	13
Good relations with manager	8	13

Source: Adapted from Rose (2003)

Figure 7.10   Job facet priorities of British workers

find interesting *and* which offer them a high degree of autonomy in how they do the work (e.g. Kinnie *et al.* 2005). The 'demand-control' model of stress argues that jobs with higher workload demands combined with low employee discretion are those that create the most strain (Gallie 2005, Mackie, Holahan and Gottlieb 2001). As Karasek (1979: 303) puts it, in a pathbreaking study of American and Swedish workers, 'the working individual with few opportunities to make job decisions in the face of output pressure is most subject to job strain'. Better-quality jobs therefore have a fair level of work demand while using the individual's capacity for decision making and learning as much as possible. There can, however, be problems in situations where jobs are intrinsically interesting and empowering but where company work norms or an individual's personality means they take on more work than is good for their health. 'Workaholism' of this kind is clearly a problem among professionals and managers (e.g. Kersley *et al.* 2006: 102–3). Job characteristics, working methods and work pressures are therefore important features of managing individual performance and well-being and point to the value of a regular dialogue between individuals and their supervisors around job design, decision making and work expectations.

A key contribution to our understanding of intrinsic job satisfaction is contained in the major study of social change and economic life (SCELI) in Britain conducted in the late 1980s. This study contains a survey of some 4,000 employees (Penn, Rose and Rubery 1994).[4] Through the SCELI study, Michael Rose (1994) has developed the theory that people are satisfied in their jobs (and more loyal to their companies) when the skills they use in their job ('job-skill') match the skills they actually have ('own-skill'). This is quite a refreshing argument because it implies that most people can be happy in their work, irrespective of how brainy they are. The key factor in intrinsic satisfaction is finding a job which uses the talents one has.

In this respect, Rose (1994) defines three categories. The first are the under-utilised whose talents are not fully engaged (own-skill greater than job-skill). University students doing low-skilled jobs while studying often fall into this category but so too does anyone working in a job which does not make good use of their talents. The second group are matched (own-skill approximates job-skill) while the third category are under-qualified (own-skill less than job-skill). These categories are refined somewhat further in

---

4 The SCELI sample was drawn from six localities – Aberdeen, Coventry, Kirkcaldy, Northampton, Rochdale and Swindon – but very closely matches the 'class composition' of Britain as a whole.

Skill situation of subgroup	Satisfaction level
Under-utilised	
Low job-skill, moderate own-skill	−27
Moderate job-skill, high own-skill	−15
Low job skill, high own-skill	−13
Matched	
Low job-skill, low own-skill	+1
Moderate job-skill, moderate own-skill	+5
High job-skill, high own-skill	+4
Under-qualified	
Moderate job-skill, low own-skill	+12
High job-skill, moderate own-skill	+13
High job-skill, low own-skill	+33

Source: Rose, M. 'Job satisfaction, job skills, and personal skills'. In Penn, R., Rose, M. and Rubery, J. (eds) *Skill and Occupational Change*. Oxford: Oxford University Press. © 1994 By permission of Oxford University Press.

Figure 7.11 Types of skill-matching and satisfaction levels

Rose's (1994) analysis of the satisfaction levels of the three groups (shown in Figure 7.11). The composite satisfaction levels indicate how people in these categories feel, on balance, about their work. The study indicates that people who feel their talents are under-employed at work are the most unhappy while those where talents needed and possessed are equivalent are generally satisfied with their work. The findings on the under-qualified represent an amusing but dangerous story. People who are obviously inadequate for their work feel quite happy. Not surprisingly, they are the group which is best pleased with management (Rose 1994: 258). After all, management's failure to deal with their incompetence has been very rewarding.

This study illustrates why half of Adams' (1965) equity theory is probably wrong. Studies confirm that people do generally adjust their effort if they feel fair rewards are not forthcoming, as predicted by equity theory (Watson 1986). Most people are concerned with what pay theory calls 'internal equity': they expect to be rewarded in a very similar way to those doing the same job or a job of equivalent importance in their organisation. However, Adams (1965) argued that individuals who felt over-rewarded would try to lift their game to compensate. While it is more than likely that some do this, the evidence in Rose's (1994) study suggests that there are personality types who are quite happy with this sort of inequity. As subsequent psychology has argued, people often find ways of rationalising unfair advantages that come their way and are capable of inflating their performance through 'self-serving bias' (e.g. Kruger 1999).

The most important point to be taken from Rose's (1994) work, however, is the value of choosing employees who are interested in the work being offered because they find it a good deployment of their abilities. This is the old notion of 'person-job' or (more broadly) 'person-organisation' fit (Kristof 1996). It implies that economic motives, while very important, cannot solely account for long-term employee behaviour. Intrinsic satisfaction, and opportunities to grow in the work, are also very important alongside economic drivers (Boxall *et al.* 2003). While people work to meet material needs and attain lifestyle aspirations, the motive of 'expressivism' is also significant, particularly among contemporary growth occupations (Rose 2000, 2003).

The adult life cycle and the drive for personal growth

The drive to express one's personality in work is supported by life-cycle theory which suggests that there will be several times over a person's adult life when they will seek major developmental challenges. According to life-cycle theorists, the adult life cycle consists of alternating periods of *stability* (structure – building) and *transition* (structure – changing) (Sheehy 1977, Levinson 1978, Levinson and Levinson 1996). In each stable period, the emphasis is on pursuing one's goals and values *within* a given structure of key choices. In the transitional periods, one 'questions and reappraises the existing structure, to explore various possibilities for change in self and world, and to move toward commitment to the crucial choices that form the basis for a new life structure in the ensuing stable period' (Levinson 1978: 49). At the transitional points, some people 'externalise' their inner turmoil more than others: changing their job, their address, their spouse, perhaps their country of domicile.

Research indicates that up to about the age of thirty, most men and women are experimenting with the workplace, finding out what kind of work they do or do not like. Labour turnover rates are generally much higher among the under-thirties than other age groups (Burgess and Rees 1998, Boxall *et al.* 2003). The pattern of stability alternating with change across the life cycle is likely to be similar for both sexes (Sheehy 1977, Levinson and Levinson 1996). There is greater variety, however, in women's patterns (e.g. Gilligan 1982). Women who focus on being mothers, and have no paid (or very incidental) employment after their first child is born, have a life pattern which is obviously very different from the typical male one. On the other hand, women who are not, or choose not to be parents, may have very similar career orientations to men. Paid employment is a very central life interest, if not the most important thing. A third pattern includes those women who try to balance family and employment (Buxton 1998), on the basis of either part- or full-time employment.

Where paid employment makes up a significant element of the life, we can expect both men and women to seek some regular growth opportunity (such as acquiring new skills in the latest technology or extending skills from one career context to another or shifting from employee to self-employed or from part-time to full-time). Periods of reflection and change will naturally occur throughout the lifespan. As a rough rule of thumb, talented people seek some kind of significant stimulation every 3 to 4 years. The challenge of retaining high performers over the long-run, then, becomes one of providing a setting in which developmental challenges can be navigated in-house.

This analysis puts an interesting spin on the issue of change in the workplace. We are frequently told that employees are resistant to change. However, research on job satisfaction and life-cycle theory suggests that people leave firms because their employer cannot offer them *enough* stimulating change (Boxall *et al.* 2003). Generally speaking, firms can do better at designing growth opportunities for individuals. A good use of performance appraisal systems (see above) lies in the way they can be used to open up a dialogue around personal growth opportunities, a use which would make them more sympathetic to the rise of 'expressivism'. From the viewpoint of improving the firm's retention of good performers, this is a better use of the appraisal interview than a tiresome review of past performance (Latham and Latham 2000). Good performance should be informally and regularly acknowledged while the annual 'appraisal' interview becomes a vehicle for encouraging the employee to discuss development interests and a forum for planning ways to match these with opportunities in the firm.

Conclusions

This chapter has underlined the value of thinking about individual employees through the lens of the performance equation ($P = f(A,M,O)$). The characteristic that firms most want from individuals is motivated capability. There is a vast range of abilities in the working population and strong competition for the best talents. This means that recruitment and selection activities are critical to all firms, even those with extensive internal labour markets. Wherever labour markets are tight, firms are well advised to make recruitment practices more proactive. Some firms have major strengths that appeal to employees but fail to maximise them through want of creativity in recruitment strategy. The greater the investment in staffing (greater inducements and more strenuous efforts to draw a better pool and better selectivity in the hiring process), the greater the benefits to be gained from building on this basis through strong training and development. While small firms can make do with good informal methods of performance feedback, large firms should aim for greater validity in performance appraisal, particularly in work involving high levels of discretion where there are major performance variations. We realise now that the task of getting 'rated' performance as close as possible to 'objective' performance is as much a problem of managing organisational politics as it is a technical one of improving system design and managerial training.

The attraction of relevant human ability is clearly of vital importance in all firms that want to perform well and grow. But this potential will be wasted if motivational strategies are neglected and employee retention is taken for granted. Agency theory emphasises the important role of aligning the economic or material interests of employer and employee. As a general rule, within the Anglo-American context, talented employees will expect to be paid close to their productivity. Ensuring that they are takes some very careful management. In terms of pay system design, good employee involvement and study of critical contingencies are vital to minimise the potential for demoralisation and perverse incentives.

Economic factors matter in motivation but the theory of psychological contracting helpfully brings in an understanding of important social and psychological processes over time. Where management is concerned to enhance employee commitment, it implies that faith in the trustworthiness of management is something that should be striven for. An organisation in which management is seen to treat employees fairly and delivers on its promises will generally enjoy greater employee loyalty. This is very valuable wherever firms need experienced employees to win and retain customers.

Extrinsic rewards such as income and employment security are important drivers of employee satisfaction but intrinsic rewards are also critical. Intrinsic satisfaction is greater when there is a good match between the skills an individual possesses and the skills needed in their job. Fortunately for firms, this matching principle is relevant to workers of all skill levels, not simply to the most highly educated or the more intelligent. It suggests that there are opportunities in all sorts of roles to foster higher levels of employee satisfaction and thus build greater commitment. Job satisfaction and life-cycle research also point to the rise of 'expressivism' (Rose 1994, 2000) in the workplace, to the fact that employees increasingly want to develop in their work. Where firms are concerned about improving the long-term retention of valuable employees, then, attention should be given to ways of opening up regular opportunities for their personal growth.

8

Linking HR systems to organisational performance

We have been searching in this part of the book for general principles underpinning better HRM. In this chapter, we draw this part together. We do so through the idea of HR systems, examining the notion of 'internal fit' within such systems, and outlining a typology of common HR systems and the contexts in which they are typically found. This helps to summarise the huge variation we see in the way firms approach HR strategy and highlights key contextual issues we have been talking about. We then review theory linking HR systems to performance outcomes. The characteristics of HR systems vary but all HR systems are intended, in some way, to reach valued organisational outcomes. What mediating or intervening variables are important in this process? Drawing particularly on the last three chapters, we outline some key principles that affect the extent to which valued outcomes will be attained.

HR systems and organisational patterns in HR strategy

As explained in Chapter 3, a firm's HR strategy is typically 'variegated': it incorporates a mix of HR systems or models. HR systems are clusters of work and employment practices that have evolved to manage major hierarchical or occupational groups in the firm. HR systems help management to build the human and social capital the firm needs to reach its overall goals in HRM.

In our discussion of the research on 'best fit' and 'best practice' in Chapter 3 and of the evolution of work systems in Chapter 5, we underlined the way in which managers generally try to ensure that HR systems fit in with their environment. These 'external' and 'organisational' fits include the need to adapt to societal factors (e.g. laws and cultural norms), industry factors (e.g. technologies and customer preferences) and organisational factors (e.g. the firm's size, its stage of development and the characteristics of its employees). In Chapter 4, which draws on the resource-based view, we explained that such a process of adaptation to context does not rule out idiosyncrasies in the firm: management ideologies, competencies, personalities and power struggles will inevitably put particular twists on HR systems. Thinking about this more positively, there is an opportunity for viable firms to create a unique form of fit in HRM: some management teams tailor and nurture HR systems which create 'human resource advantage' for the firm. A companion notion that has been emphasised in the strategic HRM literature alongside these ideas of external and organisational fits is the concept of 'internal fit'. Internal fit is seen as critical to a high quality performance in HRM (Kepes and Delery 2007).

HR systems and the problem of 'internal fit'

Those who talk of internal fit are usually making an argument for a high level of *coherence* among the HR policies and practices adopted within an HR system. MacDuffie (1995) talks of the need for positive 'bundling' in the HR practices used to support work reform in automobile assembly plants. In his terms, this means adopting the skill development and incentive practices that will support more participative styles of working among core operating workers in such plants, as discussed in Chapter 5. Positive bundling is a search for 'powerful combinations' among practices (Becker *et al.* 1997). The corollary is that HR managers should avoid 'deadly combinations' (Becker *et al.* 1997, Delery 1998): policies which work in directly opposite directions such as strong training for teamwork but appraisal which only rewards highly individualistic behaviour. Coherence in HRM implies designing policies that pull in the same direction.

Delery (1998) also warns against the costly duplication of practices, such as over-designed selection systems where extra hurdles add no further predictive power to the process. Consider the example of the firm that would benefit from structured interviewing and reference checking of job applicants but decides instead to design an 'assessment centre' with five or six kinds of test involved. Chances are that much of the assessment centre is an expensive white elephant. Little of value has been added for the considerable extra expense involved. This is not so much a point about coherence as about cost-effectiveness, which should always be borne in mind.

The notion of *consistency*, which overlaps with coherence, is also used in discussions of internal fit. One of the more useful summaries is provided by Baron and Kreps (1999: 39) who define three types of desirable consistency in HRM. The first type is 'complementary' fit or what they call 'single employee consistency': for example, ensuring that where firms use expensive selection approaches they also invest in training and promotion policies that aim to reduce labour turnover (thus increasing the chances of reaping rewards from their investment in individuals, as we explained in Chapter 7). In effect, this is about coherence in HR policy design and entails the search for 'powerful' rather than 'deadly combinations'. The second type of fit Baron and Kreps (1999) argue for is consistency across employees doing the same kind of work ('among employee consistency' but better known in everyday usage as 'standardisation' of employment conditions). There are strong normative or ethical pressures for standardisation in HR policies in firms, at least for the same class of labour: one of the main ways employers argue they are treating people equitably is by treating them all the same when it comes to employment conditions (e.g. standard working times and leave policies). The third kind of consistency is what Baron and Kreps call 'temporal consistency': consistency of employee treatment across a reasonable period of time. 'In general, how employee A is treated today should not differ radically from how she was treated yesterday' (Baron and Kreps 1999: 39). Again, and assuming employee A has not done something radically different in the last 24 hours, this principle makes good sense: employees like to be able to predict an employer's behaviour and can be seriously demotivated by violation of their 'psychological contract', as argued in Chapter 7.

As far as it goes, this kind of advice seems very reasonable. Is there anything wrong with it? Unfortunately, there is: it is somewhat over-simplified. While rightly emphasising the value of various forms of coherence and consistency, which help to build stability and trust, the notion of 'internal fit' tends to be discussed in a way that overlooks the paradoxical elements involved in managing work and people. The problem stems from the fact that, as emphasised in Chapter 1, there are multiple goals in HRM and these bring a range of strategic tensions. There are, for example, tensions between economic goals and the need for social legitimacy. There are also tensions between economic performance in the short run and preparation for the long run. The reality of these tensions means that mixed messages will often be transmitted to employees within the firm's HR systems.

As an illustration, consider work by Pil and MacDuffie (1996) on automobile manufacturing, important research we have discussed previously.

Pil and MacDuffie (*ibid.*) find a general increase in the use of high-involvement practices in the industry around the world. As we noted in Chapter 5, these are practices that foster higher skill and solicit greater commitment to, and creativity in, problem solving. However, at the same time, firms have had to pursue downsizing, often of major proportions. The same picture is described by Bacon and Blyton (2001) in the international iron and steel industry: new work systems designed to increase employee involvement in decision making have been introduced at the same time as firms have introduced more contingent employment contracts (fixed-term contracts and sub-contracting of jobs) and have continued to carry out redundancy programmes. As anyone with experience of downsizing and sub-contracting processes knows, these sorts of actions typically raise suspicions, reduce trust in management and undermine employee commitment to the firm. This climate of insecurity, however, has not prevented management in these firms from seeking higher involvement from the remaining workforce. Here, then, is a critical tension: between needing more skilful, more creative work while not being able to hold traditional staffing levels and offer traditional levels of employment security. It seems that management often needs a blend of 'forcing' and 'fostering' behaviour as it wrestles with the problem of renewing the firm (Walton, Cutcher-Gershenfeld and McKersie 1994), as we noted in Chapter 6.

We must be careful, then, with the concept of 'internal fit'. It rightly underlines the importance of seeking coherence among the HR policies aimed at a particular group of employees and consistency in their application. Where, for example, management aims to introduce a new style of working for a major occupational group, such as one that implies higher levels of skill and creativity, striving for reinforcement across the HR policies needed, and their consistent application, is obviously important. However, striving for 'internal fit' in this sense will never rule out the fact that there are competing interests in the workplace or the fact that management may have to change its HR strategy to adapt more effectively to change.

A typology of HR systems

HR systems, then, are clusters of related HR practices for particular workforce groups, which benefit from coherence in their design and consistency in their application, but which may still contain paradoxical elements. We are now in a position to consider the main HR systems we observe across firms. Our typology of HR systems or models is shown in Figure 8.1. The typology cannot be presented as something which is culture free. It mainly reflects

Type of HR system	Defining characteristics	Typical context and key HR goals
Familial model	Family members, among whom trust levels are high, provide the core labour resources and control decision making.	Common among small businesses (e.g. in agriculture, retail, construction, transport) where owners want strategy and succession under family control. High-trust relations and preferential employment conditions may be extended to key long-term employees if the firm expands.
Informal model	Workers are managed personally by owners or supervisors. Wages and skill levels are often relatively low and trade unions are rare. Temporary and part-time forms of employment are common and levels of employee turnover tend to be high.	Common in the early stages of industrialisation; remains common in low-skill services and in various types of small business for groups of labour which are outside the core. The goal of cost-effectiveness is paramount and legitimacy is typically secondary.
Industrial model	Highly specialised, low-discretion ('Taylorised') jobs, set within a hierarchy of management authority but linked to bureaucratic rules that bring standardisation and various career features ('internal labour markets'). Trade unions are common.	Developed in the late nineteenth century and in the early to mid decades of the twentieth century to support efficiency-oriented mass production with greater workplace stability and higher levels of social legitimacy.
Salaried model	Managers and white collar specialists are employed in jobs in which they enjoy higher levels of discretion, responsibility, pay and security than other employees. Their career development is actively fostered within the firm.	The necessary, more trusting corollary of the industrial model designed to build strong identification with the company. Provides the authority and decision-making structure that enables the industrial model to function.
High-involvement model	Work organisation is reformed to break down Taylorism. Specific practices vary but teamworking, higher levels of training and better pay incentives are common. Managerial roles change to facilitate greater employee participation.	Common in capital-intensive or high-tech firms where it is often accompanied by high levels of mechanisation and computerisation. Also used in service firms targeting higher quality market segments. Intended to enhance cost-effectiveness through greater worker involvement, skills and commitment.
Craft-professional models	Work practices reflect roots in 'craft' control and long periods of professional education and socialisation. Employee skills, discretion and pay levels are all high. Professionals may work in teams but cannot rotate across (contd.)	Craft models survived in high-skill parts of manufacturing where Taylorist practices would not work or were successfully resisted. Professional models are the natural approach in private sector professional services where (contd.)

Figure 8.1   A typology of HR systems

Type of HR system	Defining characteristics	Typical context and key HR goals
	their specialisations. Democratic decision making is often practised among the partners although this tends to become representative rather than direct as organisations get larger.	employee ownership is the norm and in those parts of the public sector which depend on professional work (e.g. public health and education). Craft or professional autonomy and high economic rewards are typical goals.
Outsourcing model	The work concerned is outsourced to a specialist provider in the country of domicile or is offshored to a lower-cost country. This implies nothing about the nature of the outsourcer's HR system which could be any one of familial, informal, industrial, salaried, craft or professional types in their various cultural and regulatory guises.	Common in globalised and electronically connected production environments where firms seek quantum improvements in labour cost. Better quality and customer service may also be desired but is not always achieved.

Figure 8.1 (Continued)

sources which are based on studies in the Anglo-American world. However, it does recognise patterns – such as the familial model – that surface in many cultures and the typology specifically incorporates an awareness of the process of globalisation.

We begin with the 'familial' model. Family firms are important nearly everywhere in capitalism. In the UK, they make up 76 per cent of all firms while they constitute 75 per cent in Italy and 80 per cent in Germany (Colli, Fernández Pérez and Rose 2003). They are rare, of course, in industries where operations require large workforces or high levels of physical capital and account for lower percentages of total employment. In the UK, family firms currently make up 40 per cent of all firms with at least 10 employees and account for 31 per cent of private sector employment in this category (Kersley *et al.* 2006: 19). Their incidence, however, is growing and the familial HR system is something that should be recognised and better understood in HRM.

The defining characteristic of the familial model is that family members, among whom trust levels are generally high, provide the core labour resources the firm needs (often sacrificially) and control decision making. The family patriarchs and/or matriarchs at the head of these firms are highly motivated to retain their control. This is not surprising: they typically have their personal wealth, including the family home, at stake. Retaining wealth, employment opportunities and leadership succession in the family can be more important than making the highest rate of return (e.g. Colli *et al.*

2003, Marchington *et al.* 2003). A key advantage of established family firms is that they can remain viable at lower rates of financial return without shareholders kicking up a fuss. Small, specialist businesses can sometimes survive at the edge of markets where it is sub-economic for the dominant, public companies to reach them, as argued by organisational ecologists in the theory of 'resource partitioning' (Carroll and Hannan 1995: 215–21). While the familial model is family-oriented, familial conditions and trust are often extended to key 'outsiders' (non-family members) if the firm grows to the extent that this becomes necessary (Colli *et al.* 2003).

Our second HR system is the informal model. This is sometimes called a 'low-wage' HR system (e.g. Katz and Darbishire 2000: 10). We prefer to describe it as informal because its defining characteristic is that workers are managed personally and informally by owners or supervisors. This was the main way individuals were managed in the early stages of industrialisation when an overseer hired and supervised their own workers, as we described in our discussion of work systems in Chapter 5. Speaking of nineteenth-century factories in the USA, when foremen (and they were usually men) had high levels of autonomy in hiring and firing, Jacoby (2004: 15) calls the informal model the 'drive system'.

This era has largely passed (at least in the developed countries) but the informal model is still commonly used in small firms for those who are not in the family or core workforce. As noted in Chapter 3, lower levels of formalisation and standardisation are common in small organisations. For small service firms operating in mass service markets where margins are tight, cost-effectiveness matters enormously, as explained in Chapter 5. Wages and skill levels are often relatively low. Trade unions are rare and standards of social legitimacy can also be low: the more established firms are typically compliant with their obligations under labour law but some owners are unaware of them or non-compliant. In terms of the employee relations styles discussed in Chapter 6, the preference is often for union avoidance. Temporary and part-time forms of employment are common with jobs not generally linked into a longer-term career structure (Osterman 1987). Workforces often have disproportionate numbers of less experienced and more vulnerable groups: student workers, new migrants and women returning to the workforce after child-rearing. Whenever labour markets are tight, levels of employee turnover tend to be high. However, informal models can include situations where workers make high wages, as in the construction sector and in home maintenance when skills are in short supply.

Our third type, which Osterman (1987) calls the 'industrial model', grew out of the informal type, as explained in Chapter 5. As workers were gathered into factories around a common power source (first water, then steam, then electrical power) in the nineteenth century, a process of specialised working was reinforced. Jobs low in discretion, responsibility and scope were created ('Taylorised' jobs) and workers were subservient to a hierarchy of management authority. Trade union and government challenges to these work systems, however, reinforced and expanded bureaucratic rules that brought standardisation and career features ('internal labour markets') to employment conditions. Workers were not insulated from lay-offs but seniority rules negotiated by unions often protected those with longer tenure (Osterman 1987, Jacoby 2004).

The industrial model was built to foster the efficiency advantages of high degrees of specialisation and economies of scale in mass production. However, reformers within management and, more importantly, pressure from trade unions and governments helped to ensure that wages and employment conditions, including levels of job security and scope for internal promotion, were improved (e.g. Jacoby 2004). While many firms continued to adopt a style of limiting union influence or keeping the unions at 'arm's length' (Chapter 6), the overall result was greater workplace stability and higher levels of social legitimacy. The industrial model was enormously influential. Its core features of specialised jobs embedded in strong 'internal labour markets' spread into large service firms and the public sector and across the world.

The necessary corollary of the industrial model is the 'salaried' system (Osterman 1987, Pinfield and Berner 1994). This was developed to manage the managers and 'white collar' specialists who were also essential to factories and to other large-scale organisations, such as large service firms and government departments. Under the salaried system, the individual is paid an annual salary rather than a wage calculated on the actual hours worked. This in itself conveys a lot more trust and suggests a lot more flexibility is desired of managers in the way they carry out their roles. Managers and specialists employed in this way enjoy higher levels of discretion, responsibility, pay and security than other employees. Jobs are more open to interpretation and lateral thinking. Career development within the firm is fostered. While such bureaucratic practices as job descriptions, job evaluation and performance appraisal are prevalent in large organisations, there is often scope to recognise individual strengths through merit-based pay. At the highest levels of management, reward levels, including bonuses and share options, are extremely attractive. Identification with the employer is assumed to be high and unions are rare (except in the public sector and in the finance and insurance sector).

As we explained in Chapter 5, the economic and technological context has changed very significantly over the last thirty years. One outcome of the changes is that various firms have made a move from the industrial HR model to a high-involvement one. This grew among manufacturers in high-wage countries who needed to respond more effectively to competitors delivering better quality at lower unit cost. As Chapter 5 shows, leading examples of HIWSs have emerged in such industries as automobile assembly and steel manufacturing (MacDuffie 1995, Appelbaum *et al.* 2000). Under the high-involvement model, work organisation is reformed to reverse the dysfunctional aspects of Taylorism. Specific practices vary across occupations and industries but the underpinning aims are to enhance employee discretion and expand skill formation and employee incentives. Managerial roles must change to facilitate greater employee participation or the model will not work well.

The high-involvement model represents an attempt by management to reform earlier management strategies. It has features in common with craft or professional HR systems. Craft models have their genesis in 'craft' control: in direct control of work practices by highly skilled, often mobile workers whose critical skills in the production process give them greater labour market power (Osterman 1987). Taylorism did not affect all manufacturing workers: some successfully resisted it or occupied jobs which were much less amenable to it. Maintenance workers in factories, for example, who had completed apprenticeships and were responsible for machine performance, often formed an 'aristocracy of labour' (e.g. MacKenzie 1973) who were able to distance themselves from the work practices imposed on less-skilled operating workers.

In a similar way, the professions, such as law, medicine, accountancy and professional engineering, have developed their own work practices through long periods of professional education and socialisation (e.g. Combs *et al.* 2006). Professionals may work together in teams but cannot rotate across their specialisations without the requisite qualifications (e.g. Kalleberg *et al.* 2006). Professionals form organisations serving their own ends. Autonomy and high economic rewards are typical goals and customers who want advanced professional services must pay a premium, as Chapter 5 explains. Professional models are the natural approach in private sector professional services where firms are based on an elite form of employee ownership, one in which partners, who remain working members of the firm, own the firm's shares (e.g. Boxall and Steeneveld 1999, Malos and Campion 2000). Democratic decision making is practised among the partners in the professional HR system although this tends to become representative rather than direct as organisations get larger. Professional HR systems are also prevalent in those parts of the public sector which depend on professional work (e.g. public health and education). However, in these contexts, unionisation tends to be high and struggles between professional groups and between professionals and managers tend to be common (e.g. Bach and Kessler 2007).

We call our final HR system the 'outsourcing model'. As explained in Chapter 5, globalisation, deregulation, new technologies and public sector reforms have exposed more organisations to lower-cost competitors, both domestically and internationally. The outsourcing of work has grown: sometimes to firms which specialise in high-volume, back-office functions (e.g. aspects of accounting, IT and HR work) and sometimes offshore where whole operations can be performed much more cheaply. Parcelling out of non-core activities to make major cost savings is a trend with major implications for HR systems. In our typology, we use the term, 'outsourcing model', to indicate an HR system which is thus very much driven by the cost side of cost-effectiveness. However, we are implying nothing beyond this about the nature of the outsourcer's HR system. The outsourcer could adopt any one or more of the familial, informal, industrial, salaried, craft or professional models in their various cultural and regulatory guises. There are clearly major cost differences when an industrial model is adopted in China as opposed to the UK or the USA.[1] But there are also major cost differences when highly educated professionals are employed in India as opposed to Europe or North America.[2]

HR systems and organisational patterns

Having defined the most common HR systems, we now come back to the point that HR strategies in organisations typically incorporate a range of HR systems. Organisations and HR systems are rarely equivalent. It is very unusual to have a 'single status' HR system covering all employees in a firm. It is therefore helpful to use another typology, shown in Figure 8.2, which identifies the common *mixes* of HR systems across major types of organisation.

---

1 See, for example, the outsourcing survey in *Business Week*, 30 January 2006: www.businessweek.com/magazine/content/06_05/b3969401.htm
2 See, for example, Randeep Ramesh, 'Analyse this: Wall Street looks to India', *Guardian*, 6 November 2006, p. 26.

Organisational types	Typical HR systems used	Contextual factors and major variations
Family firms	Familial and informal systems	Familial models dominate in family-owned small enterprises in agriculture, manufacturing and less-skilled services. Workplaces are small, unions are rare and informal models are used for non-family members.
Professional service firms	Professional and salaried systems	In high-skill, private sector services, professional models dominate. Unions are rare. Professionals own and jointly manage the firm while employing lower-level professionals, managerial and support staff on salaried systems. Large professional service firms use more representative modes of partner democracy.
Classical bureaucracies	Salaried, industrial and craft systems	Classical bureaucracies include the large private and public sector organisations that grew strongly in the early to middle decades of the twentieth century. Salaried career managers lead large workforces which are predominantly managed through an industrial model (while some groups are employed on craft models). Trade unions are commonly involved and tend to heighten bureaucratic standardisation and restrain management power. There are three main variants: the industrial bureaucracy (typical in large manufacturers), the service bureaucracy (e.g. in the large banks and insurance companies) and the public sector bureaucracy (standard in public service departments and local authorities).
Participatory bureaucracies	Salaried and high-involvement systems; salaried and professional systems	A mix of salaried and high-involvement HR systems is common in capital-intensive or high-tech firms seeking to respond to high quality competition through higher skills, learning and innovation and in service firms trying to serve higher quality, more lucrative market segments. The main variants in the private sector concern whether employee involvement is driven by non-union practices or is built around a union–management 'partnership'.

Participatory bureaucracies are also common in the public sector for professional services (e.g. in public health and education). In these situations, unions are common and employment practices are prone to ongoing tensions between professional disciplines and struggles between professional and managerial control. |

Figure 8.2 A typology of organisational types and their HR systems

Organisational types	Typical HR systems used	Contextual factors and major variations
Flexible bureaucracies	Salaried and outsourced systems	Typical in large organisations where a salaried hierarchy remains but where it has become legitimate to outsource operations and specialist functions, downsize workforces and weaken long-term commitments to employees. Where trade unions exist, they may extract relatively high wage levels for slimmer workforces but cannot protect jobs against rounds of restructuring. Common among organisations which now see the need for a better balance between short-run efficiency and long-run agility, including multinational firms which are responding to heightened cost pressures in international markets, large service firms in deregulated industries (e.g. airlines, telecommunications) and public sector organisations which have been required to adopt the greater emphasis on flexibility and financial control in the 'new public management'.

Figure 8.2 (Continued)

We begin with two types which do not typically have external shareholders and which are generally managed by the owners rather than by career managers. The first type is the family firm in which workplaces are small and trade unions are rare. In agriculture, in small manufacturing firms and in the less-skilled service sector, family firms typically aim to use a cost-effective blend of familial and informal HR systems. The family members and their trusted associates are employed under the familial model, providing the 'backbone' to the firm, while other workers are employed under the informal model. How far the familial model is extended to non-family members is a variable. It is more likely to be extended when employees have critical skills or can affect sensitive customer relations. Thus, in a regional trucking firm, loyal, skilled and trusted drivers are likely to be 'looked after' by the family (Marchington *et al.* 2003) while student workers or new migrants picking fruit and vegetables in summer for a contracting firm are likely to be treated in a much more disposable way.

In the second type, professional service firms (PSFs), ownership resides in the hands of a group of partner-professionals. This amounts, in effect, to a restricted system of employee ownership: the partners are simultaneously owners, workers and managers (e.g. Greenwood, Hinings and Brown 1990,

Boxall and Steeneveld 1999). In small PSFs, partners work closely together and try to manage the firm in a direct, highly democratic kind of way. This does not mean that things will work out well. How long such a firm will last depends very much on the quality of relations within the partnership group. In large professional service firms, formalisation increases with staffing levels and partnership democracy tends to be more representative. The partners employ lower-level professionals and non-professional staff (e.g. clerical workers, practice managers, accounting, marketing and HR specialists) on salaried conditions. In PSFs, then, managerial specialists are subservient to the professional partners, not the other way round.

The other three types of organisation are all best understood as management-driven forms of bureaucracy. We use the term 'classical bureaucracies' to describe the large organisations that emerged in the nineteenth century and the early and middle decades of the twentieth century. In these organisations, shareholders were remote and salaried, career-oriented managers took charge of large workforces. Trade unions were common. As Chapter 5 explains, unions did not stop high levels of job specialisation but did help to lift wages, restrain management power and foster 'internal labour markets' (e.g. Jacoby 2004). In the 'industrial bureaucracy' typical in large manufacturers, Taylorist and Fordist philosophies made their marks and the main HR systems were therefore industrial models for waged workers and salaried models for line managers and management specialists. Some groups of workers, however, retained craft models (e.g. highly skilled maintenance workers and design engineers).

In the service bureaucracies that grew in the private sector (such as in the large banks and insurance companies), job specialisation was also prevalent, creating a kind of 'office factory'. Salaried systems were common but were fairly basic in terms of pay levels and discretion at entry and lower levels in the hierarchy. Salaried systems became progressively more empowering and generous as workers were promoted to higher-level, managerial cadres. This 'office factory' was also typical of public sector bureaucracies. However, unionisation became stronger and more extensive in public service departments and local authorities than in private sector services.

The final two organisational types both represent attempts to reform the classical bureaucracy. Rather than bureaucracies disappearing among large organisations, what has happened is more akin to a reform of bureaucracy (Jacoby 2004). We see two major trends here. One is the 'participatory bureaucracy' (Kelley 2000), a reform of the industrial bureaucracy designed to foster high-involvement HR systems. Managerial and specialist staff remain on salaried systems but need to adjust their relationships with core operating staff if the model is to succeed. The participatory bureaucracy is common in capital-intensive or high-tech firms seeking to respond to high quality competition through higher skills, learning and innovation, as noted in Chapter 5. As explained there, it is also a feature of large service firms, such as hotels, banks and rest homes, trying to target higher quality, more lucrative market segments. The main variants in the private sector concern whether employee involvement is supported by non-union voice practices or is built around a union–management 'partnership', as discussed in Chapter 6.

Participatory bureaucracies are also common in the public sector for professional services (e.g. in public health and education). It is fair to say, however, that the bureaucratic features are stronger in the public sector than in the private. Employee ownership is not possible and unions remain common, fighting for professional autonomy and income levels. Employment practices are prone to ongoing tensions between professional disciplines (e.g. between medical and nursing professions in hospitals). In recent times, conflict levels have been high due to major struggles between professional and managerial groups (e.g. over cost cutting and an escalation of bureaucratic controls under the 'new public management', as discussed in Chapter 5).

Finally, we see the emergence of what we call the 'flexible bureaucracy'. We use this term to recognise what Grimshaw et al. (2005) describe as a growth of fragmentation in large organisations. Like Jacoby (2004) and Grimshaw et al. (2005), we do not see this type of organisation as a repudiation of bureaucracy but, rather, a reform of it in which it is more legitimate to downsize workforces, to weaken long-term commitments to employees and to consider all sorts of outsourcing and offshoring. The flexible bureaucracy combines an inner core of salaried managerial and specialist staff, whose own contracts have often been heightened in terms of performance expectations and rewards, with outsourced HR systems. The outsourced models adopted can include any number of types, including those which foster high levels of involvement but do so with lower-cost workers. Where trade unions exist, they may extract relatively high wage levels for slimmer workforces in the developed countries but cannot protect jobs against rounds of restructuring. The flexible bureaucracy is common among organisations in which senior managers now see the need for a better balance between short-run efficiency and long-run agility. This includes multinational firms which are responding to heightened cost pressures in international markets, large service firms in deregulated industries (e.g. airlines, telecommunications) and, once again, public sector organisations which have been required to adopt the greater emphasis on financial control in the 'new public management' (Bach and Kessler 2007).

The 'black box' problem: links between HRM and performance

As we have indicated, the quality of the investment made in people varies across the models we have described. In family firms, for example, those managed informally are clearly not offered the same trust and employment terms as those managed under the familial model. Similarly, in the flexible bureaucracy, there is a core of highly paid salaried staff who provide leadership and networking coordination. However, these individuals are responsible for finding outsourced arrangements in which the whole idea is to employ people around the world who are treated more contingently and paid at much lower levels. HR systems vary in the messages they send: some are more oriented to achieving low labour costs with adequate levels of effectiveness than they are to achieving high levels of employee commitment and expert performance.

Having said this, are there some commonalities in how HR systems should operate? Are there some key links that all HR models need if they are to reach their intended outcomes? This is what HR researchers have called the 'black box' problem (e.g. Purcell *et al.* 2003, Wright and Gardner 2004): what chain of links leads from HR policies through to whatever notion of organisational performance is desired? Despite the variation in the goals of HR systems, there are some important principles here which we need to understand. These are of particular relevance to large, bureaucratic organisations where tall hierarchies, changes in ownership, and swings in ideology threaten coherence and consistency in HR strategy. Although they are much more resource-constrained, coherence and consistency are easier to achieve in small firms, as we shall explain.

The centrality of employee attitudes and behaviour

Virtually all scholars who specify a causal chain between HR policy and organisational performance see employee attitudes and behaviour as the fulcrum or critical linking mechanism. This is true on both the individual and the collective (workforce) levels, as noted in Chapters 6 and 7. To bring about valued organisational outcomes, management needs to influence individual employee ability, motivation and opportunity to perform. On the collective level, to make individual performances possible, management needs to build a sufficient degree of workforce organisation, capabilities and positive attitudes.

However, these employee variables will not move in a positive direction if things go badly wrong within the management process itself. One of the most elaborated models linking HRM and performance is that proposed by Wright and Nishii (2004). Their causal chain proposes (1) *intended* HR practices, leading to (2) *actual* HR practices, leading to (3) *perceived* HR practices, leading to (4) employee reactions, and leading, finally, to (5) organisational performance.

The problem of gaps between espoused intentions and actions

Wright and Nishii's (2004) model underlines the fact that there can be major gaps between management intention and management action that are damaging to employee attitudes and behaviour and ultimately to performance outcomes. Other scholars have made the same point in talking about a gap between management rhetoric and reality (e.g. Legge 2005). We live in a time when it has become common for senior managers to espouse a certain kind of 'culture' in their organisations: a desired way of working with employees, customers and suppliers. Some publish on the web their statements of 'vision and values'.[3] The problem is that the workforce will treat such statements as 'rhetoric' and look for the extent to which high-sounding cultural statements are manifested in reality, in the actual 'climate' of the organisation.

Grant (1999) explores the issues involved through the theory of psychological contracting, which we discussed in terms of individual employment relationships in Chapter 7. However, he raises the level of analysis to the collective level, defining four types of psychological contract between management and its workforce:

- the 'congruent contract' (where management's 'rhetoric' in HRM appeals to employees and 'coincides with their perceptions of reality'). Previous experiences 'tally with the content of the rhetoric'.
- the 'mismatched contract' (where 'the rhetoric fails because it has no appeal to the employee and does not match the perceived reality'). This can happen, for example, when past experience tells employees management cannot deliver on its rhetoric.

---

3 See, for example: www.pfizer.ca/english/pfizer %20canada/vision %20and %20values/ default.asp?s=1 and www.o2.com/cr/resource/visionandvalues.asp

- the 'partial contract' (where 'parts of the rhetoric appeal to the employees and parts do not'). 'For example, the employee may feel that rhetoric promising personal development reflects reality, while at the same time they may feel that rhetoric linking personal development to increased levels of pay does not'.
- the 'trial contract' (where 'rhetoric is given a chance to prove itself and become reality'). This can happen where employees are prepared 'to "buy in" to the rhetoric on a "wait-and-see basis"' (Grant 1999: 331).

Grant (1999) reports a case in the UK consumer electronics sector ('Renco') where data were obtained through two periods of data gathering on employee attitudes, some 18 months apart. Renco, a Japanese-owned company, opened a greenfield site at which Japanese practices of shopfloor participation and a cooperative approach to industrial relations were promised (a shift to a participatory bureaucracy). Workers were keen to give this approach a chance (a trial psychological contract). After 18 months, however, management practice had diverged significantly from the initial rhetoric. Japanese-style consultative practices were allowed to decay. Employees did not experience consistent opportunities for involvement. The trial contract passed away as employees revised their effort (for example, lowering the quality of work) in a 'quid pro quo' for a disappointing management performance. The psychological contract shifted back to a mismatched one. The case illustrates the danger of raising expectations which are then subsequently dashed because management does not care about follow-through or because the internal politics within management de-rail top management's espoused values, as we noted in our discussion of management style in Chapter 6. Cynicism is bred in this kind of environment and any future change management programmes will have serious credibility issues.

Case study research of this nature frequently underlines the importance of bringing senior management's espoused values – or cultural signals – closer into alignment with the collective actions of both senior managers and the various layers of line and specialist managers who report to them. Large organisations in which there are high levels of inconsistency in management values and, thus, in the HRM process, do not have strongly positive workplace cultures (Gordon and DiTomaso 1992). Stronger cultures are more readily built in small, owner-managed organisations where trust levels tend to be higher (Macky and Boxall 2007). Because those who own the firm directly manage employees, there is much less chance for miscommunication to occur and for debilitating internal politics to take root. Where small business owners retain control for long periods of time, they are able to bring a high degree of consistency into the way the firm is managed. This does not mean that small business owners will give employees everything they want – far from it – but they are in a much better position to say what they mean and mean what they say.

Such consistency is much harder to achieve when organisations are large and subject to frequent changes in ownership or in senior management leadership. Public sector organisations have become a paradigm case of how much can go wrong with HRM within the management process. A large part of the difficulties experienced in the quality of employee relations in the public sector occurs because governments (in effect, the owners) change frequently, introducing new philosophies, policy requirements and senior leaders. In addition, the public sector is characterised by high-level policy groups, which can 'dream up' new bureaucratic initiatives, often from elegant theory, but without in-depth managerial experience and at a great distance from the people who actually deliver public services. On the positive side, governments have often had very valid reasons for wanting to control taxation and get better value for the public from government spending. However, a rhetoric of 'partnership' with the public sector unions sits uncomfortably with processes that involve workforce downsizing, privatisation, and contracting out of services, on the one hand, and increased bureaucratic controls through performance targets and audits, on the other (Bach and Kessler 2007). Rather than feeling like partners with government in reforms, public sector workers typically feel under greater stress and less trusted than previously. A common complaint is having too much bureaucratic work to do to get the real job done. Work intensification is particularly noticeable in Britain among professionals coping with the higher levels of client demand and escalating social problems that characterise contemporary health, education and social work (Kersley et al. 2006: 101).

The critical role of line managers

The possibility for gaps between rhetoric and reality underlines the need not only for senior managers in large organisations to figure carefully what they want to achieve and then follow through on their pledges – achieving greater consistency in their own behaviour – but also indicates how dependent they are on lower-level managers to achieve the results they seek.

While this includes both staff specialists, such as HR specialists, and line managers, the latter are particularly important if consistency is going to be high in HRM. Line managers are not ciphers or simple conduits. Line manager action or inaction is often responsible for the difference between espoused HR policies and their enactment. Many HR policies can only be converted to practice by line managers. In so doing, they often reflect the 'informal' or 'real' culture of the firm rather than the values articulated by top management (Truss 2001). In doing this, line managers are not necessarily trying to be perverse. They are often trying to make the organisation function effectively. If the firm's executives are simply financiers rather than people with deep industry experience, the role of line managers in making things work on a daily level becomes even more important. Firms that are being spun off from larger ones, and in which merchant bankers may be holding temporary ownership positions, can be at risk of operational collapse. Loyal supervisors and middle managers may be all that stands between viability and ruin.

Thus, at times, line managers help to keep a sinking ship afloat. At other times, they may be letting a policy die that they think is unworkable or against their interests. This can happen if senior managers or HR specialists have introduced a policy without consultation with those who must implement it. The relationships between HR departments and line managers are important and often contested (Hope-Hailey et al. 1997, McGovern et al. 1997). There are numerous examples of line manager adjustment of HR policies to make them more suitable for specific work settings or, on the 'dark side', for their own personal or political ends (McGovern et al. 1997, Whittaker and Marchington 2003, Batt 2004). These include policies in performance appraisal (Chapter 7) and in involvement and communication (Chapter 6), to name two of the most obvious areas which rely on line managers for their success.

The quality of the relationships between line managers and their team members is starting to receive greater attention in the analysis of HRM (Purcell et al. 2003). Uhl-Bien, Graen and Scandura (2000: 138) adopt the term 'leader-member exchange' (LMX) to argue that 'one critical element of HR systems that has not been well addressed . . . is the role of interpersonal relationships'. Research on managers and their subordinates, they suggest, 'shows that more effectively developed relationships are beneficial for individual and work unit functioning and have many positive outcomes related to firm performance' (ibid.: 143).

There is no doubt that ties within a work team can be much stronger than those with higher-level managers and with remote senior executives. It is much easier to trust someone you know, especially if you share their values and find them to be a person of competence and integrity (Macky and Boxall 2007). Becker et al. (1996) find a stronger relationship between commitment to supervisors and performance than that found between commitment to the organisation and performance. As Liden, Bauer and Erdogan (2004) comment, the 'immediate supervisor plays a critical role as a key agent of the organisation through which members form their perceptions of the organization'. And, as Redman and Snape argue (2005: 304), 'there may . . . be a general tendency for the more cognitively proximal focus (i.e. supervisor or team) to exert greater influence over employee behaviour'. Thus, research on the links between HRM and performance needs to take account of the mediating role of line managers since the HR practices that employees perceive and experience will be heavily influenced by the quality of their relationship with their direct manager.

Employees, then, are going to be influenced not simply by top management values and formal policies but by the reality of what they perceive and experience on a daily basis. Some formal HR policies (such as their base rate of pay and the details of their pension) are (nearly always) directly transmitted from policy to practice without slippage but much else is filtered through line managers, positively or negatively. In addition to espoused values, styles and HR policies, employees gain experience of the quality of material and financial resourcing in their organisation. High-sounding policies for employee rewards and development that are not met with good financial allocations are unlikely to be very convincing after a while.

All of this means that employees are receiving signals on various levels in a large organisation. What they think of the intentions and trustworthiness of management, as a whole, is reflected in the social climate of the workplace (Bowen and Ostroff 2004), which then becomes an important mediator, or intervening variable, in the links between HRM and organisational performance. In healthier organisational climates, there is 'a shared perception of what the organisation is like in terms of practices, policies, procedures, routines and rewards – what is important and what behaviours are expected' (Bowen and Ostroff 2004: 205). Strong HR systems have high levels of coherence and consistency. This does not rule out the need for difficult decisions at times – such as an unavoidable period of downsizing – but workforces are likely to adjust to these more quickly when the overall pattern of management style is deemed ethical and as consistent as possible.

We are now in a position to look at an expanded model of the mediating links that influence the effectiveness of HR systems. This model, shown in Figure 8.3, draws ideas from Purcell and Kinnie (2007) and from the sources quoted in this chapter, such as Wright and Nishii (2004). The model tracks intentions, actions, perceptions and responses and aims to integrate the individual and collective levels of analysis we talked about in Chapter 1

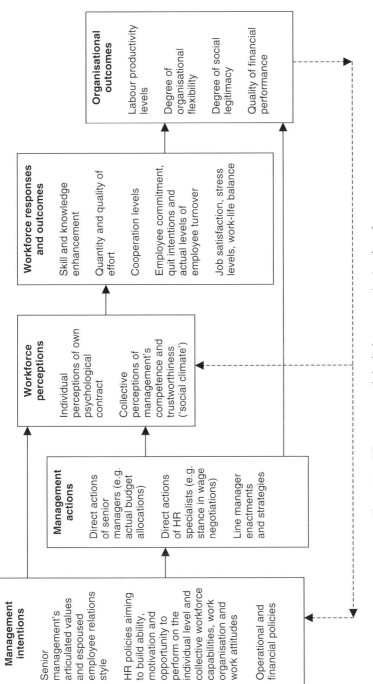

Figure 8.3 HR systems and the links to organisational performance

221

(Figures 1.1 and 1.2) and have fleshed out in the three preceding chapters in this part of the book. HRM involves attempts to build individual abilities, motivations and opportunities to perform (AMO) but this is set within a collective context in which management is trying to build relevant types of workforce capability and work organisation and a reasonably positive set of social attitudes.

At the far left of Figure 8.3 is the box containing the intended elements in HRM – such things as top management's espoused values and employee relations style and the organisation's formal HR policies, both for individuals and for larger groups. Alongside these intentions for how the firm will conduct its HRM are other relevant organisational policies, including those that structure operations and establish resource levels. What we are emphasising here is that the experience of work is not simply about policies that are explicitly called HR policies or are obviously to do with people. Much that is done in finance and in operations management, in particular, affects what people experience at work and the possibilities they have to express themselves.

The next key box in Figure 8.3 is the one where we represent management actions. There are three aspects here. First, senior managers not only form intentions but they also take direct actions, such as deciding actual budget levels in the annual budget round and deciding what they will say in an important team briefing when financial results are disappointing. There are also direct actions by HR specialists in those parts of HRM, such as collective negotiations, which depend on their expertise and networks. How senior managers and HR specialists actually behave in carrying out the organisation's espoused voice practices is a key issue, as Chapter 6 explained. Then, very importantly, there is the behaviour of line managers as they enact HR policies – to the extent that they need to and want to – and also express their own personalities in the way they do things. Line managers are responsible for converting much of HR policy into actual HR practice, given the resources they are allowed to work with and their judgement about what will work or what serves their interests. We are emphasising here that HRM is never a simple policy line. It is a much more complex spread of practice. It is useful to think of HR practice as a wide range of actual managerial behaviour around a notional policy standard.

The next box in the figure represents employee perceptions, both individual and collective. On the individual level, where there is a gap between what management promises and what it delivers, people are likely to feel their psychological contract has been violated and are therefore likely to work less effectively and to look for other options, as explained in

Chapter 7. Individual perceptions feed into, and are influenced by, the larger social climate. This consists of collective perceptions of management's competence and trustworthiness, built up over time. The way in which the larger workforce can develop a collective kind of psychological contract was illustrated in the work of Grant (1999).

Perceptions lead on to workforce responses and outcomes: to growth in skills and knowledge, to particular kinds and levels of effort in individual and group working, to degrees of cooperation between management and labour and among workers themselves, and to individual feelings of commitment, levels of employee turnover, job satisfaction, stress and the like. As we have been at pains to emphasise, these employee behavioural and attitudinal variables are key mediators which then feed into organisational performance, along with other factors in the way the organisation is resourced and managed. The figure is completed with feedback loops. This helps to make the point that more successful organisations are likely to be able to build better human and social capital over time: success often breeds success.

We are not saying through Figure 8.3 that all organisations should be aiming to achieve high levels of consistency across these links or outstanding levels of employee skill, trust, effort and commitment. This is not what all organisations are aiming for, as our discussion of HR systems should have indicated. In the informal model of HRM and in many types of outsourced HRM, for example, managers will often settle for adequate levels of employee performance at low costs. In low-skill services, where customers value low prices and are willing to take part in self-service, such an approach may be perfectly workable. However, the strategy will break down if the labour market tightens and managers have to worry about high levels of employee turnover. Weak links in the HRM-performance chain are also a strategic risk when prices are higher and customers expect careful attention from knowledgeable and accommodating staff. They are a risk whenever companies are trying to compete through higher quality and this depends on employees exercising high levels of skill and discretion.

The value in a diagram like Figure 8.3 lies in helping large organisations, in particular, identify weak links in the HRM-performance chain. Larger organisations are much more prone to internal contradictions, confusions and power struggles. As Chapter 6 explained, it can be very helpful for management in such organisations to open up more comprehensive ('dual') channels of employee voice, and institute employee opinion surveys, in order to strengthen the links in the chain. This is a very practical idea to which we will return in the final chapter.

Conclusions

The HR strategies of firms are usefully thought of as clusters of HR systems. Each HR system is a set of work and employment practices that has evolved to manage a major hierarchical or occupational group in the firm. Over time, managers inevitably put their own twists on HR systems, both positive and negative. Small firms typically depend on a blend of familial and informal models while craft-professional models are critical to professional service firms, to large parts of the public sector and to various niches in manufacturing. Industrial and salaried models emerged first in large-scale manufacturing and then spread to the large 'office factories' of the private sector and the public sector bureaucracy.

The economic and technological context has changed very significantly over the last thirty years and this has led to some key adaptations in HR systems. In various industries, firms based in high-wage countries are now seeking to compete through high skill and quality and have therefore moved from the industrial model to one which fosters higher employee involvement. Others have been seeking greater flexibility through lowering their labour cost structures and weakening their commitments to employees. They have used the opportunities presented by new information technologies, by globalisation and by weaker institutional constraints to outsource various functions and non-core parts of their operations.

The concept of 'internal fit' places a premium on achieving high levels of coherence and consistency in HR systems. Coherence is concerned with the extent to which HR policies are designed to reinforce each other while consistency is mainly to do with strengthening the links from policy to practice within the management process and over time. We should never underestimate the value of coherence and consistency but they do not rule out the possibility that at times there will be trade-offs between organisational and employee interests or that management may need to change HR systems to cope with threatening change. A management team with a high reputation for competence and integrity will negotiate these difficulties more effectively.

Firms that want to enhance the quality of their HRM need to think carefully about the 'black box' links between HRM and organisational performance. There are fragile links between what is intended, what is enacted and what is perceived in HRM that lead on to important employee behaviours and attitudes and thence to organisational outcomes. While they hold resource advantages over small firms, these links are more difficult to manage in large firms, where there can be major slippage between intentions and outcomes. This includes the highly politicised organisations in the public sector where mixed messages in HRM have contributed to low morale and ongoing problems of effectiveness. The key links in the HRM-performance chain are also important in any firm which seeks to compete through high quality or in which the satisfaction levels of customers are sensitive to the interactions they experience with the company's staff.

part 3

Managing people in dynamic and complex business contexts

9

Human resource strategy and the dynamics of industry-based competition

In this part of the book, we move from our discussion of general principles underpinning HRM to an analysis of HR strategy in dynamic and complex contexts. In Chapter 10, we examine the twin complexities of HR strategy in multidivisional and multinational firms. In this chapter, we pick up an idea first advanced by Baird and Meshoulam (1988) – that HR strategy should somehow fit with the firm's stage of development.

Our goal in the chapter is to ask: how can HR strategy support business viability and how might it lay a basis for sustained advantage as firms grapple with change in their industries? Readers will recall the argument in Chapter 2 that all firms face strategic problems. The primary problem is how to become and remain a viable player in the chosen industry. Various aspects of management – competitive positioning, technology, operational style, finance, and HRM – have a critical role to play in this. The fundamental priority of HR strategy in a firm is to secure and maintain the kind of human resources that are necessary for the firm's viability. To use mathematical terminology, a reasonably effective HR strategy is a necessary, but not sufficient, condition of firm viability. The 'second order' – or higher-level – strategic problem is that of how to develop sources of sustained competitive advantage, a problem which not all firms choose to tackle. In theory, however, there exists opportunity for any firm which remains viable in its industry to build some relatively enduring source of superior performance through outstanding management of people. In effect, HR strategy can become a competitive weapon. How it might do so is something that is usefully analysed across cycles of stability and change in industries (Boxall 1998).

229

Industry dynamics: cycles of stability and change

We begin with the basic observation that firms are located in industries (Carroll and Hannan 1995). Even when we look at firms that have grown by unrelated diversification, we find that their constituent parts – their business units – can be located in particular industries. Individual business units do not compete with every other kind of business: they compete with those who seek to serve the same set of customer needs in much the same kind of way – or in a better way. This does not mean that business units compete with every other business in their industry. It is more accurate to identify the 'strategic group' in the industry with which they associate themselves – a cluster of rivals who take significant interest in each other's products, technologies, executives, workforce skills and so on – without overlooking the fact that new competitors can come in 'from left field' (Feigenbaum and Thomas 1993, Peteraf and Shanley 1997). This is why it is useful to speak of *industry-based* rivalry.

It is important to note that the concept of rivalry does not mean that firms are constantly competing. The leaders of firms have a common interest in the health of their industry (Miles, Snow and Sharfman 1993, Nalebuff and Brandenburger 1996). They are certainly engaged in competition for survival and profitability but they also cooperate when it is helpful. Firms are frequently observed in collaborative efforts to develop foreign markets. Australian and New Zealand wine exporters benefit from the joint marketing of 'New World' wines by their national trade organisations in Europe, for example.[1] They also have interests in collaborating in the labour market. The need to build a labour market on which all can draw is often a reason for co-location of firms (Levinthal and Myatt 1994). Good institutions for skill formation and labour supply benefit all firms in the sector. All Australian and New Zealand wine-makers, for example, benefit from supporting the excellent educational institutions, such as the School of Agriculture, Food and Wine at the University of Adelaide,[2] that help to ensure a good supply of graduates for the expanding Antipodean industry.

A focus on industry-based rivalry emphasises the point that history matters, a key argument in the resource-based view of strategic management discussed in Chapter 4. Industries emerge at particular points in time and

---

1 www.wineaustralia.com/europe/Content.aspx?p=77; http://www.nzwine.com/intro/
2 www.agwine.adelaide.edu.au/school/

evolve through periods of crisis – in which there are winners and losers – and periods of relatively stable growth (Schumpeter 1950, Miller and Friesen 1980, Tushman, Newman and Romanelli 1986). This understanding of industry evolution is analogous to the well-known biological concept of 'punctuated equilibrium': the idea that the life forms we find around us are not simply the product of incredibly long periods of time, as originally argued by Charles Darwin, but result from alternating periods of intense change and periods of gradual adaptation (Gersick 1991). For convenience in the argument that follows about the nature of industry evolution, the words 'business' and 'firm' are used interchangeably.

Phases of industry evolution

At the outset of industry formation, pioneering firms introduce technological and/or organisational innovations that create new competitive space. They are typically joined by others who seek to exploit profit opportunities by imitating the pioneers (Freeman and Boeker 1984, Carroll and Hannan 1995). To get established at all, firms must either be successful leaders or successful followers. All industries, in effect, demonstrate a dynamic interplay between innovation and imitation (Schnaars 1994). Over the long haul, resilient firms exhibit an astute blend of the two processes, something than can be difficult for those business leaders who cannot accept emotionally anything 'not invented here' – NIH syndrome.

The microcomputer industry provides an interesting example of the dynamics of innovation and imitation. The legendary innovators, Apple Computer, and about a dozen other firms, entered the industry in 1976 (Carroll and Hannan 1995). Apple produced the first personal computer that could display colour graphics and which could operate with floppy disks. IBM, the industry behemoth, entered five years later, in 1981. For quite a while, David thrashed Goliath. Apple enjoyed the fruits of successful leadership through its various innovations (including the ability of Apple 11 to run spreadsheeting software). However, as we all now know, IBM showed an extraordinary ability to execute an astute 'fast follower' strategy (Utterback 1994, Carroll and Hannan 1995).

The mature context arrives when the industry or sector settles into a period of stable growth based around one or two 'dominant designs' for products or services *and* the organisations that provide them. The development of a dominant design in manufacturing industries enables firms to move quickly up what technology strategists call the S-curve (Foster 1986, Utterback 1994, Henderson 1995), depicted in Figure 9.1. High levels of R&D effort

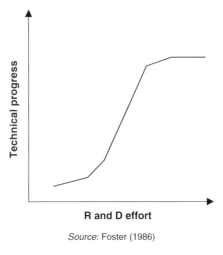

Source: Foster (1986)

Figure 9.1　The S-curve

achieve slow progress to begin with but breakthroughs associated with the dominant design create the basis for rapid improvements. Ultimately, the potential of existing technology reaches some kind of performance limit or asymptote.

In the case of personal computers, the IBM PC brought together the defining features that shaped the industry standard: 'a TV monitor, standard disk drive, QWERTY keyboard, the Intel 8088 chip, open architecture, and MS DOS operating system' (Utterback 1994: 25). Dominant designs represent the strategic configurations that have proved more successful than rival models of strategic management in the establishment phase. As Mueller (1997: 827–8) puts it:

> At some point the market begins to select its favourite model designs, producers begin to concentrate upon the best production techniques. Those firms that have selected the 'right' product designs or production processes survive, the others depart. Following this 'shake-out' period, the industry stabilizes and enters a mature phase in which the number of sellers and industry concentration do not change dramatically.

In the mature context, those who remain credible members of the industry enter a period of relative stability in which the emphasis is on continuous improvement within the prevailing business paradigm. They vary, however, in their profitability and in their readiness for change. Stable growth is punctuated by the next crisis which calls for renewal or leads to decline. Renewal crises may be the result of a new round of technological or organisational innovation within the sector – not necessarily by the original pioneers – or may be introduced by a general threat external to all firms – such as a national economic recession, the decline of tariff protection, or a technological revolution in a different field which has dramatic implications across industry boundaries. In the case of technological challenges, particular technologies tend to reach limits (the flat top of the S-curve) and firms must move to new technologies (with their own S-curves) or fail if they cling to an obsolete technology (Foster 1986).

The renewal context challenges the continuities built up over the establishment and mature phases, threatening to turn previous strengths into weaknesses. It is very hard to change the 'core features' of organisations – such as their fundamental mission, their basic technologies and their marketing strategies – so the difficulty of change in the renewal context should never be underestimated (Carroll and Hannan 1995: 26–8). Two kinds of mature firms manage to survive (Baden-Fuller 1995). One is the firm that succeeds in dominating the direction of industry change: the ultimate level of economic achievement for any firm. The other is the firm that manages to adapt to the direction of change. This kind of firm incurs serious costs of adjustment but retains its viability by making the necessary changes without insolvency or loss of investor confidence. It imitates key changes by the new innovators quickly enough to stay afloat. All other firms fail. New entrants may, of course, appear at this point and may hold a winning advantage if they can add new sources of value and behave as nimble entrepreneurial firms which out-manoeuvre the more inertial mature organisations around them.

Successful weathering of the renewal crisis ushers in another opportunity for stable growth. In effect, the cycle of stability and crisis continues for as long as the industry remains relevant to a profitable set of customer needs. If it does not, the industry enters terminal decline and firms must find something else to do or disappear altogether from the corporate landscape.

The framework shown in Figure 9.2 has been drawn to encompass both goods and service industries. As noted, the S-curve is essentially a concept that relates to manufacturing or to service industries which depend heavily

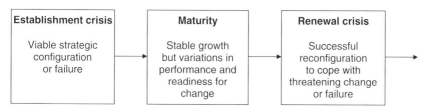

Figure 9.2 Phases of industry evolution

on manufactured technologies for customer service (such as air travel which depends greatly on aircraft technology as well as computerised reservation and passenger management systems). However, all industries – service, manufacturing, public sector etc – can be thought of as facing alternating periods of change and stability. Change need not stem from technological breakthroughs: it may stem from ecological, social or political change as well as general economic trends (such as the Asian economic crisis of the late 1990s).

It is also important to note that Figure 9.2 does not imply that all industries change at the same rate across the contexts of establishment, maturity and renewal. Some, like the profession of law, in which precedent and personal service are so engrained, seem to change only in a slow, stately manner. New information technologies have been adopted in law offices but the fundamental nature of legal research and representation has changed very little over the last 100 years or more. Others, such as consumer electronics, seem characterised by what some consultants call 'permanent white water'.

A useful typology of differences in rates of industry change has been developed by Jeffrey Williams (1992). He distinguishes between slow-cycle, standard-cycle and fast-cycle industries (Figure 9.3). One might usefully imagine a dental practice. The dentistry itself (extraction of teeth, filings etc) is an example of a slow-cycle industry. Little has changed in the fundamental nature of dental work for a long period of time. On the other hand, the toothpaste used by the dentist and his/her clients is an example of a standard-cycle industry. The product is mature, controlled by huge oligopolists, and advertising budgets jostle to hold and enlarge market share. Finally, the accounting and client management software on the computer in the dentist's office may be an example of a fast-cycle industry. New upgrades, new versions are almost constantly available.

	Class 1: slow cycle	Class 2: standard cycle	Class 3: fast cycle
Competitive analogue	Local monopoly	Traditional oligopoly	Schumpeterian
Rivalry	Relaxed: sheltered markets, isolated competition	Extended market share battles, competition on scale	Dynamic: intense rivalry, focus on innovation
Market scope	Narrow: company markets localised	Defined broadly: national or global mass markets and advertising	Varies: overlaps traditional markets, in state of redefinition

Source: Williams (1992)

Figure 9.3   Three types of industry

Despite variations in rates of change, the three-phase model of industry evolution – establishment, maturity and renewal/decline – is well supported by research in industrial economics (Mueller 1997) and provides a useful basis for our analysis. Similar models are commonly used to analyse firm and industry evolution in strategic management textbooks (e.g. Walker 2003).

HR strategy and industry dynamics

With this understanding of industry dynamics, we are now in a position to explore the challenges facing HR strategy in each phase or context. Much more research needs to be conducted on the dynamics of HR strategy. Where they are available, key studies are cited but the discussion is necessarily tentative and suggestive of further lines of enquiry. Our concern in each context is with what HR strategy needs to do to help secure the viability of the firm and, secondly, with what it might do to help create some form of sustained advantage.

The establishment context

Any serious search of the HRM literature will confirm that the establishment or founding phase of industry is the least studied of all by HRM researchers. Apart from the work of Hendry, Arthur and Jones (1995) on the role of human resources in the formation of small firms, the typical HRM textbook assumes a ready-made, large-scale, bureaucratic corporation with an HR department whose staff are concerned with choosing and improving an appropriate set of human resource policies. Few HR researchers have studied small, entrepreneurial start-ups or even new ventures spawned by large corporations. Yet if we are to take the point seriously that history matters to competitive advantage, we must try to understand the roles human resources play in the establishment phase. Strategic management research indicates that that key decisions taken at founding have profound consequences, establishing a pattern of behaviour that is difficult (though not impossible) to change (Freeman and Boeker 1984, Boeker 1989, Eisenhardt and Bird Schoonhovern 1990).

The need for talented entrepreneurs and entrepreneurial teams

What, then, might be said about the likely priorities of HR strategy in this phase? We must begin with the obvious point that all firms depend on appropriate human capital to make any sort of successful beginning.

Relevant human resources are a necessary, but not a sufficient, condition of success. This rather obvious point is supported by a major US study of 'entrepreneurial human capital inputs and small business longevity' (Bates 1990). Bates (*ibid.*) finds that more highly educated entrepreneurs have a better chance of succeeding and of raising finance capital. The likelihood of business failure is lower for high school graduates and for university graduates than it is for those who did not complete high school. The rate of failure drops markedly if entrepreneurs have four or more years of university education. Better-educated business founders make fewer mistakes, it seems. This result has recently been supported by a study of top management teams in the UK which finds that these teams perform better when the individuals in them are better educated (West, Patterson and Dawson 1999). The greatest benefit comes when at least some team members hold a postgraduate qualification. Not only are these people likely to be more intelligent but their abilities are likely to have been significantly enhanced by the kind of training gained through their postgraduate degrees.

As a general rule, firms are established by entrepreneurs, or 'intrapreneurial' teams in existing corporations, who are either (a) successful pioneers, or (b) successful followers (Schumpeter 1950, Porter 1985, Schnaars 1994, Freeman 1995, Mueller 1997). They are founded by people who create new sources of value or by others who quickly perceive that new value is being created and successfully join the industry. It is possible to fail at both leading and at following. As noted earlier, success depends on being good at one or the other or at demonstrating an astute blend of the two over time.

The need to stabilise a competent and well-coordinated workforce

While entrepreneurial insight is a necessary element, it is not, however, sufficient to ensure successful navigation of the establishment phase. The conventional wisdom is that firms need to be able to secure the kind of 'stable and committed labour force' (Rubery 1994: 47) that will enable them to compete, to deliver on promises to customers. They need to be able to recruit and retain a wider group of employees who work together effectively in expanding the founder's or the founding team's concept of the business. Otherwise, the business will simply not grow. As a study of 122 start-up companies in the USA emphasises, an ability to recruit employees is strategic to business growth, along with an ability to win customers and attract finance (Alpander, Carter and Forsgren 1990). Marketing ability, adequate money, and the people needed to carry out the work come in as the three biggest factors explaining success.

Lack of growth potential is fine in those businesses, such as small professional service firms, that can remain viable as permanently small firms (Storey 1985), but it does not work in other contexts. In many industries, firms need to meet a threshold for 'critical mass'. Viability depends on establishing credible operational capacity in the industry, on recruiting and retaining a pool of people with industry-relevant abilities. Whether firms can do this depends on the degree of labour scarcity in their industry and their ability to make competitive job offers. When labour markets are tight, it is often hard to attract talented people to employment 'in a relatively obscure company' (Alpander, Carter and Forsgren 1990: 14).

A classic example of an attempt to create a viable labour pool in the establishment phase comes from the automobile industry. Henry Ford I began production of the Model T in 1908, the same year in which General Motors was founded (Carroll and Hannan 1995). The Ford Motor Company experienced 370 per cent labour turnover in 1913, a level that was not uncommon in manufacturing at the time (Meyer 1981). In a context of massive product market growth, Henry Ford set out to create a large, competent and stable workforce with a highly innovative 'bundle' of personnel policies. This included a rational system of job grading and promotion based on skill differences, along with the 'Five Dollar Day', an early example of 'efficiency wages' (Meyer 1981, Lacey 1986, Main 1990).[3] Facing a major problem with literacy levels, it also included a schooling system for workforce education. Ford's spectacular and controversial adoption of profit sharing (coupled with a highly demanding pace of work on the moving assembly line) ensured that he attracted and retained much of the best labour then available in the industry. Workers queued to get in. Once recruited, those who could not cope with the pace dropped out. Ford built a workforce which was at least equal to that of his rivals, a critical achievement at a time of labour transience in the United States. (His subsequent attempts to fight union organisation are not offered here as a model.)

It is wrong to assume that a good workforce is readily available when the skill requirements of the firm are advanced and specialised. High-skill industries can only survive in particular countries if that society generates

---

3 Introduced in 1914. The effect was to roughly double the income of automotive workers employed by Ford. The length of work shifts was reduced at the same time: from 9 to 8 hours. 'Efficiency wages', in this case, means that there can be value in certain circumstances in paying a wage premium (well above the going rate) to improve the recruitment pool and reduce undesirable turnover of highly trained workers (McConnell and Brue 1995: 214).

sufficient numbers of people educated in the relevant science and technology. The great economic historian, David Landes (1998), cites the case of the chemical dye industry which grew phenomenally prior to World War One. Germany trained far more chemists than anyone else, enabling the foundation and growth of the German chemical giants: Hoechst, BASF, Bayer and Agfa, all 'equipped with well-fitted house laboratories and closely tied to the universities' (Landes 1998: 290). When key German chemists teaching in Britain were 'drawn back home by attractive offers, the British organic chemical industry shrivelled' (*ibid.*: 290). In an illustration of the role of tacit knowledge (discussed in Chapter 4), the confiscation of German industrial patents during the war did not help American firms to emulate German chemical success. Not to be outdone, they turned to the recruitment of German chemists in the 1920s (Landes 1998: 291).

Our argument, then, is that stabilising a competent workforce of the appropriate size for the industry and the firm's competitive goals is critical to viability in the establishment phase. This should not be thought about simply in terms of individualistic recruitment and retention. As Chapter 2 argued, effective teamwork is also needed. There needs to be reasonably good teamwork among top managers and right throughout the organisation. Research on the establishment of the semiconductor industry in the 1950s helps to illustrate these principles (Holbrook *et al.* 2000). One of the early leaders, Fairchild Semiconductor, combined a good mix of research and production skills in its core group of executives – the so-called 'traitorous eight' who broke away from the Shockley company (as noted in Chapter 4). Not only did this group work together well as a team but they worked hard to ensure that R&D activities were closely coordinated with the firm's production. When the ability of Fairchild to coordinate R&D and production was undermined in the mid-1960s, a subsequent breakaway formed Intel (Holbrook *et al.* 2000: 1027).

Sources of human resource advantage?

Large and growing firms that have the ability to pay wage premia, and the capacity to offer superior internal development, are likely to enjoy formidable advantages in the establishment phase. This certainly seems the case with firms such as IBM that enter new markets and helps to explain why so many small businesses fail to expand successfully or remain small, tenuous organisations with ongoing recruitment and retention stresses (Storey 1985, Hendry, Arthur and Jones 1995). The bigger firms operating in the same labour market have better financial resources and more developed 'internal labour markets' (Rubery 1994: 48–51). Large, established firms enjoy superior legitimacy with investors and bankers in the capital markets (Storey 1985). This enables them to offer greater training and career development possibilities to talented employees, something which many people want, as noted in Chapter 7.

What possible routes are available for the very small new venture, founded by an under-capitalised individual rather than a well-known, multidivisional corporation? Arguably, this often means clever use of personal networking (Hendry *et al.* 1995) at a strategic moment in the industry's development. While there is very limited research on this problem, we might consider the example of a young, and very successful, entrepreneurial software engineer (Boxall 1998). This young entrepreneur used their network from Engineering School to recruit highly intelligent individuals willing to work outside large organisations (perhaps because they preferred an informal, 'can do' environment) and swiftly offered those who generated outstanding value an ownership stake in the firm to align their interests over the longer term. Having worked with them at university, the young entrepreneur had special knowledge about the abilities and predispositions of classmates as well as personal ties based on friendship and trust. This created an edge over corporate recruiters forced to rely on formal screening processes and more opaque forms of information (such as university grades) rather than personal knowledge and close connections. In terms of resource-based theory, the young entrepreneur lacked superior financial clout and market reputation but used personal background and social networks to out-manoeuvre recruiters from large, established organisations.

Our knowledge about sources of human resource advantage in the establishment phase is still very limited. It seems likely, however, that *early alignment* of interests among highly talented people plays a decisive role (as was the case at Fairchild Semiconductor). This means that history – being there at the right time – matters enormously in the creation of positions of strength in industries (as argued in the resource-based view). It also implies that clever use of personal knowledge – such as an ability to network among likeminded and similarly gifted people – is needed to overcome the formidable resource barriers associated with firms that are more established in labour and capital markets.

The mature context

We can be somewhat more confident about the priorities of HR strategy in the mature context. This is the familiar terrain of the HRM textbook. Writers typically assume that a viable business has been handed on from the establishment phase. To be fair, it is only the firms which have grown beyond about 150 to 200 employees that employ HR specialists. This means that the vast majority of HR specialists are working in the mature context or in the renewal context into which it typically leads (see below).

Enduring principles but greater sophistication

Growth beyond the establishment phase into the mature context *does* introduce problems that require a different style of management. It is still vital to create, coordinate and retain a sufficient pool of motivated labour with appropriate industry know-how. This principle is hardly likely to vary with time in the industry. However, the challenges of size, increasing workforce complexity, the need to comply with various employment regulations, and the possibility of unionisation, all mean that HR systems need to become more comprehensive and more formalised, as explained in Chapters 3 and 8. Reliance on the implicit philosophies and informal practices of the small, entrepreneurial firm becomes much less realistic. When recruited into a larger organisation, workers typically expect some formalisation of their role requirements in a written job description. They tend to expect some formal orientation which will introduce them, *inter alia*, to the firm's policies for training, development, pay, promotion and so on. Properly handled, formalisation eases the process of socialisation and psychological contracting by reducing uncertainty and limiting arbitrariness in management practice. Standardisation of policies also makes the management of staff more efficient because it reduces the transaction costs of employing large numbers of people.

On the other hand, the maturing of organisational structure can alienate the very people who have helped to make the firm successful so far. The trend to bureaucratisation may antagonise those who revelled in the informality and adrenalin-pumping riskiness of the firm's founding years. These individuals may experience a sense of loss, a sense that the company will never again be driven by the same white-hot creativity and sense of fun. Thus, growth can generate a tension around the desirability of bureaucratisation: on the one hand, it is needed to manage size and complexity and, on the other, it threatens the intimacy and challenge of earlier times.

Supposing this tension does not get out of hand, firms that successfully survive the establishment crisis will have reasonably competent executive leadership and will have built an adequate operating workforce. They will typically have created a sound reputation as a source of respectable employment and have laid the basis of trustworthy employee relations.

In terms of the HRM challenges facing the business, they should at least aim to retain 'competitive parity': their HR strategy may not be the best in the industry but it has not so far undermined the firm's growth. Arguably, this situation should persist providing there are no major reversals in the quality of HR strategy. At the very least, the firm's leaders should avoid turning their competitive parity in HRM into a form of competitive *dis*advantage (Purcell 1999: 241).

Figure 9.4 summarises the key dimensions of what is required in HRM to help secure a firm's viability. As indicated in our discussion, firms need talented and functioning leadership teams, along with a motivated and capable workforce which can reliably execute its work processes and deliver on promises to customers. These critical human resources are developed through an appropriate mix of HR systems and through supportive non-human resources, including adequate levels of finance. The arrows in the diagram are double-headed because of the interaction among these elements. For example, good HR systems and adequate funding will help the firm to recruit (or develop internally) good leadership teams. However, it is also true that good leadership teams will, over time, improve the quality of HR systems in the firm and make the kind of financial allocation decisions that enable it to attract and develop other people. Similarly, a motivated and capable workforce will help the firm to generate profits, part of which can be reinvested in HR systems.

Potential sources of HR advantage?

What, however, might a firm do if it wishes to develop some form of 'human resource advantage' in the mature context? What argument can be built from the resource-based view discussed in Chapter 4? Very little theory is available on this question but one argument is based on the value of improving the

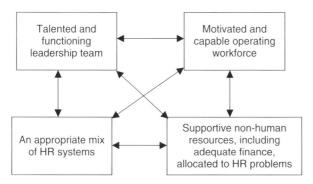

Figure 9.4 HRM and the viability of the firm: key elements

quality of management perception in HRM, the quality of HR planning, and improvements in the consistency of HR practice (Boxall 1998).

The quality of management perception in HRM
Firms vary in the quality of management's *perception* of the firm's strengths and weaknesses in HRM in relation to the strengths and weaknesses of rival employers. Specialised knowledge about *individual* HR practices is widespread (for example, the knowledge developed by recruitment consultants about selection tests or the knowledge developed by compensation consultants about pay packages) but the ability to discern the *patterns* embedded in the firm's unfolding labour management practices is more likely to be rare. The ability to perceive ways of minimising critical trade-offs in labour management (such as the trade-off between short-run employment flexibility and long-run employee commitment) is also likely to be rare (Boxall 1999).

Research suggests that few managers have a superior understanding of how to 'bundle' or integrate HR practices into HR systems that fit the firm's specific context and its unfolding strategies (MacDuffie 1995, Barney and Wright 1998). If, however, a firm employs individuals with this kind of rare knowledge and perception, and the opportunity to exercise it, what might prevent it being lost to rival firms? If much of the knowledge remains tacit, or associated with executive teamwork, it may be difficult for rivals to discern what it is or who has it (causal ambiguity and social complexity). There is little doubt, however, that this sort of skill will eventually become visible to good search consultants ('head-hunters') and therefore vulnerable to mobility. Individual perception remains, in effect, individual property.

The quality of HR planning
To build human resource advantage in the mature context, the firm needs to develop attributes which are more deeply institutionalised (Mueller 1996). A superior system of human resource *planning*, which identifies and integrates key human variables with other strategic concerns, is one way of institutionalising the perceptual insights of key HR strategists (either specialists or general managers) who may decide to resign from the firm. The kind of human resource planning which encourages firms to manage 'key value generators' proactively and plan to improve key processes (such as learning across intra-firm boundaries) is both valuable and rare (Koch and McGrath 1996). Human resource planning for concerns that transcend the short-term business context helps to avoid the all-too-common situation where financial targets, reinforced in the annual budget cycle, crowd out

longer-term strategic issues in management planning (Goold 1991), a theme we take further in Chapters 10 and 11.

Even very large firms have problems developing sophisticated strategic planning systems which incorporate a framework of strategic HR objectives capable of structuring internal debate and decision making (Purcell and Ahlstrand 1994, Boxall 1999). How might such a discipline be developed and defended? Clearly it depends on the recruitment and retention of leaders who have exceptional HR insight, as discussed above. But this is not sufficient because so much of strategic management depends on good teamwork, as argued in Chapter 2. At some point, a powerful coalition of managers must evolve the conceptual framework and generate the consensus for its ongoing application. At a minimum, a shared understanding between the firm's most influential general managers and its top HR specialists, which persuades other key managers, seems essential. Any firm that achieves this has accomplished an unusual feat in the management process given the political conflicts and paradigmatic disputes that typically afflict the management teams of large organisations. The difficulty of overcoming these internal conflicts is a powerful barrier to imitation. It is not, of course, perfect: the loss of key individuals who act as process champions can compromise the quality of any planning system.

The consistency of HR practice
The possibility of developing HR advantage will be greater to the extent that intelligent HR planning is linked to superior *consistency* of enlightened practice (Mueller 1996, Benkhoff 1997). This is an argument we developed in Chapter 8 where the problem of major gaps between management intentions and actions in HRM was discussed. Significant gaps between management rhetoric and the reality of management practice can be particularly damaging, as illustrated in the work of Grant (1999).

As mentioned in Chapter 8, there is no such thing as *the* single HR practice of the firm. HR practice in large firms typically includes all sorts of variation around the formal HR policy position. Some of this variation is good because line managers can be trying to make poorly designed policies work better in practice. Other variations are negative, stemming from personal politics or from the difficult job line managers face in reconciling HR aspirations with the resources made available to them. In those multidivisional firms where HR strategy is very devolved, for example, but managers are only rewarded in terms of short-term financial results, long-term HR priorities can suffer, as we explain in Chapter 10. While there is value in enhancing the ability of divisional or business-unit managers to make decisions that fit their circumstances, short-run performance incentives discourage long-run processes like management succession planning and development. This is not a problem if the firm's main rivals are equally weak at developing plans for long-run human resource development but it is not a recipe for building sustained advantage or undermining a more positively 'planful' competitor.

In summary, the argument here is that the possibility of creating HR advantages for a firm is greater when exceptional perception about HR strategy is embedded in sophisticated planning systems which are connected to consistent practice. The level of insight, and the degree of internal consensus, required to achieve this kind of superiority should not be underestimated. It is likely to be very rare.

The renewal context

The renewal context challenges the continuities built up over the establishment and mature phases. It threatens to turn previous strengths into weaknesses through technological (or other) shocks which call for a reconfiguration of the strategic paradigm in the firm (Schumpeter 1950, Tushman, Newman and Romanelli 1986, Barney 1991, Mueller 1997). As noted earlier, two kinds of mature firms manage to survive (Baden-Fuller 1995). One is the firm that succeeds in dominating the direction of industry change. The other is the firm that manages to adapt to the direction of change. All other firms fail. New entrants may, of course, appear at this point and may hold a winning advantage if they can behave as clever and nimble entrepreneurial firms. They needn't necessarily be small firms: they may, for example, be special business units operating within very powerful multidivisional firms.

What, then, are the implications for human resource strategy? Rather than assuming that firms are privileged by their past, we must now regard history as a double-edged sword.

Conditions for securing viability

There are, arguably, three conditions firms must meet to retain their viability during this kind of industry upheaval (Boxall 1998). Two of these conditions are primarily concerned with HR strategy but the third is not.

The first is *political*. The renewal context threatens the patterns of mutuality – of interest alignment – that have solidified over the establishment and mature phases. The renewing firm needs the kind of mandate from its core staff which enables it to bring about major change without enormous resistance. Here the impact of the established hierarchy is important. To begin with, the key players in senior management must be able to form a new 'micro-political' consensus. As noted in Chapter 2, significant, unresolved conflict in the senior management team over the need for change (possibly linked to personal career ambitions and historical power bases) will disrupt renewal efforts at the outset (Hambrick 1987, 1995).

Having said this, the ability to open the micro-political gateway at the senior level is necessary but not sufficient for successful renewal in the industry. It is also essential to achieve the necessary change to business capabilities while maintaining an adequate motivational climate throughout the core of the firm's workforce, thus ensuring wider political acceptability for the desired changes. Or, if a large part of the changes are to be formulated from the bottom up, it involves achieving a culture of change acceptability which fosters a willing acceptance of new learning trajectories as a matter of course. In general terms, as we outlined in Chapter 8, HR systems have evolved in the last thirty years to accommodate higher levels of change. Some business leaders have been seeking to evolve their organisations into 'flexible bureaucracies' which have a core workforce but also use high levels of outsourcing for non-core functions which can be obtained much more cheaply elsewhere. Others have moved to a participatory bureaucracy which embraces higher levels of employee involvement as a way of building better learning and resilience.

The second condition is *perceptual*. The firm needs leaders who can see what competencies will retain their relevance in the future while perceiving what capabilities have already become liabilities. Where, in effect, should the firm consolidate its learning and what should it 'unlearn' and to what extent (Miller and Friesen 1980, Leonard 1992, 1998, Snell, Youndt and Wright 1996)? And when, and in what order, should it make the desirable changes: how should it shape its 'strategic staircase' (Baden-Fuller and Stopford 1994)? Senior management faces a complex cognitive problem in discerning the kind, extent and timing of the change that is needed to enable the firm to survive. As noted in Chapter 2, this has been called the problem of forming a new 'mental model' (Barr, Stimpert and Huff 1992). It is highly likely, of course, that senior management does not have all the answers, in which case the firm's leadership must perceive how to design the sort of participative processes that will generate the necessary learning. The cognitive problem leaders face in renewal is not simply about content: it is also about process. It is altogether more complex than the perceptual problems associated with the mature phase.

The third condition is concerned with *related resources*. The firm must actually have the access to the financial resources it needs to make the necessary changes. As ever, human and non-human resources are interdependent (Mueller 1996). When renewal means radical change, it requires more than human willingness and cleverness. It requires the cash box to make things happen. Lots of firms fail at the renewal phase simply because they are under-capitalised (rather like the establishment phase). Despite great ideas and the best of intentions, no one will lend them any more money.

Opportunities for human resource advantage?

If these are the conditions for retaining viability in the renewal context, where do the opportunities lie for building sustained advantage through human resources? One argument is that it is simply a case of hanging on, of still being there once restructuring and rightsizing strategies – both good and bad – have made their mark on the industry landscape (Boxall 1998). Some rivals will have been fatally weakened in the process – perhaps because they divested the wrong bits – and will go into bankruptcy or suffer the sort of share price collapse that makes them easy takeover targets. The firms with the bigger cash boxes then acquire their weaker rivals, retaining the branches or plants (and people) they really want and divesting or shutting down the rest. The industry concentrates around the strongest survivors. This process may not be pleasant – and rarely, if ever, discussed in HRM textbooks – but it does suggest that superior human capital will tend to concentrate in the dominant firms despite a prevailing climate of employment insecurity in the industry. On the other hand, the dominant firms cannot afford to be complacent because processes of concentration allow some clever teams to split away from the major firms and occupy specialist market niches (Carroll and Hannan 1995: 215–21).

Human resource strategy and organisational agility

An alternative argument calls for the firm to be more proactive, asserting that the surest way to achieve human resource advantage in the renewal context lies in preparing for it more effectively in the mature context (Boxall 1998). Abell (1993) argues that the outstanding firm manages with 'dual strategies': 'mastering the present and pre-empting the future'. Duality implies superior perceptual and planning abilities in all contexts: the firm must not become locked into the inertia of a single strategy at any point in time. Providing the firm's industry does not collapse by becoming technologically irrelevant, this scenario is plausible in theory.

Based on exploratory case studies in the USA, Dyer and Shafer (1999) have developed a model of how HR strategy might support organisational agility. In their definition, agile organisations aim 'to develop a built-in capacity to shift, flex, and adjust, either alone or with alliance partners, as circumstances

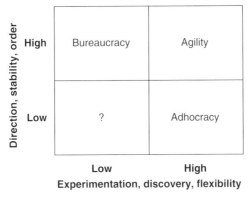

	Low	High
High	Bureaucracy	Agility
Low	?	Adhocracy

Direction, stability, order

Low   **High**

Experimentation, discovery, flexibility

Source: Dyer and Shafer (1999)

Figure 9.5 A definition of organisational agility

change, and do so as a matter of course' (Dyer and Shafer 1999: 148). In effect, they aim 'to optimise adaptability and efficiency simultaneously' (Figure 9.5). Recalling our discussion of HR objectives in Chapter 1, agile organisations can be thought of as firms that aim for high levels of cost-effectiveness (in the current context) and high levels of organisational flexibility (to cope with future contexts). In terms of technology strategy, they are firms that can maximise the gains from their current S-curve while moving when desirable to the next one and reaping its benefits. It might be worthwhile to inject a note of caution here, however. In terms of Jeffrey Williams' framework (Figure 9.3), it is firms in fast-cycle industries that most need this capacity. The idea that all industries demand this level of change readiness is exaggerated in popular accounts.

Dyer and Shafer (1999) note that organisational theorists tend to write about organisational agility with little regard for the people elements involved. To help fill this void, their model starts by defining the characteristics of agile organisations and works back through employee behaviours and competencies to desirable HR practices. We have paraphrased and summarised this model in Figure 9.6.

Dyer and Shafer incorporate resource-based thinking in their model: achievement of an agile organisation is very likely to be valuable and hard to imitate. The concept of an agile organisation is fleshed out to mean one that can read markets well (both current and emerging), can create a culture which welcomes change, and one which readily embeds organisational learning. Like Schuler and Jackson (1987), they then specify certain kinds of desirable employee behaviours and link these to HR practices (see Chapter 3). Much of this thinking is tentative and exploratory but flexible work design

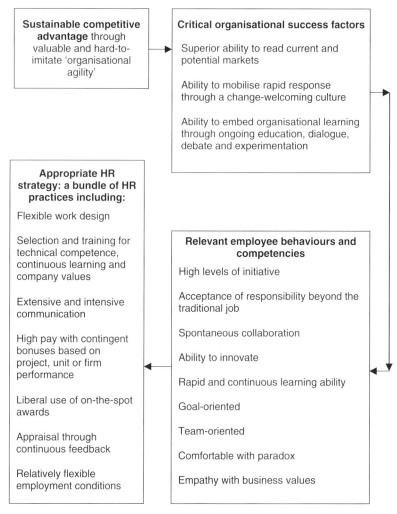

Sustainable competitive advantage through valuable and hard-to-imitate 'organisational agility'	Critical organisational success factors

Sustainable competitive advantage through valuable and hard-to-imitate 'organisational agility'

Critical organisational success factors

Superior ability to read current and potential markets

Ability to mobilise rapid response through a change-welcoming culture

Ability to embed organisational learning through ongoing education, dialogue, debate and experimentation

Appropriate HR strategy: a bundle of HR practices including:

Flexible work design

Selection and training for technical competence, continuous learning and company values

Extensive and intensive communication

High pay with contingent bonuses based on project, unit or firm performance

Liberal use of on-the-spot awards

Appraisal through continuous feedback

Relatively flexible employment conditions

Relevant employee behaviours and competencies

High levels of initiative

Acceptance of responsibility beyond the traditional job

Spontaneous collaboration

Ability to innovate

Rapid and continuous learning ability

Goal-oriented

Team-oriented

Comfortable with paradox

Empathy with business values

Source: Paraphrased and summarised from Dyer and Shafer (1999)

Figure 9.6   Dyer and Shafer's model of HR strategy in agile organisations

is central to Dyer and Shafer's model (fluid job assignments rather than fixed jobs or positions). They then suggest certain kinds of employment practice which should accompany fluid work organisation. The ideas here resonate with much of what we described as a high-involvement HR system in Chapters 5 and 8.

As Dyer and Shafer (1999) advise, we need much more research on the nature of 'organisational agility', and the kind of HR strategies that might support it. One critical question must surround the problem of incentives or mutuality. Why would talented workers want to join an agile organisation if very little security is being offered and if, as a relatively flat organisation, little career development is possible? One can imagine that some people will want to buy into the culture for the sheer thrill, the joy of learning, and quite probably, the high pay level if the firm does well. However, as Dyer and Shafer (1999: 169) imply, it is likely that an agile firm will need a stable core of long-term, talented employees if it is to be able to sustain committed learning over time:

> Most agile organisations, contrary to what might be expected, lean toward a so-called closed internal staffing system . . . They go to great lengths to retain core employees who continue to contribute; most have relatively low voluntary turnover rates and, despite having little reluctance to part company with non-performers, most make every effort to avoid lay-offs because . . . they have rather extensive investments in their core employees.

Clearly, the design of agile organisations is a 'frontier area' in strategic HRM and much more work will need to be done, particularly on the management of the strategic tensions involved (Evans and Genadry 1999). The contemporary environment contains major tensions between corporate needs for flexibility, on the one hand, and typical employee needs for certain base-line elements of stability, on the other. Talented, versatile employees have good choices in the international labour market, so the need for compromise and adjustment is not one-way. Further work on how these tensions can be better reconciled is vital.

Conclusions

This chapter has built on resource-based concepts discussed earlier in the book and examined an area that is rarely thought about in HRM texts: the ways in which HR strategy might need to adapt across cycles of change and stability in industries. Not all industries change at the same rate but change pressures are universal.

Drawing on the distinction made in Chapter 2, priorities for HR strategy were considered from two angles: what is needed for viability in the industry and what might contribute to sustained competitive advantage? To achieve viability in the establishment context, firms need talented entrepreneurial leaders and need to be able to stabilise a competent and well-coordinated workforce. Viability depends on establishing credible operational capacity.

Whether firms can do this depends on the degree of labour scarcity in their industry and their ability to make competitive job offers. Firms cannot afford to assume that all the advanced or specialised skills they require will be readily available. Large, well-funded firms are obviously at an advantage when it comes to making offers of good pay and strong internal development to talented individuals. The small, under-capitalised business has great difficulty competing against better-funded rivals but astute use of personal networking, and early alignment of interests, may help them to out-manoeuvre more bureaucratic organisations.

In the mature context, it remains important to create, coordinate and retain a sufficient pool of motivated labour with appropriate industry know-how. Firms that survive from the establishment context will have something close to competitive parity in HRM and should aim, at the least, to maintain it. However, they will find that the challenges of growth mean that the style of management will need to change: size, diversity, regulation and the likelihood of employee representation will mean that HR systems need to become more comprehensive and more formalised. Arguably, sources of advantage can be created by firms whose management teams exhibit high levels of perception in HR strategy. Talented HR strategists can be lured away, so it is better if these insights are embedded in excellent HR planning systems and consistent HR practice. This combination of strengths is likely to be very rare. It is not unusual to find ways in which the HR performance of mature firms can be enhanced.

All bets are off in the renewal context. History could now be as much a source of 'core rigidity' as 'core competence' (Leonard 1992, 1998). Simply managing the perceptual, political, and funding problems associated with survival is a major achievement. One of the most interesting questions in strategic HRM concerns the characteristics of 'agile organisations', firms that anticipate the need for renewal and are well prepared to take advantage of it (Dyer and Shafer 1999). Arguably, this is more important in fast-cycle industries. Existing work is exploratory and research in this area needs to consider ways in which tensions between company and employee goals can be managed more effectively. There is no doubt that agile organisations need greater flexibility but they are unlikely to reach high performance levels without stabilising at least a critical core of highly talented individuals and teams who work in a highly participative way. In working out the tension between stable harvesting of the current environment and preparation for radical change, firms are likely to find that at least some strong commitments need to be made to fair, interesting and reliable employment relationships if they are to attract and hold talented staff.

10

Corporate human resource strategy in the global economy

Most models of business strategy, and strategic human resource management, start with the premiss that the firm is both independent, with a direct relationship between it and the shareholders, and engaged in a single business activity. With these two assumptions in place, it is possible to model the behaviour of the firm in response to specific market and technological conditions in its industry, as we did in Chapter 9. This allows us to show the role of HR strategy within business strategy as the firm and its industry evolve over time. All models need to reduce the infinite complexity of organisational life, as revealed over time, through a process of variable reduction, enabling us to make some sense of what is going on and extrapolate trends. Sensible though this is, it can reduce complexity too far. We need in this chapter to take account of the effect on HR strategy of being a multi-business, and often multinational, firm.

It is common in advanced economies for many, if not most, workplaces to be part of larger organisations where top management is geographically remote, either domestically or internationally. For example, in the UK, 58 per cent of all workplaces with at least 10 employees in 2004 were branches of multi-site organisations (Kersley *et al.* 2006: 20). This is true of nearly every workplace in the public sector and around one in two private sector workplaces. Foreign ownership in the UK more than doubled between 1980 and 1998 (Millward, Bryson and Forth 2000: 32) and grew again in the period to 2004. By then, 31 per cent of private sector workplaces were wholly or partly controlled by foreign companies compared with 23 per cent in 1998 (Kersley *et al.* 2006: 19). The largest proportion were US-owned (37 per cent), followed by other European multinationals (23 per cent) (*ibid.*: 19). The Spanish have been particularly active in recent years: for example, in purchasing the

251

Abbey National bank. This foreign direct investment (FDI) is, of course, not restricted to Britain, although the UK has fewer restrictions on foreign ownership than its continental neighbours. 'The UK, Germany, Holland and France hosted 40 per cent of worldwide FDI in the early 1990s. There were 3500 cross-border mergers in the run-up to the creation of the Single European Market (European firms buying other European firms) . . . (while, at the same time) UK firms were investing $27 billion in the US: the largest single country-to-country movement in its history' (Sparrow 2002). A representative study of large companies in the UK in the early 1990s, each employing over 1,000 people, found that 60 per cent were multinational corporations (MNCs) (Marginson *et al.* 1993). Of the 24 per cent of these big firms which were foreign-owned, half were North American, 38 per cent had their headquarters elsewhere in Europe, with the remainder coming from other parts of the world.

To get to grips with the ways in which HRM is a strategic issue in the management of such large and dispersed firms, we need to look at trends in their structure and control, both nationally and internationally. This takes us into an understanding of the dynamics of the multidivisional company (M-form) and the way the M-form company has spread to a dominant position worldwide. Some argue that we are now seeing the emergence of a new type of M-form based around networks: the N-form (e.g. Hedlund 1994). The development of the N-form company has major implications for HRM, especially in the way the critical resources of human and social capital, including managers and professional workers, are developed and interact across boundaries, whether political-geographic or organisational.

At the same time, we need to look at the impact of ownership and control on workplace HR systems. Here a popular mantra for MNCs is to 'think global, act local' (a phrase coined by ABB Ltd).[1] This implies a separation of corporate strategy, dealing with the whole of the corporation ('think global'), from the delivery of products and services at the local level in different ways and in different forms to take account of institutional and cultural differences ('act local'). Thus, our concern is with dilemmas in structural configuration and with forms of control exercised from headquarters, the corporate office. Do firms centralise or decentralise, or try to achieve both, and with what implications? And should corporations seek to integrate the different businesses they own, or treat them as separate entities but try

---

1 See, for example, www.abb.com.cn/cawp/cnabb057/97dc03dfacc5f767c1256b0b0030a063. aspx?

to manage them better than if they were wholly independent? The crucial question is: how does the centre add value, how does it develop what has been called 'parenting advantage' (Goold, Campbell and Alexander 1994)? We need to ask: what contribution, if any, does HRM make to parenting advantage?

Most large companies have grown by buying other companies, and simultaneously selling parts of their portfolio of businesses. We need to consider the special challenges that mergers and acquisitions (M&As) pose for HRM. This is a particularly acute question since around half of all M&As are deemed failures (KPMG 1999) with implementation problems relating to people, employment and cultural issues the main reasons for failure (Hubbard and Purcell 2001: 17–18). We consider this problem in the latter part of the chapter.

The branch of HRM most concerned with MNCs is International HRM (IHRM) (e.g. Evans, Pucik and Barsoux 2002, Dowling and Welch 2004, Sparrow, Brewster and Harris 2004). Much of the research in this area has been on staffing, with a focus on the selection, socialisation and management of expatriates (see Scullion and Brewster (2001) for a summary and analysis). Formidable though some of these HR issues are, often dominating the attention of international, specialist HR managers, there are also powerful issues to do with structure – with integration and separation, centralisation and decentralisation – which have serious implications for HR strategies. In practice, virtually all MNCs adopt an M-form structure. The merging of the M-form with MNCs is, in part, an outcome of shifts in global markets. When there were predominantly national markets in, say, soap powders, cars, insurance companies and hotels, the question was: how did the MNC manage its assets (including its people) in distinct national markets? Increasingly markets are global, as we noted in Chapter 5. Soap packets can come with a whole host of languages on the back. The 'world car' is premissed on global design and global sourcing of components. Insurance companies are too small to survive in one country alone, and hotel chains straddle most parts of the world with a global branding strategy. Increasingly, the organisational form of MNCs is not one of separate companies in each country with their own national strategies but divisions based on products or services facing end-markets across boundaries. One consequence is that labour markets for managerial and professional workers have increasingly become global (Wooldridge 2006). Recruitment agencies are taking on global roles for sourcing specialist skills under global supply contracts with major employers. Manpower Inc., for example, has 4,400 offices in 73 countries and placed more than 4 million people into permanent, temporary or contract positions in 2005.[2] Its client list includes 90 per cent of the *Fortune Global 500* companies.

Thus, it is not sensible to separate a consideration of the dominant form of large firm organisation – the M-form company – from MNCs. There are key strategic factors that are common to both. The international and global issues that confront large corporations in HR terms, such as variances in cultures, forms of regulation and institutional frameworks, are woven into this chapter.

Strategy, structure and the divisionalised company

Most firms start as single businesses. As they grow and mature, and as the market they serve changes, a number of critical choices are faced. Is the competitive position in the current market sustainable given new entrants, is there sufficient capital available from revenue to fund future investment needs, is the market maturing such that growth potential and margins are likely to be eroded in the medium term? Another type of question faced is whether there are opportunities to use distinctive technologies or knowledge to enter other markets. What is certain is that doing nothing is rarely viable, and for many business leaders rather boring too. One route to growth is to branch away from the traditional market, in other words to diversify. This could be to do the same thing in a new market, as British retailer, Marks and Spencer, sought to do by buying their way into the USA and Canada. Another route is by vertical integration, seeking both to protect the supply chain and to enter new markets where there is growth potential or to make life more difficult for competitors in cornering a market position. It may also be that another firm possesses knowledge of a technology or market that the single-business firm lacks, or indeed they may feel a lack of general management expertise. Whatever the reason, the critical choice that follows is: how best to manage a diversified business, nationally and internationally, and how far should diversification go?

The traditional firm usually adopts a functional or unified form where functional specialists in marketing, operations, finance and HRM each coordinate their own areas, having representation on the board of directors under the command of the chief executive (CEO) and sometimes a separate

---

2 www.manpower.com/mpcom/content.jsp?articleid=33

chairman. The board may also contain non-executive directors drawn from the great and the good in the corporate world to provide oversight, advice and access to networks. As firms diversify, this structure is placed under strain. Executive directors are responsible for operational decisions but find that the scope of their responsibility in multiple sites and two or more markets is difficult to handle. They tend to suffer from 'bounded rationality', as we discussed in Chapter 2.

An alternative organisational form for the multi-business company is the holding company where the corporate office holds the assets of each of the companies in the portfolio but allows each to manage its own affairs and to retain a proportion of the profits that they generate. In effect, the holding company is a type of institutional shareholder or friendly banker. The problem is that the holding company does little to add value since it is not actively managing its assets, and indeed may destroy value by protecting the inefficient or preventing the good from gaining access to the capital market to fund further expansion.

The American solution to this problem of how best to manage diverse businesses was the adoption of the M-form structure. In a famous book in the early 1960s, Chandler (1962) extrapolated from the experience of General Motors under Alfred Sloan to assert that 'structure follows strategy'. This meant that decisions on the long-term direction of the firm and the scope of its activities (its corporate strategy) should be the dominant factor in decisions on the structure of the corporation. These 'second-order decisions' on internal operating procedures, and, especially for our purposes, the relationship between parts of the organisation, thus flowed from first-order corporate strategy. This had a profound influence on the location of decision making in HRM, both directly and indirectly (seen in how corporate control was exercised over operating decisions and activities). HR strategies in operating units are then best seen as a 'third-order' activities or downstream processes which are deeply influenced by first- and second-order strategy (Figure 10.1).

The distinctive feature of the M-form organisation is a clear separation of 'operational management' from 'strategy makers' in the corporate office. All profits are returned to the corporate office and regular weekly or monthly reports are required on aspects of performance, especially on rate of return on sales (ROS) or rate of return on investment (ROI). In effect, the M-form company is composed of a number of U-form-organised profit centres, or, to use the preferred term, strategic business units (SBUs). These SBUs are often limited liability companies in their own legal status. Between SBUs, which often face distinct, narrowly defined markets, and the corporate office,

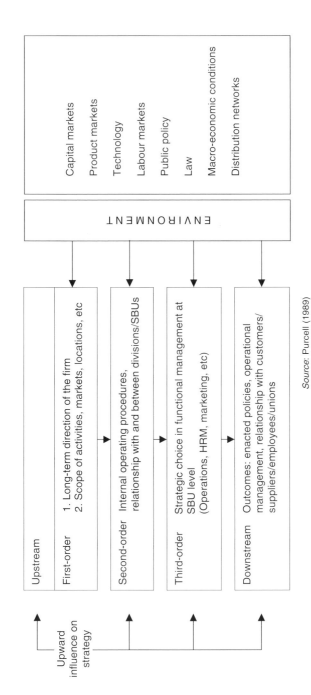

Figure 10.1 Three levels of strategic decision making in Anglo-American multidivisional firms

Source: Purcell (1989)

divisional structures often exist to coordinate whole sectors or geographic areas. M-form companies in the rational minds of industrial economists have five advantages over other forms of corporate control. Williamson (1970: 120–1) argues that these are:

1 The responsibility for operating decisions is assigned to (essentially self-contained) operating divisions.
2 The elite staff attached to the general office performs both advisory and auditing functions. Both activities have the effect of securing greater control over operating division behaviour.
3 The general office is principally concerned with strategic decisions involving planning, appraisal and control, including the allocation of resources among the (competing) operating divisions.
4 The separation of the general staff from operations provides general office executives with the psychological commitment concerned with overall performance rather than them becoming absorbed in the affairs of the functional parts.
5 The resulting structure displays both rationality and synergy: the whole is greater (more effective, more efficient) than the sum of the parts.

Whittington and Mayer (2000: 67), following the work of Jelinek (1979), note the similarity with the scientific management of F. W. Taylor (discussed in Chapter 5):

> The separation of strategy and operations . . . was the analogue of Taylor's own separation of conception from execution on the shopfloor. Divisionalisation was the scientific management of the corporation.

Seen in this way, the M-form becomes less of a structure than a process of managing: a universal theory of asset management that could be applied anywhere. The marketisation of the public service sector in the 1980s and 1990s was built on the principle of the separation of strategy from operations, adopted with new performance reporting requirements and the single-minded pursuit of efficiency or, to use the language of the private sector, 'shareholder value'.

The ultimate logic of the M-form structure or process of control was that an increasing number of firms would move from being single businesses through a process of gradual diversification and divisionalisation into a collection of related businesses, and from there to become unrelated conglomerates. At this final stage, no one business would dominate the portfolio by having 70 per cent or more of corporate turnover and there would be little or no market or technological relationships between businesses. Evidence collected in Britain by Channon (1982) between 1950 and 1980 showed a clear growth in the number of conglomerates. Firms like BTR and Hanson became known for the ruthless way in which they managed acquired businesses. Hanson typically stripped out 25 per cent of the labour costs in each of a succession of hostile acquisitions. In recent years, the attractiveness of conglomerates has waned and many have divested some of their businesses in order to refocus the corporation around a few related businesses. In a sense, the high point of the M-form was reached in the last quarter of the last century, but it still remains the dominant logic for organising and control of many multi-business firms.

The M-form company developed in the USA and spread to the UK and other parts of the Anglo-American world. Its superiority in terms of profitability and shareholder value has often been observed (Rumelt 1982, Hill and Pickering 1986). It was assumed, however, that the very different institutional environment in continental Europe would limit its impact and growth in these other societies. For example, 'in France and Germany the systems of ownership have been consistently less market-based than in the UK, control has been more personal and the technical backgrounds [of senior executives] more important' (Whittington and Mayer 2000: 121). Added to this, the regulatory and institutional frameworks in these countries are more extensive than in the Anglo-American world, especially in regard to employment matters. Despite these national and institutional differences, there is clear evidence of a growth in diversification and a move to M-form structures in these countries, as shown in Figure 10.2.

It is clear that the dominant pattern is that of the 'related diversified' company. This is where no one business contributes more than 70 per cent

	France		Germany		UK	
	1970	1993	1970	1993	1970	1993
(a) *Diversification*						
Single	20	19.4	27	12.7	6	4.5
Dominant	27	15.2	15	7.9	32	10.4
Related diversified	43	51.5	38	47.6	57	61.2
Unrelated diversified	9	17.6	19	31.7	6	23.9
(b) *Organisational structure*						
Functional	18	1.5	27	3.2	8	1.5
Functional-holding	24	9.1	21	14.3	1	0
Holding	16	13.6	14	12.7	18	9
Divisional	42	75.8	40	69.8	74	89.5

Source: Adapted from Whittington and Mayer (2000)

Figure 10.2 Trends in diversification and M-form structures in France, Germany and the UK, 1970–93, among top 100 industrial firms (%)

of the turnover to the corporate whole but where there is a market or technological relationship between different businesses in the portfolio. As we shall see, how large firms manage these relationships is crucial. Figure 10.2 also clearly indicates that the M-form or divisional structure is now by far the most important organisational form adopted by large businesses.

The HR implications of divisionalisation

What are the implications of divisionalisation for HRM? We assess this in three ways. First, there is a need to look at the form of control exercised from the centre. Second, we assess what role there is for HRM in the corporate office in determining corporate strategy and involvement in the budgetary control process. And, third, we ask specifically, what role do HR specialists play in the development of the management cadre?

Forms of control

Hill and Hoskisson (1987) examined the different approaches that divisional firms use to extract value by gaining certain economies:

Financial economies are found where the superior allocative properties of the internal capital market are maximised. That is to say that financial criteria dominate the goals set by the corporate office, compared with long-term growth or market development, for example. These enterprises are likely to have diversified into unrelated activities and to structure the firm in such a way as to minimise or ignore interdependencies between business units and between divisions.

Synergistic economies exist where common techniques, skills, or market knowledge are utilised across a range of products or services. These companies are capable of organising around key values and are usually concerned that acquisitions match and enhance their business mission. 'Second order' integration strategies are likely here.

Vertical integration happens where a closely coordinated and integrated chain of activities from raw material sourcing into final distribution allows vertical economies to be realised. Here there is likely to be a strong central planning influence and an emphasis on administrative coordination.

Relatively few firms are still organised around the principle of vertical integration, in part because of the growth in outsourcing and the focus on core markets. The choice now is more often between those firms emphasising the achievement of synergies and those focusing on financial economies and financial control. It is this latter type of company which, in HR strategy terms, is a cause for concern (we will return to synergistic companies in the next section of this chapter). As Hill and Hoskisson (1987) show, these firms place heavy emphasis on a clear separation of the centre from the operational units or SBUs, and are unlikely to have divisional offices. This decentralisation of businesses places emphasis on profit responsibility and short-term financial targets. Budgets are negotiated or imposed annually, planning horizons are short, and performance measured against targets is reported frequently: 'these companies are willing to act speedily to exit from the businesses that are not performing or do not fit...and are quicker to replace managers, fiercer in applying pressure through the monitoring process and more effective in recognising and acclaiming good performance' (Goold and Campbell 1987: 126, 132).

This decentralisation of operating decisions but strong control over budgets has important implications. First, operating units are given much greater autonomy over many aspects of HRM such as how many people to employ, the payment system to use, and decisions on recruitment, training and development (Marginson *et al.* 1993). There are exceptions: for example, few organisations give *carte blanche* to SBUs on questions of trade union recognition. The corporation will often have firm views on such matters. The logic of the financial control, M-form company is a focus on the performance control system and a minimisation of administrative controls or guidance where head office instructs on what is to be done in a particular area. As Goold and Campbell (1987) note, this can be liberating for SBU managers and the use of high-value, performance-related pay, where bonuses constitute one third or one half of salary, can be a real incentive for the SBU manager. The structure of the SBU facing a distinctive, defined market can also allow for unique product and market knowledge to be applied.

The problem with relatively high degrees of freedom for SBU managers is that they need the financial freedom to invest in HRM processes and this is much less likely. Investment decisions are made by the corporate office and the operating budget, as approved, often has no reserved area for HR issues such as training and development, for example. Short-run targets render long-run HR goals difficult to achieve, if not impossible. Since human resourcing is an indirect cost (as opposed to being directly relevant to production or service), there is always strong pressure for HR overheads to be reduced. Returning HRM to the line is as much about budgetary constraint as it is about progressive policies to encourage line managers to be responsible for the management of their own people. A survey of long-term trends in the UK's authoritative workplace employment relations survey (WERS) showed that:

> the job of workplace employee relations managers working in a multi-plant organisation appears to have become more difficult over time. First, . . . the decision-making capacity . . . has been curtailed . . . second, the facilities devoted to employee relations management have been streamlined as evidenced by the reduction in the number of non-clerical staff assisting employee relations managers. (Millward, Bryson and Forth 2000: 82)

The way these pressures are imposed will depend on the business's place in the corporation's portfolio. If a business is seen as a 'star' that is growing in a buoyant market, it may get heavy investment and be allowed to place emphasis on critical resources such as HR recruitment and development. A good business in a static or mature market is likely to be 'milked' (as a cash cow), required to strip out costs, and have its profits reinvested elsewhere in the portfolio. An unsuccessful firm in an unattractive market is squeezed before being spat out (often termed a 'dog'). Each of these types of companies in the portfolio has very different HRM consequences (Purcell 1989). Managing the portfolio means a centralisation of budgetary control. The WERS trend survey quoted above noted that 'the proportion of workplaces able to decide upon the use of any financial surplus fell from one third in 1990 to 14 per cent in 1998. In over half of the cases this decision was made elsewhere without reference to the workplace concerned' (Millward *et al.* 2000: 79). Sharing in economic success – what might be called 'gainsharing' – depends exclusively on the generosity of the corporate office, but as we noted earlier, the classic model of rationality in the M-form fosters in executives the psychological commitment concerned with overall performance rather than a psychology of absorption into the affairs of the SBUs. Thus, even if local management wished to engage in 'gainsharing', they may be prohibited from doing so.

The predominance of organising the control of SBUs through the use of financial economies is a particular feature of Anglo-American corporations. It is explained in large measure by the dominance of short-term capital markets emphasising shareholder value. Jacoby's (2005) careful analysis of US and Japanese corporations shows how, despite facing common competitive pressures unleashed by globalisation, Japanese firms retain a more stakeholder-oriented perspective which gives employees a greater role in corporate strategy and governance. Human resource departments are much more influential than in their US (or British) counterparts. This draws attention to the debate on 'varieties of capitalism', which we noted in Chapters 1 and 6.

HRM in the corporate office

The classic structure of the corporate board of the M-form is to have only one functional specialist – the finance director – as a member together with the CEO and the chairman. Other members, apart from non-executives, will tend to be the managing directors of the main operating divisions. The role of HR specialists is ambiguous. Much depends on the personal preferences of the CEO and the historical role of personnel managers in the centre. A study of the WERS trend data showed that the proportion of head offices employing specialists in HRM fell from nearly half in 1990 to just over a third in 1998 (Millward *et al.* 2000: 76). The UK 1992 Company-Level Industrial Relations Survey found that only 30 per cent of companies with a thousand employees or more had an HR director on the executive board, and as few as 14 per cent had the combination of a director, a specialist manager, and a dedicated specialist board sub-committee dealing with HR matters (Marginson *et al.* 1993: 31). As the researchers noted at the time, 'if one of the defining characteristics of human resource management is the explicit link with corporate strategies, then this survey has failed to find it for the majority of companies' (*ibid.*: 71).

However, the picture may well have changed in the last ten years. The 2004 WERS survey found that 61 per cent of managers surveyed said that there was someone 'responsible for employment relations' on the board of directors or top governing body of the organisation (Kersley *et al.* 2006: 64). And this did make a difference. Where there was someone responsible for employment relations in the boardroom, people management issues were much more likely to be included in strategic business plans. Once included in the strategic plan, there was much more concern with 'targets for productivity, labour turnover, absenteeism, workforce training, and employee job satisfaction. The inclusion of employment relations in the plan was also positively associated with targets for "customer/client satisfaction", something that well-trained and motivated staff can have a direct influence over' (*ibid.*: 66). As we discuss in the next chapter, this may imply the use of what Kaplan and Norton (1996) call a 'balanced scorecard'.

There is certainly no shortage of issues where HR or 'people-related' considerations loom large. The sort of big change decisions where HR considerations always emerge, like acquisitions, divestments, the development of greenfield site operations, plant closures etc, had taken place in the five years previously in over half of the big companies included in Marginson *et al.*'s (1993) survey. We would add to this list in the last few years, decisions on offshoring of both manufacturing and service capacity (to India and China, for example), as we discussed in Chapters 5 and 8.

Having an HR director, or at the least someone responsible for employment matters, does make a difference since this means there is someone likely to bring an HR perspective to these strategic decisions.

The management of ongoing operations is important too. This is especially the case in the budget review process. Budget formulation and control constitute one of the most important regular activities that corporate offices undertake. They establish key performance indicators (KPIs) for the SBUs and for managers themselves. These KPIs emphasise financial performance with HQ managers often 'managing by numbers'. Intangible, more human assets and behaviours tend therefore to be ignored since they cannot be 'counted' (a matter we shall pursue in Chapter 11). Once agreed, the budget sets the agenda for at least a year ahead, and more if rolling forecasts are used. By using a battery of measures, most of which include labour costs and performance data (Armstrong 1995), the process determines the boundaries for HR initiatives. Thus, budget meetings at both corporate and SBU levels are of fundamental importance, yet HR people attend these relatively rarely. At the corporate level, this was true in Marginson *et al.*'s (1993) survey in less than one third of cases but rose to half where there was an HR director. An HR director on the main board made it much more likely that HR managers locally were involved in budget setting, indicating the symbolic importance of an HR director (Purcell 1995: 79).

Management development

The most obviously important area in a corporate office for an HR role is in the management of careers for managers who populate divisions and SBUs, as noted in Chapter 2. These individuals are a critical resource for the corporation. The extent to which careers are planned varies considerably. In conglomerates and financial control companies, there is evidence that this activity is under-developed (Marginson *et al.* 1993: 38). This fits the pattern noted earlier where excessive decentralisation and separation of businesses to expose profit responsibility renders it difficult to emphasise or build on relationships between business units. Each is treated as an atomised unit. It is often the case that managers beyond head office will have contracts of employment with the operating company, not with the corporation. They are not considered as a corporate resource. In one case known to us, the only managers who moved between the SBUs to and from the corporate office were financial controllers, emphasising the dominant role of this function. Career expectations for others within the parent group were discouraged since what was required was 'focus' on local profit generation, and they competed fiercely with each other for survival and reward. Cooperation between business unit leaders was seen as a weakness. The culture favoured 'male' attributes, fighting for the survival of the fittest.

Unilever, the Anglo-Dutch, long-established, food, detergent, personal products and speciality chemicals MNC, takes a fundamentally different approach. Although it is heavily decentralised, there is a strong culture of coordination and linkages between businesses. This is achieved by building elaborate networks and lateral relationships between managers in different businesses and retaining tight control over career management and promotion decisions. All managers worldwide are considered a corporate resource. The process starts with recruitment. 'The greatest challenge of recruiting is to find the best and the brightest who will fit into the company . . . For international careers in our current operating company we look for people who can work in teams and understand the value of cooperation and consensus' (Floris Maljers, a joint chairman of Unilever, quoted in Goold, Campbell and Alexander 1994: 154). Around 1,000 graduate management trainees are recruited each year. Thereafter, career movement for the best takes on a triple spiral: between functions, between divisions, and between countries. An elaborate, knowledge-based information system for careers is widely used to aid this process. Looking at Unilever's parenting advantage in the way the centre adds value, strategy analysts conclude that:

> Unilever's system for managing its human resources creates a direct linkage benefit by providing the businesses with a larger pool of suitable management talent to draw on. It is also a mechanism that promotes other linkages. By fostering a common culture, promoting networks, and exposing managers to a broad range of experiences, the Unilever system speeds up the circulation of product knowledge and best practice. (Goold *et al.* 1994: 155)

This example of Unilever draws attention to the vital importance of the social capital built up by organisational processes which combine the generation of trust across boundaries and the building of networks aided by, but no means restricted to, information sharing. Lengnick-Hall and Lengnick-Hall (2005: 477) define social capital in an international context as 'the intangible resource of structural connections, interpersonal interactions and cognitive understanding that enables a firm to (a) capitalise on diversity and (b) reconcile differences'. Social capital helps MNCs to manage the tension between pressures for integration on a global scale and pressures for local adaptation: to cope with the challenges that arise from diverse national value systems, economic systems, and workplace conditions (Sparrow and Braun 2007). MNCs vary in how well they build social capital and reap the benefits.

Research suggests that US firms are likely to be much more centralised and formalised in managing their relationships with their subsidiaries across the world. A recent study of MNCs in the UK found that US-owned companies were much less likely to want to give subsidiaries autonomy in managing HRM and more likely to require extensive reporting of activities back to headquarters (Edwards *et al.* 2006). This, in itself, is likely to be a reflection of their short-term capital market and cultural preferences for control. It cannot be explained solely by economic rationality. Edwards and Rees (2006: 24) place emphasis on 'power relations between actors at different levels within MNCs', suggesting that 'strategies . . . are in part the result of political activity within them', a theme we explored in Chapter 2. Thus, 'MNCs, far from being stateless organisations operating independent of national borders in some purified realm of global economic competition, continue to have their assets, work-force ownership and control highly concentrated in the country where their corporate headquarters are located' (Ferner and Quintanilla 1998: 710). If we wish, therefore, to explain the origin of Unilever's social capital advantages, it would be instructive to look at the consensus model of Dutch society with its emphasis on development, learning and trust across boundaries. This is very different from the focus of many US MNCs.

From M-form to N-form?

A different word can be used to capture the Unilever experience: synergy. The modal pattern for divisionalised companies in terms of the scope of their activities, as shown in Figure 10.2, is to organise around related businesses where market or technological relationships exist between divisions. Corporations can choose to ignore these in the search for financial performance through a process of decentralisation and separation. Alternatively, the corporation can organise around these linkages in order to maximise the synergies that exist between them. One type of synergy depends on vertical integration along the supply chain, requiring integrated scheduling and development to spread, build or exploit innovations. Increasingly, however, vertical integration is giving way to outsourcing, sub-contracting and strategic alliances. A second type of synergy rests on trying to achieve 'scope' economies through shared distribution channels, for example, or the exploitation of a common root technology. One example here is the Japanese company, Canon, where 'most of the product groups share overlapping technologies that come together in the research rather than development phase, and central technologists are able to stimulate new combinations and generate new ideas' (Goold *et al.* 1994: 169). Here, organisational practices which focus on flexibility, knowledge creation, and collaboration are crucial (Volberda 1998).

A third type of synergy is achieved spatially where the same tasks are carried out in each division. This is especially the case in MNCs where product integration across boundaries is emphasised. This allows for 'economies of replication to be secured' (Marginson 1993: 6). In particular, direct comparisons between operating units in different countries can be made, enabling the centre to reward or punish in future investment decisions, and to encourage the spread of higher-performing work systems (Mueller and Purcell 1992). The Ford Production System (FPS), for example, is applied in great detail across the globe and new acquisitions, like the luxury car makers Jaguar, Land Rover and Volvo, are required to adopt the FPS with the centre using a battery of performance measures like 'Six Sigma' to encourage, cajole and sanction. Managing knowledge worldwide allows for a process innovation in, say, Brazil to be tapped into by others. This can be work team to work team, not merely restricted knowledge exchange among senior managers. Management consultancies operating globally, like McKinsey, operate in the same way through the replication of knowledge.

This does not mean doing the same thing in the same way everywhere since differences in institutional frameworks and national cultures, and in the particular histories and traditions of the operating unit, SBU or division, establish different contexts for policy implementation and innovation, as we emphasised in Chapter 3. The successful divisionalised firm, especially global ones, require strong performance but recognise the need for local diversity. Thus, there can be simultaneous divergence and convergence in multinational companies: 'think global, act local'.

The crucial point of this search for synergies between divisions, and internationally, is that corporate management cannot simultaneously seek to achieve the financial economies of separation and decentralisation and the achievement of vertical, horizontal or spatial synergies. Choices have to be made. It is here that the trade in management knowledge and ideas between generations is important. If the true divisional company is the bed-fellow of Scientific Management (the separation of strategy from operations in the former, and between planning and execution in the latter), then both were shaken to the core by the success of Japanese corporations worldwide in the 1980s, as we noted in Chapter 5. According to Whittington and Mayer (2000: 80):

The most disturbing aspect, it seemed, was that the Japanese challenge could not be attributed to the successful imitation of American management techniques but to the adoption of a completely different model . . . Being more specialised, Japanese corporations seem to have less need for the multidivisional structure . . . as a consequence while the American corporation makes a virtue of separating strategy from operations, the Japanese corporation keeps them closely interrelated.

Leading strategy analysts turned on the M-form company in the 1990s. To Bettis (1991), it was an 'organisational fossil'. Prahalad and Hamel, in a famous paper in *Harvard Business Review* in 1990, referred to the 'tyranny of the SBU' and argued for an emphasis on linked core competencies crossing the corporation's businesses, as we explained in Chapter 4. This is where the management of synergies and especially the management of critical resources in the managerial cadre become vital.

After the logic of separation in the M-form, some argue that firms seeking synergies have moved towards the N-form, organised around networks (Hedlund 1994). 'The N-form works best with the Eastern appreciation of the tacit, the embedded and the ambiguous, rather than the explicit, tightly specified knowledge systems of the West' (Whittington and Mayer 2000: 81). An interesting metaphor is between the masculinity of the M-form and the femininity of the N-form. Of course, trends in management thinking are often far in advance of practice. Just as there are plenty of examples of Scientific Management in the twenty-first century, so there are many traditional divisionalised firms still exercising strong financial control over their subsidiaries worldwide, especially US firms. Evolution and adaptation is slow but there is some evidence of the emergence of new forms of control in MNCs, giving emphasis to networks (across boundaries including suppliers) and, thus, to social capital. Whittington and Mayer's (2000) summary of these trends is shown in Figure 10.3.

	Investor	Managerial	Network
Origins	1920s–	1960s–	1980s–
Key resource	Capital	Scale and scope	Knowledge
Key technique	Accounting ratios	Planning	Exchange
Key function	Finance and accounting	Corporate planning	Human resources
Structure shape	Pyramid	Pear	Pancake
Example	DuPont	General Electric	ABB

Source: Whittington and Mayer (2000)

Figure 10.3 Evolving types of multidivisional company

Figure 10.3 argues that the human resource function is the key function in the N-form company. An example of what this might mean comes from the transformation of General Electric (GE) under the leadership of Jack Welch (who retired in 2001):

> By 1990, Jack Welch had formulated his notions of coordination and integration within his view of the 'boundaryless company'. A key element of this concept was a blurring of internal divisions so that people could work together across functions and business boundaries. Welch aimed at 'integrated diversity' – the ability to transfer the best ideas, most developed knowledge, and most valuable people freely and easily between businesses. (Grant 1998: 415)

Sparrow *et al.* (2004) suggest that there are four dominant, or super-ordinate, themes that help to provide consistency to people management worldwide in networked organisations. These are the use of strategic performance management processes, the development of global capability or competency-based HR systems, the pursuit of global talent-management strategies, and the identification of corporate and global employer brands in an attempt to socialise employee behaviour and action. This then leads on to the prospect of more sophisticated business modelling, monitoring and measurement. We show in the next chapter how the use of the 'balanced scorecard' opens up the prospect of a better dialogue between corporate and business unit management across boundaries (Kaplan and Norton 2006).

On an international scale, Bartlett and Ghoshal (1998) term the emergent organisation a 'transnational corporation'. Here, each national or regional unit operates independently but is a source of ideas and capabilities for the whole corporation. National units seek to achieve global scale through specialisation on behalf of the whole corporation. Crucially, the corporate centre manages this global network by first establishing the role of each business unit, then sustaining the system through relationships and culture to make the network of business units operate effectively. 'They must foster the process of innovation and knowledge creation. They are responsible for the development of a strong management centre in the organisation' (Johnson and Scholes 2002: 460).

These transnational firms need innovative global HR strategies but *how* their need for innovation in HRM is played out is a moot point. In Chapters 5 and 8, we argued that some firms have been trying hard to undo the dysfunctional aspects of Taylorist work design through fostering employee involvement processes and higher levels of skill formation. This is designed to enhance their capacity to deliver high quality products or services and may lay the basis for greater synergies in and across the company. They are evolving towards what some call 'participatory bureaucracies' (e.g. Kelley 2000). Others, we argued, are trying to become 'flexible bureaucracies', using high levels of outsourcing and offshoring to gain quantum improvements in cost structures. These firms are not necessarily so concerned about quality and often operate in markets where consumers are price sensitive. Here, there can be all sorts of implications for HR systems, including large-scale moves to low-cost production locations. This in turn places pressure on national systems of regulation and institutional frameworks to adapt to global competitive pressures (Katz and Darbishire 2000). As we noted in Chapters 1 and 3, however, this process means these firms can run into major problems with employment ethics and their social legitimacy. Consumer boycotts of firms reported to exploit local labour in low-skill operations like clothing manufacturing in Bangladesh or toy making in China can be very powerful.[3]

Where transnational firms are moving towards N-form structures, then, the implications for HR strategies are diverse. A highly networked approach drawing on high levels of sharing and trust and, underpinning this, high levels of commitment to employees and suppliers, is one option, to be sure. Another option is much more concerned with cost levels and leads to much more contingent commitments to employees and suppliers. Senior executives must weigh up the economic and social benefits and risks of these different approaches.

The HR implications of mergers and acquisitions

The volume of mergers and acquisitions rose considerably in the last two decades of the twentieth century (Hubbard 1999) in response to a variety of environmental changes such as the privatisation of state assets, pressures on cost reduction, especially in banking and insurance, the development of global markets, the spread of information technologies, growing costs in product development, and the availability of capital in search of higher shareholder value. Cross-border acquisitions are particularly noticeable. What is curious is that around half of acquisitions are deemed failures in the sense of either having an inability to provide shareholder value greater than the sum of the previous two companies, or an inability to maintain market dominance, achieve promised cost reductions, or manage synergies between

---

3 www.ethicalconsumer.org/boycotts.list.htm

the new firms effectively. Cross-border acquisitions are especially prone to failure, yet this is the dominant growth strategy of MNCs (Edwards and Rees 2006). Difficulty in achieving organisational fit, especially the meshing of cultures or management styles, is often identified (Buono, Bowditch and Lewis III 1985, Datta and Grant 1990).

Marks and Mirvis (1982) showed that people and employee issues accounted for a third to a half of all merger failures and there is no indication that things have improved in the last 25 years. Most often, the failure of M&As occurs not at the negotiation or purchase stages, although this can be important if a firm pays excessively for a purchase, but at the implementation stage when two firms come together. Hunt *et al.* (1987) found a positive correlation between success of implementation and the overall perceived success of the acquisition in 83 per cent of cases, making it the 'most decisive variable in success and failure'. KPMG (1999) distinguishes between 'hard keys' to successful mergers, which need to happen at the start of the process, such as synergy evaluation, integration project planning and due diligence, and 'soft keys'. These soft keys cover the classical HR issues such as the selection of the management team, resolving cultural issues, and communication inside the two companies (which needs to be compatible with communication externally to shareholders and the business press). According to KPMG, these soft or behavioural issues of implementation should be considered at the beginning of the acquisition process. Where they were, in KPMG's research, there was a strong association with success measured in terms of shareholder value. Thus, 'human factors' loom large in M&As from the beginning, but become especially acute during the post-acquisition implementation phase, and beyond in what is sometimes called the stabilisation period (Hunt *et al.* 1987, Cartwright and Cooper 1992, Hubbard and Purcell 2001).

Employee expectations and experiences

A crucial element is the uncertainty generated by the acquisition process and the response of employees to it. It is hardly surprising to find that employees suffer from uncertainty in acquisitions (Buono and Bowditch 1989) and this is linked to perceived violations of an individual's psychological contract with the employer, especially the new employer (recall Chapter 7). Such violations typically lead to a withdrawal of support for the organisation and a reduction in discretionary behaviour and motivation (Robinson 1996). In an acquisition, this psychological process can occur on a large scale, covering groups of employees leading to distinctive, and for the acquirer, damaging consequences of a withdrawal of trust and commitment. In practice, the political, and politicised, environment of an acquisition severely reduces the opportunities to participate. People often feel powerless and suffer from anomie. They may ask their manager what is happening but it is rare for her or him to know any more than they do. Trade unions may be informed one or two days before the public announcement but are generally unable, at that time, to raise issues of concern on the details of the acquisition consequences, unless provided with legal rights to do so, as in the Netherlands (Wenlock and Purcell 1991).

Beyond this, there can be a profound sense of loss – a form of bereavement (Cartwright and Cooper 1992) – when a long-established company is swallowed up and effectively dies. Symbolically, decisions such as where to locate a new head office become touchstones of the new corporation. When Lloyds Bank merged with TSB in the mid-1990s, once the decision was taken to locate the HQ in the Lloyds building, the die was cast, as it was in the 'marriage' in 1999 of CGU and Norwich Union, two giants of the insurance industry, when the head office was allocated to Norwich. A few years later Norwich Union itself was merged with Aviva and, as we saw in Chapter 5, the company has embarked on a programme of offshoring some activities to India with the loss of jobs in the UK. Mergers and acquisitions frequently lead to a round (or rounds) of job cuts. They can also lead to a substantial increase in *voluntary* labour turnover, to reductions in effort and cooperation, and to resistance to integration moves, which thus take longer and cost more in terms of performance dips than anticipated.

Senior managers can often take the view that the only HR issue of immediate concern in an acquisition announcement is to deal with job security and job loss. This is the question that is always asked by the press. In Hubbard's (1999) acquisition research, there was quite commonly an early announcement that it was to be 'business as usual' and that both companies would be stronger by coming together. This was rarely the case, and at times announcements to employees of 'business as usual' were at odds with statements to the business press on the need to reduce costs and increase margins. Of course, employees read these and note the incompatibility of the internal with the external statements.

The employee response to an acquisition announcement, especially those in the 'target' firm to be acquired, is much more multi-faceted than a single concern with job security. Hubbard (1999) calls this 'dual expectations theory'. It covers both the individual's perception of their immediate future (what will happen to *me*, do I have a job?) and their concern with their team and the wider social networks (what will happen to *us*?). Beyond that, this bifurcation between the individual and the group continues into concerns about assimilation into the new organisation and what sort of firm it is. Thus, for the individual, the issue is 'what sort of job will I have, what type of future, how do I know what is expected of me in terms of performance and will I fit into the new organisational culture?'. These concerns of individuals coalesce into wider group or collective worries about the culture and style of the new management. This 'cultural behaviour' means learning about and internalising as a group 'the shared patterns of beliefs, assumptions and expectations held by organisational members, and the group characteristic way of perceiving the organisation's environment and its norms, roles and values as they exist outside the individual' (Schwartz and Davis 1981: 33).

These expectations may come to the fore at different times in the acquisition process. Senior managers involved, directly or indirectly, in the negotiations have particular concerns at the first planning phase. Due diligence may well (and certainly should) involve an appraisal of top management capabilities with decisions taken on who is vital in terms of client or customer knowledge, or technical or product knowledge, while others are deemed less important. The issue, too, is who is to get the senior positions. If satisfied at this stage, the next stages of announcement and implementation may be of less concern to these top managers, although cultural concerns, such as the form of communication used in the new firm, often emerge later in the final, but ongoing, stabilisation phase. Middle managers, unaware of the negotiations, often find the announcement and implementation stages especially difficult. Hubbard's (1999) research showed that this group has considerable worries about organisational culture and the way they fit into the new organisation and whether they both have, and wish to have, a future in it. Quit rates for this group can be especially high in the year after an acquisition. Non-managerial employees are most concerned about job security at the point of transfer but are particularly concerned with group issues in the way redundancies are handled. The existence of legal guarantees at the point of transfer helps, but by no means overcomes, these concerns.

These types of concerns and their consequences for individuals and for the organisation seem to be common but, as the KPMG research implies, some firms are adept at handling acquisitions and learn from experience, while others are inept, especially if there is no prior experience and little understanding of behavioural issues. The finance director in one of Hubbard's cases referred to the 'abattoir effect'. 'He expressed the belief that employees actually preferred the quick, unsuspected process of redundancies . . . The brutality of the day shocked and appalled those employees being made redundant, and those remaining' (Hubbard and Purcell 2001: 24). In this case, within four months, 15 per cent of the middle managers who had stayed after 'Black Monday', as it was called, had left. The company completely failed the 'legitimacy test'. By contrast, one of the most successful acquirers, with over 40 acquisitions in the period 1993–99, is Cisco Systems based in Silicon Valley. In that period, the number of employees grew from less than four thousand to twenty-six thousand. Cisco chooses small, compatible, entrepreneurial companies and pays particular attention to cultural integration but within the dominance of the Cisco Way. This is seen in the parties having a shared vision and cultural compatibility at the start of the acquisition process:

> When we acquire a company, we do not tell them 'we'll leave you alone'. We say, 'we'll change everything'. We try to establish an environment where we are attractive to small innovative companies. We have learned that to make it (the acquisition) successful you have to tell employees up front what you are going to do, because trust is everything in this business. You've got to tell them early so you do not betray their trust later. (quoted in O'Reilly III and Pfeffer 2000: 61)

The strategic nature of acquisitions and their consequences for HRM

Strategically for Cisco, the crucial aspect of all their acquisitions is the retention of the people. Cisco is a software knowledge business. The intellectual capital of the firm is about the only 'asset' that they have. Thus, for them, capability transfer and retention is crucial (Haspeslagh and Jemison 1991). Not all acquisitions, of course, are driven by the same strategic need for talent and growth. The strategic purpose of an acquisition will deeply influence the process and the type of HR issues to be faced. In particular, the crucial issue is the degree of organisational integration required for the combined firms and the underlying reasons for it. The greater the degree of organisational integration, the greater the HR issues that come to the fore since sites are likely to close, rationalisation occurs in department amalgamations (a single sales team, a single finance office etc), and there will be 'winners' and 'losers' in the organisational musical chairs that follow (Hubbard and Purcell 2001: 21).

A whole range of issues needs to be faced in organisational integration. It is likely that most, if not all, of the HR policies and practices associated with 'AMO' will need to be integrated. Since the nature of these policies is a reflection of wider, yet ill-defined, beliefs on organisational culture, the change process can be fraught, especially if the acquired employees refuse to legitimate the new economic and social order. 'If the corporate culture makes no sense of the organisational realities experienced by the employees other than senior management, it will not be internalised outside that small sub-group' (Legge 2005: 221–2). Culture change programmes are hard at the best of times within existing companies but in acquisitions they are especially fraught. The outcome can often be no more than 'resigned behavioural compliance' (Ogbonna and Wilkinson 1990).

Stand-alone acquisitions may be easier until the new owner seeks to exercise control with the appointment of new managers or the imposition of new reporting procedures or a performance management system. These are the artefacts of cultural control. This is particularly an acute problem in cross-border acquisition, for example when a French company acquires a British utility company. The utility company is left alone in an operational sense for a while but very different forms of corporate control and expectations come from the new owners. French management is, naturally, somewhat different from British management (Barsoux and Lawrence 1990, Lawrence and Edwards 2000). More generally, 'if we accept that HRM approaches are cultural artefacts reflecting the basic assumptions and values of the national culture in which organisations are embedded, international HRM becomes one of the most challenging corporate tasks in multinational organisation' (Laurent 1986, quoted in Schneider and Barsoux 1997: 128). This is even more challenging in cross-border acquisitions. Becoming an integrated multinational, let alone a transnational corporation, building networks and powerful international systems of knowledge building, exchange and intellectual capital, as Unilever has done, often via acquisition, is a daunting task. Or in the language of the RBV (Chapter 4), it is a rare organisational attribute that combines people and processes and can become a powerful source of sustained competitive advantage that others find extremely hard to copy.

The most frequent way acquisitions are intended to create value, for the shareholder at least, but not for the employee, is by 'resource sharing' (Haspeslagh and Jemison 1991). Primarily, although often dressed up in terms of synergistic value creation, this means a focus on cost reduction while at times increasing the scope of business activities. Analysis of bank mergers in the 1990s concluded that value came more from cost reduction than from enhanced revenue generation (Houston, James and Ryngaert 2001). 'Resource sharing' is seen in branch closures where there is overlap in a town, operational rationalisation in the home country or overseas, and call and contact centre amalgamations, often linked to offshoring of certain activities. Significant savings can occur within management, too, from specialist departments coming together and from property sales and other direct savings. The problem is how this can be done quickly, leaving behind a committed, integrated, innovative workforce able to maximise customer service. Just taking one issue alone, that of IS integration, the J-curve problem, where performance dips in a change programme at the start, is painfully clear. The J-curve (Figure 10.4) draws attention to the requirements for 'competency destruction' or 'unlearning' before new learning can occur (Pil and MacDuffie 1996). It is clear even for a firm like Cisco, with all of their experience, that 'when you combine (even good) companies, for a period of time, no matter how smoothly they operate, you lose business momentum' (John Chambers, CEO of Cisco, quoted in O'Reilly and Pfeffer 2000: 56). Cisco, of course, are trying to retain talent and go for growth with all of the opportunities that can mean. Where, however, competency destruction means job loss, often in large numbers, and, for those that remain, a requirement to learn new cultures, new operating procedures and deal with new bosses, the slope of the J-curve coming out of the transitional period is tantalising but unachievable. The loss of productivity or profitability, while anticipated, is both deeper and lasts longer than hoped for, and greatly exceeds that told to the shareholders in the prospectus. It is easy to see how shareholder value is lost, let alone employee value. Cultural integration is especially hard but even system integration is difficult and requires planning,

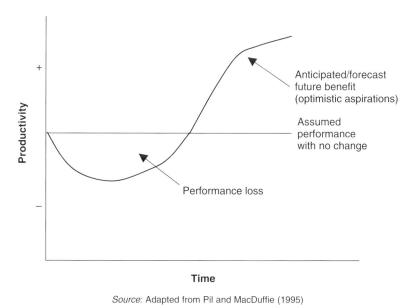

Source: Adapted from Pil and MacDuffie (1995)

Figure 10.4   The J-curve of productivity loss in the management of change

project teams and high levels of involvement at operational level between employees from the two companies, learning to work together.

One of the key, defining moments in the acquisition process, where integration is required in order to achieve cost reduction, is the way announcements are made and especially how redundancies are handled. Companies may sometimes make generous cash offers to those being made redundant and think they have done enough but this nearly always misses the crucial issue of how decision making is perceived and legitimated. Why is it that people often refer to 'survival guilt' or 'survivor syndrome' in these circumstances? This refers to those who survive the job-cutting rationalisation programmes feeling emotional, disturbed and guilty that they have been spared. Far from being grateful to management, they tend to be highly critical of it.

The role of organisational justice

In recent years, increasing attention has been given to the idea of organisational justice (e.g. Folger and Cropanzano 1998). This concept focuses on the way people evaluate the fairness of a decision. There are three elements of justice in an organisational context: distributive, procedural and interactional. Distributive justice (the fairness of the outcome) and procedural justice (the fairness with which the decision was taken, including the extent to which there is an employee voice (Chapter 6)) are strongly related. 'Procedural justice both mediates perceptions of distributive justice and has important independent effects from distributive justice' (Cox 2000: 370). As Folger and Greenberg (1985: 32) put it, 'The more someone considers a process fair, the more tolerant the person is about the consequences of the process'. In redundancy (and closure) decisions, this means that open communication and discussion on the need for, and procedures of, selection, and the design of compensation and assistance programmes (procedural justice) are important in their own right but also affect perceptions of the outcome of the programme in terms of who is selected (distributive justice). People sometimes use the term 'equality of misery' here to signify that the pain of downsizing is shared across the organisation with no group especially favoured or protected. Interactional justice focuses on how decisions are communicated to those affected by them. This covers the sincerity with which procedures are followed, the politeness and courtesy with which the individual is treated, which affects the maintenance of their sense of dignity and self-worth, and the way in which apologies, explanations and justifications are communicated (Cox 2001: 17–18). This is particularly important when the outcome is adverse for the individual, as in most cases of redundancy. The notion of interactional justice places emphasis on the capability and conduct of line managers, thus reinforcing a key message in this book on the crucial role these managers play, both in their personal leadership style and in enacting HR policies.

Referring back to the finance director who valued 'the abattoir effect' in dealing with post-acquisition redundancies, it is abundantly clear that he failed all three elements of organisational justice. The outcome, as one of the employees put it, was to destroy trust in management: 'I do not know if they (the employees) will trust again, it will take a long time if they do. People can forget things and go on but it never goes away completely. Once it has been done, you never forget it totally' (Hubbard and Purcell 2001: 26).

Conclusions

The fundamental problem for large multi-business firms, and especially those organised internationally, is to find an effective way to manage the relationships between parts of the business. This is no simple matter. It is a problem both vertically, in the relationship between the centre and the outposts, and horizontally in the way in which parts of the business collaborate or compete with each other, and the extent to which networks develop and synergies are emphasised or denied. One of the key influences on this complex problem is the extent to which the firm operates in related markets and related businesses, or has a wide range of unrelated activities. We have seen how the logic, in economic terms, of the multidivisional firm has tended to favour decentralisation and the separation of the firm into discrete accounting units, allowing the centre to 'manage by numbers'. This can fail to grasp synergies in knowledge-based competencies that stretch across business units. It can over-emphasise short-run profits at the expense of longer-run investment in skill formation, management development and organisational agility. It takes some astute leadership at corporate headquarters to ensure that a global company is not severely weakened in the long run by the dysfunctional aspects of divisionalised structures.

Quite how far large organisations are moving from the M-form model towards the networked or N-form or, in multinationals towards the 'transnational' model, is hard to say. There are some powerful and persuasive examples but they are relatively few in number. What we can say is that when networks are fostered, the way people, especially managers and professional workers, are managed plays a crucial, if not *the* crucial role. Once knowledge is defined as the key resource and a more liberal exchange of it is encouraged, HR practices that support and facilitate horizontal networking and organisational integration between markets, countries and technologies become vital. Growing by acquisition – rather than organically – makes knowledge-based synergies harder to achieve since different company cultures and different operating procedures need to be understood. Some may be eradicated but others are a source of value and imposing a standardised, internally consistent solution may destroy more value than it creates in these cases.

Despite differences in national cultures and the different forms and strength of institutions in the labour market, MNCs are naturally trying to use HRM to enhance their global performance. Globalisation is opening up huge opportunities for multinational firms to hire capable workforces at much lower cost. It is possible for powerful firms (and large firms have resources and access to capital denied to smaller organisations) to push for productivity improvements in nearly all countries, and if they fail, many have the capacity to relocate at relatively low cost, but often with a high cost to the host country. Thus, multinational HR strategies, especially those linked to major cost reductions, can spark widely different responses among employees and citizens with some welcoming the choice of their country for a new production site while others lament its departure and the loss of well-paid jobs (Edwards and Rees 2006: 39–41).

Once again, we see that ethical and legitimacy issues are inescapable in HRM. Multidivisional and multinational firms ought to give careful attention to issues of organisational justice. Questions of distributive, procedural and interactional justice come strongly into play, for example, in the redundancy programmes often associated with corporate acquisitions and divestments. In these situations, local requirements for, and expectations of, employee voice and personal redress become important. Local laws ought to be followed and are a vital part of social legitimacy. But there is also an economic pragmatism to organisational justice because the way decisions are made and communicated, and their internal logic, establishes the base-line of internal legitimacy necessary for successful change management.

11

Conclusions and implications

The purpose of this final chapter is twofold. First, we summarise the book's most important themes. The book has covered a complex and expanding terrain. We have traversed numerous studies, examined a range of frameworks and theories, and reached a number of important conclusions by the end of each of the chapters. We cannot summarise all of our chapter conclusions but what we do here is underline the most important themes that we would like readers to take away from the book as a whole. In so doing, we take the chance to offer our personal views on some key trends and implications associated with these themes. We then turn to an important 'So what?' question: how can managers in firms improve strategic management processes in their organisations to deal more effectively with the critical HR problems they face and, if possible, to take advantage of the competitive opportunities that HRM presents? This includes a review of the debate over the value of strategic planning and an examination of the question of how to design HR planning systems. It then leads into a discussion of the more integrative approaches to strategic management that have become associated with the notion of the 'balanced scorecard' (Kaplan and Norton 1996, 2001).

The main themes of this book

If we were to boil down the book's messages to a few key themes, what would they be? We think seven major themes underpin the book:

Theme one: human resource strategy is an essential element in business strategy, not some kind of dubious appendage to it, and plays a critical role in organisational viability and relative performance.

HRM is about the management of work and people in organisations. As such, HRM is an essential organisational process, which occurs irrespective of whether the organisation has its own HR specialists, and which has strategic significance in all organisations. Organisations fail if they cannot organise work appropriately and cannot attract, motivate and retain the kind of people they need to meet their goals and develop the organisation over time. A reasonably effective HR strategy is therefore a necessary, though not a sufficient, condition of business survival or viability. In organisations that do survive, the quality of HR strategy has impacts on relative performance. This means that HR strategy may help to lay a basis for sustained competitive advantage.

This theme has implications for the two business disciplines we bring together in this book: strategic management and HRM. In terms of strategic management, we take issue with anyone who thinks HRM lacks strategic significance. We live in an era of knowledge-intensive competition in which HR strategy is assuming more, not less, strategic significance in developed economies. We also live in an era of globalisation and offshoring in which uncompetitive work systems in high-wage countries – in both manufacturing and in services – are under enormous pressure from firms operating in developing countries who are offering more cost-effective and increasingly sophisticated sources of production. Because it is so critical to organisational success, greater attention should be given to HR strategy within the theory, teaching and practice of strategic management.

In terms of HRM, we challenge approaches to teaching and practice that lay too much emphasis on individual techniques and not enough on understanding HRM's role in helping firms manage the strategic problems they face across diverse contexts. This book is not a compendium of 'micro-HR' techniques, organised across the major sub-functions of HRM, such as job analysis, recruitment, selection, training, remuneration and so on. It is often useful for students to take their first course in HRM by looking at a text which covers the main elements of micro-HRM but no one who wishes to contribute meaningfully to the strategic debate and direction in an organisation should limit their reading to this kind of text.

Theme two: the goals of HRM are plural and subject to strategic tensions.

If the first theme underlines the strategic significance of HRM, the second key lesson is that HRM's role should not be thought of only in terms of a single, profit-oriented 'bottom line'. Because the firm is an economic entity located in social and political context, a good performance in HRM will always be multidimensional. To be sure, HRM's contribution to short-run economic performance is vital but a good performance in HRM will incorporate more than this. Managers face the need to develop a cost-effective system of labour management to support the firm's economic viability in the industries in which it competes while *at the same time* needing to secure legitimacy in the societies in which the firm operates. Cost-effectiveness and social legitimacy need to be pursued simultaneously.

The concept of social legitimacy as an important goal in its own right, and not simply as a means to an end, has been emphasised in this book. At a minimum, firms should employ labour according to legal requirements and should seek to work positively with important social norms for employee management. Reaching the situation where the vast majority of firms operate legitimately in this way is a major step forward in any society.

On top of cost-effectiveness and social legitimacy, there are other strategic goals that we observe in HRM. Over time, successful firms also embed significant elements of flexibility into their HRM to enable them to cope better with change. The challenge of doing so should never be underestimated. The natural tendency in organisations is to focus on stabilising performance in the immediate context (the 'short run'). The more this is done, the more difficult it is to generate a capacity to flex the organisation over the longer run. In the dynamic picture, we also observe management seeking to enhance its autonomy or power to act. Much of this is rational because firms do depend on having management teams that can react sensibly to change. However, too much emphasis on management power typically compromises the firm's ability to empower and motivate other employees and has consequences for trust levels within the organisation.

This theme, then, underlines the fact that pursuing multiple goals in HRM inevitably involves grappling with a range of strategic tensions. Among the most important of these are the tensions between employer control and employee motivation, between short-run productivity and long-run adaptability, between corporate survival and employee security, and between the drive for managerial autonomy and the need for social legitimacy. The management of these dilemmas is so important that it is useful to understand the goals of HRM as fundamentally about the management of strategic tensions.

Theme three: managers typically adapt HR strategy to the firm's specific context and they are wise to do so.

A key part of the book's review of the theory of strategic HRM examines the debate between two perspectives: 'best fit' and 'best practice'. Advocates of best fit have emphasised the contingent nature of HRM while advocates of best practice have gone in search of a universally superior set of HR practices. The idea of best practice does not stand up well under close scrutiny, including questions about whose interests are being served by a particular HR practice and how practices evolved in Anglo-American contexts can work in cultural contexts where people have different underpinning values or simply have different employment laws. Best fit is an easy winner in this debate.

When we look at the research and at organisational experience in the widest possible terms, it is readily apparent that firms either adapt their HR strategies to their specific contexts or they risk under-performance and failure. In a nutshell, there is a 'law of context' in HRM, which firms ignore at their peril. Firms are embedded in industries, networks and societies and managers in particular firms never have full control over the shape of their HRM. In this book, we have highlighted a range of important contextual differences in the way HR strategy is shaped. There are typically major differences in HRM between labour-intensive and capital-intensive / high-tech manufacturing: firms are much more likely to recruit selectively, pay high wages and invest heavily in employee development in the latter. Within private sector services, we see major differentiation in HRM across different types of service markets, ranging from low-skill, mass service markets to highly differentiated service markets in which employees are educated, control-conscious professionals or have fast-changing forms of esoteric knowledge. There are also important differences in the way HRM is organised in the more highly unionised and organisationally complex public sector.

Two major models of how context affects HRM have been examined in some depth in the book. One deals with the way HR strategy needs to adapt as firms move through the industry life cycle. In the establishment phase, firms typically start as fragile, small and informal organisations. If they build the workforce capabilities they need to survive, they will inevitably need to adapt their HRM to the challenges brought about by the much more bureaucratic mature phrase and then adapt it again to cope with the need for radical change in the renewal phase. Few organisations successfully negotiate all these phases and there are major questions around how HR strategy can help to build organisational agility. We have also looked at models of HRM in multidivisional and multinational firms. There is no HRM context more complex than that faced by these firms. Multidivisional firms have major issues of internal control and coordination and take different approaches to the question of whether synergies, including synergies in management development and social capital, are valuable. They also face a much more complex external environment: every different society in which a multinational firm operates will challenge it to adapt its HR strategies in some significant way.

Theme four: lists of best HR practices are dangerous but there is still a role for thinking about underpinning principles in HRM.

While we need to dispense with the idea that there can be lists of HR practices that are universally relevant, it is still possible to take some value out of best-practice thinking. Within an Anglo-American frame of reference, there are some practices which nearly everyone agrees are dumb or dysfunctional. For example, hardly anyone would recommend unstructured employment interviewing over a set of job-relevant questions or, if at all possible, a work-sample test.

In addition, within particular industry or occupational contexts, it is possible to identify HR systems that have a kind of 'functional equivalence' and which can benefit firms which apply them in a way that involves careful adaptation at the level of particular practices. Thus, it is possible for us to identify critical design features underpinning high-involvement work systems (an emphasis on empowering workers whose jobs have been overly Taylorised and enhancing their skills and performance incentives) while leaving open the question of which HR practices will best serve a particular company and group of workers. For example, there will be some contexts in which managers will see self-managing teamwork as critical to building an HIWS while in others they may well prefer job rotation or off-line problem-solving activities. Similarly, there will be some contexts in which contingent pay systems will be evolved to enhance performance incentives and others in which higher salaries, without contingent components, will be preferred. The role of HR strategy consultants should not be one of selling a static and de-contextualised set of 'best practices' but one of helping firms perceive the underpinning principles of these systems and make sensible adaptations in their unique context.

At the most fundamental level, it is possible to identify some underpinning general principles that can help all firms to improve their HRM. The first and third parts of the book work hard at stressing the general themes that a good performance in HRM depends on meeting multiple goals, that managers typically adapt their HRM to their specific context and that they are wise to do so, and that viable firms can evolve ways of creating superior value through somewhat unique clusters of human and social capital. The middle part of the book is designed to look at more specific principles and theoretical frameworks within the key components of HR systems and within the chain of links that connects HR policies to organisational outcomes. This part underlines the fact that choices about a firm's work systems are inevitably connected to its economic performance and matter enormously to workers, being a principal driver of job satisfaction levels and a major factor in employee turnover. It stresses the importance of voice practices for social legitimacy and underlines research showing that well-embedded voice systems are strongly associated with higher levels of employee discretion, job satisfaction and organisational commitment. In terms of understanding the management of individuals, we stressed the value of the AMO framework, which argues that individual performance improves when individuals have the ability, the motivation and the opportunity to perform. Assuming that firms can recruit effectively the individual capabilities they need (and many cannot), the AMO framework helps to highlight the importance of the ongoing management of the fragile variable of employee motivation in most employment relationships. This principle also resonates at the collective level. The social climate in workplaces is sensitive to the extent to which employees find that management is open to their voice and the extent to which they find management to be trustworthy over time.

Theme five: HR strategy is usefully understood as a cluster of HR systems, an approach that helps us to analyse strategic HR trends affecting companies and countries.

The HR strategies of firms are usefully thought of as clusters of HR systems. Each HR system is a set of HR practices that has evolved to manage a major hierarchical or occupational group in the firm. The two fundamental building blocks of any HR system are a set of practices for organising work and a set of practices for managing the people to do the work. It is quite common for there to be one HR system for management, another for core operating staff, and one or more models for support workers of various kinds. Questions of social legitimacy and internal political pressures mean there will usually be some overlaps in HR practices across HR systems within an organisation: for example, there may be common ways of handling leave entitlements and common ways of dealing with personal grievances. However, there are also substantial differences that are needed to build and manage a particular type of worker. How managers are identified, developed and incentivised necessarily needs to be somewhat different from how operating workers are selected, motivated and managed. While flexibility is an issue in all models of HRM, models for managing managers should pay particular attention to ways of encouraging creative thinking and collaborative working.

The identification of HR systems or HR models helps us to track changes in patterns of HRM in a way that can be useful for strategic analysis in firms and for public policy making in societies. In small firms, we typically observe a blend of familial and informal HR systems while craft-professional models are critical to professional service firms, to large parts of the public sector and to various niches in manufacturing. Industrial and salaried models emerged first in large-scale manufacturing and then spread to the large 'office factories' of the private sector and the public sector bureaucracy. Key changes in current patterns of HRM include the development of high-involvement models by various Western manufacturers and service firms in order to respond to, and take advantage of, quality-based or knowledge-intensive competition. More controversial is the trend towards outsourcing models of HRM, which are common in globalised and electronically connected production environments where firms seek quantum leaps in labour costs. Clearly, we are living in an era when managers need to be able to regularly evaluate the fit of their HR systems with their unfolding context if companies are to make astute shifts in HR strategy that help to support their survival.

A key implication we want to stress here is that the interests of governments are not exactly the same as those of companies. Companies ultimately have loyalties to shareholders and this means that they are not necessarily able to commit indefinitely to production sites which have become uneconomic in a particular country. In a globalised environment, company survival comes ahead of the survival of particular production sites. Governments, on the other hand, have interests in retaining high quality production sites in their particular country and keeping local communities viable. Governments in the high-wage countries increasingly favour the development of high-involvement HR models. To be successful in promoting them, public policy needs to foster the labour-market and societal institutions, including high-quality educational and vocational training systems, that encourage and support firms trying to adopt HIWSs.

Theme six: some degree of idiosyncrasy is inevitable in a firm's HRM and positive, high quality idiosyncrasies in HRM can be sources of superior performance.

Although requirements for social legitimacy and for 'table stakes' in particular industries make firms similar, managers inevitably put their own twists on HR systems, and firms build a somewhat idiosyncratic pattern of human and social capital, as the resource-based view (RBV) of the firm indicates. There is always some degree of strategic choice available to managers and particular leadership personalities will inevitably put their mark on HRM, sometimes in ways that generate competitive *dis*advantage rather than competitive advantage. A key interest in this book has been on the question of what it is that can be competitively most valuable in HRM and how such sources of value can be built and defended. The RBV lays emphasis on the ways in which valuable, hard-to-imitate resources are built up over time as a result of critical choices ('path dependency') and thus become socially complex and causally ambiguous. The book's argument is that companies acquire exceptional strengths in HRM when they attract and retain highly talented individuals (high quality human capital) and combine their talents through clever organisational processes (powerful forms of social capital). Clever individuals often make a disproportionate impact but the ongoing impact is much greater when shared, collective processes, such as teamwork and cross-functional learning, harness and expand individual talent.

A key implication must be that carefully enacted HR systems which build human and social capital can be sources of superior and hard-to-imitate value. Knowledge of individual HR techniques or policies is hardly rare or particularly valuable. However, knowledge of how to build and customise appropriate HR systems (which are clusters of key work and employment practices) and create a positively reinforcing blend of HR systems *within* a particular context is likely to be very rare. The value is greater when these astute HR decisions and processes are complemented by other intangible and tangible assets: senior management commitment, consistent line manager support for critical HR practices over significant time periods, (at least) adequate financial resourcing, sympathetic management accounting systems, and so on.

Theme seven: in any organisation where management wants to achieve higher value through HRM, careful attention will need to be paid to the chain of critical links between HR policy and performance outcomes.

The previous theme leads directly to this one. Suppose management wants to enhance the quality of products to better serve a niche market or improve the quality of the interactions between employees and customers in order to improve customer satisfaction and retention. How can management enhance the performance of its HR systems in order to create these sources of value? This is often called the 'black box' problem. It centres on the chain of links or set of mediators that leads from HR policies through to whatever type of performance is desired. This chain of links stretches from (1) management intentions, to (2) management actions, to (3) workforce perceptions, to (4) workforce responses and outcomes, and, finally, to (5) organisational outcomes. Major gaps between management's espoused intentions and managerial actions will usually engender mistrust and cynicism. Individuals may feel their psychological contracts have been violated and become less committed while trust levels and the quality of cooperation may deteriorate across entire workforces.

Large organisations may have resource and legitimacy advantages but they often have much greater problems than small firms in terms of slippage between HR intentions and performance outcomes. The possibility of gaps between rhetoric and reality underlines the need not only for senior managers in large organisations to figure carefully what they want to achieve and then follow through on their pledges – achieving greater consistency in their own behaviour – but also underlines how dependent they are on lower-level managers to achieve the results they seek. While this includes the roles of both HR specialists and line managers, the latter are particularly important if consistency is going to be high in HRM. How line managers are themselves managed by senior managers is thus critical to the overall effectiveness of the firm's HR systems.

Employees are influenced not simply by top management values and formal policies but by the reality of what they perceive and experience on a daily basis, including the quality of material and financial resourcing in their organisation. High-sounding policies for employee rewards and development that are not met with good financial allocations are unlikely to be very convincing after a while. All of this means that employees are receiving signals on various levels in a large organisation. What they think of the intentions and trustworthiness of management, as a whole, is reflected in the social climate of the workplace, which then becomes an important intervening variable in the links between HRM and organisational performance. Management teams that want to improve the mediating links between their intentions and their outcomes in HRM are well advised to open up more comprehensive ('dual') channels of employee voice, and institute employee opinion surveys, in order to improve their understanding of the strengths and weaknesses in this chain.

Can strategic planning be a valuable resource in the firm?

The final theme we have discussed leads naturally into issues surrounding strategic planning in firms and how data on critical HRM variables, such as employee attitudes to management, can be more effectively incorporated into this process. Before examining this area, we begin with a fundamental question that has attracted controversy in the management literature. The resource-based view (RBV) of the firm has occupied an important role in this book but is it actually supportive of the discipline of strategic planning? Does it suggest that better planning, with all the effort it entails, is a valuable use of executive time and the firm's money? Doesn't the RBV say that 'causal ambiguity' helps to protect a firm's key resources? In which case, does this imply, paradoxically, that we cannot plan for improved performance in HRM? Furthermore, surely Henry Mintzberg's (1990, 1994) stinging criticisms of strategic planning should caution us against bureaucratic planning routines? Could it be that long-range planning suits static rather than dynamic environments and undermines the very flexibility that firms need today?

Like Ansoff (1991) and Wilson (1994), we reject this anti-planning perspective. Chapter 4 considered three barriers to imitation: unique timing and learning, social complexity, and causal ambiguity. It argued that the notion of causal ambiguity is the least significant of the three. Ambiguity around key causes of a firm's success (and especially the way these interact) must be present to some extent in any firm. As Chapter 2 explained, strategic management is cognitively or intellectually challenging. If there were no ambiguities, senior management teams would never make blunders. However, we all know they do, and often with disastrous consequences.

Having said this, we argued that unique timing and learning ('path dependency') and social complexity (patterns of collaboration and teamwork in the firm) are more important barriers to imitation than causal ambiguity. First-mover or fast-follower strategies, when well executed, build positions of competitive strength which other firms find very difficult to emulate. There are therefore advantages to be gained from planning to build the firm's human and social capital and create faster learning in the firm.

Research does support this interpretation, as we noted in Chapter 9 in our discussion of the value of planning skills in the mature and renewal contexts of the firm's life cycle. Koch and McGrath's (1996) study of human resource planning practices and business outcomes is instructive. The sample studied consists of 319 business units drawn from the Standard and Poors' database of companies in the USA. Measures of business performance include labour productivity (defined as sales per employee). Their main finding is that:

> Labor productivity . . . tend(s) to be better in firms that both formally plan how many and what kinds of people they will need, as well as where employers systematically evaluate their recruitment and selection policies . . . *proactive* firms that *plan* for their future labor needs, as opposed to reacting to changes, as well

as those firms making investments in getting the right people for the job *at the outset*, tend to be the ones with better labor productivity. (Koch and McGrath 1996: 350)

Koch and McGrath (1996) go on to argue that superior HR planning skills, which enhance the quality of the firm's investment in human capital, can provide a form of resource-based advantage.

This is only one study and we should be cautious about concluding anything from a single study. What other evidence is there? The largest study so far is associated with a 'convenience sample' of 656 firms,[1] located mainly in the USA and in South Africa (Brews and Hunt 1999). This study was set up to examine the debate between Ansoff's 'planning school' and Mintzberg's 'learning school'. While based on executive assessments of planning practice and business performance, the study argues that unstable environments require *more* rather than less planning, thus challenging the idea that planning systems make firms inflexible. It also argues that firms gain greater advantages from planning when they persist with it: benefits are greater after four or more years of working at a planning system (Brews and Hunt 1999: 905). This finding is consistent with the analysis of the US railway companies – the Chicago and North Western (C&NW) and the Chicago, Rock Island and Pacific (Rock Island) – discussed in Chapter 2 (Barr *et al.* 1992). Both firms faced an unstable environment in the 1950s (as railroads faced serious threats from alternative forms of transport) but the directors of C&NW began to change their mental model and take responsibility much more quickly than those at Rock Island (which subsequently went bankrupt).

These studies suggest that 'learning to plan' counts for something. They imply that successful firms find ways of incorporating lessons from learning-by-doing into their planning routines and of making their planning systems more flexible. Formal planning processes, when they involve the key line managers who manage the majority of staff, offer a way of surfacing informal learning about what does and does not work in the management of people. When designed competently, planning systems provide a means for periodic review: they can be used both to make emergent learning explicit and to consider new external threats and opportunities. Rather than upholding the Mintzbergian criticisms of formal planning, these studies imply that planning systems can be reformed in ways that make them more valuable in changing times. As Brews and Hunt (1999: 906) put it: 'When the going gets tough, the

---

1 The sample was constructed from executives attending certain business education programmes in the USA but is large and covers a diverse set of industry circumstances.

tough go planning: formally, specifically, yet with flexibility and persistence. And once they have learned to plan, they plan to learn'.

The value to be gained does not lie solely in the capacity to improve the analytical abilities of the firm but also has a political dimension, something which is always present in strategic management. As Lam and Schaubroeck (1998) explain, formal planning processes can be used to bring together key constituencies in the firm, thus hammering out new compromises and building commitment for desirable change. We conclude that strategic planning systems should not be abandoned but their design should be reviewed on a regular basis and enhanced. Part of this enhancement should involve improving the way they tackle the HR challenges facing the firm.

This is obviously of great relevance to large firms, including the multidivisional and multinational firms discussed in Chapter 10, but the principles we will discuss here are also relevant to smaller ones. Small firms do not use the level of formality seen in management processes in large firms. More importantly, small firms are typically at a resource and legitimacy disadvantage (they have fewer resources and are much less well-known). However, as we showed in our discussion of recruitment strategy in Chapter 7 and in the discussion of the establishment and renewal contexts in Chapter 9, their leaders can use proactive thinking and nimble responses in a way that is very hard to do in large organisations. What matters is that managers in small firms regularly take time to examine their context and to think ahead in terms of the threats they face and the opportunities they could grasp.

The design of HR planning processes

The argument that HR planning should be linked to strategic planning did not suddenly emerge with the advent of practitioner and business school interest in HRM in the 1980s. Planning the human aspects of business strategy has a long tradition. For example, the role of planning in personnel management, including planning for recruitment and succession, was emphasised in the publication of the Institute of Personnel Management's booklet on *Functions and Organisation of a Personnel Department* in 1964 (Crichton 1968: 42–3). And it should surely be obvious that military and industrial planning techniques were absolutely central to labour force planning, training and production management in both world wars and, indeed, much earlier than this (Smith and Bartholomew 1988). The idea that we are finally discovering the value of good integration between the planning of organisational goals and labour requirements is an insult to former generations of managers. We are, however, in a position to identify some key lessons about how HR planning can be conducted more effectively.

Improving the quality of HR planning: process principles

Drawing on research and historical learning about HR planning, what principles can be used by executive teams to improve the quality of HR planning in their firm?

The stakeholder principle

As explained in Chapter 1, it is vital to recognise that HRM does not belong to HR specialists. HR planning should aim to meet the needs of the key stakeholder groups involved in people management in the firm. In the broadest sense, stakeholder groups include shareholders, creditors, managers, employees, customers, suppliers, competitors, the local community and environmental interests. In HR planning, however, we need to focus on those stakeholder groups who are most affected by the quality of labour management in the firm. This means the process ought to be designed to consider the interests of:

Line managers. As emphasised in Chapter 8, these are the managers who manage the vast majority of people in any firm. Their responses and strategies are critical to shaping psychological contracts and the social climate of the firm and, thus, to the success of any major HR initiative. Their views can be canvassed in various ways. For example, all line managers might be surveyed on HR issues in the firm. Alternatively, or in addition, a representative group of line managers might be involved in the planning team. As part of their perspective, line managers should bring into the process an assessment of how other stakeholder groups, such as customers and competitors, are affected by the firm's HR systems.

Employees themselves. It should be obvious that employees and potential recruits are 'clients' of HRM in the firm. Any HR planning process will be better if it allows for employee involvement. A common practice now in large firms is to conduct regular staff surveying, as we shall illustrate further below. Some also use focus groups – smaller samples of staff in a facilitated discussion – to look more qualitatively at key issues. Data on how employees are reacting to HR policies and practices typically helps to improve the quality of HR planning in firms.

The state. Over time, governments play a key role in providing national forms of social capital. In the sense used here, this means the quantity and quality of the country's labour pool and its educational and social infrastructure. In exchange for access to these resources, governments require certain levels of compliance with labour statutes and regulations. The requirements of labour law ought always to influence the design of HR policy in firms.

The involvement principle

The stakeholder principle implies that only through dialogue among those centrally involved in managing people in the firm can the quality of HR planning be improved. As a general rule, the senior management team should drive HR planning (with the chief executive and top team leading but involving key line managers throughout the firm). HR specialists should *facilitate* the process. Managers in other domains will want HR specialists to contribute their specialist expertise (for example, in research reports on the state of internal and external labour markets, on the HR strategies of rival firms and on longer-run plans for management development (Craft 1988)), but there is a fine line to be walked here. Senior HR specialists need to provide specialist expertise without creating the situation where strategic HR planning is seen purely as their hobbyhorse or their sectarian interest.

To be valuable, planning processes, in organisations of all sizes, should enhance strategic *understanding* and build strategic *consensus*. They should open up a fertile exchange within the organisation on its context, its past, its problems and its potential. Healthy involvement processes are critical to this. In badly run organisations, strategic planning is driven by the need to have certain planning rituals and to deliver a bureaucratic output (a set of reports containing objectives and milestones). The process can sometimes be forced through quite cynically by the inner elite without any intention to listen to diverse views or face unpalatable truths about a changing environment. It is much better if haste and reporting pressure is de-emphasised and the senior management team leads a process that will allow people to share contrasting views in a supportive environment and expand their openness to a changing world and to creative ideas. As we shall note below, there are ways of reducing the likelihood that this will turn into a 'slugfest' between rival political groups.

The rivalry principle

HR planning is of little use if it is just navel-gazing. Labour markets are competitive and intelligent rivals will attempt to recruit the best workers and build the best management processes. As a result, the firm's executive team should aim to understand the HR strengths and weaknesses of key competitors (Craft 1988). Does the company have good data on the employment strengths and weaknesses of rivals? While this is a competitive question, it should not simply be seen in a competitive light (Nalebuff and Brandenburger 1996). Rival firms may be competing in the labour market but also have common interests in improving labour supply to the network or cluster of firms, a key reason for co-location of facilities in many industries (see Chapter 9). This is one of the secrets of 'Silicon Valley' in California and of many other examples of co-located firms.

The dynamic principle

As argued in Chapter 1, it is vital to accept that change is inevitable and that some preparation for the future is therefore crucial. We have not so far discussed the issue of the planning horizon but, as in all planning, this is important. Most HRM textbooks cover the techniques of short-run HR planning well and companies typically find they need at least some of them. Some short-run planning is necessary just to stay afloat. Any type of recruitment, for example, involves some kind of thinking in advance about the firm's skill deficits and desirable types of candidate (even if this thinking becomes much sharper as the selection process unfolds). Where firms tend to be much weaker, however, is in the quality of their long-run HR planning (Gratton *et al.* 1999a, 1999b). As argued in this chapter, planning for the next three to five years is a good thing providing it does not make the organisation unduly inflexible (which it can do if done badly).

The most obvious approach in this context is scenario planning which can be used to create readiness for a range of competitive futures. One thing that must be accepted about the future is that it is uncertain. As Anthony Giddens repeatedly emphasised in the 1998 BBC Reith Lectures on globalisation, we should 'expect the unexpected' and learn to manage risk. The example shown in Figure 11.1 involves defining three competitive scenarios and exploring their HR implications. One scenario is based on the most desirable business case. Such scenarios tend to assume that intelligent rivals do not exist and that the environment is generally benign, so it pays to define a second, more likely scenario in which there are rivals and the environment has some surprises. Finally, one can define a least desirable case, a scenario in which there are major downturns or reversals in business fortunes. The bombing of the World Trade Center and the Pentagon in September 2001 should

---

Step One: Identifying long-run business scenarios

- Identify the key rivals in your industry-based 'strategic group'.
- Identify three scenarios that might be played out in the group over the next five years (e.g. most desirable case, most likely case, and least desirable case).

Step Two: Assessing the firm's HR readiness

For each scenario ask:

- What are the HR challenges posed by this scenario (e.g. challenges posed by inadequate social capital, by labour market rivals, or by the attitudes to the firm of current or potential employees)?
- What are our HR strengths to meet these challenges (e.g. existing depth of know-how in a key business area; strength of reputation as an employer)?
- What are our HR weaknesses in relation to these challenges (e.g. recruitment not yet focused on capabilities needed in the future; lack of training for future competitive needs; excessive turnover of core staff)?

Step Three: Identifying key stakeholder trends relating to HRM

Over the next five years, what are the likely trends in the following and what should the company do to prepare?

- HR strategies of key rivals: What are the threats they will most likely pose (e.g. 'poaching' of star employees)? What opportunities do they present (e.g. joint training initiatives)?
- Needs and aspirations of key workers: How might they differ from current needs and aspirations? What should the company do to prepare for these possible changes?
- Quality of labour and changes in labour market regulation: How might the quality of the labour pool change? How might labour law change?

Step Four: Planning HR strategies to meet long-run business needs and cope with stakeholder trends

- Focusing on the most desirable business scenario, list the key *long-run* HR research, review, policy or programme initiatives that must be taken for this scenario to become a reality and develop milestones for them over the next five years (e.g. a staged leadership development programme with an increasing annual budget; development of an annual employee attitude survey linked to customer surveying and jointly linked to annual business planning).
- Focusing on the most likely business scenario, identify how key HR systems should be improved to enhance readiness to cope with it.
- Focusing on the least desirable business scenario, identify how key HR systems should be improved to enhance readiness to cope with it.
- Identify (a) HR initiatives that are common across all scenarios, and (b) those that are unique and will require some development of flexible skills and processes in HRM.

Figure 11.1   An example of scenario-based HR planning

remind us that there are factors well beyond business control that can disrupt business performance. Certainly, in the case of airlines, and those in their supply chains, contingency planning for downsizing helps firms to adjust to such unexpected circumstances.

In this context, Shell's multiple planning system is a celebrated case (de Geus 1988, Grant 1998). In the aftermath of the 1970s oil shocks, most oil companies in the 1980s planned for a scenario of permanently rising oil prices. Shell did this but also planned for significant price decreases, a scenario that was played out in early 1986 as oil prices fell from US$27 a barrel to $17 in February and $10 in April. As a result of the lateral thinking encouraged by its scenario planning, Shell was better prepared than other companies in the industry. Readers will recognise that the situation in the oil industry has now changed very significantly with concerns about global warming, on the one hand, and problems of oil supply, on the other, both likely to keep prices high. However, this does not rule out the possibility that such factors as alternative technologies and legislation will change the industry dramatically in the future. It is best to be open to such possibilities and this is the point of scenario planning.

The model shown in Figure 11.1 deliberately uses three scenarios. As argued by Eisenhardt, Kahwajy and Bourgeois (1997), whose work on strategic decision making is noted in Chapter 2, it helps if more than two options are generated in thinking about the future. Two decision options can degenerate into a political slugfest between two executives or two sides of the team. Three or four options helps to reduce this kind of political in-fighting and to keep us open to the possibility that we might combine ideas from different options in the eventual decisions we take.

The integration principle

The last principle is one that has been continually emphasised in the literature for many years, as noted above. Processes for HR planning ought to be integrated with processes used for:

- long-run strategic planning and business development and
- short-run planning and budgeting.

It is not a question of choosing between short-run and long-run planning systems. Both forms of planning are important and HR planning needs to play an appropriate role in both.

In reality, no one seriously challenges this principle. The key question is always: 'yes, of course, we should integrate – but how?' In the next section of this chapter, we turn to a closer examination of this issue by considering a key set of ideas about integrating financial and non-financial planning which have become very influential in contemporary strategic management.

Seeking integration: HR planning and the new management accounting

Michael Porter's works (most notably, *Competitive Strategy* (1980) and *Competitive Advantage* (1985)) were landmark contributions to the literature on strategy in the 1980s. These books offered useful analytical frameworks, particularly the notion of 'industry analysis' which helped firms to analyse the economic and political dimensions of industries. Porter's ideas were very much concerned with forging a competitive vision: with strategy as something 'out there'.

From the mid-1990s, another perspective grew up alongside the positioning model, as Chapter 4 explained. In popular reading lists, Hamel and Prahalad's (1994) *Competing for the Future* became a counterpoint alongside Porter's frameworks, encouraging firms to apply some of the internally oriented notions associated with the resource-based view of the firm. Hamel and Prahalad's work, however, has been more difficult to apply in concrete ways. If we want to locate the most practically influential ideas since the 1990s on how to reshape strategic management they are to be found in the 'new management accounting' associated with a stream of books by Robert Kaplan and David Norton: *The Balanced Scorecard* (1996), *The Strategy-Focused Organization* (2001), *Strategy Maps: Converting Intangible Assets into Tangible Outcomes* (2004) and, most recently, *Alignment: Using the Balanced Scorecard to Create Corporate Synergies* (2006). Traditional approaches to management accounting have been roundly criticised for focusing managers on short-term performance and for failing to encourage intelligent management of the links between financial and non-financial variables in the firm (Johnson and Kaplan 1991). As a discipline that heavily influences the strategic management process, traditional management accounting has to be treated with great care if it is not to produce dysfunctional outcomes.

Not unreasonably, Kaplan and Norton start from the premise that it is *executed* strategy that counts in a firm's performance. This, of course, was Mintzberg's (1978) fundamental point in his classic work on emergent strategy. Formulation of strategy may seem incredibly important but what customers and business rivals take most seriously is the strategy that is actually implemented. Business failure is seen to stem mostly from failing to implement and not from failing to have wonderful visions (Kaplan and Norton 2001: 1). In their view, good implementation of well-formulated strategy is rare, an argument consistent with the resource-based view of the firm. This stems from lack of consensus about what the firm's strategy actually is. All too often, they argue, senior managers overestimate what people understand about the firm's espoused strategy.

Balancing performance measures in the firm

There are two fundamental sets of ideas that underpin Kaplan and Norton's (1994, 2001) framework. The first is concerned with balancing the measures that focus management attention. The balanced scorecard involves a process of developing goals, measures, targets and initiatives in four perspectives on business performance (Figure 11.2).

An edited example of a balanced scorecard, based on a US retail chain store ('Store 24'), is shown in Figure 11.3 (Kaplan and Norton 2001: 82). This edited version is depicted in vertical format rather than as a wheel. It does not show all the links involved and only includes some measures that the company uses (in the top and bottom perspectives). Kaplan and Norton recognise that financial outcomes are important to shareholders (the perspective at the top of the scorecard) but that they are 'lagging' and short-term indicators. To improve a business, management needs to look at desirable long-term outcomes and improve the 'leading indicators' or 'performance drivers' that generate them.

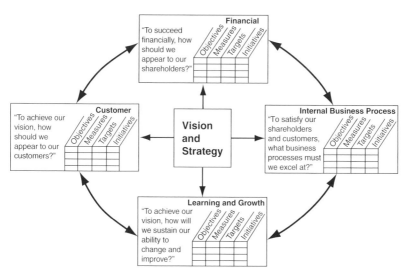

Figure 11.2 The four perspectives in the balanced scorecard

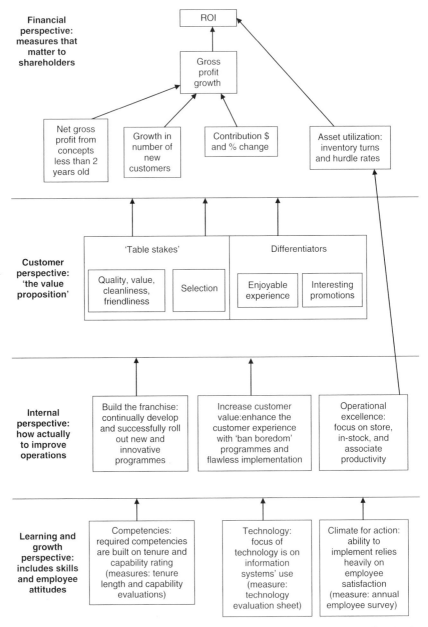

Financial
perspective:
measures that
matter to
shareholders

ROI

Gross
profit
growth

Net gross
profit from
concepts
less than 2
years old

Growth in
number of
new
customers

Contribution $
and % change

Asset utilization:
inventory turns
and hurdle rates

Customer
perspective:
'the value
proposition'

'Table stakes'

Differentiators

Quality, value,
cleanliness,
friendliness

Selection

Enjoyable
experience

Interesting
promotions

Internal
perspective:
how actually
to improve
operations

Build the franchise:
continually develop
and successfully roll
out new and
innovative
programmes

Increase customer
value:enhance the
customer experience
with 'ban boredom'
programmes and
flawless implementation

Operational
excellence:
focus on store,
in-stock, and
associate
productivity

Learning and
growth
perspective:
includes skills
and employee
attitudes

Competencies:
required competencies
are built on tenure and
capability rating
(measures: tenure
length and capability
evaluations)

Technology:
focus of
technology is on
information
systems' use
(measure:
technology
evaluation sheet)

Climate for action:
ability to
implement relies
heavily on
employee
satisfaction
(measure: annual
employee survey)

Figure 11.3   Example of a strategy map and some balanced scorecard measures

Performance drivers are located in the three perspectives that underpin the financial one. Customers must perceive a 'value proposition' if they are to reward the firm financially. As we noted in our discussion of capabilities or competencies in Chapter 4, this typically involves some 'table stakes' (in common with other firms in the sector) and some differentiators. In the case of Store 24 shown in Figure 11.3, the company's executives tried to differentiate based on providing greater shopping excitement. The motto, posted in every store, became 'Store 24 bans boredom' and special promotions were organised in an attempt to amuse customers.

The customer value proposition depends on carrying out certain key operations. This means that Kaplan and Norton's framework does not demean the role of good operational systems, something we argued is very important in Chapters 2 and 5. In Store 24's case, this was split into three internal operational themes. Two of these were targeted at generating sales growth while the third was focused on productivity or margin improvement. This is fairly typical. Balanced scorecards very often contain dual strategic thrusts: one aimed at raising the top line (revenue) and the other aimed at more effective cost management.

Finally, the balanced scorecard attempts to identify key human resource and technological variables that drive performance. In the 'learning and growth' base of the scorecard, employee skills and satisfaction are nearly always identified as critical to improving internal processes and, thus, enhancing customer satisfaction and financial outcomes. As Kaplan and Norton (2001: 93) describe it:

> The learning and growth strategy defines the intangible assets needed to enable organisational activities and customer relationships to be performed at ever-higher levels of performance. There are three principal categories in this perspective:
>
> 1. Strategic competencies: the strategic skills and knowledge required by the workforce to support the strategy
> 2. Strategic technologies: the information systems, databases, tools, and network required to support the strategy
> 3. Climate for action: the cultural shifts needed to motivate, empower, and align the workforce behind the strategy.
>
> The learning and growth strategies are the true starting point for any long-term, sustainable change.

Although Kaplan and Norton do not use the rubric, their conception of 'learning and growth', including their notions of 'strategic competencies' and 'climate for action', resonates with key ideas in this book: with the

'AMO' model of individual performance and with the issue of building workforce capabilities and social climate (see Figure 8.3 in Chapter 8 which summarises these ideas). In the notion of 'strategic technologies', they also identify part of what it means to provide workers with the opportunity to perform because such tools are needed if people are to work effectively. However, their thinking here does not go as far as we would like. It helps to see the structure of work – the forms of work organisation used in the firm – as facilitating or constraining employee opportunity to make a difference, as we argued in Chapter 5.

Through this kind of framework, then, Kaplan and Norton encourage business unit managers to define desirable long-run strategic goals and make short-run plans based on 'milestones' toward long-run goals. This provides a simple, practical way of integrating strategic planning and annual budgeting. Budgeting is a very strong corporate ritual which tends to over-emphasise short-run profitability and undermine long-run efforts to build the business. The balanced scorecard can be used to rework budgets around steps towards the desired long-run strategy. Some short-run targets are always needed (because survival into the long run depends on surviving today) but such targets should not create perverse long-run consequences. Given business unit goals, the scorecard can then be used to create departmental and personal scorecards for individual managers.

It can also be used in multidivisional firms to open up a better dialogue between corporate and business unit management about the role of each (Kaplan and Norton 2001, 2006). Rather than simply considering figures on return on investment, balanced scorecards can open up debate around the performance drivers of financial outcomes, including HR variables. Such an approach challenges some of the modes of corporate control discussed in Chapter 10. Corporate or 'enterprise scorecards' in multidivisional firms, argue Kaplan and Norton, should identify synergies across the group (why else have a group?). This includes ways in which central service units (such as corporate finance, IT and HR departments) can add value to particular business units. In those companies moving from M-form to N-form structure (see Figure 10.3 in Chapter 10), the balanced scorecard could be a valuable tool for identifying synergies across business units and between business units and corporate service centres.

The Kaplan and Norton scorecard is thus better balanced than typical financial reports that only report history and which do not identify underpinning sources of success. Our discussion indicates that it is also better balanced in the sense that it recognises outcomes that matter to other stakeholders (particularly customers and employees) besides stockholders.

This emphasis is consistent with a range of contemporary efforts to encourage broader reporting, such as the notion of the 'triple bottom line' (financial, environmental and social) (Elkington 1997).

Building a theory of the business or 'strategy map'

The second key idea in the balanced scorecard is that senior managers should build a 'theory of the business' or what Kaplan and Norton (2001, 2004) call a 'strategy map'. This is a map of causes-and-effects, of performance drivers and their key outcomes. In the edited version of a scorecard depicted in Figure 11.3, key elements of a strategy map become apparent, including the role of skill building and employee motivation in producing good encounters with customers and, thus, better financial returns.

Another example of a strategy map is shown in Figure 11.4. This map depicts the 'service-profit' or 'employee-customer-profit chain' at Sears (Heskett *et al.* 1994, Rucci, Kirn and Quinn 1998). Sears uses the idea that the company will become a 'compelling place to invest' if it is a 'compelling place to shop' and a 'compelling place to work'. The map argues that differences in employee satisfaction and capabilities have direct impacts on customer satisfaction in service firms and important indirect impacts on profitability. As Becker, Huselid and Ulrich (2001) note, the links between HR strategy, employee behaviour and what happens to customers are very clear in this kind of service business. The vast majority of employees are working directly with customers and their attitudes to the work and the company become very apparent to the customers, something to which we can all attest.

The key point about strategy maps is that they open up debate about what really makes the business successful or could make it more successful, particularly when staff at all levels of the business are included in the process (Kaplan and Norton 2001). 'Making strategy everyone's everyday job' is one of the key principles (as opposed to making it the exclusive knowledge of a top-management 'secret society'). Over time, management should postulate and measure various hypotheses about cause-and-effect in the business, for example exploring the relationship between employee and customer satisfaction, and thus improve their 'theory of the business', something that is emphasised by HR scholars such as David Guest (1997), Becker, Huselid and Ulrich (2001) and Fulmer, Gerhart and Scott (2003). All of this helps to build consensus about what the business should be doing. According to Kaplan and Norton, consensus about where the business should be heading is often lower than people think. 'We cannot expect to implement strategy if we cannot describe it' (Kaplan and Norton 2001: 100).

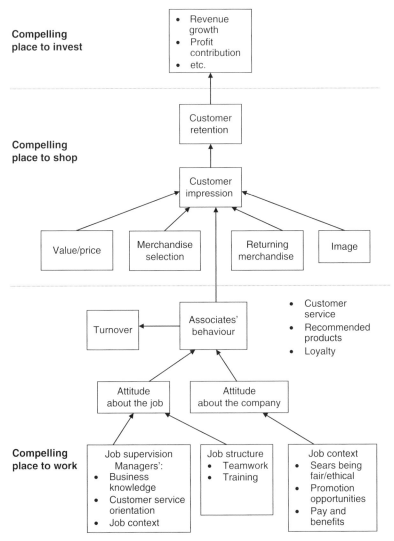

Compelling
place to invest

- Revenue growth
- Profit contribution
- etc.

Compelling
place to shop

Customer retention

Customer impression

Value/price

Merchandise selection

Returning merchandise

Image

Turnover

Associates' behaviour

- Customer service
- Recommended products
- Loyalty

Attitude about the job

Attitude about the company

Compelling
place to work

Job supervision
Managers':
- Business knowledge
- Customer service orientation
- Job context

Job structure
- Teamwork
- Training

Job context
- Sears being fair/ethical
- Promotion opportunities
- Pay and benefits

Figure 11.4   The employee-customer-profit chain at Sears

Strategic HRM and the balanced scorecard: an evaluation

In terms of the practice of strategic HRM, the balanced scorecard is clearly an interesting development. While Kaplan and Norton (1996: 144) are critical of the weak measures often used historically in companies on HR issues, they do not doubt the fundamental role of HRM in building a business over time.

Nor do they doubt the way in which employee satisfaction can contribute to operational performance, something which is increasingly affirmed in research (e.g. Koys 2001, Harrison, Newman and Roth 2006).

The 'learning and growth' perspective is essentially about people management activities. It typically encourages surveying of employee attitudes, recognising the role of these in linking HR activities to performance. The scorecard thus provides a practical methodology for integrating key HR performance drivers into the strategic management framework. There is no doubt this is helpful. Despite the growing attention to HRM over the last twenty years, senior management debates have been hamstrung by lack of agreement on how reports on strategic HR matters should be structured (Purcell and Ahlstrand 1994).

The need for strategic flexibility and 'meta-planning' skills

While seeing the major potential for better HRM–strategy integration through the balanced scorecard, caution should be exercised with some of Kaplan and Norton's ideas, or certainly with a simplistic application of them. The emphasis of the balanced scorecard is very much on improving the quality of the implementation of a *given* strategy. This is important enough, as Kaplan and Norton argue. However, arguments made above about change and dynamic planning suggest it should not be pursued to an inflexible degree. Arguably, those parts of the process which encourage openness to the environment ought to be highlighted more fully. Alongside skills in building particular strategy maps, firms ought to develop what might be called 'meta-planning' skills. These include the ability to sense new environmental directions and to switch to different competitive scenarios, something that was shown to be valuable in our earlier discussion of the US railway cases.

This criticism is increasingly recognised by Kaplan and Norton. In the *Strategy Focused Organization* (2001: Chapter 12), they accept the role and importance of environmental and competitor analysis prior to formulating strategy. They also discuss examples of 'dynamic simulation' and note the value of calibrating scorecard measures against industry rivals (thus benchmarking the firm in terms of industry change). They further argue that the firm's leaders should aim to identify and support the Mintzbergian 'emergent learning' that occurs in their organisation. They note, for example, that Store 24 (Figure 11.3) has now modified its strategy because the 'ban boredom' approach did not impress customers (Kaplan and Norton 2001: 318–19). It turns out the customers valued fast service and good selection rather than in-store entertainment. The slogan has changed to 'Cause you just can't wait', and the scorecard has been revised accordingly. All these points help to underline the value of strategic flexibility and meta-planning skills.

However, more is needed. Building the capacity for strategic management depends heavily on the quality of the *management* of managers, something we emphasised in Chapters 2, 8 and 10 and which does not figure in typical scorecards. Recruitment, development and team-building activities at the top levels of management (and at the middle levels which supply them) need to be planned for in astute ways. This point, too, has increasingly been recognised in Kaplan and Norton's latest work (e.g. 2004: 289–99, 2006: 91–3). The balanced scorecard does contain an emphasis on the management of the non-management workforce and is obviously a way of structuring executive performance measurement. This is absolutely critical but it needs to be complemented with a more comprehensive conception of HR strategy for managing managers, including processes for leadership development and processes for stimulating creative, flexible thinking.

The need to recognise multiple 'bottom lines' in HRM

A second caution is closely related to the first. The importance of productive pursuit of the current strategy is the key theme in Kaplan and Norton's framework. This is, of course, vital in any business. However, this should not make us blind to the fact that some HR policies are not connected directly to cost-effectiveness or indeed to organisational flexibility. Social legitimacy has a role to play in HRM irrespective of competitive goals, one of the key themes of this book. At the very least, all reputable firms should comply with labour laws in their countries of domicile. This means that the firm's scorecard for HRM should never be totally dominated by a single 'bottom line'. Again, Kaplan and Norton have responded somewhat to this point, recognising the importance of regulatory and social processes (2004: Chapter 6). They place more emphasis, however, on social legitimacy as a means to an end (building business reputation and shareholder value) and do not go as far as we do in seeing it as an end in itself.

How can firms practically deal with the need for multiple bottom lines in HRM without getting bogged down in too much complexity? We can work with an idea mentioned in Chapter 9. This is Derek Abell's (1993) suggestion that firms should manage with 'dual strategies': 'mastering the present and pre-empting the future'. We depict our thinking in Figure 11.5 which shows HR strategy simultaneously serving two major strategic priorities: cost-effectiveness and social legitimacy in the current context and organisational flexibility and an appropriate level of management autonomy in the long

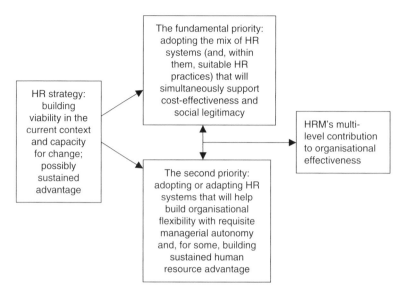

Figure 11.5   Multiple goals in HR strategy and organisational effectiveness

run. It is also possible in the long run that some firms will build sustained competitive advantage through HRM. Together, these sets of activities contribute to a multi-level understanding of organisational effectiveness.

Figure 11.5 argues that the first duty of HRM is to help the firm adopt a cost-effective and socially legitimate set of HR systems. This is needed to underpin viable operations in the current organisational context. The task here is not simply about picking HR systems out of a framework but requires sensitivity to the particular HR practices that are needed in the specific context. HR systems are broad types which inevitably need to be tailored to the actual environment. A key part of this is ensuring that cost-effectiveness is pursued in socially legitimate ways. At a minimum, this means complying with labour law and important social customs in the countries in which the firm operates. Supporting the firm's viability through cost-effective and socially legitimate HR activities must come first or the firm simply will not survive in the industries and societies in which it is located.

The second priority in HR strategy shown in Figure 11.5 is concerned with preparing for the future and with the possibility of building sustained competitive advantage through HRM. Building some degree of organisational flexibility implies an appropriate degree of managerial autonomy or power to act (but we think firms should be careful not to foster the sort of power and reward differences that undermine employee contribution and commitment). Steps to create greater flexibility could mean adopting HR systems that are inherently more flexible, such as moving from industrial models to high-involvement ones or adopting greater use of outsourcing HR models. In other cases, it could mean adding some HR practices to basically resilient HR systems. For example, a firm may have the kinds of HR systems that are serving its short-run profit goals well but find it is not doing enough to build long-run succession and development opportunities, both among managers and in the workforce generally. The response might include fostering forms of management team-building that enhance creative thinking, sponsoring more lateral shifts across the company (including across functions and countries), and reworking training and career structures for the operating workforce. This will not necessarily throw the baby out with the bath-water but should make the company better prepared for change.

All of this implies, as argued in Chapter 8, that there will be tensions in any firm's HR strategy: 'internal fit' in the sense of a single, uncomplicated theme is not possible. Multiple themes are needed in an effective HR strategy. At the very least, there needs to be a balancing of economic drivers with the ethical responsibility of the firm to behave in ways that comply with laws and important social customs. And, at the very least, there needs to be some thinking about organisational flexibility given the pervasiveness of change in today's world. As discussed in Chapters 4 and 9, more ambitious and proactive management teams will go beyond the management of these fundamental tensions to try and build the kinds of human and social capital that create sustained human resource advantage.

The need for caution with specific HR practices

A final criticism of the balanced scorecard concerns Kaplan and Norton's assumptions about desirable kinds of HR practice. Like many US best-practice writers, they tend to place too much faith in incentive remuneration (the 'balanced paycheque') (see also Becker *et al.* 2001). The principle of aligning employer and employee interests is, of course, absolutely fundamental but this does not mean that bonus systems are always desirable, a point we covered in our discussion of agency theory in Chapter 7. There are many situations in which the better focus a scorecard can bring will work well alongside high wage levels but without mechanistic bonuses. If, however, the scorecard process encourages firms to find out more about employee motivations (through, for example, encouraging greater use of employee surveying), it should improve the design of work and reward systems over time. The stakeholder and involvement principles we noted earlier in relation to HR planning systems do imply this kind of consultative process. What is needed is a way of identifying that mix or bundle of HR practices that will be relevant in a particular context. While some practices have almost universal relevance in the Anglo-American world (certain kinds of selection practice, for example), others are heavily shaped by organisational, industry and societal contexts.

Conclusions

This chapter has summarised the major themes that underpin this book and then turned to the practical question of how managers can use these ideas to enhance strategic management processes in their firms. While recognising that strategic management is broader than strategic planning, many of the ideas about how to improve strategic management come back to ideas about how to improve planning and decision-making processes in the firm. In most situations, there is competitive value in finding ways to improve the quality of strategic planning, including finding ways in which human resource problems and opportunities can be better understood and tackled. Far from being outdated or inappropriate in changing times, the discipline of strategic planning is something that can yield greater value, particularly when firms show persistence and develop 'meta-planning' skills in environmental analysis and flexible thinking. Scenario planning is important in this regard, particularly those models that involve planning for the HR challenges presented by different scenarios.

At the base of all strategies, there are things that firms need to do with people, as Kaplan and Norton's stream of work on 'balanced scorecards' and 'strategy maps' indicates. Human resources may not be sufficient for competitive success but they are a necessary part of the system of resources that is. There is no doubt that in many firms, the creation and testing of a strategy map would constitute a major breakthrough by helping to identify the key linkages between HRM and a desired competitive position. As the new management accountancy recognises, there is then less likelihood that critical resources, including human ones, will be subject to counter-productive forms of cost-cutting in the firm. Such frameworks represent an important, integrating step forward, one in which management can move beyond mere assertion about the value of human and social capital to a planning regime in which measurement and modelling of causes-and-effects confirm these important assertions by making them specific, data-based and transparent.

As Kaplan and Norton argue, human resource variables, such as employee skills and satisfaction levels, are 'performance drivers' in all firms. However, this perspective cannot encompass all that is important about HR strategy. The strategic goals of HRM should be understood in a broader sense. At the very least, they include cost-effectiveness and social legitimacy in the current context, twin goals that support viability in the firm's industries and the societies in which it is embedded. If the firm wishes to survive, they also involve some measure of flexibility and power to act over the longer term. For some high-performing firms, they involve sustained 'human resource advantage'. These goals involve strategic tensions that are never easy to handle even where measurement is improved. The 'bottom line' for HRM in organisations, including both private and public sector ones, is more complex than it first appears. A good performance in HRM is multidimensional. New frameworks in strategic management have lessons for HRM and are more embracing of HRM. The traffic, however, is not all one way. Human resource management also has some enduring lessons for the new strategic management.

References

Abell, D. F. (1993) *Managing with Dual Strategies: Mastering the Present, Preempting the Future*. New York: Free Press.

Adams, J. S. (1965) 'Inequality in social exchange'. In Berkovitz, L. (ed.) *Advances in Experimental Social Psychology, Vol. 2*. New York: Academic Press.

Adler, P. S., Goldolftas, B. and Levine, D. I. (1999) 'Flexibility versus efficiency? A case study of model changeovers with Toyota production system'. *Organization Science* 10(1): 43–68.

Alpander, G., Carter, K. and Forsgren, R. (1990) 'Managerial issues and problem-solving in the formative years'. *Journal of Small Business Management* 28(2): 9–19.

Amit, R. and Shoemaker, P. (1993) 'Strategic assets and organizational rent'. *Strategic Management Journal* 14: 33–46.

Ansoff, I. (1991) 'Critique of Henry Mintzberg's "The design school: reconsidering the basic premises of strategic management" '. *Strategic Management Journal* 12(6): 449–61.

Appelbaum, E. and Batt, R. (1994) *The New American Workplace*. Ithaca, NY: ILR Press.

Appelbaum, E., Bailey, T., Berg, P. and Kalleberg, A. (2000) *Manufacturing Advantage: Why High-Performance Systems Pay Off*. Ithaca, NY: ILR Press.

Appleyard, M. and Brown, C. (2001) 'Employment practices and semiconductor manufacturing performance'. *Industrial Relations* 40(3): 436–71.

Armstrong, P. (1995) 'Accountancy and HRM'. In Storey, J. (ed.) *Human Resource Management: A Critical Text*. London: Routledge.

Arthur, J. (1994) 'Effects of human resource systems on manufacturing performance and turnover'. *Academy of Management Journal* 37(3): 670–87.

Atkinson, J. (1984) 'Manpower strategies for flexible organisations'. *Personnel Management* 28–31 August.

Audit Commission (2002) *Recruitment and Retention*. London: Audit Commission.

Aycan, Z. (2005) 'The interplay between cultural and institutional/structural contingencies in human resource management practices'. *International Journal of Human Resource Management* 16(7): 1083–1119.

Bach, S. and Kessler, I. (2007) 'Human resource management and the new public management'. In Boxall, P., Purcell, J. and Wright, P. (eds) *The Oxford Handbook of Human Resource Management*. Oxford: Oxford University Press.

Bacon, N. and Blyton, P. (2001) 'High involvement work systems and job insecurity in the international iron and steel industry'. *Canadian Journal of Administrative Sciences* 18(1): 5–16.

Baden-Fuller, C. (1995) 'Strategic innovation, corporate entrepreneurship and matching outside-in to inside-out approaches to strategy research'. *British Journal of Management* 6(S): 3–16.

Baden-Fuller, C. and Stopford, J. (1994). *Rejuvenating the Mature Business*. London: Routledge.

Baird, L. and Meshoulam, I. (1988). 'Managing two fits of strategic human resource management'. *Academy of Management Review* 13(1): 116–28.

Barker, J. (1993) 'Tightening the iron cage'. *Administrative Science Quarterly* 38(3): 408–37.

Barnard, C. (1938) *The Functions of the Executive*. Boston, MA: Harvard University Press.

Barney, J. (1991) 'Firm resources and sustained competitive advantage'. *Journal of Management* 17(1): 99–120.

Barney, J. and Wright, P. (1998) 'On becoming a strategic partner: the role of human resources in gaining competitive advantage'. *Human Resource Management* 37(1): 31–46.

Baron, R. and Kreps, D. (1999) *Strategic Human Resources: Frameworks for General Managers*. New York: Wiley.

Barr, P., Stimpert, J. and Huff, A. (1992) 'Cognitive change, strategic action, and organizational renewal'. *Strategic Management* Journal 13: 15–36.

Barsoux, J. and Lawrence, P. (1990) *Management in France*. London: Cassell.

Bartlett, C. and Ghoshal, S. (1998) *Managing Across Boundaries: The Transnational Corporation*. New York: Random House.

Bartol, K. and Durham, C. (2000) 'Incentives: theory and practice'. In Cooper, C. and Locke, E. (eds) *Industrial and Organizational Psychology*. Oxford: Blackwell.

Bates, T. (1990) 'Entrepreneur human capital inputs and small business longevity'. *Review of Economics and Statistics* 72(4): 551–9.

Batt, R. (2000) 'Strategic segmentation in front-line services: matching customers, employees and human resource systems'. *International Journal of Human Resource Management* 11(3): 540–61.

Batt, R. (2002) 'Managing customer services: human resource practices, quit rates, and sales growth'. *Academy of Management Journal* 45: 587–97.

Batt, R. (2004) 'Who benefits from teams? Comparing workers, supervisors, and managers'. *Industrial Relations* 43(1): 183–212.

Batt, R. (2005) 'Organizational performance in services'. In Holman, D., Wall, T., Clegg, C., Sparrow, P. and Howard, A. (eds) *The Essentials of the New Workplace*. New York: Wiley.

Batt, R. (2007) 'Service strategies: marketing, operations and human resource practices'. In Boxall, P., Purcell, J. and Wright, P. (eds) *The Oxford Handbook of Human Resource Management*. Oxford: Oxford University Press.

Baumeister, A. and Bacharach, V. (2000) 'Early generic educational intervention has no enduring effect on intelligence and does not prevent mental retardation: the infant health and development program'. *Intelligence* 28(3): 161–92.

Becker, B. and Gerhart, B. (1996) 'The impact of human resource management on organizational performance: progress and practice'. *Academy of Management Journal* 39(4): 779–801.

Becker, B., Huselid, M. A., Pickus, P. S. and Spratt, M. F. (1997) 'HR as a source of shareholder value: research and recommendations'. *Human Resource Management* 36(1): 39–47.

Becker, B., Huselid, M. and Ulrich, D. (2001) *The HR Scorecard: Linking People, Strategy, and Performance*. Boston, MA: Harvard Business School Press.

Becker, T., Billings, R., Eveleth, D. and Gilbert, N. (1996) 'Foci and bases of employee commitment: implications for job performance'. *Academy of Management Journal* 39: 464–82.

Beer, M., Spector, B., Lawrence, P., Quinn Mills, D. and Walton, R. (1984) *Managing Human Assets*. New York: Free Press.

Belanger, J., Giles, A. and Murray, G. (2002) 'Towards a new production model: potentialities, tensions and contradictions'. In Murray, G., Belanger, J., Giles, A. and Lapointe, P. (eds) *Work and Employment Relations in the High-Performance Workplace*. London and New York: Continuum.

Belbin, M. (1981) *Management Teams: Why They Succeed or Fail*. Oxford: Butterworth-Heinemann.

Bendix, R. (1956) *Work and Authority in Industry*. Berkeley, CA: UCLA Press.

Benkhoff, B. (1997). 'A test of the HRM model: good for employers *and* employees'. *Human Resource Management Journal* 7(4): 44–60.

Benson, G. and Lawler, E. (2005) 'Employee involvement: utilization, impacts and future prospects'. In Holman, D., Wall, T., Clegg, C., Sparrow, P. and Howard, A. (eds) *The Essentials of the New Workplace*. New York: Wiley.

Berg, P. (1999) 'The effects of high performance work practices on job satisfaction in the United States steel industry'. *Relations Industrielles* 54(1): 111–34.

Berggren, C. (1992) *The Volvo Experience: Alternatives to Lean Production in the Swedish Auto Industry*. London: Macmillan (now Palgrave Macmillan).

Bettis, R. (1991) 'Strategic management and the straight-jacket: an editorial essay'. *Organization Science* 2(3): 315–19.

Bhargava, S. (1994) 'Profit sharing and the financial performance of companies: evidence from UK Panel Data'. *Economic Journal* 104: 1044–56.

Black, S. and Lynch, L. (2001) 'How to compete: the impact of workplace practices and information technology on productivity'. *Review of Economics and Statistics* 83(3): 434–45.

Blau, P. (1964) *Exchange and Power in Social Life*. New York: Wiley.

Blumberg, M. and Pringle, C. (1982) 'The missing opportunity in organizational research: some implications for a theory of work performance'. *Academy of Management Review* 7(4): 560–9.

Blyton, P. and Turnbull, P. (2004) *The Dynamics of Employee Relations*. London: Palgrave Macmillan.

Boeker, W. (1989) 'Strategic change: the effects of founding and history'. *Academy of Management Journal* 32(3): 489–515.

Bowen, D. and Ostroff, C. (2004) 'Understanding HRM-firm performance linkages: the role of the "strength" of the HRM system'. *Academy of Management Review* 29: 203–21.

Bowey, A. and Thorpe, R. (1986) *Payment Systems and Productivity*. Basingstoke: Macmillan (now Palgrave Macmillan).

Boxall, P. (1992) 'Strategic human resource management: beginnings of a new theoretical sophistication?'. *Human Resource Management Journal* 2(3): 60–79.

Boxall, P. (1994) 'Placing HR strategy at the heart of business success'. *Personnel Management* 26(7): 32–5.

Boxall, P. (1995) 'Building the theory of comparative HRM'. *Human Resource Management Journal* 5(5): 5–17.

Boxall, P. (1996) 'The strategic HRM debate and the resource-based view of the firm'. *Human Resource Management Journal* 6(3): 59–75.

Boxall, P. (1998) 'Achieving competitive advantage through human resource strategy: towards a theory of industry dynamics'. *Human Resource Management Review* 8(3): 265–88.

Boxall, P. (1999), 'Human resource strategy and industry-based competition: a conceptual framework and agenda for theoretical development'. In Wright, P., Dyer, L., Boudreau, J. and Milkovich, G. (eds) *Research in Personnel and Human Resource Management (Supplement 4: Strategic Human Resources Management in the Twenty-First Century)*. Stamford, CT and London: JAI Press.

Boxall, P. (2003) 'HR strategy and competitive advantage in the service sector'. *Human Resource Management Journal* 13(3): 5–20.

Boxall, P. (2007) 'The goals of HRM'. In Boxall, P., Purcell, J. and Wright, P. (eds) *The Oxford Handbook of Human Resource Management*. Oxford: Oxford University Press.

Boxall, P., Freeman, R. and Haynes, P. (2007) 'Conclusions: what workers say in the Anglo-American world'. In Freeman, R., Boxall, P. and Haynes, P. (eds) *What Workers*

Say: Employee Voice in the Anglo-American Workplace. Ithaca, NY: Cornell University Press.

Boxall, P. and Gilbert, J. (2007) 'The management of managers: a literature review and integrative framework'. *International Journal of Management Reviews* 9(2): 1–21.

Boxall, P. and Haynes, P. (1997) 'Strategy and trade union effectiveness in a neo-liberal environment'. *British Journal of Industrial Relations* 35(4): 567–91.

Boxall, P., Macky, K. and Rasmussen, E. (2003) 'Labour turnover and retention in New Zealand: the causes and consequences of leaving and staying with employers'. *Asia Pacific Journal of Human Resources* 41: 195–214.

Boxall, P. and Purcell, J. (2000) 'Strategic human resource management: where have we come from and where should we be going?'. *International Journal of Management Reviews* 2(2): 183–203.

Boxall, P., Purcell, J. and Wright, P. (eds) (2007a) *The Oxford Handbook of Human Resource Management.* Oxford: Oxford University Press.

Boxall, P., Purcell, J. and Wright, P. (2007b) 'Human resource management: scope, analysis, and significance'. In Boxall, P., Purcell, J. and Wright, P. (eds) *The Oxford Handbook of Human Resource Management.* Oxford: Oxford University Press.

Boxall, P. and Steeneveld, M. (1999) 'Human resource strategy and competitive advantage: a longitudinal study of engineering consultancies'. *Journal of Management Studies* 36(4): 443–63.

Boyer, K., Keong Leong, G., Ward, P. and Krajewski, L. (1997) Unlocking the potential of advanced manufacturing technologies'. *Journal of Operations Management* 15: 331–47.

Bracker, J. (1980) 'The historical development of the strategic management concept'. *Academy of Management Review* 5(2): 219–24.

Bradley, K. and Gelb, A. (1983) *Worker Capitalism: The New Industrial Relations.* London: Heinemann Educational.

Bradley, L. and Ashkanasy, N. (2001) 'Formal performance appraisal interviews: can they really be objective and are they useful anyway?'. *Asia Pacific Journal of Human Resources* 39(2): 83–97.

Braverman, H. (1974) *Labor and Monopoly Capital.* New York and London: Monthly Review Press.

Brews, P. and Hunt, M. (1999) 'Learning to plan and planning to learn: resolving the planning school / learning school debate'. *Strategic Management Journal* 20: 889–913.

Brewster, C. and Harris, H. (eds) (1999) *International Human Resource Management: Comtemporary Issues in Europe.* London: Routledge.

Brown, C. and Reich, M. (1997) 'Micro-macro linkages in high-performance work systems'. *Organization Studies* 18(5): 765–81.

Brown, W., Deakin, S., Hudson, M., Pratten, C. and Ryan, P. (1998) 'The individualisation of the employment contract in Britain'. *Employment Relations Research Series* No. 4. London: Department of Trade and Industry.

Bruce, A. and Buck, T. (1997) 'Executive reward and corporate governance'. In Keasey, K., Thompson, S. and Wright, M. (eds) *Corporate Governance: Economic and Financial Issues.* Oxford: Oxford University Press.

Brynjolfsson, E. and Hitt, L. (2000) 'Beyond computation: information technology, organizational transformation and business performance'. *Journal of Economic Perspectives* 14(4): 23–48.

Bryson, A. (2004) 'Managerial responsiveness to union and nonunion worker voice in Britain'. *Industrial Relations* 43(1): 213–41.

Bryson, A., Charlwood, A. and Forth, J. (2006) 'Worker voice, managerial response and labour productivity: an empirical investigation'. *Industrial Relations Journal* 37(5): 438–55.

Bryson, A. and Freeman, R. (2007) 'What voice do British workers want?'. In Freeman, R., Boxall, P. and Haynes, P. (eds) *What Workers Say: Employee Voice in the Anglo-American Workplace.* Ithaca, NY: Cornell University Press.

Budd, J. (2004) *Employment with a Human Face*. Ithaca, NY: Cornell University Press.

Buono, A. and Bowditch, J. (1989) *The Human Side of Mergers and Acquisitions*. San Francisco: Jossey-Bass.

Buono, A., Bowditch, J. and Lewis III, J. (1985) 'When cultures collide: the anatomy of a merger'. *Human Relations* 53(5): 477–500.

Burawoy, M. (1979). *Manufacturing Consent*. Chicago: University of Chicago Press.

Burch, G. and Anderson, N. (2004) 'Measuring person-team fit: development and validation of the team selection inventor'. *Journal of Managerial Psychology* 19(4): 406–26.

Burgess, S. and Rees, H. (1998) 'A disaggregate analysis of the evolution of job tenure in Britain, 1975–1993'. *British Journal of Industrial Relations* 36(4): 629–55.

Buxton, J. (1998) *Ending the Mother War*. London: Macmillan (now Palgrave Macmillan).

Campbell, J. P., McCloy, R., Oppler, S. and Sager, C. (1993) 'A theory of performance'. In Schmitt, N. and Borman, W. (eds) *Personnel Selection in Organizations*. San Francisco: Jossey-Bass.

Cappelli, P. and Neumark, D. (2001) 'Do "high performance" work practices improve establishment level outcomes?'. *Industrial and Labor Relations Review* 54(4): 737–76.

Carroll, G. R. and Hannan, M. T. (eds) (1995) *Organizations in Industry: Strategy, Structure and Selection*. New York and Oxford: Oxford University Press.

Cartier, K. (1994) 'The transaction costs and benefits of the incomplete contract of employment'. *Cambridge Journal of Economics* 18: 181–96.

Cartwright, S. and Cooper, C. (1992) *Mergers and Acquisitions: The Human Factor*. Oxford: Butterworth-Heinemann.

Challis, D., Samson, D. and Lawson, B. (2005) 'Impact of technological, organizational and human resource investments on employee and manufacturing performance: Australian and New Zealand evidence'. *International Journal of Production Research* 43(1): 81–107.

Chandler, A. (1962) *Strategy and Structure: Chapters in the History of Industrial Enterprise*. Cambridge, MA: MIT Press.

Channon, D. (1982) 'Industry structure'. *Long Range Planning* 15(5): 79–93.

Child, J. (1972) 'Organizational structure, environment and performance: the role of strategic choice'. *Sociology* 6(3): 1–22.

Child, J. (1997) 'Strategic choice in the analysis of action, structure, organizations and environment: retrospect and prospect'. *Organization Studies* 18(1): 43–76.

Child, J. and Smith, C. (1987) 'The context and process of organizational transformation: Cadbury Limited in its sector'. *Journal of Management Studies* 24(6): 564–93.

Clegg, H. (1975) 'Pluralism in industrial relations'. *British Journal of Industrial Relations* 13(3): 309–16.

Clegg, H. (1994) *The History of British Trade Unions since 1889, Vol. III*. Oxford: Oxford University Press.

Coff, R. (1997) 'Human assets and management dilemmas: coping with hazards on the road to resource-based theory'. *Academy of Management Review* 22(2): 374–402.

Coff, R. (1999) 'When competitive advantage doesn't lead to performance: the resource-based view and stakeholder bargaining power'. *Organization Science* 10(2): 119–33.

Collard, R. and Dale, B. (1989) 'Quality circles'. In Sisson, K. (ed.) *Personnel Management in Britain*. Oxford: Blackwell.

Colli, A., Fernández Pérez, P. and Rose, M. (2003) 'National determinants of family firm development? Family firms in Britain, Spain, and Italy in the nineteenth and twentieth centuries'. *Enterprise and Society* 4: 28–64.

Colling, T. (1995) 'Experiencing turbulence: competition, strategic choice and the management of human resources in British Airways'. *Human Resource Management Journal* 5(5): 18–32.

Collins, C. and Smith, K. (2006) 'Knowledge exchange and combination: the role of human resource practices in the performance of high-technology firms'. *Academy of Management Journal* 49(3): 544–60.

Combs, J., Yongmei, L., Hall, A. and Ketchen, D. (2006) 'Ho much do high-performance work practices matter? A meta-analysis of their effects on organizational performance'. *Personnel Psychology* 59: 501–28.

Commission on the Skills of the American Workforce (1990) *America's Choice: High Skills or Low Wages!* Rochester, NY: National Center on Education and the Economy.

Conner, K. (1991) 'A historical comparison of resource-based theory and five schools of thought within industrial organization economics: do we have a new theory of the firm?'. *Journal of Management* 17(1): 121–54.

Conyon, M. (1997) 'Institutional arrangements for setting directors' compensation in UK companies'. In Keasey, K., Thompson, S. and Wright, M. (eds) *Corporate Governance: Economic and Financial Issues*. Oxford: Oxford University Press.

Cooke, W. N. (2001) 'The effects of labor costs and workplace constraints on foreign direct investment among highly industrialised countries'. *International Journal of Human Resource Management* 12(5): 697–716.

Cooke, W. N. (2007) 'Multinational companies and global human resource strategy'. In Boxall, P., Purcell, J. and Wright, P. (eds) *The Oxford Handbook of Human Resource Management*. Oxford: Oxford University Press.

Cordery, J. and Parker, S. (2007) 'Work organization'. In Boxall, P., Purcell, J. and Wright, P. (eds) *The Oxford Handbook of Human Resource Management*. Oxford: Oxford University Press.

Cox, A. (2000) 'The importance of employee participation in determining pay system effectiveness'. *International Journal of Management Reviews* 2(4): 357–75.

Cox, A., Zagelmeyer, S. and Marchington, M. (2006) 'Embedding employee involvement and participation at work'. *Human Resource Management Journal* 16(3): 250–67.

Coyle-Shapiro, J. (1999) 'Employee participation and assessment of an organizational change intervention'. *Journal of Applied Behavioural Science* 35(4): 439–56.

Coyle-Shapiro, J. and Kessler, I. (2000) 'Consequences of the psychological contract for the employment relationship: a large scale survey'. *Journal of Management Studies* 37(7): 903–30.

Craft, J. (1988) 'Human resource planning and strategy'. in Dyer, L. (ed.) *Human Resource Management: Evolving Roles and Responsibilities*. Washington, DC: Bureau of National Affairs.

Crichton, A. (1968) *Personnel Management in Context*. London: Batsford.

Cronshaw, M., Davis, E. and Kay, J. (1994) 'On being stuck in the middle or good food costs less at Sainsbury's'. *British Journal of Management* 5(1): 19–32.

Datta, D. and Grant, J. (1990) 'Relationships between types of acquisition, the autonomy given to the acquired firm, and acquisition success: an empirical study'. *Journal of Management* 16: 29–44

de Geus, A. (1988) 'Planning as learning'. *Harvard Business Review* March–April: 70–4.

Deane, P. (1969) *The First Industrial Revolution*. Cambridge: Cambridge University Press.

Deephouse, D. (1999) 'To be different, or to be the same? It's a question (and theory) of strategic balance'. *Strategic Management Journal* 20: 147–66.

Deery, S. J., Iverson, R. D. and Walsh, J. P. (2002) 'Work relationships in telephone call centers: understanding emotional exhaustion and employee withdrawal'. *Journal of Management Studies* 39(4): 471–97.

Delbridge, R. (2005) 'Workers under lean manufacturing'. In Holman, D., Wall, T., Clegg, C., Sparrow, P. and Howard, A. (eds) *Essentials of the New Workplace*. New York: Wiley.

Delbridge, R. (2007) 'HRM and contemporary manufacturing'. In Boxall, P., Purcell, J. and Wright, P. (eds) *The Oxford Handbook of Human Resource Management*. Oxford: Oxford University Press.

Delbridge, R., Kenney, M., and Lowe, J. (1998) 'UK manufacturing in the 21st century'. In Delbridge, R. and Lowe, J. (eds) *Manufacturing in Transition*. London: Routledge.

Delbridge, R. and Whitfield, K. (2001) 'Employee perceptions of job influence and organizational participation'. *Industrial Relations* 40(3): 472–88.

Delery, J. (1998) 'Issues of fit in strategic human resource management: implications for research'. *Human Resource Management Review* 8(3): 289–309.

Delery, J. and Doty, D. (1996) 'Modes of theorizing in strategic human resource management: tests of universalistic, contingency, and configurational performance predictions'. *Academy of Management Journal* 39(4): 802–35.

Delery, J. and Shaw, J. (2001) 'The strategic management of people in work organizations: review, synthesis, and extension'. *Research in Personnel and Human Resources Management* 20: 165–97.

Deming, W. E. (1982) *Out of the Crisis*. Boston, MA: MIT Press.

Dierickx, I. and Cool, K. (1989). 'Asset stock accumulation and sustainability of competitive advantage'. *Management Science* 35(12): 1504–14.

DiMaggio, P. and Powell, W. (1983) 'The iron cage revisited: institutional isomorphism and collective rationality in organizational fields'. *American Sociological Review* 48(2): 147–60.

Doeringer, P., Lorenz, E. and Terkla, D. (2003) 'The adoption of high-performance management: lessons from Japanese multinationals in the West'. *Cambridge Journal of Economics* 27: 265–86.

Doeringer, P. and Piore, M. (1971) *Internal Labor Markets and Manpower Analysis*. Lexington, MA: Heath.

Donaldson. T. and Preston, L. (1995) 'The stakeholder theory of the corporation: concepts, evidence, and implications'. *Academy of Management Review* 20(1): 65–91.

Doorewaard, H. and Meihuizen, H. (2000) 'Strategic performance options in professional service organisations'. *Human Resource Management Journal* 10(2): 39–57.

Dowling, P. J. and Welch, D. E. (2004) *International Human Resource Management. Managing People in a Multinational Context*. London: Thomson.

Dubin, R. (1954) 'Constructive aspects of industrial conflict'. In Kornhauser, A., Dubin, R. and Ross, M. (eds) *Industrial Conflict*. New York: McGraw-Hill.

Dunlop, J. (1958) *Industrial Relations Systems*. New York: Henry Holt.

Dyer, L. (1984) 'Studying human resource strategy'. *Industrial Relations* 23(2): 156–69.

Dyer, L. and Holder, G. (1988) 'A strategic perspective of human resource management'. In Dyer, L. (ed.) *Human Resource Management: Evolving Roles and Responsibilities*. Washington, DC: Bureau of National Affairs.

Dyer, L. and Reeves, T. (1995) 'Human resource strategies and firm performance: what do we know and where do we need to go?'. *International Journal of Human Resource Management* 6(3): 656–70.

Dyer, L. and Shafer, R. (1999). 'Creating organizational agility: implications for strategic human resource management'. In Wright, P., Dyer, L., Boudreau, J. and Milkovich, G. (eds) *Research in Personnel and Human Resource Management (Supplement 4: Strategic Human Resources Management in the Twenty-First Century)*. Stamford, CT and London: JAI Press.

Eaton, S. (2000) 'Beyond "unloving care": linking human resource management and patient care quality in nursing homes'. *International Journal of Human Resource Management* 11(3): 591–616.

Edvinsson, L. and Malone, M. (1997). *Intellectual Capital*. London: Piatkus.

Edwards, P. and Wright, M. (2001) 'High-involvement work systems and performance outcomes: the strength of variable, contingent and context-bound relationships'. *International Journal of Human Resource Management* 12(4): 568–85.

Edwards, P., Edwards, T., Ferner, A., Marginson, P. and Tregaskis, O. (2006) *Employment Practices of Multinational Companies in Organisational Context: A Large Scale Survey*. Feedback to participating companies. Unpublished report.

Edwards, T. and Rees, C. (2006) *International Human Resource Management: Globalization, National Systems and Multinational Companies.* Harlow: Pearson Education.

Eilbert, H. (1959) 'The development of personnel management in the United States'. *Business History Review* 33: 345–64.

Eisenberger, R., Huntingdon, R., Hutchison, S. and Sowa, D. (1986) 'Perceived organizational support'. *Journal of Applied Psychology* 79: 617–26.

Eisenberger, R., Stinglhamber, F., Vandenberghe, C., Sucharski, I. and Rhoades, L. (2002) 'Perceived supervisor support: contributions to perceived organizational support and employee retention'. *Journal of Applied Psychology* 87: 565–73.

Eisenhardt, K. and Bird Schoonhovern, C. (1990) 'Organizational growth: linking founding team, strategy, environment, and growth among US semiconductor ventures, 1978–1988'. *Administrative Science Quarterly* 35(3): 504–29.

Eisenhardt, K., Kahwajy, J. and Bourgeois, L. (1997) 'How management teams can have a good fight'. *Harvard Business Review* July–August: 77–85.

Eisenhardt, K. and Zbaracki, M. (1992) 'Strategic decision making'. *Strategic Management Journal* 13: 17–37.

Elkington, J. (1997) *Cannibals with Forks: The Triple Bottom Line of 21st Century Business.* Oxford: Capstone.

Evans, P. and Genadry, N. (1999) 'A duality-based perspective for strategic human resource management'. In Wright, P., Dyer, L., Boudreau, J. and Milkovich, G. (eds) *Research in Personnel and Human Resources Management (Supplement 4: Strategic Human Resources Management in the Twenty-First Century)*, Stamford, CT and London: JAI Press.

Evans, P., Pucik, V. and Barsoux, J.-L. (2002) *The Global Challenge: Frameworks for International Human Resource Management.* New York: McGraw-Hill.

Feigenbaum, A. and Thomas, H. (1993) 'Industry and strategic group dynamics: competitive strategy in the insurance industry'. *Journal of Management Studies* 30: 9–105.

Ferguson, N. (1998) *The Pity of War.* London: Penguin.

Ferlie, E., Ashburner, C., Fitzgerald, L. and Pettigrew, A. (1996) *The New Public Management in Action.* Oxford: Oxford University Press.

Ferner, A. and Quintanilla, J. (1998) 'Multinationals, national business systems and HRM: the enduring influence of national identify or a process of "Anglo-Saxonization"?'. *International Journal of Human Resource Management* 9 (4): 710–31.

Florida, R., Jenkins, D. and Smith, D. (1998) 'The Japanese transplants in North America: production organization, location, and research and development'. In Boyer, R., Chanaron, J.-J., Jurgens, U. and Tolliday, S. (eds) *Between Imitation and Innovation: The Transfer and Hybridization of Production Models in the International Automotive Industry.* Oxford: Oxford University Press.

Folger, R. and Cropanzano, R. (1998) *Organizational Justice and Human Resource Management.* Thousand Oaks, CA: Sage.

Folger, R. and Greenberg, J. (1985) 'Procedural justice – an interpretive analysis of personnel systems'. *Research in Personnel and Human Resources Management* 3: 141–83.

Foster, R. (1986) *Innovation: The Attacker's Advantage.* New York: Summit.

Fox, A. (1974). *Beyond Contract: Work, Power and Trust Relations.* London: Faber and Faber.

Freeman, J. (1995) 'Business strategy from the population level'. In Montgomery, C. (ed.) *Resource-Based and Evolutionary Theories of the Firm: Towards a Synthesis*, Boston, MA: Kluwer.

Freeman, J. and Boeker, W. (1984) 'The ecological analysis of business strategy'. *California Management Review* 26(3): 73–86.

Freeman, R. (2007) 'Can the US clear the market for representation and participation?'. In Freeman, R., Boxall, P. and Haynes, P. (eds) *What Workers Say: Employee Voice in the Anglo-American Workplace*. Ithaca, NY: Cornell University Press.

Freeman, R., Boxall, P. and Haynes, P. (eds) (2007) *What Workers Say: Employee Voice in the Anglo-American Workplace*. Ithaca, NY: Cornell University Press.

Freeman, R. and Medoff, J. (1984) *What Do Unions Do?* New York: Basic Books.

Frege, C. and Kelly, J. (2004) 'Union strategies in comparative context'. In Frege, C. and Kelly, J. (eds) *Varieties of Unionism: Strategies for Revitalization in a Globalizing Economy*, Oxford: Oxford University Press.

Frenkel, S., Korczynski, M., Shire, K. and Tam, M. (1999) *On the Front Line: Organization of Work in the Information Economy*. Ithaca, NY: ILR Press.

Fulmer, I., Gerhart, B. and Scott, K. (2003) 'Are the 100 best better? An empirical investigation of the relationship between being a "great place to work" and firm performance'. *Personnel Psychology* 56: 965–93.

Gall, G. (2004) 'Trade union recognition in Britain, 1995–2002: turning a corner?'. *Industrial Relations Journal* 35(3): 249–70.

Gallie, D. (2005) 'Work pressure in Europe 1996–2001: trends and determinants'. *British Journal of Industrial Relations* 43(3): 351–75.

Gallie, D. and White, M. (1993) *Employee Commitment and the Skills Revolution*. London: Policy Studies Institute.

Gallie, D., White, M., Cheng, Y. and Tomlinson, M. (1998) *Restructuring the Employment Relationship*. Oxford: Clarendon Press.

Geare, A. J. (1977) 'The field of study of industrial relations'. *Journal of Industrial Relations* 19(3): 274–85.

Gelade, G. and Ivery, M. (2003) 'The impact of human resource management and work climate on organizational performance'. *Personnel Psychology* 56: 383–404.

Gerhart, B. (2007) 'Modelling HRM and performance linkages'. In Boxall, P., Purcell, J. and Wright, P. (eds) *The Oxford Handbook of Human Resource Management*. Oxford: Oxford University Press.

Gersick, C. (1991) 'Revolutionary change theories: a multilevel exploration of the punctuated equilibrium paradigm'. *Academy of Management Review* 16(1): 10–36.

Ghemawat, P. and Costa, J. E. (1993) 'The organizational tension between static and dynamic efficiency'. *Strategic Management Journal* 14: 59–73.

Giangreco, A. and Peccei, R. (2005) 'The nature and antecedents of middle manager resistance to change: evidence from an Italian context'. *International Journal of Human Resource Management* 16(10): 1812–29.

Gilligan, C. (1982) *In a Different Voice: Psychological Theory and Women's Development*. Cambridge, MA: Harvard University Press.

Godard, J. (1991) 'The progressive HRM paradigm: a theoretical and empirical re-examination'. *Relations Industrielles* 46(2): 378–400.

Godard, J. (2001) 'Beyond the high-performance paradigm? An analysis of variation in Canadian managerial perceptions of reform programme effectiveness'. *British Journal of Industrial Relations* 39(1): 25–52.

Godard, J. (2004) 'A critical assessment of the high-performance paradigm'. *British Journal of Industrial Relations* 42(2): 349–78.

Godard, J. and Delaney, J. (2000) 'Reflections on the "high performance" paradigm's implications for industrial relations as a field'. *Industrial and Labor Relations Review* 53(3): 482–502.

Gollan, P., Poutsma, E. and Veersma, U. (2006) 'Editors' introduction: new roads in organizational participation?'. *Industrial Relations* 45(4): 499–511.

Gooderham, P., Nordhaug, O. and Ringdal, K. (1999) 'Institutional and rational determinants of organizational practices: human resource management in European firms'. *Administrative Science Quarterly* 44: 507–31.

Goodrich, C. (1975) *The Frontier of Control*. London: Pluto Press.

Goold, M. (1991) 'Strategic control in the decentralised firm'. *Sloan Management Review* 32(2): 69–81.

Goold, M. and Campbell, A. (1987) *Strategies and Styles: The Role of the Centre in Managing Diversified Corporations*. Oxford: Blackwell.

Goold, M., Campbell, A. and Alexander, M. (1994) *Corporate-level Strategy: Creating Value in the Multibusiness Company*. New York: Wiley.

Gordon, G. and DiTomaso, N. (1992) 'Predicting corporate performance from organizational climate'. *Journal of Management Studies* 26(6): 783–98.

Goshal, A. and Nahapiet, J. (1998) 'Social capital, intellectual capital and the organizational advantage'. *Academy of Management Review* 23(2): 242–66.

Gospel, H. (1973) 'An approach to a theory of the firm in industrial relations'. *British Journal of Industrial Relations* 11(2): 211–28.

Gospel, H. and Pendleton, A. (2003). 'Finance, corporate governance and the management of labour: a conceptual and comparative analysis'. *British Journal of Industrial Relations* 42(3): 557–82.

Gouldner, A. (1960) 'The norm of reciprocity: a preliminary statement'. *American Sociological Review* 25: 161–78.

Granovetter, M. (1985) 'Economic action and social structure: the problem of embeddedness'. *American Journal of Sociology* 91(3): 481–510.

Grant, D. (1999) 'HRM, rhetoric and the psychological contract: a case of "easier said than done" '. *International Journal of Human Resource Management* 10(2): 327–50.

Grant, R. (1991) 'The resource-based theory of competitive advantage: implications for strategy formulation'. *California Management Review* 33(2): 114–35.

Grant, R. (1996) 'Toward a knowledge-based theory of the firm'. *Strategic Management Journal* 17: 109–22.

Grant, R. M. (1998) *Contemporary Strategy Analysis*, 3rd edition. Oxford and Malden, MA: Blackwell.

Grant, R. M. (2005) *Contemporary Strategy Analysis*, 5th edition. Oxford and Malden, MA: Blackwell.

Gratton, L., Hope-Hailey, V., Stiles, P. and Truss, C. (1999a) 'Linking individual performance to business strategy: the people process model'. *Human Resource Management* 38(1): 17–31.

Gratton, L., Hope-Hailey, V., Stiles, P. and Truss, C. (1999b) *Strategic Human Resource Management: Corporate Rhetoric and Human Reality*. Oxford: Oxford University Press.

Green, F. (2001) 'It's been a hard day's night: the concentration and intensification of work in late Twentieth-Century Britain'. *British Journal of Industrial Relations* 39(1): 53–80.

Green, F. and McIntosh, S. (2001) 'The intensification of work in Europe'. *Labour Economics* 8: 291–308.

Greenwood, R., Hinings, C. and Brown, J. (1990) 'P2-form strategic management: corporate practices in professional partnerships'. *Academy of Management Journal* 33(4): 725–55.

Griffeth, R., Hom, P. and Gaertner, S. (2000) 'A meta-analysis of the antecedents and correlates of employee turnover: update, moderator tests, and research implications for the next millennium'. *Journal of Management* 26(3): 563–88.

Grimshaw, D., Marchington, M., Willmott, H. and Rubery, J. (2005) 'Introduction: fragmenting work across organizational boundaries'. In Marchington, M., Grimshaw, D., Rubery, J. and Willmott, H. (eds) *Fragmenting Work: Blurring Organizational Boundaries and Disordering Hierarchies*. Oxford: Oxford University Press.

Grimshaw, D. and Rubery, J. (2007) 'Economics and HRM'. In Boxall, P., Purcell, J. and Wright, P. (eds) *The Oxford Handbook of Human Resource Management*. Oxford: Oxford University Press.

Guest, D. (1987) 'Human resource management and industrial relations'. *Journal of Management Studies* 24(5): 503–21.

Guest, D. (1995) 'Human resource management, trade unions and industrial relations'. In Storey, J. (ed.) *Human Resource Management: A Critical Text*. London: Routledge.

Guest, D. (1997) 'Human resource management and performance: a review and research agenda'. *International Journal of Human Resource Management* 8(3): 263–76.

Guest, D. (1998) 'Is the psychological contract worth taking seriously?'. *Journal of Organizational Behavior* 19: 649–64.

Guest, D. (2007) 'Human resource management and the worker: towards a new psychological contract?'. In Boxall, P., Purcell, J. and Wright, P. (eds) *The Oxford Handbook of Human Resource Management*. Oxford: Oxford University Press.

Guest, D. and Conway, N. (1997) 'Employee motivation and the psychological contract'. *Issues in People Management No. 21*. London: CIPD.

Guest, D. and Conway, N. (2002) *The State of the Psychological Contract*. London: CIPD.

Gumbrell-McCormick, R. and Hyman, R. (2006) 'Embedded collectivism? Workplace representation in France and Germany'. *Industrial Relations Journal* 37(5): 473–91.

Guthrie, J. (2001) 'High-involvement work practices, turnover, and productivity: evidence from New Zealand'. *Academy of Management Journal* 44(1): 180–90.

Guthrie, J. (2007) 'Remuneration: pay effects at work'. In Boxall, P., Purcell, J. and Wright, P. (eds) *The Oxford Handbook of Human Resource Management*. Oxford: Oxford University Press.

Guy, F. (2003) 'High-involvement work practices and employee bargaining power'. *Employee Relations* 25(5): 453–69.

Hackman, J. R. and Oldham, G. R. (1980) *Work Redesign*. Reading, MA: Addison-Wesley.

Hall, M. (2006) 'A cool response to the ICE regulations? Employer and trade union approaches to the new legal framework for information and consultation'. *Industrial Relations Journal* 37(5): 456–72.

Hall, P. and Soskice, D. (2001) 'An introduction to varieties of capitalism'. In Hall, P. and Soskice, D. (eds) *Varieties of Capitalism: the Institutional Foundations of Comparative Advantage*. Oxford: Oxford University Press.

Hall, R. (1993) 'A framework linking intangible resources and capabilities to sustainable competitive advantage'. *Strategic Management Journal* 14: 607–18.

Hambrick, D. (1987) 'The top management team: key to strategic success'. *California Management Review* 30(1): 88–108.

Hambrick, D. (1995) 'Fragmentation and the other problems CEOs have with their top management teams'. *California Management Review* 37(3): 110–27.

Hamel, G. and Prahalad, C. (1993). 'Strategy as stretch and leverage'. *Harvard Business Review* 71(2): 75–84.

Hamel, G. and Prahalad, C. (1994) *Competing for the Future*. Boston, MA: Harvard Business School Press.

Hannan, M. (1995) 'Labor unions'. In Carroll, G. R. and Hannan, M. T. (eds) *Organizations in Industry: Strategy, Structure and Selection*. Oxford and New York: Oxford University Press.

Harley, B. (2001) 'Team membership and the experience of work in Britain: an analysis of the WERS98 data'. *Work, Employment and Society* 15(4): 721–42.

Harrison, D., Newman, D. and Roth, P. (2006) 'How important are job attitudes? Meta-analytic comparisons of integrative behavioural outcomes and time sequences'. *Academy of Management Journal* 49(2): 305–25.

Hart, S. L. (1992) 'An integrative framework for strategy-making processes'. *Academy of Management Review* 17(2): 327–51.

Hart, S. L. and Banbury, C. (1994) 'How strategy-making processes can make a difference'. *Strategic Management Journal* 15: 251–69.

Haspeslagh, P. and Jemison, D. (1991) *Managing Acquisitions: Creating Value through Corporate Renewal*. New York: Free Press.

Haynes, P. and Allen, M. (2000) 'Partnership as union strategy: a preliminary evaluation'. *Employee Relations* 23(2): 164–87.

Haynes, P. and Fryer, G. (2000) 'Human resources, service quality and performance: a case study'. *International Journal of Contemporary Hospitality Management* 12(4): 240–8.

Hedlund, G. (1994) 'A model of knowledge management and the N-Form corporation'. *Strategic Management Journal* 15: 73–90.

Heery, E. and Adler, L. (2004) 'Organizing the unorganized'. In Frege, C. and Kelly, J. (eds) *Varieties of Unionism: Strategies for Revitalization in a Globalizing Economy*. Oxford: Oxford University Press.

Helfat, C. and Peteraf, M. (2003) 'The dynamic resource-based view: capability life cycles'. *Strategic Management Journal* 24: 997–1010.

Heller, F., Pusic, E., Strauss, G. and Wilpert, B. (1998) *Organizational Participation: Myth and Reality*. Oxford: Oxford University Press.

Henderson, R. (1995) 'Of life cycles real and imaginary: the unexpectedly long old age of optical lithography'. *Research Policy* 24: 631–43.

Hendry, C., Arthur, M. and Jones, A. (1995). *Strategy Through People*. London and New York: Routledge.

Herzberg, F. (1968) 'One more time: How do you motivate employees?'. *Harvard Business Review* 46: 53–63.

Herzenberg, S., Alic, J. and Wial, H. (1998) *New Rules for a New Economy: Employment and Opportunity in Postindustrial America*. Ithaca, NY: ILR Press.

Heskett, J., Jones, T., Loveman, G. and Schlesinger, A. (1994) 'Putting the service-profit chain to work'. *Harvard Business Review* March–April: 164–74.

Hill, C. and Hoskisson, R. (1987) 'Strategy and structure in the multi-product firm'. *Academy of Management Review* 12(2): 331–41.

Hill, C. and Pickering, J. (1986) 'Divisionalisation, decentralisation and performance of large United Kingdom companies' *Journal of Management Studies* 23(1): 26–50.

Hill, C. W. L. and Jones, T. M. (1992) 'Stakeholder-agency theory'. *Journal of Management Studies* 29(2): 131–54.

Hill, S. (1991) 'Why quality circles failed but total quality management might succeed'. *British Journal of Industrial Relations* 29(4): 541–68.

Hochschild, A. (1986) *The Managed Heart: Commercialization of Human Feeling*. Berkeley, CA: University of California Press.

Holbrook, D., Chen, W., Hounshell, D. and Klepper, S. (2000) 'The nature, sources, and consequences of firm differences in the early history of the semiconductor industry'. *Strategic Management Journal* 21: 1017–41.

Hood, C. (1991) 'A public management for all seasons'. *Public Administration* 69(1): 3–19.

Hoopes, D., Madsen, T. and Walker, G. (2003) 'Guest editors' introduction to the special issue: why is there a resource-based view? Toward a theory of competitive heterogeneity'. *Strategic Management Journal* 24: 889–902.

Hope-Hailey, V., Gratton, L., McGovern, P., Stiles, P. and Truss, C. (1997) 'A chameleon function? HRM in the '90s'. *Human Resource Management Journal* 7(3): 5–18.

Hornsby, J. and Kuratko, D. (2003). 'Human resource management in US small businesses: a replication and extension'. *Journal of Developmental Entrepreneurship* 8(1): 73–92.

Hoskisson, R., Hitt, M., Wan, W. and Yiu, D. (1999) 'Theory and research in strategic management: swings of a pendulum'. *Journal of Management* 25(3): 417–56.

Houston, J., James, C. and Ryngaert, M. (2001) 'Where do merger gains come from? Bank mergers from the perceptive of insiders and outsiders'. *Journal of Financial Economics* 60(2–3): 285–331.

Hubbard, N. (1999) *Acquisition Strategy and Implementation*. Basingstoke: Macmillan (now Palgrave Macmillan).

Hubbard, N. and Purcell, J. (2001) 'Managing employee expectations during acquisitions'. *Human Resource Management Journal* 11(2): 17–33.

Huber, V. and Fuller, S. (1998) 'Performance appraisal'. In Poole, M. and Warner, M. (eds) *The IEBM Handbook of Human Resource Management.* London: Thomson Business Press.

Hunt, J. and Boxall, P. (1998) 'Are top human resource specialists "strategic partners"? Self-perceptions of a corporate elite'. *International Journal of Human Resource Management* 9(5): 767–81.

Hunt, J., Lees, S., Grümber, J. and Vivian, P. (1987) *Acquisitions: The Human Factor.* London: London Business School and Egon Zehnder International.

Hunt, S. (1995) 'The resource-advantage theory of competition'. *Journal of Management Inquiry* 4(4): 317–22.

Hunter, J. E. and Hunter, R. F. (1984) 'Validity and utility of alternate predictors of job performance'. *Psychological Bulletin* 96: 72–98.

Hunter, J. E., Schmidt, F. L. and Judiesch, M. K. (1990) 'Individual differences in output variability as a function of job complexity'. *Journal of Applied Psychology* 75(1): 28–42.

Hunter, J. E., Schmidt, F. L., Rauschenberger, J. and Jayne, M. (2000) 'Intelligence, motivation, and job performance'. In Cooper, C. and Locke, E. (eds) *Industrial and Organizational Psychology.* Oxford: Blackwell.

Hunter, L. (2000) 'What determines job quality in nursing homes?'. *Industrial and Labor Relations Review* 53(3): 463–81.

Hutchinson, S., Kinnie, N., Purcell, J., Rees, C., Scarbrough, H. and Terry, M. (1996) *The People Management Implications of Leaner Ways of Working.* Issues in People Management No. 15. London: Institute of Personnel and Development.

Hutchinson, S., Kinnie, N., Purcell, J., Collinson, M., Scarborough, H. and Terry, M. (1998) *Getting Fit, Staying Fit: Developing Lean and Responsive Organisations.* London: Institute of Personnel and Development.

Hyman, J. (2000) 'Financial participation schemes'. In White, G. and Drucker, J. (eds) *Reward Management: A Critical Text.* London: Routledge.

Hyman, R. (1975) *Industrial Relations: A Marxist Introduction.* London: Macmillan (now Palgrave Macmillan).

Hyman, R. (1987) 'Strategy or structure? Capital, labour and control'. *Work, Employment and Society* 1(1): 25–55.

Ichniowski, C., Shaw, K. and Prennushi, G. (1997) 'The effects of human resource management practices on productivity: a study of steel finishing lines'. *American Economic Review* 87(3): 291–313.

Ichniowski, C. and Shaw, K. (1999) 'The effects of human resource management systems on economic performance: an international comparison of US and Japanese plants'. *Management Science* 45(5): 704–21.

Isenberg, D. J. (1984) 'How senior managers think'. *Harvard Business Review* November– December: 81–90.

Jackson, S. and Schuler, R. (1995). 'Understanding human resource management in the context of organizations and their environments'. *Annual Review of Psychology* 46: 237–64.

Jacoby, S. (1984) 'The development of internal labor markets in American manufacturing firms'. In Osterman, P. (ed.) *Internal Labor Markets.* Cambridge, MA: MIT Press.

Jacoby, S. (2004) *Employing Bureaucracy: Managers, Unions, and the Transformation of Work in the 20th Century.* Mahwah, NJ: Lawrence Erlbaum.

Jacoby, S. (2005) *The Embedded Corporation: Corporate Governance and Employment Relations in Japan and the United States.* Princeton, NJ: Princeton University Press.

Janis, I. (1972) *Victims of Groupthink.* Boston, MA: Houghton Mifflin.

Jelinek, M. (1979) *Institutionalizing Innovation: A Study of Organizational Learning.* New York: Praeger.

Jensen, J. and Kletzer, L. (2005) 'Tradable services: understanding the scope and impact of services offshoring'. www.brookings.edu/es/commentary/journals/tradeforum/agenda2005.htm

Jensen, M. and Meckling, W. (1976). 'Theory of the firm: managerial behavior, agency costs and ownership structure'. *Journal of Financial Economics* 3: 305–60.

Johnson, G. (1987) *Strategic Change and the Management Process*. Oxford: Blackwell.

Johnson, G. and Scholes, K. (2002) *Exploring Corporate Strategy: Text and Cases*. Harlow: Pearson Education.

Johnson, H. and Kaplan, R. (1991) *Relevance Lost: the Rise and Fall of Management Accounting*. Boston, MA: Harvard Business School Press.

Jones, S. (1994) 'The origins of the factory system in Great Britain: technology, transaction costs or exploitation?'. In Kirby, M. and. Rose, M. (eds) *Business Enterprise in Modern Britain*. London: Routledge.

Judge, T., Higgins, C., Thoresen, C. and Barrick, M. (1999) 'The big five personality traits, general mental ability, and career success across the life span'. *Personnel Psychology* 52: 621–52.

Juravich, T. and Hilgert, J. (1999) 'UNITE's victory at Richmark: community-based union organizing in communities of color'. *Labor Studies Journal* 24(1): 27–41.

Kalleberg, A., Marsden, P., Reynolds, J. and Knoke, D. (2006). 'Beyond profit? Sectoral differences in high-performance work practices'. *Work and Occupations* 33(3): 271–302.

Kamoche, K. (1996). 'Strategic human resource management within a resource-capability view of the firm'. *Journal of Management Studies* 33(2): 213–33.

Kaplan, R. and Norton, D. (1996) *The Balanced Scorecard: Translating Strategy into Action*. Boston, MA: Harvard Business School Press.

Kaplan, R. and Norton, D. (2001) *The Strategy-Focused Organization*. Boston, MA: Harvard Business School Press.

Kaplan, R. and Norton, D. (2004) *Strategy Maps: Converting Intangible Assets into Tangible Outcomes*. Boston, MA: Harvard Business School Press.

Kaplan, R. and Norton, D. (2006) *Alignment: Using the Balanced Scorecard to Create Corporate Synergies*. Boston, MA: Harvard Business School Press.

Karasek, R. (1979) 'Job demands, job decision latitude, and mental strain: implications for job redesign'. *Administrative Science Quarterly* 24: 285–308.

Katz, H. and Darbishire, O. (2000) *Converging Divergences: Worldwide Changes in Employment Systems*. Ithaca, NY: Cornell University Press.

Kaufman, B. (2004) 'Prospects for union growth in the United States in the early 21st Century'. In Verma, A. and Kochan, T. (eds) *Unions in the 21st Century*. Basingstoke and New York: Palgrave Macmillan.

Kay, J. (1993) *Foundations of Corporate Success*. Oxford: Oxford University Press.

Keenoy, T. (1992) 'Constructing control'. In Hartley, J. and Stephenson, G. (eds) *Employment Relations: The Psychology of Influence and Control at Work*. Oxford: Blackwell.

Keenoy, T. and Anthony, P. (1992) 'HRM: metaphor, meaning and morality'. In Blyton, P. and Turnbull, P. (eds) *Reassessing Human Resource Management*. London: Sage.

Kelley, M. (2000) 'The participatory bureaucracy: a structural explanation for the effects of group-based employee participation programs on productivity in the machined products sector'. In Ichniowski, C., Levine, D., Olson, C. and Strauss, G. (eds) *The American Workplace: Skills, Compensation and Employee Involvement*. Cambridge: Cambridge University Press.

Kelly, J. (1998) *Rethinking Industrial Relations: Mobilization, Collectivism and Long Waves*. London: Routledge.

Kepes, S. and Delery, J. (2007) 'HRM systems and the problem of internal fit'. In Boxall, P., Purcell, J. and Wright, P. (eds) *The Oxford Handbook of Human Resource Management*. Oxford: Oxford University Press.

Kersley, B., Alpin, C., Forth, J., Bryson, A., Bewley, H., Dix, G. and Oxenbridge, S. (2006) *Inside the Workplace: Findings from the 2004 Workplace Employment Relations Survey*. London: Routledge.

Kessler, I. (1998) 'Payment systems'. In Poole, M. and Warner, M. (eds) *The IEBM Handbook of Human Resource Management*. London: Thomson Business Press.

Kessler, I. and Purcell, J. (1992) 'Performance-related pay: objectives and application'. *Human Resource Management Journal* 2(3): 16–33.

Kessler, I. and Purcell, J. (1996) 'The value of joint working parties'. *Work, Employment and Society* 10(4): 663–82.

Kets de Vries, M. and Miller, D. (1984) *The Neurotic Organization*. San Francisco: Jossey-Bass.

King, A. and Zeithaml, C. (2001) 'Competencies and firm performance: examining the causal ambiguity paradox'. *Strategic Management Journal* 22: 75–99.

Kinnie, N., Hutchinson, S., Purcell, J., Swart, J. and Rayton, B. (2005) 'Satisfaction with HR practices and commitment to the organisation: why one size does not fit all'. *Human Resource Management Journal* 15(4): 9–29

Kinnie, N., Swart, J., Lund, M., Morris, S., Snell, S. and Kang, S. (2006) *Managing Knowledge and People in Professional Services Firms*. London: CIPD.

Kintana, M. Alonso, A. and Olaverri, C. (2006) 'High-performance work systems and firms' operational performance: the moderating role of technology'. *International Journal of Human Resource Management* 17(1): 70–85.

Kirkpatrick, I.. Ackroyd, S. and Walker, R. (2005) *The New Managerialism and Public Service Professions*. Basingstoke: Palgrave Macmillan.

Knox, A. and Walsh, J. (2005) 'Organisational flexibility and HRM in the hotel industry: evidence from Australia'. *Human Resource Management Journal* 15(1): 57–75.

Koch, M. and McGrath, R. (1996) 'Improving labor productivity: human resource management policies do matter'. *Strategic Management Journal* 17: 335–54.

Kochan, T. (2007) 'Social legitimacy of the human resource management profession: a U.S. perspective'. In Boxall, P., Purcell, J. and Wright, P. (eds) *The Oxford Handbook of Human Resource Management*. Oxford: Oxford University Press.

Konzelmann, S., Forrant, R., and Wilkinson, F. (2004) 'Work systems, corporate strategy and global markets: creative shop floors or "a barge mentality"?'. *Industrial Relations Journal* 35(3): 216–32.

Kossek, E. and Pichler, S. (2007) 'EEO and the management of diversity'. In Boxall, P., Purcell, J. and Wright, P. (eds) *The Oxford Handbook of Human Resource Management*. Oxford: Oxford University Press.

Koys, D. (2001) 'The effects of employee satisfaction, organizational citizenship behavior, and turnover on organisational effectiveness: a unit-level, longitudinal study'. *Personnel Psychology* 54: 101–14.

KPMG (1999) 'Unlocking shareholder value: the key to success'. In *Mergers and Acquisitions: A Global Research Report*. London: KPMG.

Kristof, A. (1996) 'Person-organization fit: an integrative review of its conceptualisations, measurement, and implications'. *Personnel Psychology* 49: 1–49.

Kruger, J. (1999) 'Lake Wobegon be gone! The "below-average effect" and the egocentric nature of comparative ability judgments'. *Journal of Personality and Social Psychology* 77(2): 221–32.

Krugman, P. (1997) *Pop Internationalism*. Cambridge, MA: MIT Press.

Lacey, R. (1986). *Ford: The Men and the Machine*. London: Heinemann.

Lam, S. and Schaubroeck, J. (1998) 'Integrating HR planning and organisational strategy'. *Human Resource Management Journal* 8(3): 5–19.

Landes, D. (1998) *The Wealth and Poverty of Nations*. London: Abacus.

Lane, C. (1990) 'Vocational training and new production concepts in Germany: some lessons for Britain'. *Industrial Relations Journal* 21(4): 247–59.

Lashley, C. (1998). 'Matching the management of human resources to service operaions'. *International Journal of Contemporary Hospitality Management* 10(1): 24–33.

Latham, G. and Latham, S. (2000) 'Overlooking theory and research in performance appraisal at one's peril: much done, more to do'. In Cooper, C. and Locke, E. (eds) *Industrial and Organizational Psychology*. Oxford: Blackwell.

Latham, G. and Pinder, C. (2005) 'Work motivation theory and research at the dawn of the twenty-first century'. *Annual Review of Psychology* 56: 485–516.

Latham, G., Sulsky, L. and MacDonald, H. (2007) 'Performance management'. In Boxall, P., Purcell, J. and Wright, P. (eds) *The Oxford Handbook of Human Resource Management*. Oxford: Oxford University Press.

Laurent, A. (1986) 'The cross-cultural puzzle of international human resource management'. *Human Resource Management* 25(1): 91–102.

Lawler, E. (1986) *High-Involvement Management*. San Francisco: Jossey-Bass.

Lawrence, P. and Edwards, V. (2000) *Management in Western Europe*. Basingstoke: Palgrave Macmillan.

Lazear, E. (1999) 'Personnel economics: past lessons and future directions'. *Journal of Labor Economics* 17(2): 199–236.

Leana, C. and Van Buren, H. (1999) 'Organizational social capital and employment practices'. *Academy of Management Review* 24(3): 538–55.

Lees, S. (1997) 'HRM and the legitimacy market'. *International Journal of Human Resource Management* 8(3): 226–43.

Legge, K. (1978) *Power, Innovation, and Problem-solving in Personnel Management*. London: McGraw-Hill.

Legge, K. (1995) *Human Resource Management: Rhetorics and Realities*. Basingstoke: Macmillan (now Palgrave Macmillan).

Legge, K. (2005) *Human Resource Management: Rhetorics and Realities*, 2nd edition. Basingstoke and New York: Palgrave Macmillan.

Lengnick-Hall, M. and Lengnick-Hall, C. (2005) 'International human resource management research and social network/social capital theory'. In Bjorkman, I. and Stahl, G. (eds) *Handbook of Research into International HRM*. Cheltenham: Edward Elgar.

Leonard, D. (1992) 'Core capabilities and core rigidities: a paradox in managing new product development'. *Strategic Management Journal* 13: 111–25.

Leonard, D. (1998) *Wellsprings of Knowledge: Building and Sustaining the Sources of Innovation*. Boston, MA: Harvard Business School Press.

Lepak, D. and Snell, S. (1999) 'The strategic management of human capital: determinants and implications of different relationships'. *Academy of Management Review* 24(1): 1–18.

Lepak, D. P. and Snell, S.A. (2002) 'Examining the human resource architecture: the relationships among human capital, employment, and human resource configurations'. *Journal of Management* 28: 517–43.

Lepak, D. and Snell, S. (2007) 'Employment sub-systems and the "HR architecture"'. In Boxall, P., Purcell, J. and Wright, P. (eds) *The Oxford Handbook of Human Resource Management*. Oxford: Oxford University Press.

Levinson, D. (1978) *The Seasons of a Man's Life*. New York: Knopf.

Levinson, D. and Levinson, J. (1996) *The Seasons of a Woman's Life*. New York: Knopf.

Levinthal, D. and Myatt, J. (1994) 'Co-evolution of capabilities and industry: the evolution of mutual fund processing'. *Strategic Management Journal* 15: 45–62.

Liden, R., Bauer, T. and Erdogan, B. (2004) 'The role of leader-member exchange in the dynamic relationship between employer and employee: implications for employee socialization, leaders, and organizations'. In Coyle-Shapiro, J. Shore, L. Taylor, S. and Tetrick, L. (eds) *The Employment Relationship: Examining Psychological and Contextual Perspectives*. Oxford: Oxford University Press.

Littler, C. (1982) *The Development of the Labour Process in Capitalist Societies: A Comparative Study of the Transformation of Work Organization in Britain, Japan, and the USA*. London: Heinemann.

Lloyd, C. (2005) 'Competitive strategy and skills: working out the fit in the fitness industry'. *Human Resource Management Journal* 15(2): 15–34.

Lovas, B. and Goshal, S. (2000) 'Strategy as guided evolution'. *Strategic Management Journal* 21: 875–96.

MacDuffie, J. (1995) 'Human resource bundles and manufacturing performance: organizational logic and flexible production systems in the world auto industry'. *Industrial and Labor Relations Review* 48(2): 197–221.

MacKenzie, G. (1973) *The Aristocracy of Labor: The Position of Skilled Craftsmen in the American Class Structure*. London: Cambridge University Press.

Mackie, K., Holahan, C. and Gottlieb, N. (2001) 'Employee involvement management practices, work stress, and depression in employees of a human services residential care facility'. *Human Relations* 54(8): 1065–92.

Macky, K. and Boxall, P. (2006) 'Work intensification, high-involvement work processes and employee well-being'. Paper presented to KCL-ACREW conference, Prato, 1–4 July.

Macky, K. and Boxall, P. (2007) 'The relationship between high-performance work practices and employee attitudes: an investigation of additive and interaction effects'. *International Journal of Human Resource Management* 18(4): 537–67.

MacNeil, I. (1985) 'Relational contract: what we do and do not know'. *Wisconsin Law Review* 3: 483–525.

Mahoney, J. and Pandian, J. (1992). 'The resource-based view within the conversation of strategic management'. *Strategic Management Journal* 13(5): 363–80.

Main, B. (1990) 'The new economics of personnel'. *Journal of General Management* 16(2): 91–103.

Malos, S. and Campion, M. (2000) 'Human resource strategy and career mobility in professional service firms: a test of the option-based model'. *Academy of Management Journal* 43: 749–60.

Marchington, M. (1989) 'Joint consultation in practice'. In Sisson, K. (ed.) *Personnel Management in Britain*. Oxford: Blackwell.

Marchington, M. (1995) 'Involvement and participation'. In Storey, J. (ed.) *Human Resource Management: A Critical Text*. London: Routledge.

Marchington, M. (2007) 'Employee voice systems'. in Boxall, P., Purcell, J. and Wright, P. (eds) *The Oxford Handbook of Human Resource Management*. Oxford: Oxford University Press.

Marchington, M., Carroll, M. and Boxall, P. (2003) 'Labour scarcity and the survival of small firms: a resource-based view of the road haulage industry'. *Human Resource Management Journal* 13(4): 3–22.

Marchington, M. and Grugulis, I. (2000). ' "Best practice" human resource management: perfect opportunity or dangerous illusion?'. *International Journal of Human Resource Management* 11(6): 1104–24.

Marchington, M. and Wilkinson, A. (2000) 'Direct participation'. In Bach, S. and Sisson, K. (eds) *Personnel Management: A Comprehensive Guide to Theory and Practice*. Oxford: Blackwell.

Marchington, M., Wilkinson, A., Ackers, P. and Dundon, T. (2001) *Management Choice and Employee Voice*. Research report. London: CIPD.

Marginson, P. (1993) 'The multi-divisional structure and corporate control: explaining the degree of corporate coordination over decisions in labour relations'. *Papers in Organization* No. 12. Copenhagen: Institute of Organization and Industrial Sociology, Copenhagen Business School.

Marginson, P., Armstrong, P., Edwards, P. and Purcell, J. with Hubbard, N. (1993) 'The control of industrial relations in large companies: an initial analysis of the second company level industrial relations survey'. *Warwick Papers in Industrial Relations* No, 45. Coventry: University of Warwick.

Marginson, P., Edwards, P., Martin, R., Purcell, J. and Sisson, K. (1988) *Beyond the Workplace. Managing Industrial Relations in the Multi-Establishment Enterprise.* Oxford: Blackwell.

Marginson, P., Hall, M., Hoffman, A. and Muller, T. (2004) 'The impact of European works councils on management decision-making in UK and US multinationals: a case study comparison'. *British Journal of Industrial Relations* 42(2): 209–33.

Marks, M. and Mirvis, P. (1982) 'Merging human resources: a review of current research'. *Mergers and Acquisitions* 17(2): 38–44.

Marks, A., Findlay, P., Hine, J., McKinlay, A. and Thompson, P. (1998) 'The politics of partnership? Innovation in employment relations in the Scottish spirits industry'. *British Journal of Industrial Relations* 36(2): 209–26.

Marshall, V. and Wood, R. (2000) 'The dynamics of effective performance appraisal: an integrated model'. *Asia Pacific Journal of Human Resources* 38(3): 62–90.

Marsick, V. and Watkins, K. (1990) *Informal and Incidental Learning in the Workplace.* London and New York: Routledge.

Martell, K. and Carroll, S. (1995) 'Which executive human resource management practices for the top management team are associated with higher firm performance?'. *Human Resource Management* 34(4): 497–512.

Martin, J. (1992) *Cultures and Organizations: Three Perspectives.* New York: Oxford University Press.

Martin, R. (1981) *New Technology and Industrial Relations in Fleet Street.* Oxford: Clarendon Press.

Martínez Lucio, M. and Stuart, M. (2004) 'Swimming against the tide: social partnership, mutual gains and the revival of "tired" HRM'. *International Journal of Human Resource Management* 15(2): 410–24.

McConnell, C. and Brue, S. (1995) *Contemporary Labor Economics.* New York: McGraw-Hill.

McGovern, P., Gratton, L., Hope-Hailey, V., Stiles, P. and Truss, C. (1997). 'Human resource management on the line?'. *Human Resource Management Journal* 7(4): 12–29.

McKersie, R. and Hunter, L. (1973) *Pay, Productivity and Collective Bargaining.* London: Macmillan (now Palgrave Macmillan).

McLean Parks, J. and Kidder, D. (1994). '"Till death us do part...": changing work relationships in the 1990s'. In Cooper, C. and Rousseau, D. (eds) *Trends in Organizational Behaviour, Vol. 1.* New York: Wiley.

McMillan, J. (1992) *Games, Strategies and Managers.* Oxford and New York: Oxford University Press.

McWilliams, A. and Smart, D. (1995) 'The resource-based view of the firm: does it go far enough in shedding the asssumptions of the S-C-P paradigm?'. *Journal of Management Inquiry* 4(4): 309–16.

Meyer, A. D., Tsui, A. S. and Hinings, C. R. (1993) 'Configurational approaches to organizational analysis'. *Academy of Management Journal* 36(6): 1175–95.

Meyer, S. (1981). *The Five Dollar Day: Labor Management and Social Control in the Ford Motor Company 1908–1921.* Albany, NY: State University of New York Press.

Miles, G., Snow, C. C. and Sharfman, M. P. (1993) 'Industry variety and performance'. *Strategic Management Journal* 14: 163–77.

Miles, R. and Snow, C. (1984) 'Designing strategic human resources systems'. *Organizational Dynamics* Summer: 36–52.

Miller, D. (1981) 'Toward a new contingency approach: the search for organizational gestalts'. *Journal of Management Studies* 18(1): 1–26.

Miller, D. (1992) 'Generic strategies; classification, combination and context'. *Advances in Strategic Management* 8: 391–408.

Miller, D. and Friesen, P. (1980) 'Momentum and revolution in organizational adaptation'. *Academy of Management Journal* 23(4): 591–614.

Miller, D. and Shamsie, J. (1992) 'The resource-based view of the firm in two environments: the Hollywood film studios from 1936 to 1965'. *Academy of Management Journal* 39(3): 519–43.

Millward, N. and Stevens, M. (1986) *British Workplace Industrial Relations 1980–1984: The DE/ESRC/PSI/ACAS Surveys.* Aldershot: Gower.

Millward, N., Bryson, A. and Forth, J. (2000) *All Change at Work: British Employment Relations 1980–1998 as portrayed by the Workplace Industrial Relations Survey Series.* London: Routledge.

Mintzberg, H. (1978) 'Patterns in strategy formation'. *Management Science* 24(9): 934–48.

Mintzberg, H. (1990) 'The design school: reconsidering the basic premises of strategic management'. *Strategic Management Journal* 11(3): 171–95.

Mintzberg, H. (1994) 'Rethinking strategic planning part 1: pitfalls and fallacies'. *Long Range Planning* 27(3): 12–21.

Morgan, G. (1997) *Images of Organization.* Thousand Oaks, CA: Sage.

Mueller, D. (1997) 'First-mover advantages and path dependence'. *International Journal of Industrial Organization* 15(6): 827–50.

Mueller, F. (1996) 'Human resources as strategic assets; an evolutionary resource-based theory'. *Journal of Management Studies* 33(6): 757–85.

Mueller, F. and Purcell, J. (1992) 'The Europeanisation of manufacturing and the decentralisation of bargaining: multinational management strategies in the European automobile industry'. *International Journal of Human Resource Management* 3(2): 15–35.

Murphy, K. and Cleveland, J. (1991) *Performance Appraisal: An Organizational Perspective.* Boston, MA: Allyn and Bacon.

Murray, A. (1988), 'A contingency view of Porter's "generic strategies"'. *Academy of Management Review* 13(3): 390–400.

Nalebuff, B. and Brandenburger, A. (1996) *Co-opetition.* London: HarperCollins Business.

Nelson, R. (1991) 'Why do firms differ, and how does it matter?'. *Strategic Management Journal* 12: 61–74.

Nelson, R. and Winter, S. (1982) *An Evolutionary Theory of Economic Change.* Cambridge, MA: Belknap Press.

Nissen, B. (2000) 'Living wage campaigns from a "social movement" perspective: the Miami case'. *Labor Studies Journal* 25(3): 29–50.

Noe, R., Hollenbeck, J., Gerhart, B. and Wright, P. (2005) *Human Resource Management: Gaining a Competitive Advantage.* Boston, MA: Irwin McGraw-Hill.

O'Reilly III, C. and Pfeffer, J. (2000) *Hidden Value: How Great Companies Achieve Extraordinary Results with Ordinary People.* Boston, MA: Harvard Business School Press.

Oakeshott, R. (2000) *Jobs and Fairness: The Logic and Experience of Employee Ownership.* Norwich: Michael Russell.

Odiorne, G. (1985) *Strategic Management of Human Resources.* San Francisco: Jossey-Bass.

Ogbonna, E. and Harris, L. (1998) 'Managing culture: compliance or genuine change?'. *British Journal of Management* 9(4): 273–89.

Ogbonna, E. and Wilkinson, B. (1990) 'Corporate strategy and corporate culture: the view from the checkout'. *Personnel Review* 19(4): 9–15.

Ohno, T. (1988) *Just-in-Time: For Today and Tomorrow.* Cambridge, MA: Productivity Press.

Oliver, C. (1997) 'Sustainable competitive advantage: combining institutional and resource-based views'. *Strategic Management Journal* 18(9): 697–713.

Organ, D. (1988) *Organizational Citizenship Behavior: The Good Soldier Syndrome.* Lexington, MA: Lexington Books.

Orlitzky, M. (2007) 'Recruitment strategy'. In Boxall, P., Purcell, J. and Wright, P. (eds) *The Oxford Handbook of Human Resource Management.* Oxford: Oxford University Press.

Orlitzky, M. and Frenkel, S. J. (2005) 'Alternative pathways to high-performance workplaces'. *International Journal of Human Resource Management* 16(8): 1325–48.

Osterman, P. (1987) 'Choice of employment systems in internal labor markets'. *Industrial Relations* 26(1): 46–67.

Osterman, P. (1994) 'How common is workplace transformation and who adopts it?'. *Industrial and Labor Relations Review* 47(2): 173–88.

Osterman, P. (2000) 'Work reorganization in an era of restructuring: trends in diffusion and effects on employee welfare'. *Industrial and Labor Relations Review* 53(2): 179–96.

Osterman, P. (2006) 'The wage effects of high performance work organization in manufacturing'. *Industrial and Labor Relations Review* 59(2): 187–204.

Ouchi, W. (1980) 'Markets, bureaucracies and clans'. *Administrative Science Quarterly* 25: 129–41.

Paauwe, J. (2004) *HRM and Performance: Achieving Long-Term Viability*. Oxford: Oxford University Press.

Paauwe, J. and Boselie, P. (2003) 'Challenging "strategic HRM" and the relevance of the institutional setting'. *Human Resource Management Journal* 13(3): 56–70.

Paauwe, J. and Boselie, P. (2007) 'Human resource management and societal embeddedness'. In Boxall, P., Purcell, J. and Wright, P. (eds) *The Oxford Handbook of Human Resource Management*. Oxford: Oxford University Press.

Parker, S. and Wall, T. (1998) *Job and Work Design: Organizing Work to Promote Well-being and Effectiveness*. Thousand Oaks, CA: Sage.

Pascale, R. (1985) 'The paradox of "corporate culture": reconciling ourselves to socialization'. *California Management Review* 27(2): 26–41.

Peel, S. and Boxall, P. (2005) 'When is contracting preferable to employment? An exploration of management *and* worker perspectives'. *Journal of Management Studies* 42(8): 1675–97.

Pendleton, A. (2000) 'Profit sharing and employee share ownership'. In Thorpe, R. and Homan, G. (eds) *Strategic Reward Systems*. Harlow: Pearson Education.

Pendleton, A. (2006) 'Incentives, monitoring and employee stock ownership plans: new evidence and interpretations'. *Industrial Relations* 45(4): 753–77.

Penn, R., Rose, M. and Rubery, J. (eds) (1994) *Skill and Occupational Change*. Oxford: Oxford University Press.

Penrose, E. (1959) *The Theory of the Growth of the Firm*. Oxford: Blackwell.

Peteraf, M. (1993) 'The cornerstones of competitive advantage: a resource-based view'. *Strategic Management Journal* 14: 179–91.

Peteraf, M. and Shanley, M. (1997) 'Getting to know you: a theory of strategic group identity'. *Strategic Management Journal* 18(S): 165–86.

Peters, T. and Waterman, R. H. (1982) *In Search of Excellence: Lessons from America's Best-Run Companies*. New York: Harper and Row.

Pfeffer, J. (1994) *Competitive Advantage through People*. Boston, MA: Harvard Business School Press.

Pfeffer, J. (1998) *The Human Equation: Building Profits by Putting People First*. Boston, MA: Harvard Business School Press.

Pfeffer, J. and Salancik, G. R. (1978) *The External Control of Organizations: A Resource Dependence Perspective*. New York: Harper and Row.

Pil, F. K. and MacDuffie, J. P. (1996) 'The adoption of high involvement work practices'. *Industrial Relations* 35(3): 423–55.

Pinfield, L. and Berner, M. (1994) 'Employment systems: toward a coherent conceptualisation of internal labour markets'. In Ferris, G. (ed.) *Research in Personnel and Human Resources Management*. Stamford, CT and London: JAI Press.

Piore, M. and Sabel, C. (1984) *The Second Industrial Divide: Prospects for Prosperity*. New York: Basic Books.

Polanyi, M. (1962) *Personal Knowledge*. New York: Harper.

Poole, M. (1986) *Industrial Relations: Origins and Patterns of National Diversity*. London: Routledge.

Poole, M. (1990) 'Editorial: human resource management in an international perspective'. *International Journal of Human Resource Management* 1(1): 1–15.

Porter, M. (1980) *Competitive Strategy*. New York: Free Press.

Porter, M. (1985) *Competitive Advantage: Creating and Sustaining Superior Performance*. New York: Free Press.

Porter, M. (1990) *The Competitive Advantage of Nations*. London: Macmillan (now Palgrave Macmillan).

Porter, M. (1991) 'Towards a dynamic theory of strategy'. *Strategic Management Journal* 12(S): 95–117.

Porter, M. (1996) 'What is strategy?'. *Harvard Business Review* November–December: 61–78.

Poutsma, E., Ligthart, P. and Veersma, U. (2006) 'The diffusion of calculative and collaborative HRM practices in European firms'. *Industrial Relations* 45(4): 513–46.

Prahalad, C. and Hamel, G. (1990) 'The core competence of the corporation'. *Harvard Business Review* May–June: 79–91.

Priem, R. and Butler, J. (2001) 'Is the resource-based "view" a useful perspective for strategic management research?'. *Academy of Management Review* 26(1): 22–40.

Pudelko, M. (2006) 'A comparison of HRM systems in the USA, Japan and Germany in their socio-economic context'. *Human Resource Management Journal* 16(2): 123–53.

Purcell, J. (1974) *Good Industrial Relations: Theory and Practice*. Basingstoke: Macmillan (now Palgrave Macmillan).

Purcell, J. (1987) 'Mapping management styles in employee relations'. *Journal of Management Studies* 24(5): 533–48.

Purcell, J. (1989) 'The impact of corporate strategy on human resource management'. In Storey, J. (ed.) *New Perspectives on Human Resource Management*. London: Routledge.

Purcell, J. (1996) 'Contingent workers and human resource strategy: rediscovering the core/periphery dimension'. *Journal of Professional HRM* 5: 16–23.

Purcell, J. (1999) 'The search for "best practice" and "best fit": chimera or cul-de-sac?'. *Human Resource Management Journal* 9(3): 26–41.

Purcell, J. and Ahlstrand, B. (1994) *Human Resource Management in the Multidivisional Company*. Oxford: Oxford University Press.

Purcell, J. and Georgiades, K. (2007) 'Why should employers bother with worker voice?'. In Freeman, R., Boxall, P. and Haynes, P. (eds) *What Workers Say: Employee Voice in the Anglo-American Workplace*. Ithaca, NY: Cornell University Press.

Purcell, J. and Hutchinson, S. (2007) 'Front-line managers as agents in the HRM-performance causal chain: theory, analysis and evidence'. *Human Resource Management Journal* 17(1): 3–20.

Purcell, J. and Kinnie, N. (2007) 'HRM and business performance'. In Boxall, P., Purcell, J. and Wright, P. (eds) *The Oxford Handbook of Human Resource Management*. Oxford: Oxford University Press.

Purcell, J., Kinnie, N., Hutchinson, S., Swart, J. and Rayton, B. (2003) *Understanding the People and Performance Link: Unlocking the Black Box*. London: CIPD.

Purcell, J., Purcell, K. and Tailby, S. (2004) 'Temporary work agencies: here today, gone tomorrow?'. *British Journal of Industrial Relations* 42(4): 705–25.

Quinn, J. B. (1980) *Strategies for Change: Logical Incrementalism*. Homewood, IL: Irwin.

Redman, T. and Snape, E. (2005) 'Unpacking commitment: multiple loyalties and employee behaviour'. *Journal of Management Studies* 42(2): 301–28.

Reed, R. and DeFillippi, R. (1990) 'Causal ambiguity, barriers to imitation, and sustainable competitive advantage'. *Academy of Management Review* 15(1): 88–102.

Riordan, M. and Hoddeson, L. (1997) *Crystal Fire: the Birth of the Information Age*. New York: Norton.

Robertson Cooper Ltd (2003) *Teamable Technical Manual*. © Robertson Cooper Ltd.

Robinson, S. (1996) 'Trust and the breach of the psychological contract'. *Administrative Science Quarterly* 41(4): 574–99.

Robinson, S. and Rousseau, D. (1994) 'Violating the psychological contract: not the exception but the norm'. *Journal of Organizational Behavior* 15: 245–59.

Rose, M. (1994) 'Job satisfaction, job skills, and personal skills'. In Penn, R., Rose, M. and Rubery, J. (eds) *Skill and Occupational Change*. Oxford: Oxford University Press.

Rose, M. (2000) 'Work attitudes in the expanding occupations'. In Purcell, K. (ed.) *Changing Boundaries in Employment*. Bristol: Bristol Academic Press.

Rose, M. (2003) 'Good deal, bad deal? Job satisfaction in occupations'. *Work, Employment and Society* 17(3): 503–30.

Rosenthal, P., Hill, S. and Peccei, R. (1997) 'Checking out service: evaluating excellence, HRM and TQM in retailing'. *Work, Employment and Society* 11(3): 481–503.

Rousseau, D. (1995) *Psychological Contracts in Organizations*. Thousand Oaks, CA: Sage.

Rowlinson, M. (1997) *Organisations and Institutions: Perspectives in Economics and Sociology*. London: Macmillan (now Palgrave Macmillan).

Rubery, J. (1994) 'Internal and external labour markets: towards an integrated analysis'. In Rubery, J. and Wilkinson, F. (eds) *Employer Strategy and the Labour Market*. Oxford: Oxford University Press.

Rubery, J., Earnshaw, J. and Marchington, M. (2005) 'Blurring the boundaries of the employment relationship: from single to multi-employer relationships'. In Marchington, M., Grimshaw, D., Rubery, J. and Willmott, H. (eds) *Fragmenting Work: Blurring Organizational Boundaries and Disordering Hierarchies*. Oxford: Oxford University Press.

Rubery, J. and Grimshaw, D. (2003) *The Organization of Employment*. Basingstoke and New York: Palgrave Macmillan.

Rucci, A., Kirn, S. and Quinn, R. (1998) 'The employee-customer-profit chain at Sears'. *Harvard Business Review* 76(1): 82–97.

Rumelt, R. (1982) 'Diversification strategy and profitability'. *Strategic Management Journal* 3: 359–69.

Rumelt, R. (1987) 'Theory, strategy and entrepreneurship'. In Teece, D. (ed.) *The Competitive Challenge*. New York: Harper and Row.

Rutherford, M., Buller, P. and McMullen, P. (2003) 'Human resource management over the life cycle of small to medium-sized firms'. *Human Resource Management* 42(4): 321–35.

Rynes, S., Barber, A. and Varma, G. (2000) 'Research on the employment interview: usefulness for practice and recommendations for future research'. In Cooper, C. and Locke, E. (eds) *Industrial and Organizational Psychology*. Oxford: Blackwell.

Sako, M. (1998) 'The nature and impact of employee "voice" in the European car components industry'. *Human Resource Management Journal* 8(2): 6–13.

Schein, E. (1977) 'Increasing organizational effectiveness through better human resource planning and development'. *Sloan Management Review* 19(1): 1–20.

Schein, E. (1978) *Career Dynamics: Matching Individual and Organizational Needs*. Reading, MA: Addison-Wesley.

Schmitt, N. and Kim, B. (2007) 'Selection decision making'. In Boxall, P., Purcell, J. and Wright, P. (eds) *The Oxford Handbook of Human Resource Management*. Oxford: Oxford University Press.

Schnaars, S. (1994) *Managing Imitation Strategies*. Basingstole and New York: Macmillan (now Palgrave Macmillan).

Schneider, S. and Barsoux, J.-L. (1997) *Managing Across Cultures*. London: Prentice-Hall.

Schuler, R. (1989) 'Strategic human resource management and industrial relations'. *Human Relations* 42(2): 157–84.

Schuler, R. (1996) 'Market-focused management: human resource management implications'. *Journal of Market-Focused Management* 1: 13–29.

Schuler, R. and Jackson, S. (1987) 'Linking competitive strategies and human resource management practices'. *Academy of Management Executive* 1(3): 207–19.

Schumpeter, J. (1950) *Capitalism, Socialism and Democracy.* New York: Harper and Row.

Schwartz, H. and Davis, S. (1981) 'Matching corporate culture and business strategy'. *Organizational Dynamics* 60: 30–48.

Scullion, H. and Brewster, C. (2001) 'The management of expatriates: messages from Europe?'. *Journal of World Business* 36(4): 346–65.

Sheehy, G. (1977) *Passages: Predictable Crises of Adult Life.* New York: Bantam.

Shore, L., Tetrick, L., Taylor, S., Coyle-Shapiro, J., Liden, R., McLean Parks, J., Wolfe Morrison, E., Porter, L., Robinson, S., Roehling, M., Rousseau, D., Schalk, R., Tsui, A. and Van Dyne, L. (2004) 'The employee–organization relationship: a timely concept in a period of transition'. *Research in Personnel and Human Resources Management* 23: 291–370.

Simon, H. A. (1947) *Administrative Behavior.* New York: Free Press.

Simon, H. A. (1985) 'Human nature in politics: the dialogue of psychology with political science'. *American Political Science Review* 79(2): 293–304.

Sisson, K. (2000) *Direct Participation and the Modernisation of Work Organisation.* Dublin: European Foundation for the Improvement of Living and Working Conditions.

Smith, A. (2001) 'Perceptions of stress at work'. *Human Resource Management Journal* 11(4): 74–86.

Smith, A. R. and Bartholomew, D. J. (1988). 'Manpower planning in the United Kingdom: an historical review'. *Journal of the Operational Research Society* 39(3): 235–48.

Snape, E., Redman, T. and Wilkinson, A. (1993) 'Human resource management in building societies: making the transformation?'. *Human Resource Management Journal* 3(3): 44–61.

Snell, S. (1999) 'Social capital and strategic HRM: it's who you know'. *Human Resource Planning* 22(1): 62–5.

Snell, S. and Dean, J. (1992) 'Integrated manufacturing and human resources management: a human capital perspective'. *Academy of Management Journal* 35(3): 467–504.

Snell, S., Youndt, M. and Wright, P. (1996). 'Establishing a framework for research in strategic human resource management: merging resource theory and organizational learning'. *Research in Personnel and Human Resources Management* 14: 61–90.

Solar, P. (2006) 'Shipping and economic development in nineteenth century Ireland'. *Economic History Review* 59(4): 717–42.

Sparrow, P. (2002) 'Globalization as an uncoupling force: internationalization of the HR process?'. In Gunnigle, P. (ed.) *The John Lovett Lectures: A Decade of Development of Human Resource Management in Ireland.* Dublin: Gill and Macmillan.

Sparrow, P. and Braun, W. (2007) 'Human resource strategy in international context'. In Harris, M. (ed.) *Handbook of Research in International Human Resource Management.* Mahwah, NJ: Lawrence Erlbaum.

Sparrow, P., Brewster, C. and Harris, H. (2004) *Globalising Human Resource Management.* London: Routledge.

Sprigg, C., Jackson, P. and Parker, S. (2000) 'Production teamworking: the importance of interdependence and autonomy for employee strain and satisfaction'. *Human Relations* 53(11): 1519–43.

Steedman, H. and Wagner, K. (1989) 'Productivity, machinery and skills: clothing manufacture in Britain and Germany'. *National Institute Economic Review* May: 40–57.

Stewart, T. A. (1998) *Intellectual Capital.* London: Nicholas Brealey.

Storey, D. J. (1985) 'The problems facing new firms'. *Journal of Management Studies* 22(3): 327–45.

Storey, J. (1993) 'The take-up of human resource management by mainstream companies: key lessons from research'. *International Journal of Human Resource Management* 4(3): 529–53.

Storey, J. (1995) *Human Resource Management: A Critical Text*. London: Routledge.

Strauss, G. (2006) 'Worker participation: some under-considered issues'. *Industrial Relations* 45(4): 778–803.

Streeck, W. (1987) 'The uncertainties of management in the management of uncertainty: employers, labour relations and industrial adjustment in the 1980s'. *Work, Employment and Society* 1(3): 281–308.

Suarez, F. and Utterback, J. (2005) 'Dominant designs and the survival of firms'. *Strategic Management Journal* 16: 415–30.

Suchman, M. (1995) 'Managing legitimacy: strategic and institutional approaches'. *Academy of Management Review* 20(3): 571–610.

Swart, J. (2007) 'HRM and knowledge workers'. In Boxall, P., Purcell, J. and Wright, P. (eds) *The Oxford Handbook of Human Resource Management*. Oxford: Oxford University Press.

Swart, J. and Kinnie, N. (2003) 'Sharing knowledge in knowledge-intensive firms'. *Human Resource Management Journal* 13(2): 60–75.

Tailby, S. and Winchester, D. (2000) 'Management and trade unions: towards social partnership?'. In Bach, S. and Sisson, K. (eds) *Personnel Management: A Comprehensive Guide to Theory and Practice*. Oxford: Blackwell.

Taira, K. (1993) 'Japan'. In Rothman, M., Briscoe, D. and Nacamulli, R. (eds) *Industrial Relations Around the World*. Berlin: de Gruyter.

Tayeb, M. (1995) 'The competitive advantage of nations: the role of HRM and its socio-cultural context'. *International Journal of Human Resource Management* 6(3): 588–605.

Taylor, M. S. and Collins, C. (2000) 'Organizational recruitment: enhancing the intersection of research and practice'. In Cooper, C. and Locke, E. (eds) *Industrial and Organizational Psychology*. Oxford: Blackwell.

Teece, D., Pisano, G. and Shuen, A. (1997) 'Dynamic capabilities and strategic management'. *Strategic Management Journal* 18(7): 509–33.

Tomer, J. (2001) 'Understanding high-performance work systems: the joint contribution of economics and human resource management'. *Journal of Socio-Economics* 30: 63–73.

Towers, B. (1997) *The Representation Gap: Change and Reform in the British and American Workplace*. Oxford: Oxford University Press.

Trevor, C., Gerhart, B. and Boudreau, J. (1997) 'Voluntary turnover and job performance: curvilinearity and the moderating influences of salary growth and promotions'. *Journal of Applied Psychology* 82: 44–61.

Trist, E. L. and Bamforth, K. W. (1951) 'Some social and psychological consequences of the long-wall method of coal-getting'. *Human Relations* 4: 3–38.

Trompenaars, F. and Hampden-Turner, C. (1997) *Riding the Waves of Culture: Understanding Cultural Diversity in Business*. London: Nicholas Brealey.

Truss, K. (2001) 'Complexities and controversies in linking HRM with organisational outcomes'. *Journal of Management Studies* 38(8): 1121–49.

TUC (1997) *Partners for Progress*. London: TUC.

Tuchman, B. (1996) *The March of Folly: From Troy to Vietnam*. London: Papermac.

Turnbull, P., Woolfson, C. and Kelly, J. (1992) *Dock Strike: Conflict and Restructuring in British Ports*. Aldershot: Avebury.

Tushman, M., Newman, W. and Romanelli, E. (1986). 'Convergence and upheaval: managing the unsteady pace of organizational evolution'. *California Management Review* 29(1): 29–44.

Uhl-Bien, M., Graen, G. and Scandura, L. (2000) 'Indicators of leader–member exchange (LMX) for strategic human resource management systems'. *Research in Personnel and Human Resources Management* 18: 137–85.

Utterback, J. (1994) *Mastering the Dynamics of Innovation*. Boston, MA: Harvard Business School Press.

Vandenberg, R. J., Richardson, H. A. and Eastman, L. J. (1999) 'The impact of high involvement work processes on organizational effectiveness: a second-order latent variable approach'. *Group & Organization Management* 24(3): 300–39.

Veliyath, R. and Srinavasan, T. (1995) 'Gestalt approaches to assessing strategic coalignment: a conceptual integration'. *British Journal of Management* 6(3): 205–19.

Volberda, J. (1998) *Building the Flexible Firm: How to Remain Competitive.* New York: Oxford University Press.

Waddington, J. (2006) 'The performance of European works councils in engineering: perspectives of the employee representatives'. *Industrial Relations* 45(4): 681–708.

Walker, G. (2003) *Modern Competitive Strategy.* Boston, MA: McGraw-Hill.

Wall, T., Corbett, M., Martin, R., Clegg, C. and Jackson, P. (1990). 'Advanced manufacturing technology, work design and performance: a change study'. *Journal of Applied Psychology* 75(6): 691–7.

Wall, T., Jackson, P. and Davids, K. (1992) 'Operator work design and robotics system performance'. *Journal of Applied Psychology* 77(3): 353–62.

Wallace, T. (1998) 'Fordism'. in Poole, M. and Warner, M. (eds) *The IEBM Handbook of Human Resource Management.* London: Thomson Business Press.

Walton, R. and McKersie, R. (1965) *A Behavioural Theory of Labor Negotiations.* New York: McGraw-Hill.

Walton, R., Cutcher-Gershenfeld, J. and McKersie, R. (1994) *Strategic Negotiations: A Theory of Change in Labor–Management Relations.* Boston, MA: Harvard Business School Press.

Warner, M. (1998) 'Taylor, Frederick Winslow (1856–1915)'. In Poole, M. and Warner, M. (eds) *The IEBM Handbook of Human Resource Management.* London: Thomson Business Press.

Watson, T. (1986) *Management, Organization and Employment Strategy: New Directions in Theory and Practice.* London: Routledge.

Watson, T. (2005) 'Organizations, strategies and human resourcing'. In Leopold, J., Harris, L. and Watson, T. (eds) *The Strategic Managing of Human Resources.* Harlow: Pearson Education.

Watson, T. (2007) 'Organization theory and HRM'. In Boxall, P., Purcell, J. and Wright, P. (eds) *The Oxford Handbook of Human Resource Management.* Oxford: Oxford University Press.

Way, S. (2002) 'High performance work systems and intermediate indicators of firm performance within the US small business sector'. *Journal of Management* 28(6): 765–85.

Webb, S. and Webb, B. (1902) *Industrial Democracy.* London: Longman.

Wernerfelt, B. (1984). 'A resource-based view of the firm'. *Strategic Management Journal* 5(2): 171–80.

Wenlock, J. and Purcell, J. (1991) 'The management of transfer of undertakings: a comparison of employee participation practices in the United Kingdom and the Netherlands'. *Human Resource Management Journal* 1(2): 45–59.

West, G. and DeCastro, J. (2001) 'The Achilles heel of firm strategy: resource weaknesses and distinctive inadequacies'. *Journal of Management Studies* 38(3): 417–42.

West, M., Patterson, M. and Dawson, J. (1999) 'A path to profit? Teamwork at the top'. *CentrePiece* 4(3): Winter.

Wever, K. (1995) *Negotiating Competitiveness: Employment Relations and Organizational Innovation in Germany and the United States,* Boston, MA: Harvard Business School Press.

Whitener, E. M. (2001) 'Do "high commitment" human resource practices affect employee commitment? A cross-level analysis using hierarchical liner modelling'. *Journal of Management* 27: 515–35.

Whitener, E. M., Brodt, S. E., Korsgaard, M. A. and Werner, J. M. (1998) 'Managers as initiators of trust: an exchange relationship framework for understanding managerial trustworthy behaviour'. *Academy of Management Review* 23(3): 513–30.

Whittaker, S. and Marchington, M. (2003) 'Devolving HR responsibility to the line: threat, opportunity or partnership?'. *Employee Relations* 36(3): 245–61.

Whittington, R. (1993) *What is Strategy – And Does it Matter?* London: Routledge.

Whittington, R. and Mayer, M. (2000) *The European Corporation: Strategy, Structure and Social Science.* Oxford: Oxford University Press.

Wilkinson, A. and Willmott, H. (1995) *Making Quality Critical: New Perspectives on Organisational Change.* London: Routledge.

Williams, J. (1992) 'How sustainable is your competitive advantage?'. *California Management Review* 34(3): 29–51.

Williamson, O. E. (1970) *Corporate Control and Business Behavior.* Englewood Cliffs, NJ: Prentice-Hall.

Williamson, O. E., Wachter, M. L. and Harris, J. E. (1975) 'Understanding the employment relation: the analysis of idiosyncratic exchange'. *Bell Journal of Economics* 6(1): 250–78.

Wilson, I. (1994) 'Strategic planning isn't dead – it changed'. *Long Range Planning* 27(4): 12–24.

Windolf, P. (1986). 'Recruitment, selection, and internal labour markets in Britain and Germany'. *Organization Studies* 7(3): 235–54.

Winterton, J. (2007) 'Training, development and competence'. In Boxall, P., Purcell, J. and Wright, P. (eds) *The Oxford Handbook of Human Resource Management.* Oxford: Oxford University Press.

Wolfe Morrison, E. and Robinson, S. (1997) 'When employees feel betrayed: a model of how psychological contract violation develops'. *Academy of Management Review* 22(1): 226–56.

Womack, J., Jones, D. and Roos, D. (1990) *The Machine that Changed the World: The Triumph of Lean Production.* New York: Rawson/Macmillan.

Wood, S. (1996) 'High commitment management and payment systems'. *Journal of Management Studies* 33(1): 53–77.

Wooldridge, A. (2006) 'The battle for brainpower'. *The Economist* 7 October: 3–20.

Wright, P. and Gardner, T. (2004) 'The human resource – firm performance relationship: methodological and theoretical challenges'. In Holman, D., Wall, T, Clegg, C., Sparrow, P. and Howard, A. (eds) *The New Workplace.* New York: Wiley.

Wright, P., Gardner, T., Moynihan, L. and Allen, M. (2005) 'The relationship between HR practices and firm performance: examining causal order'. *Personnel Psychology* 58(2): 409–46.

Wright, P., McMahan, G. and McWilliams, A. (1994). 'Human resources and sustained competitive advantage: a resource-based perspective'. *International Journal of Human Resource Management* 5(2): 301–26.

Wright, P. and Nishii, L. (2004) 'Strategic HRM and organizational behaviour: integrating multiple level analysis'. Paper presented at the 'What Next for HRM?' conference, Rotterdam, June.

Wright, P. and Snell, S. (1998) 'Toward a unifying framework for exploring fit and flexibility in strategic human resource management'. *Academy of Management Review* 23(4): 756–72.

Youndt, M., Snell, S., Dean, J. and Lepak, D. (1996) 'Human resource management, manufacturing strategy, and firm performance'. *Academy of Management Journal* 39(4): 836–66.

Author index

Hill, C., 43, 48, 258, 260
Hill, S., 154, 169
Hinings, C., 42, 212
Hitt, L., 121
Hochschild, A., 134
Hoddeson, L., 92
Holahan, C., 125, 176
Holder, G., 63
Hom, P., 185
Hood, C., 129
Hoopes, D., 89
Hope-Hailey, V., 219
Hornsby, J., 21
Hoskisson, R., 87, 99, 260
Houston, J., 274
Hubbard, N., 253, 269, 270, 271, 273, 277
Huber, V., 181, 182
Huff, A., 45, 46, 245
Hunt, J., 50
Hunt, J.,W., 270
Hunt, M., 289
Hunt, S., 88
Hunter, J., 50, 101, 175, 176, 181, 183
Hunter, L., 16, 68, 135, 161
Hunter, R., 175
Huselid, M., 203, 301
Hutchinson, S., 130, 166
Hyman, R., 25, 145, 147, 155

Ichniowski, C., 80, 81, 82, 124, 155
Isenberg, D., 45
Ivery, M., 152

Jackson, P., 125
Jackson, S., 64, 65, 66, 67, 69, 247
Jacoby, S., 117, 207, 208, 213, 214, 261
James, C., 274
Jelinek, M., 257
Jemison, D., 273, 274
Jenkins, D., 122
Jensen, J., 112
Jensen, M., 184
Johnson, G., 37, 268
Johnson, H., 296
Jones, A., 21, 179, 235, 238
Jones, D., 119
Jones, T., 43, 48
Judge, T., 175
Judiesch, M., 50, 101, 176
Juravich, T., 25

Kahwajy, J., 52, 54, 295
Kalleberg, A., 7, 10, 69, 123, 137, 138, 139, 209

Kamoche, K., 89
Kaplan, R., 43, 59, 93, 262, 268, 279, 296, 297, 298, 299, 300, 301, 302, 304
Karasek, R., 196
Katz, H., 208, 269
Kaufman, B., 116
Kay, J., 67, 102
Keenoy, T., 8, 23
Kelley, M., 214, 269
Kelly, J., 23, 145, 162
Kenney, M., 122
Kepes, S., 202
Kersley, B., 11, 138, 151, 152, 159, 160, 181, 182, 196, 206, 218, 251, 262
Kessler, I., 10, 128, 131, 138, 139, 155, 186, 187, 188, 189, 192, 210, 215, 218
Kets de Vries, M., 182
Kidder, D., 189
Kim, B., 75, 177
King, A., 93
Kinnie, N., 99, 101, 196, 220
Kintana, M., 69
Kirkpatrick, I., 139
Kirn, S., 301
Kletzer, L., 112
Knox, A., 68
Koch, M., 242, 288, 289
Kochan, T., 74, 187
Konzelmann, S., 126
Kossek, E., 82
Koys, D., 303
KPMG, 253, 270
Kreps, D., 63, 104, 129, 203
Kristof, A., 198
Kruger, J., 197
Krugman, P., 126
Kuratko, D., 21

Lacey, R., 116, 237
Lam, S., 290
Landes, D., 238
Lane, C., 39, 180
Lashley, C., 68
Latham, G., 75, 82, 181, 182, 183, 199
Latham, S., 181, 182, 199
Laurent, A., 274
Lawler, E., 77, 120, 122, 152
Lawrence, P., 274
Lawson, B., 121
Lazear, E., 184, 185, 186
Leana, C., 7
Lees, S., 17, 69
Legge, K., 10, 11, 73, 100, 169, 216, 274

Subject index

'new public management', 129, 139–40, 214–15
newspaper industry, 163
non-substitutability, 89–90
North American Free Trade Agreement (NAFTA), 128
Norwich Union, 113, 271
nuclear power industry, 12
NUMMI (Toyota plant), 123

occupational safety and health, 18
offshoring, 13, 105, 112, 126–31, 134, 135, 137–8, 141, 161, 179, 269, 271
oil shocks, 119
oligopoly, 40
operational planning, 35
operational strategy, 42
operations management, 112, 255
opportunity to perform, 5–7, 172–3, 284
organisational agility, 14, 15–16, 180, 246–50, 282
organisational behaviour, 23
organisational citizenship behaviours, 191
organisational climate, 6–7, 106, 155–6, 216, 220, 221, 223, 284, 287
organisational commitment, *see* employee commitment
organisational culture, 93, 169, 216–19, 245, 264, 272, 273–6
organisational ecology, 15, 41
organisational flexibility, 14–16, 20, 73, 244–50, 281, 304–6
organisational justice, 276–8
organisational life cycle, 64–5, 71–2, 229–50
organisational performance, 5–7, 20, 221, 255, 280
organisational politics, 27, 47–9, 166, 244–5
organisational process advantage, 16, 101–2
organisational psychology, 23
outsourcing, 13, 105, 126–31, 179, 206, 210, 214, 245, 269
Owen, Robert, 114

parenting advantage, 44, 253, 264
participatory bureaucracies, 211, 213–14, 245, 269
partnership, *see* social partnership, trade unions
path dependency, 91, 239, 288

'Pax Victoriana', 126
pay, 117, 122, 176, 192, 195–6, 198, *see also* wages
People's Express, 128
perceived organisational support, 194
perfect competition, 40
performance, *see* employee performance, organisational performance
performance appraisal, 75, 82, 180–3, 186, 188, 199
performance drivers, 297–303, 307
performance equation, 5–7, 172–5, 193
performance management, 181
performance-related pay, 115, 176, 185–8, 192, 306
performance variation, 50, 101, 176, *see also* employee performance, organisational performance
personal growth, 198–201
person-job fit, 50, 198
person-organisation fit, 198
person-team fit, 50
personnel economics, 184
personnel management, 171
PEST, 37n.2
'Peter Principle', 174
poaching, 180
politics, *see* organisational politics
power, *see* employee autonomy, labour power, management autonomy/power, organisational politics
powerholic personality, 182
pre-school childcare, 18
PricewaterhouseCoopers, 57
privatisation, 128–9
production systems, 11, 70–2, 125
productivity, 12–13, 116, 119, 121, 125–6, 130, 161–2
productivity bargaining, 161–2
professional services, *see* services
profit sharing, 155, 237
provisioning motive, 185
psychological contracting, 23, 188–95, 216–17, 270–1, 287
public sector, 9–10, 11–12, 128–9, 138–41, 163, 210, 213–14, 218, 257
punctuated equilibrium, 231
putting-out system, 114

quality circles, 154, *see also* total quality management

speed-up, 116
stakeholder perspective, 48, 291–2
standardisation, 203, 208, 240
'stars', 174–5
start-up firms, 64
states, *see* nation states
steel manufacturing industry, 80–1, 96–7,
   124, 126, 127–8, 204
'Store 24', 297–9, 303
strategic business units (SBUs), 94, 255–6,
   261, 267
strategic choice perspective, 34, 42–3, 55,
   57, 103
strategic groups, 58, 230
strategic HRM
   and balanced scorecard, 302–8
   and best fit versus best practice, 61–84
   defined, 57–61
   and industry dynamics, 229–50
   key themes in, 279–87
   and multidivisional/multinational firms,
      251–78
   and the resource-based view, 85–108
   see also human resource management,
      human resource strategy
strategic management
   and cognition, 44–7
   defined, 44–9, 55
   and executive appointments, 50
   and team building, 50–4
   and organisational politics, 47–9
   and the resource-based view, 86–8
strategic planning, 34, 287–90, 307
strategic problems/tensions, 36–44, 54,
   87–8, 249
strategy
   and the resource-based view, 86–8
   corporate, 43–4, 255–9
   defined, 33–44, 54
   emergent, 42, 296, 303
   maps, 301–8
   versus operations, 35
   versus strategic plan, 34
   versus tactics, 35
   see also strategic management
strain, 196
stress, 125, 134, 196, *see also* work
   intensification
strikes, 24, 25
'success trap', 47
supplemental capabilities, 97–8
survival, 37–9
survivor syndrome, 276

sustained competitive advantage, *see*
   competitive advantage
'sweetheart unionism', 168
SWOT, 87–8
synergistic economies, 259–60
synergy, 76, 87, 96, 202, 242, 265–69, 277,
   300
systemic thinking, 45–6, 97

'table stakes', 37, 55, 97–8, 124, 135–6,
   299
tacit knowledge, 93
take-overs, *see* acquisitions
Taylorism, 78, 115–16, 126, 132, 134,
   140–1, 208, 213, 257, 283
teamwork, 50–4, 92, 94, 102, 118, 125,
   137, 152
technical interdependence, 104–5, 125
technology, 12–13, 68–9, 71–2, 116, 121,
   127, 130, 135, 137, 231–4, 247, *see*
   also advanced manufacturing
   technology, information technology
telecommunications industry, 129
textile industry, 93
Thatcherism, 8, 128–9, 139
themes of the book, 279–90
theory of the business, 301–2
time-and-motion study, 115, *see also*
   Scientific Management, Taylorism
top management teams, 50–4
top-team building, 50–4
total quality management (TQM), 70–1,
   119
'town hall' meetings, 152
toy manufacturing industry, 127
Toyota production system, 119–20,
   123
Toys R Us, 26
Trade unions
   and acquisitions, 271
   and challenge to factory system, 116–17,
      208
   and change management, 164–5
   and conflict management, 117, 163
   and demarcation disputes, 117
   employee attitudes to, 147, 165, 170
   and employee voice, 143–4, 148,
      158–65
   growth of, 25, 116–17
   and HIWSs, 164–5
   and internal labour markets, 117
   and multidivisional firms, 260